Research Methods in Defence Studies

This textbook provides an overview of qualitive and quantitative methods used in different social sciences to investigate defence issues.

Recently, defence issues have become of increasing interest to researchers in the social sciences, but they raise specific methodological questions. This volume intends to fill a gap in the literature on defence studies by addressing a number of topics not dealt with sufficiently before. The contributors offer a range of methodological reflections and tools from various social sciences (political science, sociology, geography, history, economics and public law) for researching defence issues. They also address the increasingly important question of data and digitalization. The book introduces the added value of quantitative and qualitative methods, and calls for a cross-fertilization of methods in order to facilitate better research on defence topics and to fully grasp the complexity of defence in the 21st century.

This book will be of much interest to students, researchers and practitioners of defence studies, war studies, military studies, and social science research methods in general.

Delphine Deschaux-Dutard is an Associate Professor in Political Science at the University Grenoble Alpes, France. She is also a researcher at CESICE and Vice-Dean for International Relations at the Faculty of law at the same institution.

Research Methods in Defence Studies
A Multidisciplinary Overview

Edited by
Delphine Deschaux-Dutard

LONDON AND NEW YORK

First published 2021
by Routledge
2 Park Square, Milton Park, Abingdon, Oxon OX14 4RN

and by Routledge
52 Vanderbilt Avenue, New York, NY 10017

Routledge is an imprint of the Taylor & Francis Group, an informa business

© 2021 selection and editorial matter, Delphine Deschaux-Dutard; individual chapters, the contributors

The right of Delphine Deschaux-Dutard to be identified as the author of the editorial material, and of the authors for their individual chapters, has been asserted in accordance with sections 77 and 78 of the Copyright, Designs and Patents Act 1988.

All rights reserved. No part of this book may be reprinted or reproduced or utilised in any form or by any electronic, mechanical, or other means, now known or hereafter invented, including photocopying and recording, or in any information storage or retrieval system, without permission in writing from the publishers.

Trademark notice: Product or corporate names may be trademarks or registered trademarks, and are used only for identification and explanation without intent to infringe.

British Library Cataloguing-in-Publication Data
A catalogue record for this book is available from the British Library

Library of Congress Cataloging-in-Publication Data
Names: Deschaux-Dutard, Delphine, editor.
Title: Research methods in defence studies : a multidisciplinary overview / edited by Delphine Deschaux-Dutard.
Description: Abingdon, Oxon ; New York : Routledge, [2020] |
Includes bibliographical references and index.
Identifiers: LCCN 2020006852 (print) | LCCN 2020006853 (ebook) |
ISBN 9780367187859 (hardback) | ISBN 9780367187866 (paperback) |
ISBN 9780429198236 (ebook)
Subjects: LCSH: Military policy--Study and teaching. |
Military research--Methodology. | Sociology, Military--Methodology.
Classification: LCC UA11 .R47 2020 (print) |
LCC UA11 (ebook) | DDC 355.0072/1--dc23
LC record available at https://lccn.loc.gov/2020006852
LC ebook record available at https://lccn.loc.gov/2020006853

ISBN: 978-0-367-18785-9 (hbk)
ISBN: 978-0-367-18786-6 (pbk)
ISBN: 978-0-429-19823-6 (ebk)

Typeset in Times New Roman
by Taylor & Francis Books

I want to dedicate this volume to my students: they are the ones who keep alive my wish to mix rigorous analysis and didactical methods. May this volume be of help for anyone interested in investigating defence issues.

Contents

List of illustrations	ix
List of contributors	xi
List of abbreviations	xv

Introduction: why methods matter in defence studies 1
DELPHINE DESCHAUX-DUTARD

PART I
Qualitative methods in defence studies 13

1 Defence studies and geographic methodology: from the practical to the critical approach 15
AMAËL CATTARUZZA

2 Defence studies and public law: emergence, affirmation and methodology of a research field 31
ANNE-SOPHIE TRAVERSAC

3 Historical methods in defence and war studies: the case of historical defence studies in France 47
CHRISTOPHE LAFAYE

4 Secondary analysis of qualitative data in defence studies: methodological opportunities and challenges 60
LAURENT BORZILLO AND DELPHINE DESCHAUX-DUTARD

5 Public policy and defence studies 76
CATHERINE HOEFFLER

6 Sociological Methods in defence studies 93
GREGOR RICHTER

PART II
Quantitative methods and defence studies 107

7 Quantitative analyses in defence studies 109
MAYEUL KAUFFMANN

8 Databases for defence studies 129
MAYEUL KAUFFMANN

9 Economics methods for defence studies 151
JULIEN MALIZARD

10 Voting on the use of armed force: challenges of data indexing, classification, and the value of a comparative agenda 170
FALK OSTERMANN, FLORIAN BÖLLER, FLEMMING J. CHRISTIANSEN, FABRIZIO COTICCHIA, DAAN FONCK, ANNA HERRANZ-SURRALLÉS, JULIET KAARBO, KRYŠTOF KUČMÁŠ, MICHAL ONDERCO, RASMUS B. PEDERSEN, TAPIO RAUNIO, YF REYKERS, MICHAL SMETANA, VALERIO VIGNOLI AND WOLFGANG WAGNER

11 The other civil-military gap: researching public opinion on security and defence policy 189
MARKUS STEINBRECHER AND HEIKO BIEHL

Conclusion: a plea for cross-fertilization of methods in defence studies 210
DELPHINE DESCHAUX-DUTARD

Index 215

Illustrations

Figures

1.1	Scale of analysis and the operational environment (Galgano 2011)	23
8.1	Various classifications of conflict based on the Iraq Body Count event data	134
8.2	World Bank Data platform (circles added by the author).	135
8.3	Automatic analysis of conflict event by NLP	137
8.4	Sample query and result from the ICEWS database	137
8.5	Military events per month based on ICEWS	139
8.6	US versus Iran events from Phoenix (Goldstein score)	141
8.7	Sample query and result from the ICEWS database	143
8.8	Collaborative validation workflow for a database in defence studies	145
10.1	Number of deployment votes over time (all chambers), 1990–2017	173
10.2	Average Agreement Index (AI) of deployment votes	175
10.3	Number of Cases [votes] (all chambers)	177
10.4	Frequencies of Shares of Yes-Votes	179
10.5	Party family-cabinet cases by country (lower chambers only)	180
10.6	Average number of no-votes per party family with outliers	181
10.7	Average number of no-votes for party families in government or in opposition with outliers during specific cabinets	182
11.1	Support for postures in France, Germany, and the United Kingdom 2003–2013	199
11.2	Trust in the Armed Forces in the EU, France, Germany, and the United Kingdom 2001–2018	200
11.3	Support for increase of/higher defence spending in France, Germany, and the United Kingdom 2002–2016	201
11.4	Support for increase and keeping the number of troops at the same level combined in France, Germany, and the United Kingdom 2009–2012	203

Tables

1.1	The geopolitical analysis grid (Cattaruzza and Limonier 2019)	25
7.1	Poverty and civil war (1993–1994, 4 countries)	113
7.2	Poverty and civil war (1993–1994, 4 other countries)	114
7.3	Civil wars after 1993 (2 countries)	116
7.4	Comparative study (two countries, two explanatory variables)	119

7.5 Comparative study (two countries, three explanatory variables) 119
7.6 Comparative study (three countries, three explanatory variables) 119
8.1 Sample databases in defence studies 131
8.2 Sample violent event from Phoenix database 140
8.3 US/Iran event with Goldstein score of -2, second half of June 2019 142
10.1 ANOVA analysis of no-votes per party family and cabinet 181

Contributors

Heiko Biehl is head of the research unit on military sociology at the Bundeswehr Centre for Military History and Social Sciences in Potsdam, Germany. He is a guest lecturer at the University of Potsdam. His main research fields are military sociology and political sociology.

Florian Böller is Junior Professor of International Relations at the University of Kaiserslautern, Germany. His research interests include US foreign policy, NATO, and executive–legislative relations.

Laurent Borzillo holds a PhD in Political Science from the University of Montpellier and from the University of Montreal (cotutelle de thèse / international double doctoral degree). His research focuses on military cooperations in Europe and specifically on French–German military cooperation through binational military units since the 1990s. His recent publications deal with German defence policy.

Amaël Cattaruzza holds a PhD in geography from University Paris IV-Sorbonne and is a professor at University Paris 8. He is a geographer and associate researcher at the Military academy Saint-Cyr Coetquidan. He has worked on the Balkans geopolitics, and, more generally, on the mutation of contemporary conflicts. For the past ten years he has also been studying the geopolitics of cyberspace (in particular, through the notions of sovereignty, cyberwar and cybersecurity).

Flemming Juul Christiansen is Associate Professor at the Department of Social Sciences and Business at Roskilde University, Denmark. He is a legislative studies expert with a focus on parties and parliaments.

Fabrizio Coticchia is Associate Professor of Political Science at the University of Genova, Italy. His research fields are foreign policy analysis, strategic culture, and contemporary military operations. His latest book, published together with J.W. Davidson, is *Italian Foreign Policy during Matteo Renzi's Government* (Lexington Books, 2019).

Delphine Deschaux-Dutard is an associate professor in political science at the University Grenoble Alpes (France). She holds a PhD from Sciences Po Grenoble (2008) dedicated to the role of French and German diplomatic and military actors in European Defence Policy and more precisely in CSDP since the 1990s. She spent two research stays in the Sozialwissenschaftliches Institut des Bundeswehr and at the Centre March Bloch in 2006 and 2007 and. Her current research interests focus on CSDP, French-German military cooperation, parliamentary control of the use of military force in France and Germany, and lately cybersecurity and cyber defence in the EU. She teaches international relations and political science in Grenoble and Paris (ILERI, Ecole de Guerre), and is supervisor of an online master's program on International Security and Defence. Her latest publications deal with methods in the study of the military, NATO and CSDP military operations, emerging powers, cybersecurity strategy of the EU and international security. She is also the former treasurer of the French Association pour les Etudes sur la Guerre et la Stratégie (AEGES; guerre-strategie.com).

Daan Fonck obtained his PhD at the Leuven International and European Studies Institute of KU Leuven, Belgium. His research focuses on parliamentary behaviour in foreign policy. He is currently a government advisor for EU and international affairs.

Anna Herranz-Surrallés is Assistant Professor of International Relations at Maastricht University's Department of Political Science, the Netherlands. Her research deals with EU external energy policy and global energy governance, focusing on the relationship between energy, security and democracy.

Catherine Hoeffler is an associate professor at Sciences Po Bordeaux, Centre Emile Durkheim, where she specializes in comparative public policy, political economy of security and European integration. Her research has been published in – among others – *the Journal of European Public Policy, the Journal of Legislative Studies*, and (in French) *Gouvernement et Action Publique and Politique européenne*.

Juliet Kaarbo is Professor of International Relations and founding Co-Director of the Centre for Security Research at the University of Edinburgh, UK. Her research focuses on leader personality and decision-making, group dynamics, parliaments, parties, and national roles in foreign policy. She was the 2018 Distinguished Scholar of Foreign Policy Analysis in the International Studies Association.

Mayeul Kauffmann studied political science at Sciences Po Paris and economics (including econometrics) at Paris XI University, McGill University (Canada) and the University of Grenoble, where he earned a PhD in International Economics (thesis dissertation on global economic governance and armed conflicts). He has research experience of more than 20 years in the quantitative analysis of international security issues and has published numerous articles, books and reports on these issues. He has served as a senior data scientist and director of research at various public and private research institutes (including the European Commission Joint Research Centre and other renowned international NGOs); is a member of the EU Group of Experts on Quantitative Conflict Modelling, and has international experience as lecturer at various universities. He currently teaches statistical methods for the study of international security and defence issues at master's level (University of Grenoble) and is the Database Manager at CartONG (an NGO devoted to digital information management in the humanitarian world), where he also serves as a GIS expert.

Kryštof Kučmáš is a student of security studies at Charles University and junior research assistant at the Peace Research Center Prague, Czech Republic. His main research interests are security studies and social network analysis.

List of contributors xiii

Christophe Lafaye Gained a PhD in History in 2014 for *French Engineers in Afghanistan (2001–2012). Field's adaptation process in Counter-Insurgency's War. Men, materials and doctrines* (under the supervision of Rémy Porte). He won three prizes for this work (Military history national prize, 2014; IHEDN prize, 2014–2015; and UNOR price ("Raymond Poincaré") in 2016). This work is published in French: *L'armée Française en Afghanistan (2001–2012). Le génie au Combat* (Paris, CNRS editions, 22 may 2016, 512 pp.).

Julien Malizard holds a PhD in Economics (2011, University of Montpellier) dedicated to military expenditures and economic growth. He currently teaches at the Chair of Defence economics in Paris. He wrote several articles in academic reviews such as Defence and Peace Economics. His research focuses on macroeconomic effects of defence expenditures, the impact of budgetary constraints on defence expenditures and geographic analysis of defence.

Michal Onderco is Assistant Professor of International Relations at Erasmus University Rotterdam, The Netherlands, where he also coordinates the master's program "International Public Management and Public Policy". His research interests include domestic politics of foreign policy and Central European security policy (when he is not busy studying nuclear proliferation).

Falk Ostermann is Assistant Professor of International Relations at the Justus Liebig University Giessen, Germany. He holds a PhD in Political Science from Vrije Universiteit, Amsterdam. He is a specialist on French security and defence policy and works on the party politics of foreign policy, NATO, European defence, and foreign policy identity. He is the author of *Security, Defense Discourse and Identity in NATO and Europe: How France Changed Foreign Policy* (Routledge, 2019).

Rasmus Brun Pedersen is Associate Professor at the Department of Political Science at Aarhus University, Denmark. His research areas cover foreign policy, small states and their participation in coalition warfare.

Tapio Raunio is Professor of Political Science at Tampere University, Finland. His research interests cover legislatures and political parties, the Europeanization of domestic politics, semi-presidentialism, and the Finnish political system.

Yf Reykers is Assistant Professor of International Relations at the Department of Political Science at Maastricht University, The Netherlands. He studies issues relating to the accountability of security and defence policy, multinational military operations, and rapid response mechanisms.

Gregor Richter, PhD, is a researcher at the Bundeswehr Center of Military History and Social Sciences, Potsdam, and lecturer at the University of Potsdam, Germany. He studied sociology, statistics, and economics at Ludwig-Maximilians-University in Munich, Germany. His fields of work and research interests are empirical organization research and military sociology.

Michal Smetana is a researcher and Assistant Professor at Charles University and coordinator of the Peace Research Center Prague, Czech Republic. He is the author of *Nuclear Deviance: Stigma Politics and the Rules of the Nonproliferation Game* (Palgrave, 2020).

Markus Steinbrecher is a research associate in the research unit on military sociology at the Bundeswehr Centre for Military History and Social Sciences in Potsdam, Germany. He received his PhD from the University of Bamberg in 2008. His main research fields are political behaviour, political attitudes, political psychology, and military sociology.

Anne-Sophie Traversac holds a PhD in public law from University Paris II Panthéon-Assas. She has been an associate professor in public and international law at the University Paris II Panthéon-Assas (France) since 2010. She is also acting as a member of the Research Center in French Military Academy of Saint-Cyr (CREC), and teaches European Defence Issues to Cadets. She is member of French Association of Law of Security and Defence (AFDSD) and member of the Board of this Association. Her research focuses on Constitutional Law and Defence Studies from a law perspective, including external and internal issues.

Valerio Vignoli is a postdoctoral researcher at the Department of Social and Political Science at the University of Milan. His research interests are foreign policy analysis, international relations, party politics, Italian politics, and quantitative methods.

Wolfgang Wagner is Professor of International Security at the Vrije Universiteit Amsterdam, The Netherlands. His most recent book is *The Democratic Politics of Military Interventions: Political Parties, Contestation and Decisions to Use Force Abroad* (Oxford University Press).

List of abbreviations

A400M	Military Aircraft
ACDA	Arms Control and Disarmament Agency
ACLED	Armed Conflict Location & Event Data Project
AEGES	Association for War and Strategic Studies
AI	Agreement Index
AIK	Bundeswehr Academy for Information and Communication
AKUF	Arbeitsgemeinschaft Kriegsursachenforschung
ANOVA	Analysis of Variance in Statistical Models
ANQAR	Afghanistan Nationwide Quarterly Assessment Research survey
ATL	Advanced Technology Laboratories
BFA	French-German Brigade
BPM	Business Process Management
C2SD	French Social Sciences Research Center on Defence
CAMEO	Conflict and Mediation Event Observations
CBA	Cost-Benefit Approach
CDEC	Center for Doctrine and Command Instruction
CEHD	Center for Defence History Studies
CEREMS	Research Center for French Military Higher Education
CESA	Center for Strategic Airspace Studies
CESM	Center for Advanced Studies of the French Marine
CHEAR	Center for Advanced Studies on Arm Procurement in France
CHEM	Center for Advanced Studies of the Military School in Paris
CHES	Chapel Hill Expert Survey
CIA	Central Intelligence Agency
CIDCM	Center for International Development and Conflict Management
CFHM	French Military History Commission
CFSP	Common Foreign and Security Policy
COW	Correlates of War
CMP	Comparative Manifesto Project
CNIL	National Commission on Informatics and Liberty in France
CNRS	French National Center for Scientific Research
CREA	Research Center of the French Airforce
CREC	Research Center of the French Army in Saint-Cyr Coëtquidan
CREV	Countries at Risk of Electoral Violence Database

xvi *List of abbreviations*

CSDP	Common Security and Defence Policy
CSFRS	French High Council for Strategic Research
CSP	Center for Systemic Peace
CYBIS	Cybersecurity and International Security Research Project of University Grenoble Alpes
DARPA	Defence Advanced Research Projects Agency
DFG	Deutsche Foschungsgemeinschaft
DGA	General Directorate for Arm procurement of the French Ministry of Defence
DIB	Defence Industrial Database
DoD	Department of Defence (USA)
DS	Defence spending
ECAAR	Economists Against the Arms Race
ECSC	European Coal and Steel Community
EDC	European Defence Community
EPS	Economists for Peace and Security
ERGOMAS	European Research Group on Military and Society
ESDP	European Security and Defence Policy
ESRC	Economic and Social Research Council
EU	European Union
EUG (or EUBG)	European Union Battlegroups
EUFOR	European Union Force
EUTM	European Force Training Mission
EUR	Euro
FELIN	Integrated Infantryman Equipment and Communications
FLOSS	Free/Libre/Open-source Software
FPA	Foreign Policy Analysis
GCRI	Global Conflict Risk Index
GDP	Gross Domestic Product
GDELT	Global Database of Events, Language, and Tone)
GEOINT	Geospatial Intelligence
GIDD	Global Internal Displacement Database
GNAD	Global Nonviolent Action Database
GRIP	Group for Research and Information on Peace and Security
GTD	Global Terrorism Database
GTI	Global Terrorism Index
HDI	Human Development Index
HIIK	Heidelberger Institut für Internationale Konfliktforschung
ICEWS	Integrated Conflict Early Warning System
ICOW	Issue Correlates of War Research Project
ICPSR	Interuniversity Consortium for Political and Social Research
IDMC	Internal Displacement Monitoring Center
IE	Information Extraction
IHEDN	French Institute for Advanced Studies on Defence
IISS	International Institute for Strategic Studies
IMF	International Monetary Fund
IR	International Relations
IRSEM	Institute for Strategic Research of the Military School in Paris

List of abbreviations

IRNAV	Research Institute of the French Navy
ISA	International Sociological Association
ISAF	International Security Assistance Force in Afghanistan
ISO	Organization for Standardization
ITU	International Telecommunication Union
IUS	Inter-University Seminar on Armed Forces & Society
MAR	Minorities at Risk Database
MoD	Ministry of Defence
MoP	Member of Parliament
MV&R	Monitoring Verification and Reporting
NATO	North Atlantic Treaty Organization
NAVCO	Nonviolent and Violent Campaigns and Outcomes
NLP	National Language Processing
NSA	National Security Agency
OECD	Organisation for Economic Co-operation and Development
OEDA	Open Event Data Alliance
OMGUS	Office of the Military Government of the US
OSint	Open Source Intelligence
ParlGov	Parliaments and Governments Database
PDVD	Parliamentary Deployment Votes Database
PESCO	Permanent Structured Cooperation
PPP	Purchasing power parity
PRIO	International Peace Research Institute in Oslo
QPC	Priority Question on Constitutionality
R&D	Research and Development
RGI	Resource Governance Index
SAS	Small Arms Survey
SHD	Historical Defence Service of the French Ministry of Defence
SIPRI	Stockholm International Peace Research Institute
SOWI	German Social Science Institute of the Federal Armed Forces
TIV	Trend Indicator Value
UAV	Unmanned Aerial Vehicle
UK	United Kingdom
UN	United Nations
UNDP (or PNUD)	United Nations Development Programme
USD	American Dollar
USIA	United States Information Agency
USSR	Union of Soviet Socialist Republics
WB	World Bank
WHO	World Health Organization
WU	Western Union
WZB	Wissenschaftszentrum Berlin für Sozialforschung
ZInfoABw	Bundeswehr Center for Public Relations
ZMSBw	Bundeswehr Center for Military History and Social Sciences

Introduction*

Why methods matter in defence studies

Delphine Deschaux-Dutard

"One cannot do without a method to be seeking the truth of things."
René Descartes, *Discours de la méthode* (1637).

The past three decades have witnessed a significant growth in social science research on defence issues. With the rise of global terrorism, the return of the use of armed force in international relations after the Cold War, the growing professionalization and the rising technologization of defence matters, academic research on defence is not only relevant but also indispensable. Indeed, the use of violence, as defence's core issue, is probably one of the most unpredictable topics in human society (e.g. Soeters et al. 2014). And though numerous works on defence issues have been published in recent decades,[1] only a limited number of these are specifically dedicated to methodological questions (see Soeters et al. 2014; Williams et al. 2016; Carreiras et al. 2016). However, in the past few years, some methodological reflections have arisen on how to conduct research on the military. Researchers from different countries have started to consider method as a research topic *per se* when it comes to investigating defence issues (see in particular Carreiras and Castro 2011; Soeters et al. 2014; Carreiras et al. 2016). Boëne proposed for instance a stimulating thinking on methods and theories in military studies (Boëne 2008). In the past decade, five academic books and handbooks more precisely fuelled this emerging academic literature: one exclusively focuses on the use of qualitative methods (Carreiras and Castro 2011), while the others aim at a wider perspective and also question military sociology, reflexivity, publishing or even ethics (Soeters et al. 2014; Williams et al. 2016; Carreiras et al. 2016; Caforio and Nuciari 2018). The *Routledge Handbook of Research Methods in Military Studies* (Soeters et al. 2014) is very rich but focuses mainly on methods on military questions, when researching conflict, war and military actors. The project of this book is different in that it focuses on defence as a whole, which means also as a public policy ruled by norms, historical, economical and geographical aspects, and reliant on many factors such as public opinion or parliamentary votes. Thus, this edited book puts a specific focus on conflict and war, as explained in the sections below. Last, but not least, another recently published handbook raises some methodological challenges but with a very particular focus on international security: the *Oxford Handbook of International Security* (Gheciu and Wohlforth 2018). As for the French academic sphere, it seems to have taken a little more time as defence studies emerged later and with more difficulty in the French academic landscape, as compared with the British or American ones (see Holeindre and Vilmer 2015; Holeindre 2015). Yet we can recently observe positive developments in two ways. On the one hand, a special issue of the French journal *Les Champs de Mars* dedicated to defence researches by social scientists has been published on methodological issues with a focus on interviews in the defence milieu (Lafaye et al. 2015). On the other hand, the Institute for Strategic Studies (IRSEM) located in Paris organized a special doctoral workshop on methodology in strategic studies in June 2019.[2] But aside from these recent works, questioning methods in defence research remains quite marginal compared to the increasing number of academic publications dedicated to defence issues in the past three decades. And yet this subject is not only interesting for young and senior researchers, but also for students and practitioners, since defence and the military raise the question of the specific features of this social field.

Why publish this volume now?

What does this book aim to bring to the literature on methods while investigating defence issues? The volume intends to complete this emerging literature by addressing a number of topics that have either not been dealt with sufficiently or even not at all before. If the case of geographical methods, public policy methods, or quantitative methods, for instance, has been much under-investigated in defence studies until then, some of the issues raised here are even a first, like secondary analysis in defence studies. In this later case the authors of the chapter dedicated to this topic could not find any substantial publications on the subject and propose a reflexive analysis of a unique research experience (see Borzillo and Deschaux-Dutard in this volume). The contributors to this edited book, all high-profile French and German scholars, have been chosen not only for their acknowledged specialization in defence studies in their own disciplinary field but also for their innovative methodologies and openness to cross-disciplinary research in several cases. Thus this volume aims at adding value to the emerging literature dedicated to methodological questions regarding research on defence issues. It will also give a valuable access in English to a large amount of the literature developed in French and German synthesized for the first time in the contributions of this volume, and not previously accessible to a wider non-native speaking audience.

Yet one could question the timing: why this volume now? The rise in academic interest in defence issues in the aftermath of the terror attacks in France in 2015 and more generally in Europe has been a strong impetus for the development of defence studies in France in particular. The terror attacks in Paris in November 2015 revealed a critical lack of social sciences scientific resources on defence and security issues, which prompted the French Ministry of Defence to dedicate specific funding for research in social science on defence topics in the widest sense. Even though doctoral and postdoctoral funding had been introduced since the end of the 1990s,[3] the aftermath of the terror attacks witnessed a radical increase in such funding facilities for universities that are independent from the defence institution. In parallel, scholars have also worked at promoting the emergence of defence and war studies in France by witnessing the success of this field in Anglo-Saxon countries where war studies have for long time become an established research field in the academia (Holeindre and Vilmer 2015; Holeindre 2015). Yet if research on defence issues is encouraged by the new capital inflow released by defence institutions in France but also in some other countries as Germany in the last decade (see for instance Gareis and Klein 2006: 12), the question of how to investigate such topics also increases, as a recent controversy on these funding has shown in the French political science community.[4] As the defence sphere is characterized by its social specificity, it is important to give intense thought to the way it can be investigated by social sciences using both quantitative and qualitative epistemologies.

The other important reason why this volume is being published now is the increasing interest of students in defence issues in the past decade. At the University of Grenoble Alpes alone, the only pluridisciplinary master's degree on defence and international security (existing both in face-to-face and online teaching) welcomes over 400 applications each academic year for only 50 places. The same is true in many universities offering master's degrees in International Relations, or security and defence issues. Thus the growing number of students engaging in defence studies not only in France but also in other European countries makes it all the more important to give them the tools to address defence issues with solid methods and informed knowledge.

Scope of the book

Yet we need to explain more precisely what we understand under the term "defence studies" in this volume, as it is the common ground for all the contributions. It is important to define the scope of this book and what makes it different from the other existing handbooks. As Galbreath and Deni define it, defence studies constitutes "a multi-disciplinary field examining how agents, predominantly states, prepare for, prevent, avoid and/or engage in armed conflict" (Galbreath and Deni 2018: 1). Thus defence studies can be considered as a coherent area of study encompassing the way defence policies are set up and evolve over time under a large set of constraints and the action of multiple public and private actors. It is therefore important to distinguish defence studies from security studies, covering almost the totality of international and internal affairs,[5] and also from war studies, focusing mainly on the fighting aspects of the military (operations, strategy, tactics but also soldiers' experience). As Schmitt underlines, the link between defence studies and war studies consists in understanding war in all its aspects as a necessity to build an efficient defence policy able to cope with threats (Schmitt 2018: 18). Therefore defence studies are a natural component of war studies (Schmitt 2018: 26). Here we understand defence studies following the definition of defence as a policy and a strategic action aiming at preparing for conflicts and opposing efficiently to threats. We also include a larger sense of defence when considering civil wars in the contribution on databases, for instance, as they constitute the majority of the 21st century's armed conflicts.

The term "defence" has been used in a narrow sense in the military context since the end of the 12th century as the means mobilized by a state to make war (Joana 2017). The signification of the term has then evolved towards a much broader meaning from the 19th century and designates two main elements: a specific domain of state public action (a policy) (Vennesson 2000; Battistella et al. 2012; Joana 2017) and a peculiar type of strategic action (Brown et al. 2004). Broadly speaking defence can be considered as the way to translate foreign policy, and more and more often also security objectives,[6] into military means (encompassing financial means but also troops, arm procurement and even public opinion support). Defence policies result from the interaction of a multiplicity of actors: civilian, military and administrative actors (Vennesson 2000). Therefore, defence studies lies at the intersection between internal and international issues. The scope of the book is to propose epistemological and methodological food for thought based on defence as a specific field which not only entails the overall means public authorities dedicate to the defence of their territory, the protection of their citizen through military forces and the support of their interests in international security but also the norms surrounding this field of public action and the strategies adopted in order to develop an effective defence. This global understanding of defence studies leads us to adopt a multi-disciplinary approach to methods in defence studies, as defence encompasses not only political and social issues, but also normative and legal, economic, historical and geographic issues. Defence also requires quantification, be it for defence spending purposes or to measure the level of public support or the implication of states in defence issues such as military deployment. We then consider defence studies together as studies of a specific type of policy developed by political authorities within the framework of a political regime, as a specific type of normative and legal production and as a form of strategic action relying on multiple material and immaterial factors such as geography, history (Part I) but also statistics and data, public opinion and democratic control (Part II). With our definition of the scope of the book clarified, we can now deal with general methodological questions raised by defence studies and how we conceive of them in this volume.

Why do defence topic raise specific methodological questions?

Researching defence issues raises a singular question: is the defence field a specific social field or not? And if it is, what makes it special?[7] We will only outline the main arguments from the debate around the specific feature of the defence field, as this is not the main point of this introduction but it still has some implications in the key debates we will discuss below. On the one hand, the defence field has a clearly identified social function in human societies: defence and the military are consubstantial with state monopoly of violence (Elias 1991; Tilly 1985). Many researchers endorse this conception of defence as a specific social field (Boëne 1990; Bardiès 2011; Soeters et al. 2014), and we subscribe to it. Defence issues are most of the time characterized by technicality and secrecy (think about the decision to launch a military intervention, or to develop a new military device as drones for instance). Even if most of the armies of democratic industrialized countries have become professional armies after the Cold War, one cannot affirm that defence and the military are such common professions (Janowitz 1974; Moskos and Wood 1988; Gresle 2005). Their core social characteristic is violence and the implementation of state violence outside the national territory, and even sometimes inside as the increasing use of the military for securing purposes against the terrorist threat has shown for few years in many European countries, with the case of the Sentinelle operation in France for instance. Therefore producing research on defence requires to take this specificity into account (we will discuss shortly the insider/outsider dilemma for the researcher below). This also implies reflexivity (see interesting developments on this issue in Carreiras and Caetano 2016). In the next two sections we will focus on two core debates on methodological issues when researching defence and that all the contributors of this edited book experienced at least once: the insider/outsider dilemma, and the choice for qualitative or quantitative methods.

Uncovering the insider/outsider dilemma[8]

The insider/outsider dilemma is closely linked with the question of accessing the field and/or data in defence studies. Most of this volume's contributors have experienced it, be it for the purposes of interviews, data or archive collection. All of the authors gathered here either had to negotiate their way to access the defence field, or became embedded (for a short or longer time) in defence institutions as researchers and thus had to keep a critical distance from the field (see Pajon and Martin 2015).

The access to the defence field can be difficult for different reasons: danger in some cases (like a field research during some military operations; see Leonhard et al. 2008), but also frequently mistrust from defence institutions. The researcher often faces a common fear of secrecy-breaking towards external members who do not belong to the defence field (see Schmitt 2015 on confidentiality and secrecy issues). Researching the defence field, either by interviews, polls, statistics or archives, implies that if he/she wants to collect valid data, the researcher should not be perceived as an "intruder" by defence actors. It is therefore crucial to raise trust not only towards the hierarchy (officers or unity commander for instance), but also towards the soldiers or administrative actors if needed. In that matter, we experienced in our own researches that some contacts offer "open sesames": name-dropping can be quite fruitful (Deschaux-Beaume 2012).

Getting along with the hierarchy can be even more crucial when the researcher needs to reach soldiers. If the respondents feel that hierarchy mistrusts the researcher, its introduction in the field can be difficult and sometimes even impossible: Pajon uses the expression "managing mistrust" to describe this situation (Pajon 2005). However, being granted trust from the hierarchy does not guarantee that the researcher will be well introduced among troops: he/she can still be seen as a relay of the hierarchy sent to scrutinize the soldiers (Hockey 2016). Thus many researchers contributing to this volume not only had to ask for an authorization to access classified documents, but also sometimes chose immersion to become a "native". Mastering the culture and technical language of the defence sphere is not only a way of being trusted but also a way of understanding the field behind the technicality surrounding it. To put it simply: the closer one gets mentally, culturally, cognitively, to the defence field, the higher the chances to get access, and vice versa. However, this insider strategy raises a connected dilemma: how to publish in the open the results of research if one needs an authorization from the defence field? How to manage the "resurfacing" by making sure the researcher does not only write what the defence institution would like him to say? There again, reflexivity on what method is applied and for what research purpose is crucial so as to manage to produce valid research results not necessarily in line with the official defence narrative. Therefore, depending on the aim of the research, the question of the access to the defence field is directly linked with methodological choices.

Qualitative, quantitative ... or both methods?

Is there a method better suited to analyse defence issues with social sciences tools? The choice of method is not only driven by the aim of the enquiry but is also problem-driven in defence studies. We won't enter the quantitative versus qualitative debate here as it would take us far from our scope (on this question, see Goertz and Mahoney 2006, 2012). We will only outline some implications of research on defence issues both for quantitative or qualitative methods.[9]

Starting with qualitative methods, though this methodology often meets the insider/outsider dilemma, it constitutes a very fruitful way of enquiring into the defence field.[10] Following the idea that "if one wants to know society, one first has to know it first-hand" (Becker 2007: 44), qualitative methods relying on semi-directed interviews, participant observation, focus groups or the ethnographical methodology provide a stimulating methodology to study defence issues.[11] More precisely, in the case of a social science research on defence, qualitative interviews fulfil two main objectives: getting first-hand information, and having interesting access to the military actors and their representations and practices (Deschaux-Beaume 2011, 2012). The same applies to archives directly gathered from the soldiers for instance (see Lafaye in this volume). The ethnographic method seems to be particularly popular among scholars working on defence, as it offers a unique access to this usually closed field (Lafaye et al. 2015; Schmitt 2015). But some also experiment with other techniques, such as focus groups (Haddad in Carreiras and Castro 2011), participant observation (Carreiras and Castro 2011; Schmitt 2015; Hockey 2016), data collection through databases or computing devices (Kauffmann in this volume), and of course archives when it is possible (Deschaux-Beaume 2011; Schmitt 2015; Lafaye in this volume).

Concerning quantitative methods,[12] they raise the question of accessing enough data and/or respondents (in the case of a wide survey, for instance) so as to build a valid sample. The epistemology and methodological choices implied by quantitative methods will be discussed in Chapter 7, as Kauffmann explains the epistemological founding principles of these methods and their implementation in defence studies. The choice for quantitative methods relying on multiple cases or surveys not only necessitates the agreement of the hierarchy but also the effective presence of the respondents. For instance, if one wants to conduct an opinion survey inside a military unit, one challenge is the rapid turnover of the soldiers: as Pajon states, in some cases, about 80% of the unit troops are outside the national territory and sometimes for many months (Pajon 2005). The same problem occurs when the researcher wants to reiterate interviews with officers or soldiers several months or even years after the first research phase (Settoul 2015). Another related problem is the researcher's freedom to build his/her own sample when sometimes defence institutions would rather propose "representative" individuals chosen from the inside to prevent any critical judgement to be expressed before external persons (Pajon 2005).

Thus any method can be well suited while researching defence matters as long as the method is problem-driven (Soeters et al. 2014; Deschaux-Dutard 2018). Several contributors of this book also tend to mix quantitative and qualitative methods by choosing a dominant method (for instance, the qualitative one) and complementing it by a second one: the case is particularly striking in the collection and management of archives by Lafaye (Chapter 3).

The aim of this book is thus to provide the reader with an overview of methods used in different social sciences (political science, sociology, history, public law, economics, geography) in order to investigate the defence field and analyse defence issues using both qualitative and quantitative tools and in some cases mixing methods from different disciplinary backgrounds.

Structure of the book

Broadly speaking, defence can be considered as the way to translate foreign policy, and more and more often also security objectives (with the growing implication of military actors in the internal fight against terrorism, as in the framework of the operation Sentinelle in France since 2015), into military means (encompassing financial means but also troops, arm procurement and even public opinion support). All

Introduction   7

the contributors have significant experience in research on defence topics, which they can draw upon to propose original and synthetic reflections on methods in the multiple areas covered by defence studies. The book also addresses the multiplicity of defence studies by covering not only organizational and legal aspects, but also operational and even political topics such as the measurement of public opinion on defence matters or the construction of an international index to scrutinize parliamentary votes on military deployment in several Western countries.

Thus this edited volume follows a structured logic. The methods presented here and put to the test by the contributors aim at exploring the different elements surrounding defence policies. For clarity reasons, the book adopts a classical divide between qualitative and quantitative approaches, which does not mean that one is exclusive of the other, as a researcher investigating defence issues may use both, depending on what he/she aims at demonstrating. We will come back to this idea in the conclusion of this book. Many contributors not only explain the status of defence issues in their own disciplinary field but also propose original reflexions on the methods used from their disciplinary perspective. Several contributors underline their use of both methodologies, but with a bigger place dedicated to one or the other (see, in particular, the chapters by Lafaye, Cattaruzza, Kauffmann and Ostermann et al. in this volume). Most of the contributors also explain how they deal with the digitalization of data, not only when using databases but also when using archives, geographical information or even interviews. The book is composed of six chapters focusing primarily on qualitative methods, and five chapters more orientated towards quantitative methods.

The structure of the book starts with the physical, normative, political, social and historical dimensions of defence studies. The first part deals more precisely with qualitative methods to uncover these dimensions. The logic underpinning this part is to explore the different elements having an impact on defence policies and defence issues, starting with material and objective ones (geography, law, history) to come to the more social and subjective ones implying representations and social practices. Therefore many chapters not only analyse methods from a disciplinary point of view but also need to recall first the place of defence issues in some of the disciplines represented in this volume as geography, law or history, so as to better reflect on methodological aspects. More precisely in Chapter 1, Amaël Cattaruzza discusses methodological questions raised by the geographical approach to defence issues. Therefore he first draws the links between geography and defence studies so as to better show how geographic methods can give us interesting insights to investigate defence topics on the wider sense. He more precisely focuses on the question of data and big data, and how the spatialization of data impacts defence studies. In Chapter 2, Anne-Sophie Traversac focuses on the law methodology when researching defence on the perspective of public law (international, European and national law). She demonstrates how defence studies have started to spread into public law by developing more precisely from the case of French public law and its growing interest for defence issues in the last decade. She also pleads for cross-fertilization of methods between public law and political science to grasp the complexity of defence legal measures. In Chapter 3, Christophe Lafaye proposes an analysis of the emergence of defence and war studies in the French university system and how the historical discipline found its way in this emerging field. He then reflects on the use of archives and how to deal with immediate and digitalized archives, advocating the training of social science researchers in computing methods. In

Chapter 4, Laurent Borzillo and Delphine Deschaux-Dutard explore an under-investigated issue: secondary analysis of qualitative data in defence studies. They propose a reflexion on the potentialities and limits of this method in defence studies, as it also raised ethical questions to be addressed by the researcher. Both researchers more precisely focus on the re-use of qualitative interviews in defence studies and formulate propositions to archive this kind of material in a digitalized way. In Chapter 5, Catherine Hoeffler addresses the question of method using policy analysis to investigate defence and focuses on some of the key issues pertaining to the links between policy analysis and defence studies. Uncovering among others the question of agenda setting, governance, implementation and effectivity or internationalization of defence public policies, she furthermore advocates for methodological pluralism and underlines some challenges of qualitative methods when researching defence using conceptual and methodological tools from policy analysis. In Chapter 6, Gregor Richter gives a critical overview on empirical sociological methods in defence-related research. He particularly explores the way research questions are generated using sociological analytic tools on defence issues and the challenges of embedded sociological research, the access to the field and how to deal with research results.

The second part of the book has been conceived to focus more thoroughly on the use of quantitative methods and statistics to investigate the defence field in several social sciences such as political science, sociology or economics. This part logically starts with a general reflection about quantitative methods in defence studies before more precisely focusing on some specific uses of these methods to build and analyse databases and data, create indexes or even opinion surveys on defence topics. This part opens with Chapter 7, in which Mayeul Kauffman proposes a general overview of the main categories of quantitative methods applied to defence studies, presenting various examples illustrating their strength and weaknesses. His primary reflections about the founding principles of quantitative methods and their epistemological foundations furthers understanding of how useful such methods can be used to investigate defence issues, but also the limits of such methods. In Chapter 8, Kauffmann relies on his dual background as defence economist and computer scientist to draw synthetic methodological observations from the use of databases and big data in defence studies, even introducing a state-of-the-art of techniques and technologies so as to make them accessible and fruitful to non-technical readers by providing guidelines for the creation of databases on defence issues. In Chapter 9, Julien Malizard follows the reflection on the use of quantitative methods by addressing the issue of economic methods in defence studies. He first explores the different possible economic methods used to investigate the defence topic with a particular focus on the calculation of defence spending, and then addresses the important question of economic data production and its limits, before proposing a critical review of the main topics and methods used in defence economics. In Chapter 10, collectively written by Falk Ostermann and his colleagues from the research project Parliamentary Deployment Vote Database (PDVD),[13] the authors analyse and explain the method used to build indexes in defence studies, with a specific case study on parliamentary votes on military deployment in several countries during the last decade. Last but not least, in Chapter 11, Markus Steinbrecher and Heiko Biehl pursue the exploration of quantitative data by explaining how public opinion surveys on defence issues can be developed and what are their potential and limits to analyse the relationship between defence and public support with a case study focusing on German public opinion. The book finishes with a Conclusion by Delphine

Deschaux-Dutard pleading for more cross-fertilization between the different methods and disciplines and relying on examples so as to grasp more in depth the complexity of the defence field in the 21st century.

Notes

* The editor of this book would like to thank three anonymous reviewers for their fruitful suggestions on an earlier version of this introduction.
1. When typing the key words "defence" and "military" and browsing only in titles, Google Scholar finds over 1180 pages of results from 1990, all disciplines included.
2. https://www.irsem.fr/agenda-enhancer/agenda/journee-d-etude-des-doctorants-de-l-irsem.html (Accessed 24 July 2019).
3. The editor of this volume herself benefited from a doctoral funding from the Ministry of Defence for her doctoral dissertation in the early 2000s.
4. See the arguments of this controversy online: https://zilsel.hypotheses.org/3052 and https://zilsel.hypotheses.org/3071 (Consulted on 19 July 2019). This controversy started raising after the signature of two memoranda of understanding: one between the French National Research Center (CNRS) and the Ministry of Defence in 2017, and one between the CNRS and the Direction for Military Intelligence in 2018.
5. See for instance the concept of securitization linking the internal and external levels of security developed by the Copenhagen school of security studies (Buzan 2008).
6. The growing implication of military actors in the internal fight against terrorism, as in the framework of the operation Sentinelle in France since 2015, participates in this process.
7. A more extensive analysis on this point can be found in Deschaux-Dutard (2018).
8. For more elements on this issue, see Deschaux-Dutard (2018).
9. For more details see Deschaux-Dutard (2018).
10. See also *Qualitative Methods in Military Studies* (Carreiras and Castro 2011), and the second part of the *Routledge Handbook of Research Methods in Military Studies* (Soeters et al. 2014), which come as two very useful complements of this volume as it has been conceived.
11. Samy Cohen incidentally underlines how much more fruitful than archives those interviews turn out to be in the defence field (Cohen 1999: 19).
12. The case of quantitative methods in the study of the military is interestingly investigated in the third part of the *Routledge Handbook of Research Methods in Military Studies* (Soeters et al. 2014). For an original perspective on the use of statistics in the study of international questions (among which armed conflicts), see also Kauffmann (2008).
13. See the website of the project: http://deploymentvotewatch.eu/ (Accessed 25 July 2019).

References

Bardiès, L. (2011). Du concept de spécificité militaire. *L'Année sociologique*, 61 (2), 273–295.
Battistella, D., Petiteville, F., Smouts, M. C., Vennesson, P. (2012). *Dictionnaire des relations internationales: approches, concepts, doctrines*, Paris, Dalloz.
Becker, H. S. (2007). Les ficelles du métier: comment conduire sa recherche en sciences sociales. Paris, La Découverte. [Original publication: Becker, H. S. (1998). *Tricks of the Trade: How to Think about Your Research While You're Doing It*, University of Chicago Press.]
Boëne, B. (1990). *La spécificité militaire*. Actes du colloque de Saint-Cyr Coëtquidan, Paris, Armand Colin.
Boëne, B. (2008). Method and substance in the military field. *European Journal of Sociology/ Archives Européennes de Sociologie*, 49(3), 367–398.
Brown, M. E., CotéJr, O. R., Lynn-Jones, S. M., Miller, S. E. (Eds.) (2004). *Offense, Defense, and War*, Cambridge, MA, MIT Press.
Buzan, B. (2008). *People, States and Fear: An Agenda for International Security Studies in the Post-Cold War Era*, Colchester, ECPR Press.

Caforio, G., Nuciari, M. (2018). Social research and the military: A cross-national expert survey, 27–58. In: Caforio, G. (ed.) (2018). *Handbook of the Sociology of the Military*. 2nd ed., York, Springer.

Carreiras, H., Castro, C. (Eds.) (2011). *Qualitative Methods in Military Studies*, London, Routledge.

Carreiras, H., Caetano, A. (2016). Reflexivity and the sociological study of the military, 8–22. In: Carreiras, H., Castro, C., Frederic, S. (Eds.). (2016). *Researching the Military*, London, Routledge.

Carreiras, H., Castro, C., Frederic, S. (Eds.). (2016). *Researching the Military*, London, Routledge.

Cohen, S. (1999). Enquêtes au sein d'un « milieu difficile »: les responsables de la politique étrangère et de défense, 17–50. In: Cohen, S. (ed.) (1999). *L'art d'interviewer les dirigeants*, Paris, PUF, Coll. "Politique d'aujourd'hui".

Deschaux-Beaume, D. (2011). Studying the military in a comparative perspective: methodological challenges and issues. The example of French and German officers in European Defence and Security Policy, 132–147. In: Carreiras H., Castro C. (Eds.) (2011). *Qualitative Methods in Military Studies*, London, Routledge.

Deschaux-Beaume, D. (2012). Investigating the military field: Qualitative research strategy and interviewing in the defence networks. *Current Sociology*, 60 (1), January 2012, 100–116.

Deschaux-Dutard, D. (2018). Methods in defence studies, 40–52. In: Galbreath, D., Deni, J. R. (eds.) (2018). *Routledge Handbook of Defence Studies*, London, New York: Routledge.

Elias, N. (1991) [German ed.]: Suhrkamp Verlag, (1987). *La société des individus*, Paris, Fayard.

Galbreath D., Deni J. (Eds.) (2018). *Routledge Handbook of Defence Studies*, London, Routledge.

Gareis, S. B., Klein, P. (2006). *Handbuch Militär und Sozialwissenschaft*, Wiesbaden: VS Verlag für Sozialwissenschaften.

Gheciu, A., Wohlforth, W. (Eds.) (2018). *The Oxford Handbook of International Security*, Oxford, Oxford University Press, 2018.

Goertz, G., Mahoney, J. (2006). A tale of two cultures: Contrasting quantitative and qualitative research. *Political Analysis*, 14(3), 227–249.

Goertz, G., Mahoney, J. (2012). *A Tale of Two Cultures: Qualitative and Quantitative Research in the Social Sciences*, Princeton, Princeton University Press.

Gresle F. (Ed.) (2005). *Sociologie du milieu militaire. Les conséquences de la professionnalisation sur les armées et l'identité militaire*, Paris, L'Harmattan.

Holeindre, J. V. (2015). Des strategic studies aux war studies. La structuration d'un champ d'études, 499–512. In: Henrotin, J., Schmitt, O., Taillat, S. (2015). *Guerre et stratégie: approches, concepts*, Paris, Presses Universitaires de France.

Holeindre, J. V., Vilmer, J. B. J. (2015). Pour des war studies en France: un diagnostic et des propositions. *Revue défense nationale*, 785, 53–59.

Hockey, J. (2016). Participant observation with infantry. In: Williams, Alison J.*et al.* (Eds.) (2016) *The Routledge Companion to Military Research Methods*, London, Routledge.

Janowitz, M. (1974; 1st ed: 1960). *The Professional Soldier: A Social and Political Portrait*, Glencoe, The Free Press.

Joana, J. (2017). Défense (politique de), 359–366. In: Durieux, B., Jeangène Vilmer, J.-B., Ramel, F. (2017). *Dictionnaire de la guerre et de la paix*, Paris, PUF.

Kauffmann, M. (2008). *Building and Using Datasets on Armed Conflicts*, Amsterdam: IOS Press.

Lafaye, C, Paya y Pastor, A., Thura, M. (Eds.) (2015). Special issue: La pratique des sciences sociales en milieu militaire: une opération spéciale? *Les Champs de* Mars, 27.

Leonhard, N., Aubry, G., Casas Santero, M., Jankowski, B. (Eds.) (2008). *Military Co-operation in Multinational Missions: The Case of EUFOR in Bosnia and Herzegovina* (SOWI Forum International 28), Strausberg: Sozialwissenschaftliches Institut der Bundeswehr.

Moskos, C., Wood, F. (1988). *The Military: More Than Just a Job?*, Washington DC, Pergamon-Brassey's.

Pajon, C. (2005). Le sociologue enrégimenté: méthodes et techniques d'enquête en milieu militaire, 45–57. In: Gresle F. (Ed.) (2005). *Sociologie du milieu militaire. Les conséquences de la professionalisation sur les armées et l'identité militaire*, Paris, L'Harmattan.

Pajon, C., Martin, C. (2015). La sociologie militaire par les personnels de la défense: une sociologie d'insiders? *Les Champs de* Mars, 27, 23–30.

Schmitt, O. (2015). L'accès aux données confidentielles en milieu militaire: problèmes méthodologiques et éthiques d'un "positionnement intermédiaire". *Les Champs de* Mars, 27, 50–58.

Schmitt, O. (2018). Defence as war, 18–28. In: Galbreath, D., Deni, J. R. (Eds.) (2018). *Routledge Handbook of Defence Studies*, London, New York: Routledge.

Settoul, E. (2015). Analyser l'immigration postcoloniale en milieu militaire: retour sur les enseignements d'une méthode ethnographique. *Les Champs de* Mars, 27, 31–41.

Soeters, J., Shields, P., Rietjens, S. (Eds.) (2014). *Routledge Handbook of Research Methods in Military Studies*, London, Routledge.

Tilly, C. (1985). War making and state making as organized crime, 161–191. In: Evans P., Rueschemeyer D., Skocpol T. (Eds.) (1985). *Bringing the State Back In*, Cambridge: Cambridge University Press.

Williams, Alison J.*et al.* (Eds) (2016). *The Routledge Companion to Military Research Methods*, London, Routledge.

Vennesson, P. (2000). *Politiques de défense: institutions, innovations, européanisation*, Paris, L'Harmattan.

Part I
Qualitative methods in defence studies

1 Defence studies and geographic methodology

From the practical to the critical approach

Amaël Cattaruzza

Introduction

The relationship between geography and defence issues may seem old and obvious. Maps have always been tools for soldiers on the battlefield and in staffs, from tactical to the strategic scale. Military geography also appeared as an autonomous discipline at the end of the 19th century. At the same time, the first geopolitical works were published in the United States and Europe. The link between defence studies and geography is complex. It concerns the study of the terrain as a place of confrontation, the study of the military organization and its geographical distribution, and also the study of the spatial distribution of power in its various dimensions (political, strategic, economic, and symbolic).

Geographers have thus been integrated into military staffs and have developed a technical approach of places in order to serve as a decision-making tool for military purposes both for strategists and politicians. This tradition still exists today through the use of geospatial intelligence. Relying on a set of digital technologies, military geography aims at informing the military staff about the battlefield, and it is now crucial in operational planning. However, geographers have also sought to guide the strategies and policies of their leaders and rulers with their discipline. Relying on geostrategy and geopolitics, they talk about the distribution of forces and power games worldwide. By studying geographical factors, they provide an interpretation that was once considered purely objective and scientific, and that could have served as a legitimization for imperialist claims (American imperialism, Third Reich conquest strategy, among others). The place of the military issues in these studies has always been important. It would, therefore, be difficult to discuss the methodological questions raised by defence issues investigated by geography without considering both approaches.

The geographical perspective on war and defence issues has nevertheless evolved in the last decades with the development of a critical school in geography and geopolitics. The critical approach aims at revealing the balance of power at stake behind all territorial and political constructions. In this sense, the military field, and more generally, the question of war, was the subject of a revival within the geography field during the 1990s. The goal of critical geography is to reveal power relations and strategies hidden behind the spatial dimensions of the military domain.

In this chapter, we consider the question of methodology by first presenting a genealogy of the links between geography and defence studies and show how intertwined geography and military issues have been for a long time. In the second part, we focus on the recent evolutions of geography in defence studies by examining more precisely the critical turn and the new methodologies developed. Finally, we analyse the crucial role of data and digitalization processes and stress on their consequences for methods in defence studies.

Geography, a science serving military action or an ideological tool dedicated to the legitimization of power?

Geography, as a discipline, has always had a dual dimension: both physical and human geography, natural and social science. Thus, it provides both an expert voice on the interactions between man and his physical and social environment, and develops a critical approach about how knowledge and control of places may strengthen and legitimize the expression of power in society. Therefore the knowledge of the field has early been considered as a strategic knowledge. From Sun Zi to Clausewitz, the great thinkers of military strategy have always stressed the importance of this field knowledge in the context of armed conflicts (Motte 2018).

From a tactical point of view, geographical knowledge enables military forces to adapt the intervention of troops to different environments in which they can evolve (land, sea, air, mountain, desert, etc.) and to reflect on the most relevant action needed to take the lead over the opponent. Geography is also primarily conceived as an objective tool to investigate theatres of operation. The emergence of military geography in the 19th century is part of this framework. But knowledge of the geographical context also makes it possible to formulate analyses on a broader scale. The gradual and parallel structuring of disciplines such as geostrategy and geopolitics also need to be taken seriously and indeed, officers or former officers have played a role in this development (such as Giacomo Durando, inventor of the term "geostrategy" in 1846, or in the early 20th century Karl Haushofer, thinker of German *Geopolitik*). Whether at the tactical or strategic level, the objective of this use of geography was to support political and military decision-making based on an scientific-analysis considered objective, since it was based on undeniable physical factors.

The 19th century, a time for the emergence of strategic geographic knowledge

This desire to "technicize" the decision-making process tells us a lot about the intellectual context of the 19th and early 20th centuries, marked by the industrial revolution and the progress of social sciences on the one hand, and by colonial domination by the European powers on the other hand. These powers were seeking intellectual tools to strengthen and legitimize their leadership positions in the world.

On a scientific level, several developments contributed to making geography a first-rate science in the military and strategic fields. First of all, the progress in cartography made during the 17th and 18th centuries made the map a significant tool for the conduct of wars. The publication in 1793 of the first scientific map of a State, the Geometric Map of France, produced by the Cassini family, marked a turning point in cartographic science. As Luca Muscarà points out, this evolution of geography has quickly become a tool of political and military power and control:

> With Napoleon, the French army was reorganized and mapping was the key to military conquest and administration. The *ingénieurs-géographes* (engineers-

geographers) of the renamed *Dépôt général de la Guerre et de la Géographie* accompanied and sometimes preceded the army in mapping operations designed to consolidate French control.

(Muscarà 2018: 368).

This use of geography to support decision-making is in line with the perspectives established by the tenants of positivism. In the continuity of the Enlightenment, this school of thought intended to apply the scientific method to the social field in order to go beyond knowledge based on tradition (Kremer-Marietti 2017). In doing so, the foundation of social sciences building was based on the recognition of positive facts and systematic data collection. Thus, social scientists believed they could deduce universal laws and be able to anticipate social phenomena. First, this approach has led to enormous progress in the geographical and geological sciences. Viktor Mayer-Schönberger and Keneth Cukier refer in particular to the case of the US Navy naval officer, Matthew Fontaine Maury, who drew up the first maritime cartography for navigation (Mayer-Schönberger and Cukier 2014: 95). In 1855, he published a *Geography of the Sea* based on more than 1.2 million data points. Significant progress has therefore been made insofar as intuitive assumptions, once taken for granted, could finally be confirmed or invalidated by a systematic empirical approach. These advances have been put to good use in the military field, and fostered the illusion of certainty that would be dictated by the intrinsic characteristics of the regions and the geographical terrain.

However, the development of military geography is also due to a particular political context. Indeed, the colonization carried out by the European powers required the various armies to adapt to environments that were very different from their traditional theatres of operations. The neutral and "apolitical" knowledge offered by physical geography allowed the military to learn about operations in desert environments, or in exotic climates, while limiting thinking to simple technical and operational arguments. Nevertheless, colonial anthropology and geography offered an often caricatured and essentialized vision of local societies. Thus, they strengthened the idea of the civilizing dimension of Western administration. As Rachel Woodward notes, "Military geography has a long history, its roots tangled up with the imperial ambitions and military requirements that late-nineteenth-century Geography emerged to serve" (Woodward 2004: 6). Thus, Anne Godlewska's observation concerning the *ingénieurs-géographes* (engineers-geographers) of the Napoleonic administration still finds echoes in the practice of this kind of military geography. For her, military geographers believed in "a developing certainty that the inherent value of a region, terrain or people could be accurately measured through the use of French scientific methods… of which the non-European cultures appeared incapable" (Godlewska 1994: 41–42). In parallel, the rise of Geostrategy and Geopolitics has also been used as a legitimization discourse for colonization.

So, the 19th and early 20th centuries were key periods in the relationship between geography and defence studies, through three different approaches, military geography, geostrategy and geopolitics. If strategists have always taken into account the field in the art of warfare, advances in the geographical sciences made it possible to move from practical use to a rigorous and systematic study of operations theatres. Nevertheless, this period also brought a particular vision of geography within the military, tinged with determinism.

Military geography, or the application of geographic methodology to the conduct of military campaigns

The emergence of an autonomous military geography within geography dates back to the second half of the 19th century, with the first works by Théophile Lavallée, professor of geography at the *Ecole spéciale Militaire de Saint-Cyr* in France (Boulanger 2002). Strongly inspired by the German school, Lavallée sketched a discipline in which topographical and geological data were put in perspective with the strategic thinking of the time, and in particular with the works of Jomini. For the first time, he raised the idea that knowledge of the natural environment could be used for military purposes (Boulanger 2002: 26).

Subsequently, new specialists emerged in Europe (Coutau-Bégarie 2006). Nevertheless, the discipline remained very academic and developed at the beginning of the 20th century "very systematic geological inspirations theories, increasingly disconnected from the operational needs of the armies" (Coutau-Bégarie 2006). As Rachel Woodward notes, military geography

> is primarily concerned with how military activities and armed conflict are shaped by terrain and environment. (…) Yet, as an academic discipline, Military Geography has failed to evolve. The application of topographical and environmental knowledge to the conduct of military campaigns, and the strategic and tactical considerations to be taken into account, were set out by T. Miller Maguire in 1899. Over the 20th century and in the 21st century, this understanding of Military Geography held fast.
>
> (Woodward 2004: 6)

In fact, the discipline suffered in the United States and Europe from the anti-war opinions of the 1960s and 1970s caused by the movements surrounding the decolonization wars and the Vietnam War. Military geography had practically disappeared in France after World War II, supplanted by geostrategic thinking (Boulanger 2002). While Military Geography in the United States has a specialty group within the Association of American Geographers, its definition in the early 2000s remained traditional: "Military Geography is (…) the application of geographic information, tools, and techniques to military problems" (Woodward 2004: 6). In France, Philippe Boulanger's work shed light on the history of this discipline between 1871 and 1945 (Boulanger 2002) and helped to update its practice, by taking into account new environments and issues (Boulanger 2006, 2011). Nevertheless, the work of Military Geography remains attached to a utilitarian vision of geography, often considered in a descriptive and essentialized way.

Geostrategy, a strategy for large areas

General Giacomo Durando first used the term geostrategy in 1846. He gave two definitions to this word. Geostrategy would be both the study of how geographical data determine the "social bonds" that found the nation, but also, in a more military sense, the study of the influence of geography on the use of organized forces at the national level (Motte 2006). Unlike military geography, geostrategy is not about tactical and operational dimensions, but about the "strategy of large areas" (Motte 2018). This discipline has had a strong resonance in diplomatic circles and quickly led to the definition of strategies dedicated to each environment (land and naval strategies, and soon air, space, and cybernetics strategies). This way of thinking based on the geographical constraints of each environment leads to broader analysis about the nature of power, involving classical oppositions like land/sea, land power/sea power, upon which geopolitics is subsequently based. It is sometimes difficult to classify thinkers and to distinguish what in their thinking is geostrategic or geopolitical. The case of Admiral Mahan (1840–1914) is exemplary in this respect.

Mahan's researches are mainly focused on Sea Power. Mahan was first and foremost a sailor marked by his experience in the US Navy, from 1856 to 1896. He took part in the American secession wars and analysed the innovations they brought. At the time, the southerners' maritime blockade had been decisive in winning the victory. This strategy had only been possible thanks to the technical progress of the navy and the switch from steam sailing to sailing. One of his major contributions has been to perceive the consequences of the industrial revolution in world geopolitics. From 1885 onwards, he became a teacher and devoted himself to historical research, which led him to formulate a theory based on maritime power or Sea Power.

With Mahan, strategic thinking is combined with a detailed knowledge of geographical environments and the physical constraints imposed by geographical factors. This geostrategic approach later spread within military thinking, particularly with the French Admiral Raoul Castex. Without calling into question the notion of Sea Power, Castex considers that it must be nuanced, taking into account the economic, political, diplomatic, and above all technological contexts. The invention of new weapons can reverse Sea Power. In this sense, Castex's thinking is less deterministic than Mahan's. Geostrategy, therefore, proposes a militarized vision of the earth's space, in which geography is thought of as the basis for the deployment of armed forces. This discipline was very successful during the Cold War when these concepts (shutter zone, containment, etc.) were put forward in East/West rivalry.

Geopolitics, "science" or ideology?

At the beginning of the 20th century, geopolitics emerged and aimed at discerning the geographical foundations of power on the international scene. Its thinkers, geographers or soldiers, have made these analyses ideological tools to serve an imperialist idea of power. Until World War II, two major trends emerged within geopolitics: a naturalistic approach, centred on social Darwinism, and a broader approach, focusing on a study of the "great game" at work between the major powers in international relations. In both cases, the State, as a political structure, remains the central unit of measurement for this first discipline. On the one hand, the German school developed around the work of the geographer Friedrich Ratzel and Officer Karl Haushofer; on the other hand, the English-speaking approach drew from the work of the British academic Halford Mackinder.

Considered as the father of political geography, Friedrich Ratzel (1844–1904) is a leading scientific figure of the second half of the 19th century. In his book *Anthropogeographie* published in 1882, he laid the foundations of human geography by focusing on the relationship between societies and their environment. In *Political Geography* published in 1897, the State is referred to as an organism (i.e. an organized structure in Ratzel vocabulary). The borders would be the peripheral organs, while power would be the centre. Through these theories, the concerns for a German unified state in the making with expansionist views were backed up.

On the other hand, the British academic Sir Halford Mackinder developed at the beginning of the 20th century another kind of discourse based on the analysis of the geographical factors of power. His most famous work, *The Geographical Pivot of History* published in 1904, ambitiously aimed at formulating "certain aspects of geographical causality in Universal History" (1992). He defined the notion of Heartland, a Central Asian space that extends beyond the borders of the Russian Empire, to which he conferred the role of "geographical pivot of History". This area would have a strategic role due to its geography: a low-lying area favouring rapid traffic and contact between Asia and Europe, with significant resources. Thus, it effectively reversed Mahan's reasoning, which saw Sea Power as the alpha and omega of global power. On the contrary, Mackinder emphasized continental power. He based this argument on the invention of the railway, which considerably transformed mobility and favoured land travel.[1] For Mackinder, this gave Russia a significant strategic advantage, as location can serve as a promontory to Asia, the Middle East, and Europe, regions where more than two-thirds of the world's population where concentrated at this period. The strength of its reasoning was to introduce a global approach in the analysis of the international scene.

Ratzel and Mackinder's approaches have influenced the birth of the haushoferian *Geopolitik*. In the 1920s, Karl Haushofer (1869–1946) proposed an autonomous structuring of this discipline and made it grow on the intellectual scene of the interwar period. A former officer of the Bavarian army, he was deeply affected by the German humiliation inflicted by the Treaty of Versailles.[2] Under his impetus, the *Zeitschrift für Geopolitik* (Journal of Geopolitics) was created in 1924. For Haushofer, *Geopolitik* had to differ from political geography: he wanted it to be a science that would serve political action and enable Germany to regain its status as a Great power. In this sense, he revisited Ratzel's concepts, in particular that of *Lebensraum*, which allowed him to claim for Germany a "natural" sphere of expansion in Central and Eastern Europe, which would give him access to economic self-sufficiency. Geopolitik was the subject of numerous criticisms from that time on, because it seemed to justify a conquering and belligerent policy through "natural laws". Nevertheless, the most virulent criticisms have been levelled at the Nazi regime's use of these ideas, by reinterpreting the work of geopoliticians.

Military geography, geostrategy and geopolitics therefore appear as three traditional uses of geography in defence studies. The involvement in each of its specialties of military personnel as thinkers undoubtedly explains the importance given to the military dimensions of power. At that time, these three disciplinary fields shared a very static vision of geography, considered as the physical foundation on which military force was deployed.

The critical turn of geography and its methodological consequences on defence studies

In the 1970s, international relations were characterized by decolonization and the conflicts of the Cold War. The interventions of the Great powers have never been so debated and criticized within civil society. The problems under discussion were indeed geopolitical. At the same time, the perspectives and methodologies in social sciences have utterly changed, with the works of thinkers such as Fernand Braudel, Michel Foucault and Henri Lefebvre. The influence of Marxism led some young geographers (David Harvey, Edward Soja, and Kevin Cox) to develop political analyses that were increasingly critical of the governments and detached from the state level, taking into account issues related to other actors and local and regional levels. According to their radical approach, the geographical location of a phenomenon must be interpreted as the product of a balance of power that produces socio-spatial inequalities.

Critical approaches in Geography: discovering power behind the spatiality of military issues and war

In France, while regional geography and its economical approach were mostly dominant, Yves Lacoste developed an analysis on colonialism and the strategies at work in the Vietnam War, and proposed to rebuild the analytical frameworks of the discipline. In his book *La Géographie, ça sert d'abord à faire la guerre* (Lacoste 1982), he asserts that geography is not neutral. On the contrary, it informs strategists and justifies domination. Maps are not only representations of places and areas, they are instruments of battle and propaganda tools. By showing borders, they seem to give "scientific" legitimacy to artificial territories and their governments. Lacoste's approach is a critical one. He aims at building analytical and methodological tools to reveal the strategies of domination at work through geography and spatial organization.

In the English-speaking academia, the main evolution of the discipline is based on a change of perspective. Indeed, since the 1990s, Critical Geopolitics has integrated a more reflective dimension into the geopolitical analysis under the impetus of geographers such as John Agnew, Simon Dalby, or Gearoid O'Tuathail (or Gerard Toal). The latter defines this discipline as opposed to Geopolitics: "Geopolitics can be described as a problem-solving theory for the conceptualization and practice of statecraft. (…) In contrast, Critical Geopolitics is a problematizing theoretical enterprise that places the existing structures of power and knowledge in question" (O'Tuathail, 1999: 107). Thus Critical Geopolitics implies a rigorous reflexive approach, which questions all its research objects as material forms of power, and which also questions political or scientific discourses aiming at legitimizing them.

In this perspective, geography is no more conceived as a fixed background, but as a social construct uncovering power relations. As Flint states in his book, *Geography of War and Peace*:

> In the current academic jargon, war/peace and geography are mutually constituted and socially constructed. In other words, geography and war are the products of human activity; war creates geographies of borders, states, empires, and so on, and in turn, these geographic entities are the terrain over which peace is maintained or new wars are justified. Rather than being as permanent and sedate as a mountain range, the geography of war is as fluid and volatile as a lava flow.
>
> (Flint 2005: 4).

In this perspective, geography does not determine the strategy of the actors. On the contrary, the actors, through their strategies, produce new geographies. The study of war geography has thus been wholly renewed.

Nevertheless, military geography has been little affected by this evolution of the discipline, except for the work of Rachel Woodward (Woodward 2004). Together with her colleagues, she laid the foundations for a critical approach to military geography (Rech et al. 2015). According to them:

> A geographical approach (...) has much to offer critical military studies, not just by emphasizing that key foci – war, militarism, militarization, and military organizations, institutions, capabilities, and activities – take place in places, but also by insisting on the multiplicity of ways in which these phenomena are geographically constituted and expressed. At the heart of the critical military studies project is an understanding of these phenomena as the outcome of social practices, rather than as given categories beyond interrogation, in direct contrast to the normative approaches prevalent in much traditional military geography (and, indeed, traditional military and war studies).
>
> (Rech et al. 2015: 55–56)

Such an approach would allow military geography to take its full place in a global strategic reflection, integrating the social, cultural, and political dimensions specific to each military intervention.

The methodologies of human geography and their implementation in defence studies

The turning point in human geography in the 1970s *de facto* changed its methodologies and discourses, which are now more analytical than descriptive. The purpose of the discipline is not only to accumulate geographic data collections (maps, name of countries and capitals, characteristics of regional climate, mountain's altitudes, etc.), but to analyse spatial processes, to understand and explain the location of human activities, and to formulate a critical point of view on spatial environment (Cattaruzza and Limonier 2019). It is a method of thinking, which could be summed up in a few simple questions. *What?* The researcher needs to define his object. *Where?* He needs to locate this object in space and time. *Why here and not somewhere else?* He needs to understand the singularity of this object based on geographic analysis and comparisons. *Why and how?* He needs to explain the spatiality of the phenomena he studies.

To do this, the geographer observes and analyses each phenomenon at different scales (local, regional, national, continental, and global) and over different time periods. One of the main specificities of geographical reasoning is to highlight the multiple interactions between different scales of analysis. For example, a local event, such as the Battle of Aleppo in Syria (2012–2016), may be interpreted differently depending on the scale of observation. While a local analysis would focus on battles within the city, a national perspective would reveal other processes (ethnic and political distribution of populations, movements of displaced persons and refugees, etc.), as well as an international perspective. However, all these observation scales influence each other. The specificity of geography is also to combine different fields of analysis, such as geology, biology, climatology, demography, anthropology, urban and rural studies, history, or political science. The discipline is integrative, with many sub-domains such as geomorphology, biogeography, political or cultural geography, population geography, etc.

The common perspective of all these different approaches is to analyse phenomena in terms of spaces, places, territories, and landscapes. Today, human geography focuses the actors influencing the construction of territories.

As said above, geography has always played an important role in defence studies because of the strategic dimension of space and places in wartime. The use of concepts such as battlefield, area of operations (local level), theatre of operations (local level), and theatre of war (regional level) illustrates the contributions of geography at the operational level. Yet, from a military point of view, the study of space phenomena is not an end in itself and remains a means to obtain strategic advantages in the field or to reveal power relations at different scales. Therefore the methodology must take into account the strategic dimension of research.

In his seminal work *Paix et guerre entre les nations* (Aron 1962), the French philosopher Raymond Aron distinguished between the notions of "environment" and "theatre". According to the author, the study of environment is part of a scientific process and requires the intervention of technicians and scientists. On the contrary, theatre is an abstract, simplified notion, a representation making sense in the context of a given operation. Thus, the study of theatre of operations or theatre of war depends on the goal to be achieved defined by strategists and politicians. This is not just a technical issue. It is also a political issue. *De facto*, the "theatre of operations", for the strategist, is not an exhaustive description of the field, but a simplified vision that depends on the objectives to be achieved and the nature of the actors involved. Thus, in the context of defence studies, the geographer must adapt geographical concepts to the strategic and military objectives of the actors involved, and must, therefore, be introduced to strategic literature.

For example, the notion of scale has a particular meaning in strategic thinking (see Figure 1.1 below). As geographer Francis A. Galgano states (Galgano 2011: 46):

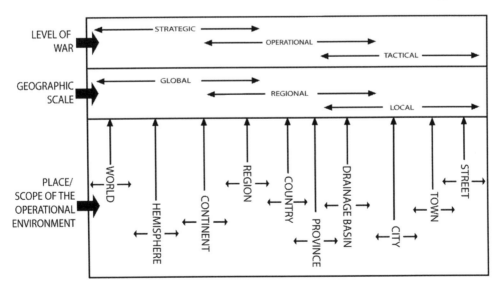

Figure 1.1 – Scale of analysis and the operational environment (Galgano 2011)

> The scale of a place is, in a military sense, a function of the level of war. At the strategic level, a place or operating environment may be an entire continent. At the operational level, it may be a region or country. At the tactical level, it could be something as small as a city block.

Thus, the geographical study of defence issues must always correlate the different level of war with different geographic scales, and highlight the influence of each level with the others.

The same adaptation process must be carried out for concepts as simple and essential as site and location, distance, size, or regions. The site is used to describe the internal characteristics of the site (morphology, relief, climate, infrastructure, etc.). Battlefield site investigation can offer crucial strategic advantages during a battle. The notion of location, on the other hand, refers to the relative location of a place in a geographical context. A place is always more or less linked to other places, and the relationship between them can be interpreted functionally and hierarchically (as for a centre and peripheries, or for dominant and dominated places). Distance is also a fundamental concept in geography, whether considered in an absolute or relative sense.[3] With the spread of the Internet and cyberspace, the notion of distance need to be reinterpreted in this new context. Cyberattacks, for example, can be launched regardless of the distance between the attacker and the victim.

Last but not least, the notion of region is perhaps the most commonly used geographical concept nowadays. However, its definition is difficult to define because it refers to different meanings and scales according to the authors. In most cases, the word region is used to refer to contiguous spaces sharing one or more common characteristics. But it can also be used in the case of areas polarized around an economic or political centre, or even in a more general sense, in the case of areas integrated into a spatial interaction system, such as border regions (Mareï and Richard 2018). In a military operation, regional analysis is fundamental at all levels (strategic, operational, and tactical) because it allows defining the spatial units in which military action must be carried out. These sets can refer to different parameters (geographical, political, cultural, economic, etc.) and make it possible to highlight different types of spatial relationships (domination, rivalries, cooperation, etc.) at different scales of analysis.

The geopolitical methods and the critical perspectives

Geopolitical methods introduce a more critical perspective. Unlike geography, the geopolitical approach focuses more particularly on actors, their rivalries, and spatial representations. The principles of geopolitical reasoning, as they have been practiced since the early 1970s, can be evoked in the form of a grid (see Table 1.1). Among the methods and factors used to formulate a geopolitical analysis, we can mention the identification of the actors involved, the study of the territories they draw or invoke, the analysis of the relations and rivalries of various kinds (political, economic, cultural, etc.) involved. From these elements power relations emerge on territories, at several spatial and temporal scales. But this geopolitical analysis grid also informs us about another specificity of this method, namely the attention given to rivalries and conflicts. Indeed, this practice does not imply studying the actors *ex nihilo* but describing them in their relational context (power relations, conflicts, cooperation, etc.).

Table 1.1 – The geopolitical analysis grid (Cattaruzza and Limonier 2019)

	Actors	Territory	Rivalry/Conflict
Nature	State Individual(s) Social Group Ethnic group Organization Religious institution Party Armed group Company Media and media Etc.	**Political territory** (state issues: borders, power) **Economic and/or socio-economic territory** (social justice issues, struggle for resources, appropriation conflicts, etc.) **Sociocultural and/or "identity" territory** (demographic and symbolic issues, protection of minority populations, symbolic places, religious sites, monuments, etc.)	Political, economic, symbolic, identity rivalries, property conflict, land-use conflict, etc.
Status	Aggressor (point of view) Defender (point of view) Victim (point of view) Ombudsman Combatant Non-combatant Etc.	**Territory as a framework** (framework of power rivalries) **Territory as an issue** (territory at stake in power rivalries) **Territory as a theatre** (theatre of operation)	Open or latent rivalry Armed or unarmed conflict Symmetric or asymmetric conflict Etc.
Scale	Scale(s) of action and influence of actors	Territorial scales subject to conflict (multiscalar approach from global to local)	Scales of materialization of rivalry or conflict (circumscribed conflict, diffuse, repercussions at various scales, etc.)
Temporality	Temporality of the actors (long time of economic actors; average or short time of political actors, etc.)	Temporality of the territories (average time of political territories, long time of cultural territories, etc.)	Temporality of the rivalries and conflicts (short, medium, long time)
Representation	Argumentations or representations that allow actors to legitimize their positions vis-à-vis other	Territorial representations of the actors (mapped or not)	Actors' representation of the conflict (as in the notion of "just war", "holy war", etc.)

In this context, the notion of power, which implies a subordinate relationship between two actors, and the study of the different representations of the actors involved, occupy a central place in the analysis. Indeed, each geopolitical actor develops its representation of the world, which legitimizes in its eyes its way of acting and being part of it. Beyond strategies of domination, rivalries of power are also conflicts of representation (representations of the world, territorial representations, representations of authority and justice, cultural, and political representations, etc.). The geopolitical analysis, therefore, requires the ability to account for the different representations at stake or even to question its own analysis, however complex it may be. This reflexive approach makes it possible to introduce critical methodologies when researching defence issues using geographical and geopolitical methods and to avoid formulating expert opinions based on positivist and normative approaches to spatial phenomena, without explanations and analytical perspectives.

Geodata and Geospatial Intelligence and their methodological implications: evolution or revolution?

Today, technological advances in the field of geographical sciences seem to make these methodologies partly obsolete. Indeed, with new technical and commercial data capture and acquisition capabilities, geographic intelligence can be based on an increasingly important set of information and data (satellite images, geospatial data, etc.). Faced with these new sources of information, it is, therefore, necessary to question the relevance of qualitative and critical methods derived from contemporary human geography.

The promises of battlefield digitalization

The Geoint (for Geospatial Intelligence), a concept invented in the 1990s, became the main focus of the new National Geospatial Intelligence Agency in 2003. This agency, dedicated to the production and dissemination of geodata for the US military, aim at meeting the strategic needs for information superiority (Boulanger 2016). However, while the critical approach invites the researcher to deconstruct the social and political dimensions of geographical space, geospatial intelligence, on the contrary, seems to lead military geography into a technological mutation that produces and processes data without ever questioning them. In recent years, the emergence of new tools such as Big Data and Intelligence have maximized expectations. The hypothesis is that massive real-time data processing would significantly improve our knowledge of the environment, and could even allow to predict events and behaviours.

Therefore in the last decades, the military sector has dedicated a lot of researches and investments to this field. The most enthusiastic speeches in strategic circles see it as a major opportunity to predict and anticipate future threats of all types (social, economic, political or natural) and thus to build a tool to prevent potential wars. One of the main consequences of these programmes and investments is the increasing datafication of the battlefield. In France, the so-called FELIN programme[4] (FELIN for Integrated Infantryman Equipment and Communications), which integrates several sensors directly into military equipment, or the SCORPION program[5] illustrates this phenomenon within the French army. Other recent technical progress has also enabled the development of new tools, including autonomous land vehicles (robotic vehicles) and unmanned aerial vehicles (UAVs). These autonomous machines capture, store and analyse different types of data. The aim is to collect as much data as possible and to increase the volume of information flows between all components of the military ecosystem. This process leads to the progressive transcription of the entire battle environment into digital data and its networking. As far as data is concerned, their networking makes it possible to exchange, centralize, and enhance them. *De facto*, the value of data mainly depends on its processing. Indeed, via data mining, even the most common digital data can acquire strategic value by being correlated with other data. The role of the Geoint engineer is, therefore, crucial in this valorization process. It is undeniable that geospatial intelligence makes it possible to produce relevant, accurate, and localized information, both at the tactical and strategic levels.

Finally, another dimension of digitalization concerns the potentially predictive nature of data and the ability of geospatial intelligence to anticipate events in the field. Indeed, because of the structural changes that these techniques bring to the way knowledge is built by promoting correlation on causality, it would be possible to make statistical predictions using models applied to a corpus of data. These algorithmic techniques are now used in the field of security and defence to anticipate crises and conflicts. Many programmes have been launched in recent years by the US Department of Defense and the CIA (Himelfarb 2014). For example, the CIA's Open Source Indicators programme seeks to predict political crises, epidemics, economic crises, shortages, and natural disasters in specific regions. This kind of initiative has multiplied over the past decade, bringing together new private actors specialized in this activity. This appeals to more pluridisciplinary competences (and precisely computing competences) from the researcher investigating defence issues with geographical methods.

War and geodata, consequences and limits in terms of methodology

Nevertheless, the widespread use of Geoint techniques as a decision-making tool in the field may have its limitations. Indeed, the various sensors on the battlefield and the multiple sources of accessible data can have significant consequences in terms of intelligence and on the conduct of operations. One possible consequence could be the *hyper-personalization* of war (Dunlap 2014). Based on the model of the realization of consumer profiles in trade, similar processes have been applied in the military field in the United States to identify real or potential enemies. With this in mind, the National Security Agency (NSA) collects millions of facial images every day and maintains a database that can be used by sophisticated facial recognition programmes. Combined with the increasing use of drones, alone or in swarms, it would become possible to identify each combatant on the battlefield and to perform targeted strikes. The consequences are important. With regard to the conduct of operations, Dunlap referred to three possible developments. These technologies would enable the defence institutions to focus on key targets, allowing them to destabilize enemy armies profoundly, either by "decapitating" the leaders or by targeting technicians and individuals who are difficult to replace because of their specific skills. Then, the mere fact of being able to select the targeted individuals according to their own identity would have an effect on the psychology of force as a whole (Dunlap 2014). Finally, the identification of the combatants also makes it possible to contact them individually to weaken their determination.

More recently, the case of the Strava application illustrates the digitalization of the battlefield as a bottom-up process, showing that a lot of geospatial data can be entirely out of control of the leadership holder. Strava is a sports application, enabling the user to track his activity in both time and space, using geospatial data. Soldiers have widely used it in their private lives. In January 2019, an Australian student found out that the map listing the routes was fully available as open-source data on the Internet. However, the only concern of the defence institutions at the time was the risk of unveiling military bases. But a French journalist uncovered that, besides this threat, the use of cross-referenced data available on the Internet could allow the identification of the people behind the map. To prove this, he was able to associate geospatial data from the application with the identities of five members of the French intelligence services. This case shows that the digitalization of the battlefield has raised vulnerabilities generated by geodata that are beyond control. There again, this appeals for more awareness of researchers in social sciences towards technical competences to be found in computer and statistical sciences.

Finally, the promise of predictive information can be seriously nuanced. Indeed, similar attempts have already been developed in the case of "predictive policing". These techniques intended to produce predictive analysis of the most likely areas where future crimes will occur, have had mixed results. Two types of predictive policing practices can be distinguished: predictive mapping, which formulates predictive analyses on when and where crimes could take place based on aggregate data, and predictive identification, which attempts to define, at the collective or individual level, profiles of potential criminals or victims. The most widely used technique to date is predictive mapping, which has led to the implementation of various programmes around the world, such as PredPol in the United States and Great Britain, Criminality Awareness System in the Netherlands, Precobs in Germany and Switzerland, and KEYCRIME in Italy. It is still too early to assess the results of such devices, although many biases have already been reported. Thus, in the case of PredPol, initial feedback highlighted the lack of transparency of the algorithms used by the company to carry out its processing, and errors in data collection that lead to causal prediction errors[6]. If these digital tools are likely to continue to develop for economic reasons, their relevance can yet be questioned. In any case, the same reservations can be made about the notion of Anticipatory Intelligence implemented under Geoint.

Therefore it seems necessary to articulate Geoint's development with a critical approach that puts the information produced and data generated in perspective with the potential biases created by this type of analysis and the vulnerabilities that can result from this use. In other words, this means that these digital tools must be combined with critical and qualitative methodologies in the social sciences, and that the generalization of geodata technology does not make human geography approaches any less relevant.

Conclusion

The scientific use of geography by military organizations in their operations spread in the 19th century at all levels (tactical, operational, and strategic). However, at that time, the geography used in defence studies was mostly deterministic, with an emphasis on physical geography, geology or climatology supposed to condition human actions. Nevertheless, the use of German *Geopolitik* by the Nazi regime has revealed the dangers of such an approach. However, the same deterministic and technicist approach seems to be promoted, in a more or less conscious way, with the development of the Geoint. Even if the accuracy of the information given by digital tools is not called into question here, there is a risk of hiding the political dimension of human action behind technical expertise. Geographer Louise Amoore has clearly shown the reasons why governments and decision-makers base their security and defence policies on statistical expertise (Amoore 2013). Indeed, how can such a decision be challenged when the political choices seem to be hidden behind numbers?

Also, the question of the future of geography in defence studies, and more particularly human geography, is now more important than ever. Several calls have already been made for critical reflection on geodata and its uses (Amoore 2013; Kitchin 2014; Davadie et al. 2016). Geography must, therefore, take its rightful place in this evolving strategic reflection. Geographers must be able to combine technical approaches, based on the processing of geodata, with qualitative and critical approaches from human geography and the social sciences. Indeed, data analysis should not be limited to technical criteria. It should integrate a more global approach, combining political, social, economic, cultural, or ethical dimensions. In this sense, the methodologies of human geography and social sciences remain more relevant than ever in the interpretation of spatial phenomena in the study of defence issues.

Notes

1 Transcontinental lines in America and Europe were created at the same time.
2 Having converted to geography for health reasons, he obtained his doctorate in 1913 and became a professor at the University of Munich in 1919.
3 Galgano explains: "Distance links locations and may be viewed in both an absolute and a relative sense. The spatial separation between points, usually measured by some known standard (e.g. miles or kilometres), defines absolute distance. In contrast, relative distance translates linear measurements into other, more meaningful, spatial relationships" (Galgano 2011: 45).
4 This combat system aims at improving five functions of the warrior: communication, observation, lethality, protection, mobility and human support. The soldier on the battlefield receives and produces data.
5 Scorpion is a large modernization program aiming at replacing a variety of aging infantry vehicles. All the new vehicles employ the modern Scorpion Information and Communications System (SIC-S), which creates an integrated network of data sharing.
6 For instance, the "prediction of banalities", meaning that neighbourhoods already known as "sensitive" are systematically pointed out by the software. Therefore, it increases the probability that these neighbourhoods will reappear in future analyses.

References

Amoore, L. (2013). *The Politics of Possibility: Risk and Security Beyond Probability*, Durham, NC, Duke University Press.
Aron, R. (1962). *Paix et guerre entre les nations*, Paris, Calmann-Levy.
Boulanger, P. (2002). *La Géographie militaire française (1871–1939)*, Paris, Economica.
Boulanger, P. (2006). *Géographie militaire*, Paris, Ellipses.
Boulanger, P. (2011). *Géographie militaire et géostratégie*, Paris, Armand Colin.
Boulanger, P. (2016). De la géographie militaire au Geospatial Intelligence, 153–168. In: Boulanger, P. (ed.) (2016). *Géographie et guerre*, Bulletin de la Société de géographie, Hors-Série, Paris, Société de Géographie.
Cattaruzza, A., Limonier, K. (2019). *Introduction à la géopolitique*, Paris, Armand Colin.

Coutau-Bégarie, H. (2006). Géographie militaire. In: De Montbrial, T., Klein, J. (eds) (2000). *Dictionnaire de stratégie*, Paris, Presses universitaires de France.

Davadie, P., Kempf, O., Teboul, B. (Ed.) (2016). *La donnée n'est pas donnée*, Annecy le Vieux, Editions Kawa.

Dunlap Jr, C. J. (2014). The hyper-personalization of war: Cyber, Big Data, and the changing face of conflict. *Georgetown Journal of International Affairs* 15, International Engagement on Cyber IV, 108–118.

Galgano, F.A. (2011). An introduction to geography for non-geographer, 38–53. In Galgano, F. A., Eugene, J. P. (ed.) (2011). *Modern Military Geography*, New York, London, Routledge.

Flint, C. (ed.) (2004). *The Geography of War and Peace*, Oxford, Oxford University Press.

Godlewska, A. (1994). Napoleon's geographers (1797–1815): Imperialists and soldiers of modernity, 31–54 In: Godlewska, A., Smith N. (Eds.) (1994). *Geography and Empire*, Oxford, Blackwell.

Himelfarb, S. (2014). Can Big Data stop wars before they happen? *Foreign Policy*, 25, available online: https://foreignpolicy.com/2014/04/25/can-big-data-stop-wars-before-they-happen/ (Consulted on 2019).

Kitchin, R. (2014). *The Data Revolution*, Sage, London.

Kremer-Marietti, A. (2017). Le positivisme. *Encyclopedia Universalis*, Paris, Encyclopedia Universalis2017.

Lacoste, Y. (1982). *La Géographie, ça sert d'abord à faire la guerre*. 2nd ed., Paris, Maspero.

Lacoste, Y. (2012). Le « pivot géographique de l'histoire »: une lecture critique. *Hérodote*, (3), 139–158.

Mackinder, H. (1992). Le pivot géographique de l'Histoire [1904]. *Stratégique*, n°55, available online: http://www.institut-strategie.fr/strat_055_MACKINDERP.html (Consulted on 2019).

Mareï, N., Richard, Y. (2018). *Dictionnaire de la régionalisation du monde*, Paris, Atlande.

Mayer-Shönberger, V., Cukier, K. (2014). *Big Data. La révolution des données est en marche*, Paris, Robert Laffont.

Motte, M. (2006). Géostratégie. In: De Montbrial, T., Klein, J. (eds) (2000). *Dictionnaire de stratégie*. Paris, Presses universitaires de France.

Motte, M. (2018). La géostratégie. In: Motte, M.*et al.* (eds) (2018). *La mesure de la force*, Paris, Tallandier, 251–274.

Muscarà, L. (2018). Maps, complexity, and the uncertainty of power, 362–379. In: Coleman, M., Agnew, J. (eds) (2018). *Handbook on the Geographies of Power*, Cheltenham, Northampton, Edward Elgar Publishing.

O'Tuathail, G. (1999). Understanding critical geopolitics: Geopolitics and risk security. In: Colin, C.S., Sloan, G. (eds) (1999). *Geopolitics, Geography and Strategy*, London, Frank Cass.

O'Tuathail, G., Dalby, S. (1998). *Rethinking Geopolitics*, London, Routledge.

Rech, M., Bos, D., Jenkings, K. N., Williams, A., Woodward, R. (2015). Geography, military geography, and critical military studies. *Critical Military Studies*, 1(1), 47–60.

Woodward, R. (2004). *Military Geographies*. RGS-IBG Book Series, Malden, MA, Oxford, Victoria, Blackwell Publishing.

2 Defence studies and public law
Emergence, affirmation and methodology of a research field

Anne-Sophie Traversac

Introduction

What public law and defence have in common is that they allow us to reflect on the settlement and perpetuation of the state. Defence in this sense might be one of the key issues of public law. While taking a closer look, this intricate dependence between defence and public law seems to be established but not verified when analysing security and defence studies. It seems to be a work in progress regarding research in security and defence. This leads to an accurate need of methodology in this field, which will be further developed in this chapter.

When focusing on methods regarding defence and security issues we may first keep in mind the traditional distinction in the French legal order. Fundamental distinction for French jurists is made between public law and private law. This distinction goes back to Roman law: when the state is a party implied, public law should be enforced. Another way of defining public law confirms this distinction by mainly relying on the notion of general interest, as a goal to protect a Nation. Every system worldwide integrates a distinction between public law and private law. The essential question relies on how we conceive it. France considers that relations where the state is implied should be governed by rules that are different from the rules applying between particulars. French-law developed rules that could be defined as those of a "protecting" state. Before the French Revolution, the Fundamental Laws of the Kingdom constituted the material constitutional law of the French Monarchy. After the Revolution, the distinction between private and public law could be clearly expressed by the construction of two orders of jurisdiction: one is an administrative Supreme Court – the *Conseil d'Etat* (State Council) – the other is the Judiciary Supreme Court – the *Cour de Cassation* (Court of Cassation) dealing with civil, commercial, social or criminal cases. Even if they are organized in a similar manner, they apply different rules. One jurisdiction could distinguish any conflictual matter, the *Tribunal des Conflits* (the Court of conflicts).

The distinction between public and private law is essential to explain the classical structure of French law regarding defence issues. This explains consequently the organization of law studies in French universities. This is the point we may keep in mind for defence studies. This underlines, too, the way research is growing and how researchers can conceive their work and accordingly their career. The teaching and research methods concerning the defence field are supposed to acknowledge the powerful meaning of two separate branches. In this chapter we will particularly rely on the French case concerning methodological elements of domestic public law.

Another key to understanding French law and the place for defence in public law within French law consists in establishing a pyramidal conception of rules. The French Revolution legislators considered in 1789 that fundamental rights and rules regarding separation of powers needed to be written down clearly. In this regard French constitutional issues are henceforth mostly expressed through written laws. Methodologically this means that the core method for research in public law is the analysis of this written material and the correlation between the different texts. Public law, which comprises defence law, incarnates the pyramidal construction of norms in the French legal system. Following Kelsen's "pure theory of law" (Kelsen 2017; Herrera 1997), this means that public law (and consequently defence public law as a small branch of public law) considers the Constitution as the top of the pyramid. All the other branches of public law should thus conform to the Constitution: international (including European) law should conform to constitutional law (Art. 55 of the French Constitution), laws voted by the Parliament (or by the people directly, which is very rare) and also administrative regulatory texts (decrees, for instance). Defence issues borrow from all of these matters, and, in parallel, the same questions arise about methodology. This means there is a difficulty in correctly identifying the field, this means there is also a key challenge to determine the most effective methods. Therefore in this chapter we will concentrate in a more restrictive way on a contemporary approach and particularly focus on the last two decades. Security and defence have been the recurrent subjects of laws and moreover it has been a research topic in public law. Regarding the French conception of public law, defence studies are not a classical field from an academic point of view. This chapter thus aims at explaining how these questions have become an object of research and teaching in the last decades in public law and what consequences is has on methodology. The chapter first examines how defence issues can be investigated by relying on external law (international and European law). This raises a challenge because of the fragmentation of defence and security rules and norms in different fields. Then the second part will focus on domestic law and how defence issues tend to convey the need for mixed methods (mainly derived from law and political science) so as to better grasp the complexity of domestic legal measures concerning defence issues. In this part we will observe how defence studies emerged as a major research topic and spread into general public law in the recent years. We will draw our arguments from the case of French domestic law, as each country's normative system implies a wide variety of defence-law systems in the democratic states, let alone worldwide. This example enables yet to derive general conclusions concerning methodology.

What place for Defence Studies in public law?

When looking at the place occupied by security and defence issues in public law, they spread into classical and historical structures of French public law. In this part we will show and explain why security and defence issues are fragmented into different subfields of public law. We observe that despite the demonstrated spread, the same methodology tools are useful.

A fragmentation of security and defence studies in public law: origins and effects in external law and their methodological consequences

In the last decades, security and defence studies have spread more and more within French public law. This phenomenon is the result of both distant and more immediate origins. The distinction between domestic and international law is a good start to understand this fragmentation.

External law refers to norms having an external origin. France consents to these norms, France is also part of several international organizations which can enforce norms having a direct or indirect application (like in the case of the EU for instance). Focusing on defence issues leads us to observe the place and role of international and European laws in the French legal system and how the evolution of these laws combine with the emergence of a normative apparatus concerning defence issues.

International public law and defence: what method for a valid research?

As far as international public law is concerned it is quite clear that the place of defence and security matters. This comes from the evolution of international relations and its effects on the international normative order since World War II. After 1945 more and more treaties and international agreements have been signed coinciding with the development of more and more international organizations in different fields (and not only concerning military issues). These organizations have been created not only to offer economic forums but also to help build peace and develop human rights and democracy values worldwide. In the defence field different organizations tend to overlap and fulfil the same types of commitments: the collective defence clause of NATO in 1949 is the most common example on a regional scale (Zarka 1997). This clause concerning collective defence as set up by the Washington Treaty of 1949 is the result of different commitments. Indeed in 1947 France and United Kingdom signed the Treaty of Dunkirk. This treaty of alliance and mutual assistance was the first of its kind after World War II. In the text the enemy has been clearly pointed out: the essential motivation was to protect France and the United Kingdom against the potentiality of an act of aggression from Germany. This tells us a lot about the original way in which the European security system has been conceived. After this first attempt the idea of common assistance has been brought further to a wider scale with the Treaty of Brussels signed in 1948 between France, United Kingdom, Belgium, Luxembourg and The Netherlands (Van Ackere 1995). With this treaty these European partners gave birth to the Western Union (WU) which is the first European intergovernmental organization after World War II. The treaty aimed at different objectives including economic, social and cultural cooperation among member states. The member states essentially accepted a mutual defence clause (Art. IV).

We underline so far the need to follow the classical method used by researchers in law: the primary research tools here are mainly texts, treaties and conventions for the examples above, whatever number of states implied, whatever the success of neither the treaty nor the organization. These sources are relatively easy to obtain as many are open-source data, like in the case of a treaty or an official legal agreement for instance. But the difficulty here is the period before the text is officially released, which can be very long as long as the legal negotiations are not closed. The researcher might rely on press releasees, and even sometimes interviews (see Chapter 4 on this issue) to get information. This leads to an important challenge: first, we may ask which information can be used, and then, we must question at what stage can we use it? Regarding security and defence, a small number of blogs are very useful ("Bruxelles2" provides a good example, as a blog both in French and English), a large number of Internet sources can be helpful but can't be considered as scientific material. Law researchers are first and consequently deprived of a substantial amount of information: they need to give themselves a methodology to analyse which media can be used, with necessary discernment. This methodology is very close to the one used in political science; researchers are more used to questioning the media, and to using media sources in their own researches.

As for the content, we can underline that recalling these treaties is an important element to understanding what collective defence means and how it translates into legal norms. Studying defence clauses leads us on the one hand to take into account the United Nations Charter and its Article 51 on legitimate defence for instance (see Verhoeven 2002; Cassese 2005). Even though many criticisms had been raised in the previous decades towards the functioning of the Security Council and the use of veto by some powerful states (like Russia or China in the last decade) the UN remains the only universal international organization providing for collective security and defence and giving directives on how to achieve them by using peaceful means to solve inter-state disputes (particularly in Chapter 6 and Chapter 7 of the UN Charter) (see Anderson 2009 considering the Security Council as a Talking Shop in an age of rising multipolarity). On the other hand it also leads us to consider the regional collective or mutual defence clauses such as the famous article V from the Washington Treaty in the case of the most powerful military alliance (NATO) in the world in the contemporary era. These two examples provide the basis of collective defence at the global level and at the regional level (NATO here, but it is also true for the EU, for instance) which builds upon the international norms derived from the UN Charter as the basis of contemporary international law. Again, we can highlight the main difficulty for the researcher in public law: the main weaknesses of the Security Council are not made of classical materials for law researchers. In fact, the method needs here focus on content analysis of the positive material, but also and mostly what is not in the material texts: the analysis of the Security Council's action in this field relies more on what isn't done nor written. This leads to common methodology challenges between research in law and in political science.

Moreover, this brief analysis of collective defence clauses enable us to highlight an interesting element in line with the purpose of this edited volume: the main handbooks on international public law dedicate pages to collective security, but not more than a chapter, even not more than 20 pages (out of 800) on collective security (see, for instance, Armstrong 2009; Aust 2010). In these pages (or chapters) much attention is paid to the history of limitation of the use of force or to the focus on classical authors like Grotius (*De jure belli ac pacis*, 1625) or Vattel (*The Law of Nations*, 1758). The often cited example are the League of nations (1919) and the Briand-Kellogg Pact (1928) to explain the UN Charter: "*All Members shall refrain in their international relations from the threat or use of force*" (Art. 2 §4 of the UN Charter; see Schrijver 2005). Many pages could be written here, cross-fertilizing law and political science by relying on similar methodological tools.

Defence issues are only one matter over plenty of examples of the development of international public law. The place of these issues is yet essential given the history of war and peace between nations, but this topic is still given a minor place in most international law handbooks. As a matter of fact, defence materials and norms are mostly presented and developed in dedicated fields such as international law for armed conflicts or international humanitarian law (see for instance Fleck et al. 1999; Bothe 2013; Clapham et al. 2014; Weller et al. 2015). Security and defence are only a small part of international public law, even though collective security and peace making is the inherent aim of the United Nations given by the San Francisco Charter of 1945.

What are the consequences of this marginal position of defence norms when researching and teaching international public law? This mainly results in the fact that before reaching the master's level of study most public law students (in the French case) only tackle defence issues as one example among many others. This lack of specific teaching on defence issues in French universities is also linked to the content of security and defence on an international scale and the disciplinary divide in teaching those matters at Bachelor level. In most French universities international relations are considered as a branch of political science as much as of international law. The terror attacks of 2015 even started raising the awareness of the French academia on the lack of war studies in France (Holeindre 2015; Holeindre and Vilmer 2015). The multiplication of treaties and organizations within the international order born after 1945 leave the field of international relations open to different disciplinary investigations including in law. Even though law studies are not the only relevant matter on this kind of issue, law remains an important part of the research and teaching in defence issues.

International public law is closely linked to international relations and international politics investigated by political science. The close link between both different academic fields is also a point that we need to explore further. The French academic system tends to separate these two fields. In international public law security and defence questions are studied basically in the first years of Law studies (Bachelor degree). Deep attention is paid at master's level (4th and 5th year of study), when students choose to specialize in international public law. They are then offered a complete overview of security and defence issues. Furthermore, this insulated position of defence issues is a bit unfortunate as many issues of international law could fundamentally be treated through the prism of defence studies. One good illustration of this point could be environmental law. This is now a good example of a rapidly emerging issue both quantitatively and qualitatively. Some aspects of environmental law became, obviously, major security and defence issues: the consequences of armed conflicts on environment is the topic of a PhD in public law and of many more papers from students, as it's a subject of teachings of qualified publicists (see for instance Kiss 1989; Beurier 2017).

Methodological issues in the European Union law research investigating defence issues

The regional development of the European Union is also a good way of understanding how defence found a place in research and teaching in public law. Here we will not discuss the question of the nature of European Union, as it not crucial to our argument (see for instance Grard 2012). Indeed the legal history and development of the European Union implied first the marginalization of security and defence issues.

In 1951 six European countries created the European Coal and Steel Community (ECSC). Belgium, France, Italy, Luxembourg, the Netherlands and West Germany founded an organization to regulate the industrial production of coal and steel. Before pursuing and founding in Rome two other communities, they attempted to set up a European Defence Community (EDC) in 1950 (based on a French plan, the Pleven Plan). After years of negotiations to get all the partners' agreements on the EDC Treaty (also called the Paris Treaty), the French Assembly failed in ratifying the text in 1954 as the opposition against the Treaty won the parliament over (see Aron and Lerner 1956; Vial 1992; Buton 2004). This led to the first failure in the attempt to build a European security system by the European States themselves as they simultaneously ratified the Washington Treaty and committed to NATO ruled by the American leadership (see Deschaux-Dutard 2018). The consequence of this historical sequence is a twisted conception of European security by European States still prevailing in the 21st century.

If European defence is a current teaching subject in many Anglo-Saxon universities (in Germany, the UK, the Netherlands ...), it is still quite marginal in French law Bachelor degrees but became a raising research topic in the last two decades for PhD students and researchers in political science and public law (see for instance Irondelle and Vennesson 2002; Irondelle 2002; Mérand 2008; Terpan and Saurugger 2018). As we pointed out that security and defence issues globally occupy a small part of international public law handbooks, the same applies to handbooks on the European Union. It is of course different in the Anglo-Saxon academic literature were plenty of edited books and handbooks can be found on European defence (see for instance, Mérand 2008; Biscop and Whitman 2012; Meijer and Wyss 2018). Different reasons could explain this. First of all, European defence has had some failures and mostly relies on intergovernmental non-constraining rules. From 1954, when France decided not to continue any further in the establishment of the EDC, and sanction from the Lisbon Treaty, European defence did not generate so many binding legal rules (even though it seems to be changing in the Brexit context since 2017 and the adoption of Permanent Structured Cooperation (PESCO), for instance). European defence relies on a long list of negotiations and summits and numerous small steps. The Treaty of Maastricht (Treaty on European Union, 1992) is one of them. It adopts a cautious formulation: "The common foreign and security policy shall include all questions related to the security of the Union, including the eventual framing of a common defence policy, which might in time lead to a common defence" (Article J.4). This Article demonstrates the common progresses of European defence. From 1954 to 1992, there has been a constant construction of European "conception" of defence. In 1992 the Maastricht Treaty altered the former treaties and created a European Union based on three different pillars, including the Common Foreign and Security Policy (CFSP) which was renamed Common Security and Defence Policy (CSDP) by the Lisbon Treaty (2007). During the general evolution of the Union, moving faster on some policies also explains the minor place of defence studies even if we can underline a coherent construction of European rules of law in security and defence issues.

As well as for international public law, European law research tends to leave defence issues under-investigated. As defence has long been apart from the integration process, handbooks are progressively adding defence issues as it becomes more and more subject to discussions and analysis (see for instance, Blumann and Dubouis 2016).

Regarding the methodology to investigate European defence relying on public law, we can conclude in the same way as for international public law. Indeed, researchers in law are mostly using treaties and the rules deriving from those treaties. All materials existing before the treaties can be referred as "grey materials": these are key to understand defence issues in the EU but this soft law is not yet the first material for research in public law. This means that law researchers on this field are not numerous because their object is not yet clearly identified as a law research object. The consequence of this is major for the career of young researchers in law wanting to uncover European defence issues; when researchers are interested in this field, they can hesitate when choosing a PhD subject: one can ask if this subject, borrowing from public law and political science, can be relevant for the a researcher aspiring to a tenure position in the academia.

Regarding the teaching methodology on such issues, the situation is quite similar as the one described above concerning international public law. Bachelor degrees in law mainly focus on non-security and defence aspects of EU law. Only students who want to pursue a master's degree in international and/or European law are actually confronted with defence issues and given legal perspective on these issues. Unlike international public law researches which can focus on security and defence studies as a subpart of this academic field, European law students and researchers who want to focus on defence issues are confronted with a new reading of European history, focusing on defence. It is an interesting specialization though. For instance, legal understanding of European defence issues can help understand how neutral states have accepted to ratify articles enabling other states to cooperate further and faster on defence issues with the PESCO mechanism adopted in 2017 by the European Council without having to commit into PESCO themselves.[1] Even if defence has not yet moved from cooperation to integration, public law is more and more accurate on these issues and needs to be completed by others academic fields, such as political science or economics. Research in European law becomes all the more relevant on defence issues as the Lisbon Treaty has increased the level of norms applying in the field of European defence and security. This translates to handbooks on European Union law tend to start devoting more substance to issues related to CFSP and CSDP. Likewise the increasing role of security and defence issues in the EU will call for more defence developments in the near future with an emerging role for the Court of Justice of the European Union (see for instance Terpan and Saurugger 2018).

As shown in this part defence studies are increasingly tackled by international and European laws. We will now analyse the situation of defence issues in French domestic law and show its consequences in terms of methodology.

Understanding the fragmentation of security and defence studies in public law: the methodology of domestic law in defence studies

Research on defence issues has overcome an important evolution in the last decades. As in the case of external law, domestic law (mainly constitutional law but not only) develops a growing interest for defence issues. If the contemporary context (the aftermath of the terror attacks in France and Europe) is one of the main reasons, a reasonable and major development is also underway: when law was considered as a constraint before, it seems to be socially better accepted.

The first purpose of constitutional law is the reference to texts and practices incarnating the way a state is ruled. Devolution and separation of powers are developed in the French Constitution (the Constitution of the 5th Republic adopted in 1958). Thought and designed by General Charles de Gaulle, the Constitution of 1958 mainly relies on principles which exacerbate the role and powers of the French President. The practice of government by Charles de Gaulle during the first decade is still relevant today to investigate how French institutions work. Methodologically speaking we need to underline again here the proximity between law and political science, even though contrary to a political scientist, a public law researcher who wants to investigate the practice of legal texts is confronted with the difficulty of lacking experience concerning research interviews. So he/she needs to focus on the analysis of content, even though legal texts may sometimes be parsimonious.

Indeed regarding defence the French Constitution is not very revealing. Few clauses concern defence but the main elements on defence are not written in this very text. The only and major point is the leader's identification: defence relies on the decision of the President of the Republic. According to the Article 15: "The President of the Republic shall be Commander-in-Chief of the Armed Forces. He shall preside over the higher national defence councils and committees".[2] Furthermore the government "shall have at its disposal the civil service and the armed forces" (Article 20) and the Prime Minister "shall be responsible for national defence" (Article 21).[3] Yet confronting the text and practice under the current 5th Republic, the President is the essential player. He is the only one in charge of the nomination of his Prime Minister, who should have the confidence of the lower House of Parliament (*Assemblée nationale*). France knew three periods of distortion of majority, named "*cohabitation*" between the President and the lower House: 1986–1988, 1993–1995, and 1997–2002. French President François Mitterrand let there be no doubt about who had the power of decision in the defence field in 1986. The *cohabitation* between a president and a prime minister of different political colours raised the question of the adaptation of the text to this new practice. 1988 was the first time since 1958 that the Parliament had a political majority different from the one supporting the President. The answer of President Mitterrand to this context was clear. The Constitution should apply with a simple principle: the whole Constitution, nothing but the Constitution (address to the lower House in 1986). This practice revealed the perpetuation and confirmation that the 5th Republic is a parliamentary regime. The defence field is a very interesting subject to investigate the functioning of the regime. At this exact period when President Mitterrand analysed how the fundamental norm would apply, he tried simultaneously to preserve the fundamental powers that the Constitution gives to the President (see Howorth 1992). One aspect is particularly clear. When the Prime Minister had been chosen among the new majority in the Parliament, he had to compose the government. He expressed clear concerns about who would be appointed as defence minister and as minister of foreign affairs. This clearly shows that he wanted to keep the defence and international relations areas under his supervision. Years later the last *cohabitation* in France made no exception on this issue. From 1997 to 2002, President Chirac and Prime Minister Jospin attended together meetings on defence and foreign affairs matters. Even if the Prime Minister could have the Parliament vote on different aspects of defence, defence historically remains an issue under the private turf of the executive power (*domaine reservé*; see Howorth 1992).

The text of the French Constitution gives the main responsibility of defence to the executive. The President of the Republic "shall preside over the higher national defence councils and committees" (Article 15). Nevertheless the role of the Parliament increased slightly in the last decades in this field (see Deschaux-Dutard 2017). Historically the Parliament disposes of the war powers: "A declaration of war shall be authorized by the Parliament" (Article 35 §1). Yet in practice there has been no use of this article under the 5th Republic. For instance the "war on terror" that President Hollande launched after the terror attacks in Paris in November 2015 is legally not a war. The role of Parliament increased with regard to defence issues since the last amendment of the Constitution initiated in 2008.

The amended Article 35 states:

> The Government shall inform Parliament of its decision to have the armed forces intervene abroad, at the latest three days after the beginning of said intervention. It shall detail the objectives of the said intervention. This information may give rise to a debate, which shall not be followed by a vote.
>
> (§2)

"Where the said intervention shall exceed four months, the Government shall submit the extension to Parliament for authorization. It may ask the National Assembly to make the final decision" (§3). The 24th renewal of the text of the Constitution in 2008 was the most extensive since 1958. More than half of the articles were modified. The aim was to revalorize the Parliament and to promote a better control of the executive. Actually defence is not a pertinent illustration of the aim and result of this constitutional reform. The Parliament takes benefit of a scrutiny that had never existed before. When the government decides to send armed forces abroad, he has to inform the Parliament. The Prime Minister is also only informed. This is a positive evolution but the information is totally controlled by the government. Moreover the Parliament has also seen its scrutiny competences increased concerning French military interventions abroad: should the intervention exceed four months, the Members of Parliament (MoPs) have to authorize the extension of the intervention. This is also a new power for the legislative body (Gohin 2014). Yet the practice of the last decade shows sparsity from the MoPs. Defence matters in France usually benefit from a global national consensus among the political elites which makes it difficult for a political party to assume the burden of breaching this consensus. France has until recently not been used to debate on defence issues. This is slowly changing. More politicians are assuming discordant voices after executive decision in this field, as shown when MoPs are debating on defence matters. This could come from a stricter interpretation of the self-defence disposition of the UN Charter (Article 51) that France tended to support for few years. Terrorism has clearly influenced the way France decides to interpret this clause. The operations lead in Iraq and Syria in the recent years are a good illustration of this trend. From a methodological perspective, this means that research in public law on defence issues needs to take international relations into account so as to grasp the complexity of legal measures and their context of application. Which means press content analysis, and discourse analysis in many cases. There again, this pleads for more cross-fertilization with other disciplines, such as political science.

Back to the French case, even if the national consensus on defence is slightly weaker than before, the last Parliamentary votes on defence issues convey three remarks. First of all, all operations were extended without much debate in the Parliament. As only simple majority is required, it is not an obstacle: defence issues are traditionally not used by the opposition to tackle the government contrary to financial or social issues for instance. The Parliament would not risk a government crisis by opposing the extension of a military intervention. This is even truer given the high level of public opinion support towards the French armed forces and their interventions abroad since the terror attacks of 2015.Yet this high level of support could slightly change with the last missions in Sahel. Operations Serval (2013) and Barkhane (since 2015) tend to last for a very long time and have no precise deadlines yet (they should go on as long as terrorism destabilizes this region). Eventually the practice of the renewed Article 35 shows that the Parliament voted when the Executive decided (see Deschaux-Dutard 2017). In the French tradition, when it comes to military intervention abroad, the Executive decisions – which really means the presidential decisions – have generally been accepted with no (or very few) discussion.

However some criticisms occurred recently (yet not enough to change the executive decision). The Serval operation provides a good example here. In January 2013 President Hollande decided to send armed forces in Mali. Despite some hesitations about the first legal arguments conveyed the decision occurred after Malian authorities asked for a French military intervention (see for instance, Traversac 2014). As the operation was embedded in the global fight against terrorism outside French borders it has been easily accepted by the MoPs and the public opinion. Few voices – including the former President Giscard d'Estaing – considered this intervention in Africa as neocolonialism whereas such consideration is typical in France when it comes to relations – *a fortiori* military ones – with former colonies.

Likewise even before the terror attacks in 2015, Paris has decided to lead targeted attacks on Syria which shows an extended interpretation of self-defence. Some legal experts expressed concerns on the legality of these strikes (Fernandez 2015). If their legitimacy has not (yet?) been much of an issue, legality has become a little more of a concern than before. However, these arguments were put aside after November 2015 as France witnessed a "rally around the flag" phenomenon after the massive terror attacks in Paris.

In this section we tried to show that defence occupies a limited space in constitutional law be it in the text or in practice. Defence issues in constitutional law are essential but remain marginal in most handbooks on French constitutional law. They also clearly benefit from cross-fertilization with political science to investigate the gap between the texts and their practice. This leads to the same conclusion as in the case of international or European Law: defence studies are conceptually essential for the state and yet defence issues remain under investigated in many academia and particularly in the French academia. However, the dramatic increase of terrorism on the French ground led to an evolution with the concept of "state of emergency".

A new golden era for research on defence: methodology and the weight of political actuality in public law research on defence issues

The increase in terrorist activities both on the French territory and abroad called for renewed norms and a cultural change towards security and defence issues. The example of the amended Article 35 of the French Constitution has been extensively explained above. Defence took a more important place in the Constitution. Indeed the terror attacks of November 2015 shed a new light on the interpretation the French Constitution. At this time legal researchers discovered that some constitutional tools were of no use. To start with Article 16 has become useless. It states

> Where the institutions of the Republic, the independence of the Nation, the integrity of its territory or the fulfillment of its international commitments are under serious and immediate threat, and where the proper functioning of the constitutional public authorities is interrupted, the President of the Republic shall take measures required by these circumstances, after formally consulting the Prime Minister, the Presidents of the Houses of Parliament and the Constitutional Council.

This article was used only once since 1958 during the decolonization war in Algeria. The conditions mentioned are clearly not suited for the actual 21st-century context. A few hours after the attacks on the Bataclan Theater, and even before the situation was totally under control, the Ministers had a meeting in the presidential palace to discuss a much needed evolution on this point.

Another constitutional article turned out to be useless. Article 36 calling upon "A state of siege" which "shall be decreed in the Council of Ministers". Like Article 16, Article 36 implies powers that would have been disproportionate to the threat by transferring the decision power from civilian to military authorities.

Another tool has been developed in the field of defence and security law in France since 2015. It is the state of emergency created in a law of 1955 again in the context of the decolonization warfare in Algeria. In a state of emergency, a first decree must be issued by the executive and if the state of emergency shall continue, the Parliament should then extend its application by a law in a period of 12 days. On 16 November 2015, President Hollande pronounced a speech before the Congress[4] where he proposed a constitutional reform in order to amend the different legal tools needed if the nation is put at risk. This reform essentially aimed at introducing in the Constitution the only tool which was not of constitutional level: the state of emergency. This state of emergency had been proclaimed by decree less than three days before. We will not discuss here the question of the possibility to amend the Constitution during such a period. Such an amendment would have not been unconstitutional (Article 89 of the French Constitution does not forbid it), but this could be a means to underline the vacuity of the existing French legal tools when such a specific and dramatic context leads to the worst decisions. Surprisingly the constitutional reform did not succeed for a reason. In addition to the reform of emergency legal procedures, the French President aimed at adding a clause enabling the loss of citizenship in case of participation to a terrorist activity. This implied an important political debate on this issue among French political elites whereas the defence issues were not disputed as much ... This example provides for the relative political consensus on defence issues that we underlined above among the French political elites. It is also interesting to note that this constitutional reform could have given Parliament more competences to discuss different possibilities to answer the terrorist threat through legal defence and security tools. But as many proposals of constitutional reform before, this proposal has mainly been designed to answer the threat as quickly as possible and without taking the time for a global debate on the process of creating new legal defence and security tools.

The state of emergency (2015–2017) has had several consequences to take into account, as observed by a law researcher on defence issues. What is striking is the tremendous amount of books related to the state of emergency (see for instance Beaud and Bargues 2016; Cassia 2016). This aftermath of the terrorist attack can be qualified as a golden age for defence studies in public law in France. This increased legal materials for research on defence issues in public law. Yet again the methods should not only focus on legal measure but also on other sources of information (such as media, political discourses …) for which he/she needs to combine its method with political science methodology (see Chapters 4 and 5 in this volume).

The example of how the news also impacts research on defence issues for researchers in public law (and appeals for more multidisciplinary cross-fertilization) is well illustrated by the example of the state of emergency in France. A classical legal debate particularly found an important echo during this period: it is the debate on the balance between security and the preservation of civil liberties. By essence the state of emergency supposes measures that can result in reducing civil liberties for the sake of the nation's protection. Looking at French institutions we should highlight that after the decree proclaiming the state of emergency, the Parliament voted on the perpetuation of this exceptional legal measure concerning defence and security on the French territory. This law of 20 November 2015 could have been checked by the Constitutional Court which is entitled to give an advice on a legal text under eight days in a case of emergency. As the national consensus was strong on the issue after the terrible trauma caused by the Paris attacks no Member of Parliament (they need to be 60 Congressman or 60 Senators), nor the President of the Republic or the Prime Minister, neither the Presidents of the lower or upper House of Parliament made use of their right to ask the Constitutional Court for judicial advice. Thus there has been no control of conformity of the law declaring the state of emergency towards the French constitutional norms.

The constitutional reform in 2008 introduced the priority question on constitutionality (the so called *QPC*). This tool completes the former control tools happening *a priori* (before a text is passed as a law) with an *a posteriori* control (after the law has been passed). Beyond the constitutional field constitutional decisions (named QPC) reveal the influence of the state of emergency on different matters. For instance concerning administrative law, the chapter on administrative police was renewed and completed. In the field of Fundamental Rights number of civil liberties found a new illustration of the conciliation between security and civil liberty.

Yet this exceptional situation is not completely new in France. In the eyes of the Constitutional Court, the state of emergency played the role of a legal tool enabling the perpetuation of the Rule of Law and underlined the role of the Constitutional Court as a nonexclusive but respectful guardian of constitutional principles.

As a matter of fact security and defence studies have a paradoxical connection with public law. Indeed security and defence studies are naturally composed of measures of public law. Yet the place of public law in defence studies has long been relatively weak quantitatively speaking even though defence questions are, qualitatively speaking, essential for a state. The example of constitutional law developed above with the question of the state of emergency in France has demonstrated it well. Taking a close look at domestic law, defence studies are also developing within public law. This is a rather recent evolution that we observe spreading to all the different fields of public law, even though a classical part of administrative law has for long time dealt with security issues of policing.

The subfield of Fundamental Rights studies are also a good way of witnessing the development of defence issues in public law. Here the conciliation debate between defence of the national territory, security in the wider sense and civil liberty is a key for understanding the teaching and thinking process. The French legal Code on Internal Security states that security is a fundamental right and one of the conditions for enjoying individual and collective liberties (Article L. 111–1). This Code is quite new (2012) but the meaning of this article is older (end of 1970s). As it has been extensively developed in the last years among researchers in public law the conciliation between defence, security, and civil liberties implies judicial answers and furthermore also philosophical and political approaches.

Emerging defence issues (cyber, intelligence …): a stimulating agenda for research in public law

Finally concerning public law, some subfields have been increasingly tackled by defence issues in the recent years. Two elements can be noticed here. First military intelligence has become an issue of growing importance in the context of the fight against terrorism. This issue is by essence surrounded by secrecy and the difficulty of its regulation by law. Yet some efforts have been made to set rules concerning military intelligence. A second example is the militarization of cyberspace. This example is particularly interesting because it comes against the classical conception of national borders in public law. Cyberattacks could be initiated from everywhere around the world and from individuals, organizations or groups, more or less state-sponsored. A doctrine on this subject is being constructed where public (and more precisely international) law is witnessing a growing impact (Bannelier 2014; Tsagourias and Buchan 2015; d'Aspremont 2016; Couzigou 2018; Delerue 2019). Cyber-defence issues raise the question of the appropriateness of legal rules to the cyberspace and new potential cyber conflicts. Studying legal measures that are developing to provide protection for cybersecurity and cyber-defence issues also tend to show that aside the debate about the appropriateness of international law in cases of cyber conflict or cyber-attacks, countries tend to develop a domestic legal approach to the subject (see for instance Bannelier and Christakis 2017) while cyber means are by essence transnational.

Conclusion

As we tried to demonstrate in this chapter defence issues are spread within the different fields of public law. Defence studies are not yet a major field among the classical structure of public law. Yet recent years have witnessed a rapid evolution with the growing transnational threats surrounding not only democratic states but each and every state in the world. There is now a great number of questions linked to security and defence issues in public law. Defence is also a rising research field in public law in general and in domestic law in particular as we showed above. More and more researchers started discussing defence issues in the last decade, be they embedded or not in military formation structures such as military universities. Many of these researchers work in public universities and have no direct link to the military institution but develop a strong interest for defence issues in public law. If defence (and by extension security) issues have long tended to occupy a rather marginal position in public law this is quickly changing and will without doubt be of growing interest for public law researchers in the future. In a context of diffused and renewed security and defence threats, defence studies are offering the sovereign state the most important place in the protection of the citizen. The governments have to bear these issues in mind when deciding defence measures for domestic purposes and/or when these measures derive from consenting to apply international norms. Therefore if one wants to grab defence issues as a whole in the future, one also will have to develop research on the legal aspects of defence issues, and cross-fertilize it with other disciplines, such as political science, as we have shown in this chapter. A good way of investigating the legal aspects of defence studies may be inspired by researches on denationalized or transnational law, as defence issues have become more and more embedded with international security since the end of the Cold War (see, for instance, Ancel and Heuschling 2016).

Notes

1 The PESCO mechanism already existed in the Lisbon treaty but had not been used since its ratification in 2009.
2 Source: https://www.conseil-constitutionnel.fr/sites/default/files/2018-10/constitution_anglais.pdf (Consulted on 18 June 2019).
3 Id.
4 The Congress is the reunion of the two Chambers of the French Parliament in the Castle of Versailles.

References

Alland D., Rials S. (2003). *Dictionnaire de la culture juridique*, Paris, PUF, coll. "Quadrige".
Ancel P., Heuschling L. (2016). *La transnationalisation de l'enseignement du droit*. 1st ed., Bruxelles, Larcier.
Anderson, K. (2009). United Nations Collective Security and the United States Security Guarantee in an Age of Rising Multipolarity: The Security Council as the Talking Shop of the Nations, *Chicago Journal of International Law*, 10(1), Article 5.
Aron, R., Lerner, D. (Eds.) (1956). *La Querelle de la CED: essais d'analyse sociologique*, Paris. Armand Colin.
Armstrong, D. (Ed.). (2009). *Routledge Handbook of International Law*, London, Routledge.
d'Aspremont, J. (2016). Cyber operations and international law: An interventionist legal thought. *Journal of Conflict and Security Law*, 21(3), 575–593.
Aust, A. (2010). *Handbook of International Law*, Cambridge, Cambridge University Press.
Bannelier, K. (2014). Cyber diligence: A low-intensity due diligence principle for low-intensity cyber operations? *Baltic Yearbook of International Law*, 14.
Bannelier, K. and Christakis, T. (2017). Cyber-attacks–prevention-reactions: The role of States and private actors. *Les Cahiers de la Revue Défense Nationale*, Paris.
Beaud O., Bargues C. (2016). *L'état d'urgence: une étude constitutionnelle, historique et critique*. 2nd ed. Paris, LGDJ, coll. "Systèmes perspectives".
Beurier, J.-P. (2017). *Droit international de l'environnement*, Paris, Pedone, coll. "Etudes internationals", 5th ed., 628p.
Biscop, S., Whitman, R. (Eds.) (2012). *The Routledge Handbook of European Security*, London, Routledge.
Blumann, C., Dubouis, L. (2016). *Droit institutionnel de l'Union européenne*, Paris, Lexis Nexis, 6th ed., 922p.
Bothe, M. (2013). *The Handbook of International Humanitarian Law*, Oxford, Oxford University Press.

Buton, P. (2004). La CED, l'affaire Dreyfus de la quatrième république?. *Vingtieme Siecle. Revue d'histoire*, (4), 43–59.
Cassese A. (2005) Article 51, 1329–1360. In: Cot, J.-P., Pellet, A. (eds.) (2005). *La Charte des Nations Unies. Commentaire article par article*, Paris, Economica.
Cassia, P. (2016), *Contre l'état d'urgence*, Paris, Dalloz.
Clapham, A., Gaeta, P., Haeck, T. (Eds.) (2014). *The Oxford Handbook of International Law in Armed Conflict*, Oxford, Oxford University Press.
Couzigou, I. (2018). Securing cyber space: the obligation of States to prevent harmful international cyber operations. *International Review of Law, Computers & Technology*, 32(1), 37–57.
Delerue, F. (2019). International cooperation on the international law applicable to cyber operations. *European Foreign Affairs Review*, 24(2), 203–216.
Deschaux-Dutard, D. (2018). Das Scheitern der Europäischen Verteidigungsgemeinschaft. *Welt-Trends*, (139), 31–35.
Deschaux-Dutard, D. (2017). Usage de la force militaire et contrôle démocratique: le rôle des arènes parlementaires en France et en Allemagne. *Revue internationale de politique comparée*, 24(3), 201–231.
Clapham, A., Gaeta, P., Haeck, T. (Eds.). (2014). *The Oxford Handbook of International Law in Armed Conflict*, Oxford University Press.
Fernandez, J. (2013), Il n'y a aucun fondement juridique à une intervention en Syrie, *Le Monde*, 30 août 2013.
Fleck, D., Bothe, M., Fischer, H. (Eds.). (1999). *The Handbook of Humanitarian Law in Armed Conflicts*, New York, Oxford University Press.
Gohin O. (2014).Le contrôle parlementaire sur les opérations extérieures des forces armées françaises, 63–78. In: Vallar Ch., Latour X. (2014). *Le droit de la sécurité et de la défense en 2013*, PUAM.
Grard, L. (2012). La condition internationale de l'Union européenne après le Traité de Lisbonne. *Revue québécoise de droit international*, 2(1), 65–72.
Herrera, C. M. (1997). *Théorie juridique et politique chez Hans Kelsen*, Paris, Kimé.
Holeindre, J. V. (2015). Des strategic studies aux war studies. La structuration d'un champ d'études, 499–512. In: Henrotin, J., Schmitt, O., Taillat, S. (2015). *Guerre et stratégie: approches, concepts*, Paris, Presses Universitaires de France.
Holeindre, J. V., Vilmer, J. B. J. (2015). Pour des war studies en France: un diagnostic et des propositions. *Revue défense nationale*, 785, 53–59.
Howorth, J. (1992). François Mitterrand and the "Domaine Réservé": From cohabitation to the Gulf War. *French Politics and Society*, 43–58.
Irondelle, B. (2002). Défense européenne et sciences sociales: où en est le débat théorique? *Revue internationale et stratégique*, (4), 79–88.
Irondelle, B., Vennesson, P. (2002). La défense européenne: un objet de science politique. *Politique européenne*, (4), 5–12.
Kelsen, H. (2017). *General Theory of Law and State*, London, Routledge.
Kiss, A. (1989). *Droit international de l'environnement*, Paris, Pedone, coll. "Etudes internationals", 1st éd., 1989, 349p.
Meijer, H., Wyss, M. (Eds.). (2018). *The Handbook of European Defence Policies and Armed forces*, Oxford, Oxford University Press.
Mérand, F. (2008). *European Defence Policy: Beyond the Nation State*, Oxford, Oxford University Press.
Schrijver, N. (2005). Article 2, paragraphe 4, 437–467. In: Cot, J.-P., Pellet, A. (ed.) (2005). *La Charte des Nations Unies. Commentaire article par article*, 3rd ed. Paris, Economica.
Terpan, F., Saurugger, S. (2018). Assessing judicial activism of the CJEU the case of the court's defence procurement rulings. *Journal of European Integration*, 1–19.
Traversac, A.-S. (2014). Le cadre juridique de l'intervention française au Mali, 103–119. In: Vallar, Ch., Latour, X. (Eds) (2014). *Le droit de la sécurité et de la défense en 2013*, PUAM.

Tsagourias, N., Buchan, R. (Eds.) (2015). *Research Handbook on International Law and Cyberspace*, Cheltenham, Edward Elgar Publishing.
Van Ackere, P. (1995). *L'Union de l'Europe occidentale*. 1st ed. Paris, PUF, coll. "Que sais-je?".
Verhoeven, J. (2002). Les "étirements" de la légitime défense. *Annuaire français de droit international*, 49–80.
Vial, P. (1992). Redécouvrir la CED. *Matériaux pour l'histoire de notre temps*, 29(1), 9–16.
Weller, M., Solomou, A., Rylatt, J. W. (Eds.) (2015). *The Oxford Handbook of the Use of Force in International Law*, Oxford, Oxford University Press.
Zarka, J.-C. (1997). *L'OTAN*. 1st ed., Paris, PUF, coll. "Que sais-je?".

3 Historical methods in defence and war studies

The case of historical defence studies in France

Christophe Lafaye

Introduction

Over the last few years in France there has been a strong trend to promote War and Defence Studies among a few scholars and the Institute for Strategic Research of the Military School (IRSEM)[1] funded by the Ministry of Defence. War Studies is defined as a multidisciplinary research field having war as its object. This field of study considers that war is a global social fact since it is influences society in all its (political, economic, sociological, ethical, geographical, juridical etc.) aspects. War is an overall phenomenon escaping disciplinary boundaries. A cross-cutting approach is the only one fit to understand it in all its complexity. The same applies to defence studies, as defined in the introduction of this volume. Defence studies are by essence multidisciplinary, as defence issues not only concern the strategic aspects but also historical, social, economic, political aspects. War and defence studies thus aim at combining heterogeneous methods from various disciplinary fields. Moreover there are no simple distinctions unambiguously defining war and defence, thus enabling a variety of disciplinary perspectives (strategic studies, security studies, peace studies, military studies, defence studies etc.) to coexist. Prof. Jean-Vincent Holeindre helpfully demonstrated how to differentiate them (Holeindre 2015). As a matter of fact, they are not identical. So what is specific about defence studies and war studies? Like security studies, they were born within the academia (unlike strategic studies stemming from administrations and think tanks) and they have a distinctive inclusive approach. As Jean-Baptiste Vilmer points out: "War Studies have a narrower approach as they are limited to a particular threat, that is armed conflict, but wider than others as they are examining it from every conceivable angle" (Vilmer 2017: 51). Defence studies as well as war studies rely on a comprehensive approach seemingly fit for the complexity of the subjects at stake. In this chapter we use both terms of defence studies and war studies, as we conceive defence studies as a natural component of war studies as Schmitt states, underlying the "constitutive effects of war and defence": "defence policies are shaped by the changing character of war and the international context, and in turn influence them" (2018: 26). As Schmitt notes, understanding war is a necessity for a state in order to build a proper defence able to face a potential enemy (Schmitt 2018: 19).

Established within King's College in London in 1962, the department of War Studies is considered a global flagship in this disciplinary field. It provides education for over 2,000 students, among which many are foreigners. Its teaching capacity includes researchers from an array of disciplines (history, political science, law, philosophy, sociology etc.) as well as practitioners from various backgrounds (high-ranking military officers, diplomats, physicians etc.). From 1997 onwards the defence studies department provides higher military education to Joint Services Command and Staff College based in Shrivenham. While this kind of education is spreading in Europe (especially in Denmark) and worldwide (in Canada and the United States, where security studies, strategic studies and military history are prevailing), France appears to be lagging behind (Eulriet and Krahmann 2004; Holeindre and Vilmer 2015; Meijer 2015). Why is the development of war and defence studies so weak in France? Are there works of individuals taking this multidisciplinary perspective? In this chapter we propose to first examine the reasons for the late and still ongoing recognition of defence and war studies in France as well as the ongoing catching-up process. In a second part of the chapter we will focus more precisely on the case of history in the field of defence and war studies and show the tortuous path for military history to gain legitimacy within the academic circles and the universities in the French case. The third section of the chapter will then raise the methodological issue when studying defence in a historical perspective. In such case, the researcher has to put forward innovative transdisciplinary methodologies. We will precisely take the example of the collecting, archiving and highlighting of the 21st-century fighting experience of the French army as a test case to explain how we apply the historical methodology to defence issues. This method is borrowing its intellectual tools to immediate history, military history, archival science, sociology and computer science. The use of built archives enables the researcher to gather sufficient sources so as to study the experience lived by soldiers in the 21st century's armed conflicts. Providing a basis for transdisciplinary academic works, this method is fully adequate for defence studies and war studies. We will conclude our chapter by drawing perspectives for the future of defence and war studies using the historical method.

Defence and war studies: a slow implementation process in the French case

In France, despite many attempts since the early 1970s to establish research centres or training courses specialized on defence and war issues within the academia, this disciplinary field has been undermined by institutional instability and dissipation of the effort. The literature published on defence issues, and more specifically on issues concerning war, is not only scarce but is also scattered. As Vilmer points out:

> The fact that France was able to produce its own strategic thinking, as well as significant authors, is a testament to individual talents and to the combined efforts of associations and research institutes, including the Ministry of Defence, a consumer as well as producer of research.
>
> (Vilmer 2017: 53)

For example, the Institute for Strategic Studies (IRSEM) was created in 2009 by merging four previously existing research centres. It presently plays a significant role in the development of defence and war studies in France. Each army also develops in parallel to its own research centres. The French army land forces also disposes of a Centre for Command Teaching and Doctrine[2] as well as the Saint-Cyr School Research Centre (CREC)[3] at the superior military academy of Saint Cyr Coëtquidan. The French air Force develops a Centre for Strategic Aerospace Studies[4] and an Air School Research

Centre on its air base in southern France (Salon-de-Provence)[5] but also recently set up two Excellence Research Chair (one on drones and one on cyberdefence) dedicated to applied research for the French Air Force. The French navy disposes of a Marine Graduate Studies Centre[6] and the Naval School Research Institute based in the Superior Naval Academy in Brest.[7] The existing higher education system in the French Military School in Paris (The War College and the Military School Centre for Advanced Studies)[8] helps to invigorate strategic research. The same is also true on a lower level, which is at the joint service force level: the Joint Centre for Concepts, Doctrines and Experiments[9] has been created to perform operational foresight, develop and experiment doctrine and operational concepts for joint and combined operations in a national or multinational framework. At the inter-ministerial level the National Defence Institute of Advanced Studies[10] and the French Superior Council for Strategic Research[11] also tend to play an increasing role in strategic thinking. However, this brief overview of the specialized research centres working on strategic and defence issues in France shows how this research remains scattered. France is lagging behind compared to other developed countries. Defence and war studies are adversely affected by marginalization and fragmentation. Marginalization is partly attributable to a certain antimilitarism legacy in French universities. Originating from the interwar period it grew stronger after World War II. This marginalization has been intensified by the war in Algeria in the 1960s and its *repercussions* and then, after the fall of the Berlin Wall, by the faith in the possibility of bringing peace to international relations. As Vilmer states:

> *studies on war are also marginalized because of other factors related to the research* subject's practical aspect. Studying war involves (…) speaking freely with politicians determining it and military men waging it. (…) Some believe this position is a threat to research's independency.
>
> (Vilmer 2017: 55)

Some of these observations also apply to some other European countries' situations regarding the emergence of defence studies, like in the case of Germany for instance where the field really started to get academic recognition after the end of the Cold War and once Germany was back in military interventions in the late 1990s (Gareis and Klein 2004). This is not the case in the United States for instance where dialogue between universities and the administration are quite commonplace.

The fragmentation of defence and war studies is stemming from the French university system's structure: there are a few main subject areas hardly engaging in dialogue and mostly following disciplinary silos. Nor are the various services producing strategic thinking (academia, the military institution, companies, and think tanks) properly connected. Encouraging interdisciplinary research and creating the conditions for dialogue between the parties involved in strategic thinking therefore represent important issues to develop further defence and war studies. Some progress is currently under way. Since the beginning of the 2000s a new generation of researchers started benefiting from research-funding programmes from the Ministry of Defence (and in the first place from the French Procurement Agency),[12] which is yearly funding 130 doctoral researches not only in engineering or competing but also in social sciences. These new experts tend to hold high-level academic positions. Students are also more and more able to benefit from international mobility and use an academic stay to study abroad in countries where defence and war studies are well established within the academia. Increasing numbers of students also engage in specialized master's degrees on defence issues. A professional association to promote defence and war studies has also been set up by young scholars in the aftermath of the terror attacks against the journalist of Charlie Hebdo in Paris in January 2015: the Association for War and Strategic Studies (AEGES) aims at promoting this research area in the global French academic sphere. Increasing overseas military operations (Afghanistan, Lybia, Mali, Central African Republic, Iraq, and Syria etc.) as well as domestic ones (counter-terrorism) implying French armed forces triggered a brutal awakening of public opinion to the social significance defence issues. In 2017 Jean-Yves le Drian, the former Defence Minister made this issue one of its top priorities: "to support the emergence of an academic strategic research within the field of social sciences and the humanities (…) implying the development of War Studies *à la française*"(cited in Vilmer 2017: 54). The French Ministry of Defence (MoD) decided to launch a specific Pact for Higher Education funding for not only doctoral dissertations in social sciences, but also post-doctoral programmes and research programmes in several research centres in France (see the chapter written by Borzillo and Deschaux-Dutard in this volume). One of the benefits of this measure is to increase the employability of young researchers working on defence issues by giving universities an incentive to create positions. Other mechanisms are imagined to encourage servicemen to undertake doctoral dissertation not only in engineering or computer sciences (as in the French Air Force for instance) but also in social sciences and more precisely in history, political science, psychology and sociology. Yet, although defence and war studies benefit from an encouraging environment in France, over the last few years they have still encountered criticism from a part of the academia, as the controversy raised in the political science community in 2018 shows.[13] The same applies to history where defence and war studies also face implantation and legitimacy issues in the universities.

Military history and defence studies: a long road to gain academic legitimacy

Since the early 20th century in France, military history has neither been the most prestigious nor the liveliest sub-field of the historical discipline in academic research. Each generation produces a few famous names, but generally speaking military history still remains the poor relation of the academic world. The French history school clearly stayed behind its German and British counterparts in the period before 1914. Between 1920 and 1940 military history was conceived narrowly and conventionally. Military history was at the time written without concern for new disciplinary considerations, eliciting a strong social rejection fuelled by pacifism and anti-militarism in the 1930s. The interest in the history of institutions prompted Marc Bloch's and Lucien Febvre's harsh criticism voiced in the periodical *Annales d'histoire économique et sociale* (See for instance Huppert 1982). Both intellectuals held up to ridicule what they called the "battle history" (see Paret 2009 about the relationship of the Ecole des Annales and the history of war). This kind of history is frequently written by military officers seeking to draw lessons-learned from the past battles for the present and future actions (Offenstadt 2011: 98). Marc Bloch's work have been used for the purposes of military history in France, while Hans Delbrück censured it in Germany (Delbrück 1908).[14] The latter complained about the fact that that military history focuses on battle, which is one of the armed forces' main goal, thus shrinking the scope of the possibilities for historical inquiries. Scientific military history gradually started developing in the United States during the 1930s. It particularly became a prominent part of the intellectual formation of the officers' training in military academies. The closeness of military history to the academia provided a fertile ground to develop new research issues. Historians in English-speaking world still largely teach in higher education structures as it was the case for John Keegan (Keegan 1983)[15] in the United Kingdom. Despite the existence of promising works (Lot 1946, Launey 1949, Girardet 1953, Vidalenc 1955;[16] Contamine 1957), military history has been cast aside in France after World War II. Moreover military history tends to be taught less and less in the universities even within armed forces.

Yet this sub-field of the historical discipline experiences a form of revival based on the increasing porosity between historical subfields and on the broadening of historical methods and subjects globally (Contamine 1998). In order to secure its resurgence, military history engaged in a sociological and quantitative turn. A renewed military history started developing following the historical conception of the sub-field by the Annals School (Denys 2005). In 1963 an article about the dimensions of military history has been published by Piero Pieri (1963). Books about warfare in the Antique world have been published quasi-simultaneously (Vernant 1968, 2019; Brisson 1969). André Martel, André Corvisier, Guy Pédroncini and Philippe Contamine also played an active role in reviving military history. They constitute an outstanding generation.[17] Institutions such as the French military history commission (CFHM)[18] or the development of specialized research institutes in Montpellier, Paris and later Aix-en-Provence[19] indicate a clear trend towards the re-emergence of military history. These structures deserve credit for (re)creating a meeting facility for researchers in military history to exchange and develop collaboration with the military. The military has long been perceived – until the 1990s – by academic military history mostly through its societal, cultural and political aspects (Denys 2005: 23), whereas research related to military thinking or strategic aspects has most of the time been confined to institutional research made within the military institution itself. Yet since the 1990s historical academic schools started evolving not only in their research topics but also in their academic debates, which has provided a positive context for the re-emergence of military history. Historical analysis progressively takes into account many aspects of a historical situation (including political, diplomatic, economic, cultural aspects etc.): for instance the publication of the four-volume Histoire militaire de la France edited by Corvaisier (1998) embodies a half century of shared research between the military and the academic world, while allowing various researchers to provide a personal contribution (Jacques Frémeaux and Jean-Charles Jauffret, for example). Military history started to cover a variety of issues among which a renewed version of "battle history" (Bertaud 2013 [1970]; Duby 2014 [1984]; Drévillon 2009; Henninger and Wiederman 2012), studies about prisoners of war or history of weapons (Cochet 2012), or more broadly historical cultural interest in combat and in fighters. This widening of the issues covered by military history in the last decade indicates a dynamism going beyond the specificity of the historical disciplinary field, and even sometimes, threatening its own singularity (see for instance Branche (2011) on wartime violence and Barthelemy (2004) on peacetime violence in the medieval era). Moreover, military history has benefited from the setup of dedicated research centres in the last two decades such as the Center for Defence History Studies (CEHD) created in 1994 and integrated within the Institute for Strategic Research (IRSEM) in 2009. The IRSEM thus helps gathering researchers with different disciplinary backgrounds and researchers involved in the renewed battle history form an influential group among them. The IRSEM also includes the former Center for Social Studies in Defence,[20] the Center for Higher Military Studies and Research[21] and the Center for Advanced Armament Studies.[22] This institute thus offers an interesting venue to develop cross-disciplinary fertilization on defence research issues. Both the military and academic worlds seem to draw closer to each other in this research facility, which remains rather rare in the French research and academic sphere. Yet as evoked earlier this getting closer together has raised controversy within the academic community concerned with the independence of research funded by military funding. More precisely concerning military history, past the rejection phase in the 1960s the sub-field now has to find its place within the growing number of researches in defence studies on the one hand, and the growing interest of the military institution for social science knowledge so as to better train the future officers. Therefore, having difficulty expressing specificity within the global field of defence studies, the researchers in military history decided to go their own way and left the IRSEM in 2014 to join together the Historical Service of Defence in Paris under the supervision of Professor Hervé Drévillon. However, this evolution left unresolved until now the question of the collection of historical military sources, which was at stake in the decision of the historians to set up their own research facility. On 23 November 2015 a directive about operational archiving has been adopted by the French army general staff to give a new impetus to the historical mission of the military institution. One of the main aims of this document is to enable the military institution to document the recent French army commitment overseas. This process implies the collection of sources meant for immediate use, thus opening up opportunities for the implementation of a new oral history project driven by the Army legacy delegation working together with the historical office of the MoD (*Service Historique de la Défense*). Since 2017, new internal directives have been passed so as to coordinate the gathering of historical material within the military institution. The writing of military history is more and more conceived as a multidisciplinary process encompassing asserted global history dimensions. This aspect is apparent in the recent research work of Masha Cerovic (2018) or Elie Tenenbaum (2018). Two newly published books about war history are noteworthy and adopt a pluridisciplinary perspective: the collective work completed under the supervision of Professor Bruno Cabanes (2018) and the two-volume publication of France's military history edited by Hervé Drévillon and Olivier Wieviorka (2018). Another paper completes these funding works: the book published by Xavier Lapray and Sylvain Venayre (2018) definitely confirms the editorial liveliness of this historiographical field in defence studies, which is currently experiencing a renaissance.

Defence and war studies, by nature multidisciplinary, inspire many research projects in contemporary history. The method developed to collect, archive and highlight the 21st-century fighting experience is a perfect example of what a researcher in defence studies or military history can achieve.

An important methodological challenge for defence studies in a historical perspective: building archives to study the 21st century fighting experiences

A good example of the development of defence and war studies in France can be found with of a multidisciplinary academic research that the author of this chapter

Historical methods: defence and war studies 53

launched for a few years, which was about the gathering, archiving and highlighting of the 21st century fighting experience. This research projects asks the researcher in history to rely on a cross-disciplinary approach to achieve an improved study of the fighting experience lived by French military fighters in very recent battles. This observation was made during our doctoral research in history about the French military forces in Afghanistan (Lafaye 2014, 2016) prompted an in-depth study of how to build archives on such contemporary issues. The methodological questions about the collection of archives on this kind of issues even generated the will to complete a master's degree entitled "Archives in the 20th and 21st century" at the University of Burgundy and to write a Master thesis on how to collect, archive and increase the value of fighting experience in contemporary armed conflicts (Lafaye 2017, 2018a and 2018b).[23] A further incitation to develop reflexivity on how to collect and archive fighting memory was carried out during an internship in the historical office of the MoD within its oral archives department, which allowed us to carry out an experiment of data collection about the military deployment of the 1st Division of the French Army and the 19th Combat Engineer Regiment in the Sahel-Saharan strip from 2015 to 2017. Since the early 2000s, the French Army experienced an intense professionalization process as well as an increase in military operations outside the French territory. This raising involvement of the French armed forces in international security started raising the crucial question of the recollection of military operations and soldiers' fighting experiences in their wide variety. In an ever more digitalized era, what kind of workable traces can the researcher be able to handle so as to retrace present-day campaigns or to document the lived experiences of soldiers? In France, in spite of the existence of an up and running archiving project lead by the MoD's historical service Historical Defence Service of the French Ministry of Defence (SHD), numerous sources are not well preserved. This concerns soldiers' oral testimonies (from privates to junior officers, including the NCO Corps), e-mails exchanged with their family, journals, pictures, videos, artefacts etc. Another kind of data, such as war diaries are not available in consideration of time-based access restrictions. Therefore the researcher in contemporary, and even immediate, history has to think carefully about the forms of data gathering concerning the fighting experience of soldiers in recent or current military operations, starting from combat personnel as such. To understand more accurately the fighting experience of soldiers by working in a global history perspective, it is necessary to extend the gathering of testimonies to political actors, military families, civilians planning the missions, defence bases, local people involved in the areas of operations, non-governmental organizations (which are frequently interacting with servicemen), diplomats, international coalitions staff where appropriate, and even to the enemy wherever possible. The only collection of the oral testimonies of soldiers deployed in these armed conflicts is obviously insufficient; nevertheless the researcher has to start somewhere among the variety of actors involved, even though the researcher needs to be aware that the military institution is not the only depositary of the fighting experience in military operations. This reflexive thinking about how to collect such recent archives spread on diversified media seems to be a necessary prerequisite to the investigation and the writing on contemporary military operations and the experience of the protagonist of armed conflicts.

The historian should ideally be able to possess fully organized research materials in order to be able to produce a reflexive analysis of the collected data. Within the variety of potential sources, oral sources hold a special status. However, they should not be overestimated compared with other sources as public or privately held archives, newspapers, pictorial or audiovisual materials, etc. The researcher needs to develop rigorous methods here so as to gather and build his/her own archives, so that the collected data can not only be useful for the researchers' works in progress but also be available to other researchers or readers (reuse of research data) while respecting national legislation (on the secondary use of qualitative data, see the chapter by Borzillo and Deschaux-Dutard in this volume). These documentary resources tend to be preserved either on the shelves of material archive centres or on servers of websites and online databases (thematic digital archival centres). This practice assumes the researcher has the ability to master at least some competences in software tools: for instance he/she has to be able to index collected sources, to scan, to operate qualitative data with software tools, etc.[24] This kind of methodology raises challenges for the researcher as it stands at the crossroads of immediate history, military history, sociology, archival, and information technology. Thus it provides a good example of pluridisciplinary approach involving diversified proficiencies and technical skills complementing those of the classical historical work. In the section below we explain thoroughly how the researcher can implement this kind of method to investigate immediate history in defence studies.

Building archives: a method to preserve the soldier's fighting experiences and document immediate history in defence studies

Building archives is a key feature in this method (Lafaye 2018b). These archives are produced by an actor (researcher and/or archivist) for the purpose of building up sources enabling the completion of a research and/or to cope with an institutional expectation. This researcher collecting the archives therefore has to delineate the perimeter of the field of survey, to care for its opening (and sometimes obtain an authorization from the military institution), and to develop a collecting methodology. Once this phase has been completed the researcher has to proceed to data collection, to operate their archival treatment and to depose them so as to ensure their preservation. He/she may need to exploit the collected data and develop the whole process in accordance with the applicable laws and regulations related to archives. The collection of the fighting experience specifically requires an a posteriori testimony of the real-life experience of a witness present on the armed conflict theatre, in order to fuel further multidisciplinary research and to keep records for future generations. These collections are made up of oral testimonies, but personal archives should also include relevant information about its collector, the fieldwork procedures (data collection and production charts, systematic note-taking, all relevant sociological information concerning the interviewed witnesses etc.). Rigor is required while exercising this method. Modesty is also suitable in the presentation of the research's outcomes. The researcher's complete neutrality in respect of his/her object of investigation is a very challenging ideal to say the least. It is possible to objectivize research material through the use of reflexivity regarding the collected sources. The precarious nature of digital documents produced by people in the very recent past must also be acknowledged. This applies to private iconographic documents, battlefield-recorded videos, diaries drafted with mainstream word processing software, working papers foregoing the drafting of official documents, personal e-mails (which are frequently non-archived documents), videoconferencing discussions (frequently unrecorded, or non-archived when recorded), etc. If this kind of evanescent data is not collected soon enough, they are meant to irrevocably disappear sooner or later, thereby depriving historians from sources documenting the life of contemporary fighters. For instance, Afghanistan has been lived as an ordeal for French fighting soldiers, who formed the fourth generation to fight in an armed conflict abroad after the trauma experiences with the Algerian War: the Afghan experience here confronts the researcher and the archivist with a technological challenge resulting from the digital revolution.

The early stages of this disruption were perceptible for the researcher not only in the preliminary questionnaires but also as we experienced problems affecting the curators responsible for the preservation of the first photographic and audiovisual collections, facing the digital revolution in the late 20th century. Formats survivability, data preservation, data migration and losses resulting thereof, these themes were foretaste of future challenges that the researcher and the archivist could encounter in a society entirely driven by digital tools and the daily production of personal data in the virtual space. Which ones of these data have to be collected? When produced on a warzone by soldiers themselves, are they public archives or private ones? What kind of contract has to be chosen for collecting them? What kind of protection is needed to ensure the rights of the various personnel contributing to the collections development? In the case of archives related to armed forces, questions about confidentiality, protection of witnesses (as they may still be in activity), military secrecy, professional confidence, and communicability of collections as well as their exploitation are as a matter of fact a big concern for the researcher/archivist. Working on the collection of testimonies of contemporary fighters, be it either on the external operation theatre or in a mainland-stationed unit, raises the question of the access to the field. Required approvals must be available to the researcher so as to be able to access his intended witnesses. Additionally, it is important to possess a relatively high cultural capital and master a good knowledge about the military society and its specific codes, thus allowing researchers to carryout surveys in the military environment (see for instance Deschaux-Dutard 2015; Schmitt 2015). Collection straight from the operation theatre within close combat units – such as the collection carried out in the United States from 1942 on in the framework of the Military History Operations (Krugler 2009) – can only be performed by historians specially trained to this end and embedded in the military institution. Collection on the national territory in France concerning domestic operations (such as the Sentinelle operation launched in the aftermath of the terror attacks in 2015, for instance) can on the contrary be carried out by more diversified actors such as reservists or even students if the chain of command approves. In any case this work is required to be part of the researcher/archivist's preliminary training (interviewing methodology, technical learning of use of the tools needed for recording and exploitation, archival tools, XML-EAD computer language etc.). This training may also concern researchers in contemporary history wanting to deal with defence and war studies and relying on archive research data.

In our experience the method we use to collect fighting experiences allows the historian to dispose of original research materials which could be effectively used to document research on 21st century armed conflicts. Besides, fighting soldiers' real-life experience can also be recounted thanks to these research materials. The present work needs further development within the National Defence archives so as to prevent the potential loss of valuable data. An ambitious joint service programme could be implemented; the creation and training of a specialized team dedicated to the collection as well as to an in-depth thinking about the legal framework regulating digital data produced by individuals on the battlefield could be very beneficial for defence studies more generally. Computer equipment procurement should also be carefully thought-out before taking action because this hardware is meant to ensure total data security from the field where data are collected to the server on which they are hosted and archived. We have been granted access to units returning from operational tours in France and in our opinion, the forthcoming initiative should be to provide access to new collection areas during domestic and overseas military deployments so as to fuel the archival fieldwork. Digital revolution has therefore an influence on the organization of sources but also reshapes the research methods and approaches for historians and archivists. Such a method calls for more diversified knowledge as well as for computing skills to be developed.

Conclusion

In this chapter we commented on the slow implementation process of the defence and war studies in France and showed how difficult this emergence is within a major discipline such as history. We have therefore highlighted a research methodology drawing its tools from the multidisciplinary approach needed in defence and war studies as many topics stand at crossroads of different disciplines. Even though defence studies have faced some opposition in France, the current dynamic is powerful and seems to follow the flow of history. As Olivier Schmitt points out, the emergence of defence and war studies depends on three parameters: an awareness of the importance of the subject for the society; promotion of interdisciplinary in the academic sphere; the concern of the researcher to be useful to the policy (Schmitt 2018). Even though multidisciplinarity currently remains under-recognized in French universities and the researcher's connection with the defence field is sometimes still perceived a little suspiciously by colleagues working on other research fields, defence studies keep developing and imply that both the academic and military perceptions of defence and war studies keep evolving. In the meantime, the creation of a pluridisciplinary research institute by the French MoD in the 2000s offers a promising measure, as well as the funding facilities offered by the MoD in the last two decades.

Yet it cannot be denied that the defence studies tend to clash with the traditionally discipline-based organization of the French university system. Therefore, one important question here seems to be: how to integrate defence and war studies into the French university system based on strict disciplinary organization? By creating a new discipline like "international relations" with defence studies as sub-discipline? This solution is not yet conceivable in the French context. Currently the training courses and research centres dedicated to defence studies are mostly connected to disciplinary departments like law or political science mainly. This situation creates tensions between disciplines and competition between universities. Another problem linked with this disciplinary structure of the French academic system is the still rather low perception of the doctoral degree in the military institution, even though more military personnel tend to write PhDs not only in social sciences but also in technological sciences for instance in the last decade. Unlike in the United States, officers with a PhD are still quite rare in France. Their careers may even be slowed down by their doctoral process. The development of defence studies not only requires a real scientific recognition from the academic community but also a professional recognition within the military institution.

However, by developing diversified research skills as we tried to show here, a researcher in military history may prove very useful not only for the academia but also for the defence field, as he may be able to archive and pass on the memory of recent armed conflicts by relying on digital tools.

Notes

1. In French: *Institut de recherche stratégique de l'école militaire* (IRSEM).
2. In French: *Centre de Doctrine et d'enseignement du commandement* (CDEC).
3. In French: *Centre de Recherche des Écoles de Saint-Cyr* (CREC).
4. In French: *Centre d'études stratégiques aérospatiales* (CESA).
5. In French: *Centre de recherche de l'école de l'air* (CREA).
6. In French: *Centre d'études supérieures de la Marine* (CESM).
7. In French: *Institut de recherche de l'école navale* (IRNAV).
8. In French: *Ecole de guerre* and *Centre des hautes études de l'école militaire* (CHEM).
9. In French: *Centre Interarmées de Concepts, de Doctrines et d'Expérimentations* (CICDE).
10. In French: *Institut des Hautes Études de la Défense Nationale* (IHEDN).
11. In French: *Conseil Supérieur Français de la Recherche Stratégique* (CSFRS).
12. In French: *direction générale de l'armement* (DGA).
13. See the arguments of this controversy online: https://zilsel.hypotheses.org/3052 and https://zilsel.hypotheses.org/3071 (Consulted on 19 July 2019).
14. As Bloch used to say himself, military men may be the only ones among men of action intentionally attempting to use its research results for practical purposes. (Bloch 1937), "Que demander à l'histoire?", *Mélanges Historiques*, Paris, 1937.
15. John Keegan (1934–2012) was a British historian and journalist whose works had a very significant impact on military history's development, notably new *battle history*.
16. Jean Vidalenc, *La demi-solde, étude d'une catégorie sociale*, Paris, M. Rivière, 1955.
17. The military was present in the 1960s and 1970s thanks to the writing of general of Jean Delmas and general Fernand Gambiez, among others.
18. In French: *Commission française d'histoire militaire* (CFHM).
19. The *Centre d'histoire militaire et d'études de la défense nationale* was created in 1968 within the Paul-Valéry University (Montpellier III) under the *leadership* of André Martel. Worth mentioning are also the "Armées sociétés en Europe du XVe au XIXe siècle" *seminar chaired by* André Corvisier at the University Paris IV and the Centre d'histoire militaire comparé in the Instiotute for Political Studies of Aix-en-Provence.
20. In French: *Centre d'études en sciences sociales de la défense* (C2SD).
21. In French: *Centre d'études et de recherches de l'enseignement militaire supérieur* (CEREMS).
22. In French: *Centre des hautes études de l'armement* (CHEAr). A research support programme was implemented. Furthermore, the point of this structure is to bring young researchers' efforts together in a joint seminar, fostering transversality between research fields and a relative multidisciplinary.
23. Christophe Lafaye, *Collecter, archiver et valoriser l'expérience combattante des XXe et XXIe siècles*, Mémoire de Master II professionnel "archives des XXe et XXIe siècles européen", réalisé sous la direction du professeur Jean Vigreux, Université de Bourgogne, soutenue le 6 septembre 2018.
24. The researcher also needs to be aware of concepts such as informed consent process, copyright, professional secrecy, national defence secrecy, rights pertaining to individual data secured by the *Commission Nationale Informatique et Liberté* – CNIL (National Commission on Informatics and Liberty).

References

Barthelemy, D. (2004). *Chevaliers et miracles. La violence et le sacré dans la société féodale*, Paris, Armand Colin, coll. "Les enjeux de l'histoire".

Bertaud, J. P. (2013 [1970]). *Valmy. La démocratie en armes*, 1st ed. Paris, Editions Gallimard.

Bloch, M. (2011 [1937]). Que demander à l'histoire?, *Mélanges Historiques*, Paris, Editions du CNRS.
Branche, R. (2011). *Viols en temps de guerre*, Paris, Payot.
Brisson, J.-P. (1969). *Les problèmes de la guerre à Rome*, Paris, Éditions de l'École des hautes études en sciences sociales.
Cabanes, B., Dodman, Th., Mazurel, H., Tempest, G. (2018). *Une histoire de la guerre-Du XIXe siècle à nos jours*, Paris, Le Seuil.
Cerovic, M. (2018). *Les enfants de Staline: la guerre des partisans soviétiques, 1941–1944*, Paris, Ed. du Seuil.
Cochet, F. (2012). *Armes en guerre: XIXe-XXIe siècle. Mythes, symboles, réalités*, Paris, CNRS-éditions.
Contamine, H. (1957). *La revanche, 1871–1914*, Paris, Berger-Levrault.
Contamine, P. (1998). L'histoire militaire, 359–368. In: Bédarida, F. (ed.) (1998). *L'histoire et le métier d'historien en France: 1945–1995*, Paris, Editions de la Maison des Sciences de l'Homme.
Corvisier, A. (ed.) (1998). *Histoire militaire de la France*. 4 volumes, Paris, Presses universitaires de France.
Delbrück, H. (1908). *Geschichte der Kriegskunst im Rhamen der politischen Geschichte: Das Altertum*. 2nd ed., New York, Vol 1.
Denys, C. (2005). Die Renaissance der Militärgeschichte der fruhen Neuzeit in Frankreich: eine Historiographische Bilanz der Jahre 1945–2005. *Arbeitskreis Militär und Gesellschaft in der Frühen Neuzeit*, vol.1. Available online: https://publishup.uni-potsdam.de/opus4-ubp/frontdoor/deliver/index/docId/1083/file/MGFN_11_2007_1_Btr01.pdf.
Deschaux-Dutard, D. (2015). Stratégie qualitative et défense: l'entretien comme interaction sociale en milieu militaire. *Les Champs de* Mars, 2, 42–49.
Drévillon, H. (2009). *Batailles: scènes de guerre de la Table Ronde aux Tranchées*, 417. Paris, Seuil.
Drévillon, H., Wieviorka, O. (2018). *Histoire militaire de la France*, Volumes 1 and 2, Paris, Perrin.
Duby, G. (2014 [1984]). *Guillaume le Maréchal: ou le meilleur chevalier du monde*. 1st ed., Paris, Fayard.
Eulriet, I., Krahmann, E. (2004). Les études sur la sécurité et la défense au Royaume-Uni: institutions, débats et perspectives de recherche. *Les Champs de* Mars, 15(1), 95–117.
Gareis, S. B., Klein, P. (2004). Militär und Sozialwissenschaft—Anmerkungen zu einer ambivalenten Beziehung, 9–12. In: Gareis, S. B., Klein, P. (2004). *Handbuch Militär und Sozialwissenschaft*, Wiesbaden, VS Verlag für Sozialwissenschaften.
Girardet, R. (1953). *La société militaire dans la France contemporaine, 1815–1939*, Paris, Plon.
Henninger, L., Widemann, T. (2012). *Comprendre la guerre: histoire et notions*, Paris, Perrin.
Holeindre, J. V. (2015). Des strategic studies aux war studies. La structuration d'un champ d'études, 499–512. In: Henrotin, J., Schmitt, O., Taillat, S. (2015). *Guerre et stratégie: approches, concepts*, Paris, Presses Universitaires de France.
Holeindre, J. V., Vilmer, J. B. J. (2015). Pour des war studies en France: un diagnostic et des propositions. *Revue défense nationale*, 785, 53–59.
Huppert, G. (1982). Lucien Febvre and Marc Bloch: The creation of the annales. *The French Review*, 55(4), 510–513.
Keegan, J. (1983). *The Face of Battle: A Study of Agincourt, Waterloo, and the Somme*, London, Penguin Books.
Krugler, G. (2009). Historians in Combat. L'armée américaine et le concept de Military History Operations. *Revue Historique des Armées*, 257, 59–75.
Lafaye, C. (2014). *Le génie en Afghanistan (2001–2012). Adaptation d'une arme en situation de contre-insurrection. Hommes, matériel, emploi*. Doctoral dissertation, Université Aix-Marseille.
Lafaye, C. (2016). *L'Armée française en Afghanistan. Le génie au combat 2001–2012: Le génie au combat 2001–2012*, Paris, Cnrs Editions.

Lafaye, C. (2017). De la collecte de l'expérience combattante. *Inflexions*, (3), 203–212.

Lafaye, C. (2018a). *Collecter, archiver et valoriser l'expérience combattante des XXe et XXIe siècles*, Master Thesis, Under the supervision of prof. J. Vigreux, Université de Bourgogne.

Lafaye, C. (2018b). *La préservation de l'expérience combattante des XXe et XXIe siècles en France*. Conference paper presented at the symposium "Archiver le temps present" held in the University of Louvain, Louvain-la-Neuve, 26–27 April 2018.

Launey, M. (1949). *Recherches sur les armées hellénistiques*, Paris, Editions de Boccard.

Lot, F. (1946). *L'art militaire et les armées au Moyen-Âge, en Europe et dans le Proche-Orient*, Paris, 2 vol.

Meijer, H. (2015). L'étude de la guerre et de la stratégie aux États-Unis et au Royaume-Uni. *Revue défense nationale*, 711, available online: www.defnat.com (Consulted on 2019).

Offenstadt, N. (2011). *L'Historiographie*. Paris, Presses Universitaires de France, Coll. "Que Sais-je?" (n°3933).

Paret, P. (2009). The Annales School and the history of war. *The Journal of Military History*, 73 (4), 1289–1294.

Pieri, P. (1963, August). Sur les dimensions de l'Histoire militaire. *Annales. Histoire, Sciences Sociales*, 18(4), 625–638.

Schmitt, O. (2015). L'accès aux données confidentielles en milieu militaire: problèmes méthodologiques et éthiques d'un "positionnement intermédiaire". *Les Champs de Mars*, (2), 50–58.

Schmitt, O. (2018). Defence as war, 18–28. In: Galbraith, D., Deni, J. R. (Eds.) (2018). *Routledge Handbook of Defence Studies*, London, New York: Routledge.

Tenenbaum, E. (2018). *Partisans et centurions. Une histoire de la guerre irrégulière au XXe siècle*, Paris, Perrin.

Vernant, J. P. (1968). *Problèmes de la guerre en Grèce ancienne*, Paris, Mouton.

Vernant, J. P. (Ed.). (2019). *Problèmes de la guerre en Grèce ancienne* (Vol. 11), Berlin, Walter de Gruyter GmbH & Co KG.

Vidalenc, J. (1955). *La demi-solde, étude d'une catégorie sociale*, Paris, M. Rivière.

Vilmer, J. B. J. (2017). Le tournant des études sur la guerre en France. *Revue défense nationale*, 800, 51–61.

4 Secondary analysis of qualitative data in defence studies

Methodological opportunities and challenges

Laurent Borzillo and Delphine Deschaux-Dutard

Introduction

Secondary analysis of qualitative data has become a growing trend in social sciences for the last two decades (Heaton 1998). This method can be defined as "the use of existing data collected for the purposes of a priori study, in order to pursue a research interest which is distinct from that of the original work" (Heaton 1998: 1). The first analyst to recognize the potential of secondary analysis of qualitative data was Barney Galser, who discussed in the early 1960s the possibility of extending secondary analysis from quantitative data to qualitative data (Heaton 2004: viii). This re-use of already existing qualitative data started developing in nurse and education sciences since the late 1990s (Heaton 2008) and became a topic of interest for other social sciences (such as sociology, political science or management studies) more recently since the mid-2000s but remains "ill-defined and under-developed as a qualitative methodology" (Heaton 2004: viii). Yet secondary analysis generated an important methodological and epistemological debate in the United Kingdom or in the USA for instance (Heaton 2004; Duchesne, 2017), but its use is still very limited in France (see the example of the EDF Verbatim in Dargentas and Le Roux 2005; Duchesne and Dupuy 2017) and completely absent in defence studies. When typing the words "secondary analysis" and "defence" in the search window of the Google Scholar website for instance, no match can be found.[1] Thus, this chapter will not only explore the potentials of secondary analysis of qualitative data in defence studies but also analyse the only explicit case of the re-use of qualitative data that we could identify in defence studies more globally in the recent years.

Why can secondary analysis of qualitative data be interesting and useful in defence studies? What specific challenges does it raise? How can it be implemented? What specific challenges do the archiving of qualitative data related to defence topics raise and how can they be addressed? In order to answer these questions, we will first give an overview of secondary analysis of qualitative data and the peculiar methodological questions it raises for defence studies. We will then in a second part of the chapter focus on a case study and explore how to apply this method in defence studies. We will finish with an examination of the specific challenges that secondary analysis of qualitative data raises in terms of archiving when it comes to data on defence topics and formulate some prospective proposals to archive such data by relying on the French context of the emerging recognition of French war studies for few years.

Secondary analysis of qualitative data and defence studies: why and how to proceed?

Before assessing the potentials of secondary analysis of qualitative data in defence studies, we first need to be clear about what we are talking about here and what advantages secondary analysis brings to the researcher, generally speaking, before going more in depth into its advantages and challenges in defence studies.

Secondary analysis in social sciences: a short overview

Secondary analysis of qualitative data does not consist only in one method but relates to different types of methodologies. The first use of secondary analysis started to grow in social sciences in the 1960s and 1970s particularly in the UK mainly concerns the use of pre-existing statistical and quantitative data for the purposes of a new research. As Heaton states, the first fundamental article about the re-use of statistical data has been published by Herbert Hyman in 1972 about secondary analysis of sample surveys (Heaton 2004: 1). If this methodology is commonplace in the researches of social sciences implying quantitative data, it is much less obvious and standard when it comes to re-using qualitative data. This comes from the fact that the collection of qualitative data implies the need for reflexivity on how and under what conditions this data was produced. For instance, interview data constitute a very interesting case as this kind of data come from a specific social interaction between the researcher and the interviewee, which "colours" the produced data. This is even truer in defence studies as we will explain it later (see Deschaux-Beaume 2012; Deschaux-Dutard 2018). Yet the main objectives of secondary quantitative data tend to be similar to the objectives of secondary analysis of qualitative data: this method is supposed to provide a good and cheap (in time and in means) access to a larger amount of data and thus enable scientific cumulativity (Dale 1993).

As Heaton writes, it is hard to find a one-and-only definition of secondary analysis (Heaton 2008: 34) but one can still define secondary analysis generically with Hakim as "any further analysis of an existing dataset which presents interpretations, conclusions or knowledge additional to, or different from, those presented in the first report on the inquiry as a whole and its main results" (Hakim 1982: 1). The main purpose of re-analysing existing data is to save up time and money to reinvestigate a dataset produced for a primary research. Concerning the secondary analysis of qualitative data more precisely, the aim is to reinvestigate the data of one or several primary researches with the research questions differing from the ones raised in the primary research. This re-use of qualitative data can either be done by the primary researcher himself/herself or by another researcher (we will call him/her the secondary researcher here). The data considered here includes semi-structured interviews (recording and/or transcription), interview notes, filed notes, research diaries and even answers to questionnaires and run by the primary researcher or the primary research team. Heaton identifies five sorts of secondary analysis of qualitative data (Heaton 2004: 38):

- Supra analysis: this method transcends the focus of the primary research and examines new questions related either to the theoretical framework, the empirical investigation and the methodology;
- Supplementary analysis: this method consists of a more in-depth investigation of the primary research to uncover an issue not investigated in the primary study;

- Re-analysis: the method here consists more in a verification process so as to assess the validity of the primary study according to its dataset; this method is also called "active citation" (Moravcsik 2010, 2012, 2014a, 2014b);
- Amplified analysis: this method combines data from several primary studies so as to gather a large sample;
- Assorted analysis: this method combines secondary analysis of primary qualitative data and naturalistic qualitative data produced by the secondary researcher. It is mainly this method that we will explore in our case study on the second part of our chapter.

Archiving and re-using qualitative data: between scientific cumulativity and falsifiability

As secondary analysis started developing in several countries, an important question emerged: how and where to archive qualitative data so as it could become accessible for secondary researchers to reinvestigate this data? Several experiments have developed, among which the most successful example is Qualidata developed in the UK. Qualidata, which stand for Qualitative Date Archival Resource Center, is a pioneer experience set up in 1994 (Scot 2006). It has been supported by the main agency financing public research in the UK, the Economic and Social Research Council (ESRC), which required that researchers receiving funds from ESRC for their research must deposit their dataset in Qualidata. This experience raised an important epistemological debate opposing the supporters of the archiving process much involved in the Qualidata experience and conceiving data in a positivist perspective (data exists as such; Bishop 2005, 2006, 2009; Bishop et al. 2014; Corti and Bishop 2005; Corti and Backhouse 2005; Corti et al. 2005) to their opponents defending a constructivist approach to qualitative data production. These opponents argued that decontextualizing qualitative data produced in a primary research leads to this data being deprived of its validity as qualitative data results from the social interaction between the primary researcher and its research field. For this second group of researchers data does not exist as such but is the result of a social construction, which prevents any possibility of archiving it as it only exists in the context of the primary research (Bishop, 2005 and 2007; Mauthner et al. 1998; Parry and Mauthner 2004). Later the scientific debate around Qualidata moved to the question of the opposition between primary and secondary analysis (Hinds et al. 1997; Corti and Backhouse 2005; Parry and Mauthner 2005; Bishop 2007; Corti 2007; Hammersley 2010). The debate raised by the re-use of qualitative data met a lot of the elements of the debate about the scientific validity of qualitative data. In this respect the archiving of such data raised issues in the US in the 2000s around the concept of "active citation". With the digitization of social science research and the development of open access databases, researchers have been encouraged to submit their dataset (both quantitative and qualitative) in open access archiving resource centres and databases so that when published their result could be confronted with their data. This is what Moravcsik calls active citation (Moravcsik 2010, 2012).

The underlying logic here is not so much to capitalize qualitative data than the quest for verification, which fuelled an intense debate between the supporters and opponents of the idea (Van den Berg 2008; Moravcsik 2014a, 2014b). Another experience of archiving qualitative data has also been launched in France with the BeQuali database following a series of workshop and seminars initiated in Grenoble by the CIDSP (a research centre working on social and political data) and the research centre of the French energy provider EDF (the GRETS). BeQuali first aimed at archiving semi-structured interviews led by researchers at the Cevipof, one of the oldest French research centres working on political sociology (Duchesne and Garcia 2014; Duchesne and Brugidou 2016; Bendjaballah et al. 2017). Contrary to the positivist approach underlying Qualidata, the BeQuali proponents supported an interpretivist conception of data. Such a conception recognizes the validity of secondary analysis but insists on the fact that the data produces and the analysis made by the researchers (both primary and secondary) are successive interpretations (Chabaud and Germain 2006). BeQuali tends to go beyond the scope of Qualidata which only aims at archiving qualitative data, whereas BeQuali tends to formalize the filed data in order to induce re-use (Both and Cadorel 2015; Duchesne and Brugidou 2016). However, the success of the French databank remains underwhelming even though it is used for teaching purposes.

This short overview of secondary analysis led us to identify the advantages and challenges raised by this method generally so as to better understand what specificity of a such method means in defence studies.

Qualitative data, secondary analysis and defence studies: squaring the circle

Why should a researcher consider secondary analysis as an interesting research method? How the questions raised by this method meet some of the classical challenges of research on the defence field? We will discuss both these issues in this part.

Secondary analysis as a fruitful method in defence studies

Although secondary analysis remains under-explored as a method to investigate the defence field, it presents interesting perspectives.[2] First of all, the re-use of already existing qualitative data is a time and money saver, as the researcher does not have to invest a lot of time and money to produce field research (Heaton 2004; Corti et al. 2005; Corti 2007; Hammersely 2010). In this regard public funds invested in the primary research (via a doctoral grant, for instance, of a public research programme financed by state means) are also better put to use. Secondary analysis of qualitative data also allows more scientific cumulativity by re-investigating existing data and extending it with new data and/ or new theoretical or epistemological perspectives. This method can even help develop multi-disciplinary approaches when secondary analysis is applied to data produced in a specific scientific context (for instance the analysis of a specific kind of social actor's representations on a topic) with another focus (for instance, the same data used for the purposes of policy analysis; see Duchesne and Dupuy 2017). This advantage meets the question of the access to the field when investigating defence topics (Deschaux-Dutard 2018). In any research project on defence matters an essential methodological problem quickly emerges: the problem of access to internal documents and grey literature. This access is not always easy for the non-military researcher and can represent an important amount of time and resources to lead interviews (Deschaux-Beaume 2012, 2013). The difficulty of access to defence actors can be manifold for a civilian researcher. We can identify five reasons why secondary analysis can be a fruitful method in defence studies given the specificity of the defence field (Deschaux-Dutard 2015, 2018). First of all, the access can be difficult because of the frequent professional turnover of military personal (a position is held for a medium-term of three years in the defence services such as the ministries of defence, the position as commander of a military unit or a position at NATO or the EU for instance). Second, the access to information on defence topics can also be hindered by the embargo on archives: in many countries' public archives can only be consulted after 30 years, a period which can be extended to 50 years about defence archives. The difficulty becomes even more accurate when the researcher needs to consult classified archives (the classification usually goes from "confidential" to "top secret"), which frequently leads to the method of semi-structured interviews being chosen (Deschaux-Beaume 2013). Thus when data already exist, secondary analysis represents an interesting time and trouble saver for the secondary researcher, even though many precautions need to be taken, as we will explain below.

Yet the secondary researcher has to be conscious of the fact that the data produced via primary interviews (during which he was not present) incarnate a social interaction between the primary researcher and its interviewees of the defence sphere (Deschaux-Beaume 2012, 2013). This raises several challenges that we will explore later in this chapter. The third interest of secondary analysis is also obvious in case of death of the interviewees: the only possibility to access them is then secondary analysis of existing interview material. This method is also a good means to rapidly identify defence actors formerly interviewed for research purposes and get in contact with them through the primary research. Moreover when the reused data has been produced many years ago secondary analysis is a good way of providing for a rich diachronic analysis (see for instance Belot and Van Ingelgom 2017). The fourth advantage of secondary analysis in defence studies is directly linked to the social specificity of the defence field. Indeed interviewing defence staff in most of the countries consists in carrying out an "investigation amongst a 'difficult environment', [...] a suspicious environment and yet not hermetic to research" (Cohen 1999: 17). Working by interviews implies that if he/she wants to collect valid data, the researcher should not be perceived as an "intruder" in this social configuration. Thus the data produced can save this difficulty for secondary researchers, as far as the precautions of confidentiality and anonymity of the interviewees are respected (see, for instance Schmitt 2015). We will go back to this issue below. Last but not least re-using qualitative data already produced and investigated in a primary research on defence issues helps increase the number of sources and enables the secondary researcher to better cross and confront its sources by adding new qualitative data to the already existing data. This aim for cumulativity and cross-fertilization is not specific to defence studies but is particularly interesting when investigating defence topics.

We then showed that secondary analysis of qualitative data can be very fruitful in defence studies, but this method also raises a number of issues and challenges which need to be addressed now.

Secondary analysis and defence studies: what precautions and what challenges?

The aim here is not to come back to the specific challenges raised by the study of defence organizations as it has been explored earlier (Deschaux-Dutard 2015, 2018). We will just raise some of the specific issues raised by secondary analysis of qualitative data in defence studies in this section, which globally match the general challenges met both by researchers in defence studies and by researchers using secondary analysis of qualitative data: direct connection to the field, secrecy and anonymization, ethics and conditions of re-use of the data.

First of all secondary use of qualitative data, as thrilling and promising as it may be in defence studies, must draw the attention of the secondary researcher on a fundamental need: the direct connection to the field. If for quantitative data this direct connection is not necessary, when the researcher works on the defence organizations' or actors' representations, it is best for him/her to also have a connection to the defence field and to be aware of the functioning of this social field, so as so avoid misinterpretation of the data he/she re-uses. This connection is even more important depending on the available information surrounding the reused data: can the secondary researcher access side notes, full transcription of qualitative semi-structured interviews or even audio recordings? How can these information be archived securely? This is a very important challenge for which we will formulate some propositions in the end of this chapter. The access to a written transcription of semi-structured interviews is of course a precious basis for the secondary researcher but raises important challenges for both researchers. For the primary researcher transcription implies a lot of time (and sometimes money) and a reflexive archiving strategy. For the secondary researcher it requires the need for consent from the primary researcher and raises the issue of the consent given by the interviewees to the primary researcher. Even if the issue of consent is not specific to defence studies (Corti et al. 2005; Goodwin and O'Connor 2006; Grinyer 2009), the culture of secrecy and the difficulty of accessing some important information or actor in the defence field shines an interesting light on the issue. In some cases the consent given to the primary researcher was a one-time consent. This calls for a cooperative relationship between the primary and secondary researcher so as to re-use the produced data respecting the limits given by the primary interviewees. The strategy here can also be, when reference is made to this primary data, to cite only the minimum indication so that the primary source cannot be identified and the consent of the interviewee is not jeopardized. As we will show is our case study below, the data reused by the secondary researcher (Borzillo) had been published in the primary researcher's doctoral dissertation (Deschaux-Beaume 2008), who chose to only publish interviews without embargos from the interviewees.

The re-use of qualitative data collected via semi-structured interviews also meets the challenge of anonymization, which is a classical challenge in the study of defence organizations (Deschaux-Beaume 2011; Deschaux-Dutard 2015, 2018; Schmitt 2015). As some authors state, the researchers working with re-use of data or conducting secondary analysis of qualitative data have to find a thin balance between honouring the commitment of confidentiality made to interviewees (which is most of the time required in the defence field) at the time the primary data was collected and the possibility to re-use this data generated with an important amount of time and money from the primary researcher or research team (Thomson et al. 2005). Anonymizing means removing the information leading to a potential identification of the interviewee. Yet anonymity is a difficult issue in the defence field as the number of interviewees on a given topic is not wide and it may imply less efficiency in the researcher's effort to guarantee it. Another possibility can be to ask again the interviewee for his/her consent if he/she is reachable but this may also lead to a risk of reinterpretation of the discourse given to the primary researcher. This question of how to reconcile confidentiality and access to primarily gathered data meets two important debates in secondary analysis: the epistemological debate evoked earlier (can one really re-use qualitative data emanating from a specific interaction between a researcher and his object?) and the archiving debate vividly explored both in the UK via the Qualidata experience and in France with the BeQuali experience. We will explore an alternative possibility to archive qualitative data in defence studies in the last part of this chapter. In the case of defence organizations, confidentiality is most of the time an important prerequisite, which calls for specific attention when archiving the data and defining the conditions of access to the collected data for other researchers. These elements show that secondary analysis of qualitative data in defence studies bears very fruitful promises but must be carried out with precautions more than in any other research field, given the specificity of the defence field and its relationship towards academic research between eagerness to show openness and difficulties of trust in some sensitive issues like terrorism or nuclear dissuasion for instance (Cohen 1999). The primary researcher as well as the secondary researcher may keep far from two hurdles when interpreting and re-interpreting the qualitative data collected via semi-structured interviews in defence organizations: either refracting the institutional discourse of the interviewees by a lack of scientific distance, or putting this discourse aside too quickly by considering it as a trick (Codaccioni et al, 2012).

After having squared the circle between defence studies and secondary analysis of qualitative data in this research field, we will present a recent case study where this methodology is implemented for the purpose of a research in progress.

Secondary analysis of qualitative data in defence studies: a case study on French-German military cooperation

This part of the chapter is aimed at showing a recent implementation of secondary analysis of qualitative data in defence studies. It describes the re-use of Delphine Deschaux-Dutard's data produced during her doctoral dissertation (Deschaux-Beaume 2008) by Laurent Borzillo for his own doctoral dissertation in progress (to be defended by the end of 2019). These two studies, conducted many years apart, offer an opportunity for secondary analysis of qualitative data in the field of defence policy research. They also offer a chance to demonstrate the fruitfulness of secondary analysis of qualitative data in the larger field of European studies and more precisely in the study of European military topics.[3] More specifically the investigation consisted in a mixed analysis, that is a combination of a secondary analysis of Deschaux-Dutard's data and primary qualitative data collected during fieldwork on Borzillo's dissertation.

Borzillo's study (carried out at the universities of Montreal and Montpellier) focuses on two multinational military units: the French-German Brigade (BFA) and European Union Battlegroups (EUG or EUBG). Deschaux-Dutard's dissertation addressed a more general topic (the role of the French-German military cooperation in the development of European defence policy from 1990 to 2008; Deschaux-Beaume 2008). Her research was largely based on semi-directive interviews: 135 interviews, 36 of which were fully transcribed and can be consulted in the appendix to her dissertation. As both the BFA and EUG have been an integral part of European defence policy for several decades, she refers to them frequently. Not only did this situation enable us to implement a secondary analysis of qualitative data, but also more concretely it offered an opportunity – to use military jargon – to apply a "RETEX" (lessons learned) technique to defence policies, thereby expanding potential avenues for further research into its use in the specific context of defence policy research.

Feedback from a secondary analysis of qualitative data in a work in progress

Although this chapter clearly demonstrates the usefulness of secondary analysis of qualitative data, it is interesting to note that until recently the secondary researcher (Borzillo) was quite unaware of this method. Despite having followed an Anglo-Saxon doctoral programme (with seminars, mandatory courses and exams), the secondary researcher had never implemented or even encountered this method. The discovery was made almost by chance, underlining the awareness of secondary analysis of qualitative data. Consequently Borzillo initially applied a secondary analysis of qualitative data in empirical studies, before using it to develop theory and including it in the ongoing academic discourse.

The fortuitous discovery of the primary researcher's (Deschaux-Beaume) interviews was the main driver in this process. The secondary researcher was already familiar with the primary researcher's work in the context of his research and his own dissertation makes many references to her contribution. However, it is unfortunate that the length of Deschaux-Dutard's dissertation discourages a full reading. Written more than ten years ago, the form is typical of the former French academic requirements: running to exactly 1,195 pages, it is a classic of its time. This handicap proved difficult to overcome and initially the secondary researcher (Borzillo) focused on her other publications, skipping through the primary dissertation. Consequently it was almost by chance, as the secondary researcher's own work came to an end and he began the data processing stage that he decided to read the primary researcher's entire dissertation – including the 417 pages of appendices. To his great surprise these appendices included no less than 36 full transcriptions of interviews – some with people he had himself interviewed and others with people he had wanted to but had not been able to meet.[4] This discovery increased the number of interviews available for the secondary researcher's own research, which was particularly interesting as research in the defence field suffers from a lack of first-hand qualitative data. The opportunity to compare our sources made it possible to cross-reference the comments made by our interlocutors.[5] These two elements helped to strengthen the rigour of the secondary researcher's own assertions and hypotheses.

The primary researcher chose to use a partially anonymized system: the names and functions of her interlocutors are only given in an appended table. Nevertheless, both the body of the text and the appended transcriptions indicate the main functions of the people that were interviewed. Given that the secondary researcher's solid knowledge of the field he could quite easily identify the individuals who had been interviewed. Consequently during the first phase of the secondary analysis, the secondary researcher did not contact her colleague as he had been able to determine the identities of the persons interviewed and he had no theoretical or practical knowledge of secondary analysis of qualitative data.

These three dozen additional interviews provided an important amount of additional information.[6] Coupled with the 100 interviews the secondary researcher had already conducted, the dataset encompassed nearly 130 interviews. The presence of 100 other interviews cited extensively in the primary researcher's dissertation, of which the secondary researcher had only a few scraps, nevertheless aroused some regrets and frustrations. They motivated him to finally contact the primary researcher so as to try and get access to this apparently unavailable empirical treasure. The initiative had two consequences. First the number of available interviews increased. Second the secondary researcher discovered the theoretical aspects of secondary analysis and the academic debates surrounding it.

The reading of articles related to the academic controversy over secondary analysis (Chabaud and Germain 2006; Dargentas and Le Roux 2005; Duchesne and Brugidou 2016; Duchesne 2017; Duchesne and Dupuy 2017; Goodwin and O'Connor 2006; Heaton 2004; Le Roux, and Vidal 2000; Merkle 2009; Van den Berg 2008) and discussions of the issue with colleagues very quickly led the secondary researcher to identify his position between the three schools of thought: a clear rejection of the constructivist approach and a theoretical position that was halfway between positivism and interpretivism. This intermediate position can be explained by the risk (inherent in the positivist approach) of obscuring contextual elements, and the interpretative tendency to ultimately give greater importance to these elements than to the data targeted by the secondary analysis.[7] Consequently a significant part of the secondary researcher's methodological developments in his dissertation refers to the primary researcher's interviews[8] and his theoretical and practical understanding of secondary analysis of qualitative data. The chapter includes a detailed presentation of the primary research. More specifically in the context of the secondary researcher's own hypotheses,[9] the primary interviews were used to identify three elements related to the secondary research theoretical framework:

- any information that could identify actors (senior administrators in government departments, or key political figures such as a minister, the President of the Republic or the Chancellor) who contributed to the decisions;
- any statements referring to rivalries and conflicts, either normal or specific to the military troops being analysed, or between the actors studied;
- any comments from interviewees that revealed social representations among actors, either relating to their role or that of their country on the international stage.

The third element refers obviously to ideal aspects. Although such comments were included in the reanalysis, they were used with caution, as the secondary researcher considered them as potentially misleading. On the other hand, data related to the first two elements was considered to be less risky to interpret.

This use of interviews conducted by a third party also brought the secondary researcher face-to-face with three constraints/ questions: one of an ethical nature and two of a practical nature. The first concerns the ownership of interviews included in the primary researcher's dissertation and are a global issue for any secondary analysis of qualitative data re-using interview material. Are they the property of the first researcher? Are they in the public domain? Or are the researcher's interlocutors the true, legal owners? Given the potentially sensitive nature of the collected data and the functions of interviewees in defence policy research, this issue is far from trivial (see for instance Goodwin and O'Connor 2006; Grinyer 2009). Consequently influenced by his initial secondary analysis of the qualitative data approach (i.e. before making contact with Deschaux-Dutard, the primary researcher), the secondary researcher (Borzillo) adopted the second option: namely that the interview content was in the public domain. However, he consequently decided that all transcripts (without exception) should be fully anonymized. Under this condition he considered that his position could be justified. It is noteworthy to state that despite the sensitivity of the question in the defence domain, the secondary researcher never directly addressed the topic with the primary researcher. The anonymization of sources have been clearly designed from our first exchanges. In practice we have mutually and tacitly opted for the most favourable solution to the secondary analysis (including the requirement of automaticity of anonymity).

Accessing and archiving the primary researcher's unpublished interviews was a second major constraint. The secondary researcher was happy to learn that the primary researcher had recorded most of her interviews using a recorder, as secondary analysis is much more difficult when transcripts take the form of brief notes prepared by the researcher. However, he was the unfortunate victim of a phenomenon dreading every researcher: the crash of the primary researcher's former hard drive containing most of the transcriptions. The loss was all the more regrettable as some interviews concerned people who had since died. Nevertheless the partial anonymization system chosen by the primary researcher made it possible to clearly identify the authors of quotations included in the body of the text. This approach enabled 28 interview fragments to be reconstructed. The final secondary analysis was based on 58 interviews. However, this wealth of additional data exacerbated the question of the anonymization.

As stated above secondary analysis of qualitative data requires very strict anonymization. In the same time the secondary researcher had already adopted such a system for his own interviews as he wrote his dissertation in a French-Canadian academic framework. Canada set rigorous rules governing research ethics. Consequently Borzillo did not record the names and specific functions of his interlocutors. The aim was to protect the anonymity of interviewees while giving the reader an indication of the functions of these individuals. The list of interviews in his appendix therefore only includes the following elements: socio-professional category (military personnel, diplomat, politician or senior official), nationality, place or form of interview (telephone or email), and date. For quotations used in the body of the text Borzillo adds details regarding the service/department in which the person was working at the time.[10]

When it came to incorporating the primary researcher's interviews the secondary researcher had four options: maintaining his own anonymization system alongside her system; developing a dedicated system for the reanalysed interviews; extending his system to the primary researcher's interviews; or developing a new method for the two sets of interviews. Keeping the primary researcher's system was immediately ruled out as it contravened Canadian requirements for protecting the anonymity of individual. In addition it weakened the secondary researcher's position concerning the question of the ownership of the interviews.

Another issue concerned the fact that in some cases the same person was interviewed again ten years later. This raised the question of how to handle citations. In particular the secondary researcher needed to develop a strict anonymization method that ensured that the same person would not be identified as two different persons because of confidentiality rules. Finally he decided to extend the classification used for his interviews to those of the primary researcher's, which ensured the anonymization of all persons mentioned. With respect to the risk of confusion regarding people interviewed by both researchers, the secondary researcher decided to make a note to precise that the two anonymous sources cited were one and the same person when necessary.

Although sometimes difficult secondary analysis of qualitative data proved to be very stimulating and enriching in many ways. As it is very difficult for researchers in the defence field to conduct numerous interviews, secondary analysis represents an unexpected opportunity. It increases the amount of available data, which strengthens the validity of hypotheses and theories. It also helps to save money and time, as conducting interviews can be expensive, especially in the case of fieldwork abroad.

Archiving and re-using qualitative data in defence studies: challenges and perspectives

Using the method to build an argument implies the rejection of the so-called constructivist approach. It is also somewhat distant from the interpretivist approach. The effect of the latter may, in fact, be to focus more on research carried out in the past than on data targeted by the secondary analysis. As stated above the BeQuali catalogue is an interesting illustration of this risk. In particular the primary researcher is required to provide not only his/her data, but also the documentation used or produced during the various stages of the research process: documents relating to the preparation and conduct of fieldwork; the research project; funding; interviews; field notes; correspondence; questionnaires; summaries; drafts; communications; publications; etc. Such onerous requirements can only discourage academics from sharing their data. Therefore the requirements for reanalysis by a second researcher are equally excessive.

We argue that it is sufficient to provide the raw interview data, the publication for which these data were collected and the interview analysis. This third element may not even be necessary, as they are usually included in published material. We also argue that the secondary researcher should provide the following elements in his/her final work: a summary of the work of the primary researcher, their hypotheses and the theoretical approach, information on the selection of interviewees and the interview analysis. This information could be provided as an appendix (inclusion in the body of the text is not mandatory).

Secondary analysis of qualitative data is one of the richest methods in defence studies. However, encouraging its use raises three questions: i) the ownership of interview data, notably in relation to the anonymity of interviewees; ii) how to encourage researchers to archive their data; and, iii) who is responsible for data collection and access.

Managing the issue of the ownership of the data

Adopting the position that the content of interviews is owned by the researcher's interviewee is likely to prevent the development of the method, as it creates an administrative burden for both the secondary and primary researchers. It would require documents to be signed during the first interview, their conservation, and the implementation of time-consuming access procedures for secondary researchers. Although less onerous, the first researcher option would still be an impediment to this technique for similar administrative reasons. However, the approach would have the advantage of encouraging exchanges between the researchers in defence studies.

We assume that the most promising option is a combination of strict anonymization of data. This would not require the development of a specific anonymization system but a minimum set of mandatory criteria to ensure the anonymity of respondents. Needless to say this anonymity would be lifted for the secondary researcher in order to allow him/her to make best use of the primary data. Yet the latter would have to adopt a classification system that ensures the anonymity of sources from primary research. Paradoxically this question is the easiest to address among the three questions we listed above. Encouraging researchers to archive and clearly document their work is a much more complex issue.

Encouraging researchers to archive their data

The most efficient way to analyse secondary data is based on full transcriptions or at least audio recordings. However, the defence community is often reluctant to use this recorders. If researchers automatically required defence personnel to agree to the use of audio recorders the number of interviews would probably drop dramatically. Although it is possible to record interviews, it is unlikely that this technique would help promote secondary analysis of qualitative data in defence studies.

This latter point is an argument in favour of the use of partial transcriptions of interviews recorded by taking notes. Yet such transcriptions are rarely intelligible to third parties, as researchers do not naturally tend to consider the needs of other hypothetical researchers who could be interested by their primary field inquiry. This raises two questions. On the one hand how can the primary researcher be encouraged to make its interview notes comprehensible for someone else? On the other hand how should the secondary researcher use these data, especially in the context of secondary analysis of qualitative data?

The issue of the responsibility for data collection and access

Regarding the first question raised above, one solution could be the funding of organizations to establish suitable mechanisms. This would require the definition of standards regarding requirements to qualify for this type of assistance. The second point implies that the second researcher must be even more circumspect with regard to the reanalysed material. In practice the main difficulty remains that of deciding which institution or organization should be responsible for collecting interview data from the defence field and controlling access to them. In France, the BeQuali catalogue is well-established. But its interdisciplinary nature and extreme interpretivist approach immediately exclude its use in defence studies. A key requirement is to reassure interlocutors working in the defence sector that their anonymity can be preserved and it therefore seems inevitable that the Ministry of Defence – either directly or indirectly through institutions such as IRSEM,[11] SHD[12] or the department of foresight, research and innovation of the DGRIS[13] – would have to be involved. Does this mean that a centralized, national system is required? Not necessarily: the BeQuali catalogue is an unfortunate illustration of the dangers of French-style centralization, which tends to end in the establishment of an onerous bureaucratic structure.

Rather than adopting a national solution, we argue that a better option would be to draw upon the five research centres that have recently been pre-selected as Centres of Excellence by the Ministry of Defence in the French case. These centres are spread across the country (in Grenoble, Bordeaux, Lyon and Paris).[14]3 The initiative could well fit into the Pact for Higher Education launched by the French MoD to encourage the development of war studies in the widest sense in France and relies on providing funding and investing in the academic sector over the past few months. The main aim is to learn the lessons of the terror-strikes in Paris in 2015 which revealed the lack of research on defence and security issues in France. The aim of the French government since has been to promote work on defence and war studies, given its success in Anglo-Saxon countries (Holeindre and Vilmer 2015; Holeindre 2015). As five social sciences universities are already cooperating with the Ministry of Defence (each with its own domain of expertise), they could develop tools to support the archiving of interviews on defence issues in their domain of expertise.[15] Such a distributed network would have two consequences. First it would help to overcome the onerous bureaucratic burden typically found in national, centralised solutions. Secondly, having five centres able to archive data on defence studies might encourage healthy competition between them. However, it would require an in-depth study and a minimal consensus on the procedures to be set to access interview content and verify the identity of secondary researchers. It seems crystal clear that any debate on the formalities and procedures to be set would be no less cutting than academic quarrels over the use of secondary analysis of qualitative data.

Conclusion

In this chapter we have demonstrated that secondary analysis of qualitative data bears fruitful promises in defence studies, even though it has not yet been much implemented. The case study we presented here is the only reflexive case we could find in the academic literature. It helped us not only document the potentialities and challenges raised by secondary analysis of qualitative data in defence studies but also the challenges of this method regarding the specificity of the defence field as a field of inquiry for social science researchers. The lessons learned from our case study help uncover a potentially progressive research programme and led us to formulate propositions regarding the archiving of qualitative data in defence studies. Even though the culture of secrecy and confidentiality is very consistent in the defence field, education of both the researchers and interviewees about the benefits of secondary analysis can open interesting paths for the future as public research benefits from scarce financial and time resources on the one hand, and qualitative data is so rich that a one-time exploitation often means an under use of data primarily produced.

Notes

1 Epistemologically secondary analysis schematically opposes a positivist position held by the proponents of secondary analysis (see for instance Bishop 2005, 2006, 2009, 2014; Corti and Bishop 2005; Corti and Backhouse 2005; Corti et al. 2005) versus a constructivist position asserting that qualitative data does not exist outside the context of its production, which makes it impossible to reuse as it is the result of a specific interaction between the researcher and its object (see for instance Mauthner, Parry and Backett-Milburn 1998).
2 When searching for literature on the issue via several research catalogues and literature databases such as Google Scholar, no match could be found when typing the expressions "secondary analysis", "qualitative data", and "defence".
3 Military aspects of the EU and of Europeanization have generated a growing field of literature in the last decade. The publications are too numerous to be cited here but one can refer to some global references (Mérand 2008; Biscop and Whitman 2012; Meijer and Wyss 2018).
4 Either because the person concerned refused, or because they had died.
5 Notably, with people who were interviewed more than ten years apart.
6 Of the 36 interviews, 30 were reanalysed and reused in Borzillo's dissertation on the BFA and EUG.
7 The BeQuali catalogue is an excellent illustration of these unhelpful tendencies.
8 This includes specific information regarding the research questions and hypotheses to which these interviews related.
9 The focus of Borzillo's research is to examine and analyse decisions as the product of roles, in the sense of Karl Holsti (1970). In particular, the roles that actors who are involved in these decisions, and who are the winners and losers of the conflicts and power relations between administrative departments, attribute to their State.

10 For instance: "telephone interview with a French diplomat on 8 January 2017"; "member of the French Permanent Representation to NATO at the time of the event".
11 The Military Academy's Institute of Strategic Research, which is the social science research centre of the French Ministry of Defence located in Paris.
12 Historical Defence Service of the French Ministry of Defence.
13 General Directorate for International Relations and Strategy of the French Ministry of Defence.
14 University of Paris 1 Panthéon Sorbonne; University of Paris 8 Vincennes – Saint-Denis; University of Bordeaux; University of Grenoble Alpes; University of Lyon 3 Jean Moulin.
15 The use of armed force, Datasphere and cybersecurity, data basis, space, nuclear, missile defence.

References

Belot, C., Van Ingelgom, V. (2017). La réanalyse à l'épreuve d'une comparaison qualitative diachronique: stabilités et évolutions dans les perceptions citoyennes de l'Europe en 1995–1996 et 2005–2006, *Recherches qualitatives*, 21, 99–221.

Bendjaballah, S., Garcia G., Cadorel, S., *et al.* (2017). Valoriser les données d'enquêtes qualitatives en sciences sociales: le cas français de la banque d'enquête beQuali, *Documentation et bibliothèques*, 63(4), 73–85.

Biscop, S., Whitman, R. (Eds.). (2012). *The Routledge Handbook of European Security*, London, Routledge.

Bishop, L. (2005). Protecting respondents and enabling data sharing: Reply to Parry and Mauthner, *Sociology*, 39(2), 333–336.

Bishop, L. (2006). A proposal for archiving context for secondary analysis, *Methodological Innovations Online*, 1(2), 10–20.

Bishop, L. (2007). A reflexive account of reusing qualitative data: Beyond primary/secondary dualism, *Sociological Research Online*, 12(3), 1–14.

Bishop, L. (2009). Ethical sharing and reuse of qualitative data, *Australian Journal of Social Issues*, 44 (3), 255–272.

Bishop, L.*et al.* (2014). Re-using qualitative data: A little evidence, on-going issues and modest reflections, *Studia Socjologiczne*, 214(3), 167–176.

Both, A., Cadorel, S. (2015). Pour en finir avec l'original? Des effets du numérique sur les archives scientifiques: le cas de beQuali, 157–164. In: Bert, J.-F., Ratcliff, M. (Eds.) (2015). *Frontières d'archives: recherches, mémoires, savoirs*, Paris. Éditions des Archives Contemporaines.

Chabaud, D., Germain, O. (2006). La réutilisation de données qualitatives en sciences de gestion: un second choix? *M@n@gement*, 9(3), 199–221.

Codaccioni, V., Maisetti, N., Pouponneau, F. (2012). Les façades institutionnelles: ce que montrent les apparences des institutions: Introduction. *Sociétés contemporaines*, 88(4), 5–15.

Cohen, S. (1999), Enquêtes au sein d'un "milieu difficile": les responsables de la politique étrangère et de défense, 17–50. In: Cohen, S. (Ed.) (1999) *L'art d'interviewer les dirigeants*, Paris, PUF, Coll. "Politique d'aujourd'hui".

Corti, L., Backhouse, G. (2005). Acquiring qualitative data for secondary analysis, *Qualitative Sozialforschung/Forum: Qualitative Social Research*, 6 (3), available online at: http://www.qualitative-research.net/index.php/fqs/issue/view/1 (Consulted on 19 April 2019).

Corti, L., Bishop, L. (2005, January). Strategies in teaching secondary analysis of qualitative data. *Forum Qualitative Sozialforschung*, 6(1). FQS.

Corti, L., Witzel, A., Bishop, L. (2005). On the potentials and problems of secondary analysis. An introduction to the FQS special issue on secondary analysis of qualitative data. *Forum Qualitative Sozialforschung/Forum: Qualitative Social Research*, 6(3), available online at: http://www.qualitative-research.net/index.php/fqs/issue/view/1 (Consulted on 19 April 2019).

Corti, L. (2007). Re-using archived qualitative data—where, how, why? *Archival Science*, 7(1), 37–54.

Dale, A. (1993). Le rôle de l'analyse secondaire dans la recherche en sciences sociales. *Sociétés contemporaines*, 14 (1), 7–21.

Dargentas, M., Le Roux, D. (2005). Potentials and limits of secondary analysis in a specific applied context: The case of EDF—Verbatim. *Forum Qualitative Sozialforschung/Forum: Qualitative Social Research*, 6(3), available online at: http://www.qualitative-research.net/index.php/fqs/issue/view/1 (Consulted on 19 April 2019).

Deschaux-Beaume, D. (2008). *De l'Eurocorps à une armée européenne? Pour une sociologie historique de la politique européenne de sécurité et de défense (1991–2007)*. Doctoral Dissertation, Université Pierre Mendès-France-Grenoble II.

Deschaux-Beaume, D. (2011). Enquêter en milieu militaire: Stratégie qualitative et conduite d'entretiens dans le domaine de la défense. *Res Militaris, Res Militaris*, 2011, 1(2).

Deschaux-Beaume, D. (2012). Investigating the military field: Qualitative research strategy and interviewing in the defence networks. *Current Sociology*, 60(1), 101–117.

Deschaux-Beaume, D. (2013). *Studying the military in a qualitative and comparative perspective: methodological challenges and issues*, 114–132. In: Carreiras, H., Castro, C. (Eds.) (2013), London, Routledge.

Deschaux-Dutard, D. (2015). Stratégie qualitative et défense: l'entretien comme interaction sociale en milieu militaire. *Les Champs de* Mars, 2, 42–49.

Deschaux-Dutard, D. (2018). Methods in defence studies, 40–52. In: Galbraith, D., Deni, J. R. (Eds.) (2018). *Routledge handbook of defence studies*, London, New York: Routledge.

Duchesne, S., Garcia, G. (2014). BeQuali: une archive qualitative au service des sciences sociales, 35–56. In: Cornu, M., Fromageau, J. (2014). *Archives de la recherche. Problèmes et enjeux de la construction du savoir scientifique*, Paris: L'Harmattan.

Duchesne, S., Brugidou, M. (2016). Bequali, une archive en question. *Revue d'anthropologie des connaissances*, 10(4), 531–556.

Duchesne, S. (2017). De l'analyse secondaire à la réanalyse. Une innovation méthodologique en débats. *Recherches qualitatives*, 21, 7–28.

Duchesne, S., Dupuy, C. (2017). La réanalyse au service de l'interdisciplinarité? *Recherches Qualitatives*, 21, 76–98.

Goodwin, J., O'Connor, H. (2006). Contextualising the research process: Using interviewer notes in the secondary analysis of qualitative data. *The Qualitative Report*, 11(2), 374–392.

Grinyer, A. (2009). The ethics of the secondary analysis and further use of qualitative data. *Social Research Update*, 56(4), 1–4.

Hammersley, M. (2010). Can we re-use qualitative data via secondary analysis? Notes on some terminological and substantive issues. *Sociological Research Online*, 15(1), 1–7.

Heaton, J. (1998). *Secondary Analysis of Qualitative Data: Social Research Update*. Working Paper No. 22, Surrey, University of Surrey Guildford, England.

Heaton, J. (2004). *Reworking Qualitative Data*, London, Sage.

Heaton, J. (2008). Secondary analysis of qualitative data: An overview. *Historical Social Research/Historische Sozialforschung*, 33–45.

Holsti, K. (1970). National role conceptions in the study of foreign policy. *International Studies Quarterly*, 14(3), 233–309.

Hakim, C. (1982). *Secondary Analysis in Social Research: A Guide to Data Sources and Method Examples*, London: George Allen & Uwin.

Hinds, P. S., Vogel, R. J., and Clarke-Steffen, L. (1997). The possibilities and pitfalls of doing a secondary analysis of a qualitative data set. *Qualitative health research*, 7(3), 408–424.

Holeindre, J. V. (2015). Des strategic studies aux war studies. La structuration d'un champ d'études, 499–512. In: Henrotin, J., Schmitt, O., and Taillat, S. (2015). *Guerre et stratégie: approches, concepts*, Paris, Presses Universitaires de France.

Holeindre, J. V., Vilmer, J. B. J. (2015). Pour des war studies en France: un diagnostic et des propositions. *Revue défense nationale*, 785, 53–59.

Irwin, S. (2013). Qualitative secondary data analysis: Ethics, epistemology and context. *Progress in Development Studies*, 13(4), 295–306.

Le Roux, D., Vidal, J. (2000). VERBATIM: Qualitative data archiving and secondary analysis in a French company. *Forum Qualitative Sozialforschung/Forum: Qualitative Social Research*, 1(3), available online at: http://www.qualitative-research.net/index.php/fqs/issue/view/27 (Consulted on 19 April 2019).

Mauthner, N., Parry, O., Backett-Milburn, K. (1998). The data are out there, or are they? Implications for archiving and revisiting qualitative data. *Sociology*, 32 (4), 733–745.

Mauthner N., Parry, O. (2013). Open access digital data sharing: Principles, policies and practices. *Social Epistemology*, 27(1), 47–67.

Meijer, H., and Wyss, M. (2018). Upside down: Reframing European Defence Studies. *Cooperation and Conflict*, https://journals.sagepub.com/doi/abs/10.1177/0010836718790606.

Mérand, F. (2008). *European Defence Policy: Beyond the Nation State*, Oxford, Oxford University Press.

Merkle, P. (2009). Available online at: https://calenda.org/198605 (Consulted on 19 April 2019).

Moravcsik, A. (2010). Active citation: A precondition for replicable qualitative research. *PS: Political Science & Politics*, 43(1), 29–35.

Moravcsik, A. (2012). Active citation and qualitative political science. *Qualitative and Multi-method Research*, 10(1), 33–37.

Moravcsik, A. (2014a). Transparency: The revolution in qualitative research. *PS: Political Science & Politics*, 47(1), 48–53.

Moravcsik, A. (2014b). Trust, but verify: The transparency revolution and qualitative international relations. *Security Studies*, 23(4), 663–688.

Parry, O., Mauthner, N. (2004). *Whose data are they anyway? Practical, legal and ethical issues in archiving qualitative research data*. *Sociology*, 38(1), 139–152.

Parry, O., Mauthner, N. (2005). Back to basics: Who re-uses qualitative data and why? *Sociology*, 39(2), 337–342.

Scot, M. (2006). Les archives britanniques des sciences sociales. Deux études de cas: UK Data Archive (UKDA) et Qualidata. *Genèses*, 2, 46–65.

Schmitt, O. (2015). L'accès aux données confidentielles en milieu militaire: problèmes méthodologiques et éthiques d'un "positionnement intermédiaire". *Les Champs de* Mars, (2), 50–58.

Thomson, D., Bzdel, L., Golden-Biddle, K., Reay, T., and Estabrooks, C. A. (2005). Central questions of anonymization: A case study of secondary use of qualitative data. *Forum Qualitative Sozialforschung/Forum: Qualitative Social Research*, 6 (1). Accessed online: http://www.qualitative-research.net/index.php/fqs/article/view/511 (Consulted on 17 June 2019).

Van den Berg, H. (2008). Reanalyzing qualitative interviews from different angles: The risk of decontextualization and other problems of sharing qualitative data. *Historical Social Research/Historische Sozialforschung*, 179–192.

5 Public policy and defence studies

Catherine Hoeffler

Introduction: Public policy and Defence Studies, *Je t'aime moi non plus*

Public Policy[1] and Defence Studies have entertained an ambiguous relationship. On the one hand, defence has always been considered as a very specific if not unique policy (Boëne 1990; Deschaux-Beaume 2011; Deschaux-Dutard 2018). This supposed exceptionality has justified some reluctance to employ similar theories and methods just like the ones used for "civilian" policies. Also, because of its international dimension, defence has often quickly been associated with the discipline of International Relations (IR), and Foreign Policy Analysis (Hudson 2005; Kaarbo 2015). These two factors can explain why, overall, it seems fair to say that Public Policy has not investigated defence policies very much. This is especially true when compared to the large number of publications on some other policies: think of how much attention has been devoted to the welfare state and its various policies (Esping-Andersen 1998; Morel et al. 2012; Pierson 1996; Thelen 2014). On the other hand, notwithstanding certain methodological difficulties (Carreiras and Castro 2014; Soeters et al. 2014), defence is a fascinating policy to analyse through Public Policy *because* of its defining characteristics (Irondelle 2008; Joana 2012; Vennesson 2000). Defence constitutes one of the core sovereign competences through which Western nation-states have developed and consolidated since the 18th century: it is therefore of crucial importance to understand such policies at the core of a historically embedded (and potentially temporary) form of political organization and their evolutions.

Scholars have debated whether defence policy is as specific as often assumed: In other words, the question has been whether "normal" scientific approaches could be applied to it and if so, which one (with competing accounts from IR, Public Policy, or sociology). This debate is particularly visible in the case of the European Union and the integration of national Member States' defence policies. An originally Realist-based consensus took for granted that defence policy, because it belongs to high politics, would not be integrated, or at least not as much as other civilian, mostly economic policies. This conventional wisdom has been challenged in many ways, which we will explore later. But this debate is not settled yet. In a book analysing how the EU has encroached upon core state powers (Genschel and Jachtenfuchs 2013), the three authors dealing (albeit from partly different angles) with the EU's Common Security and Defence Policy (CSDP) do not agree on whether or not the EU has gained authority in this policy (Menon 2013; Mérand and Angers 2013; Weiss 2013). While they explain why according to them their findings do not contradict each other, it seems to the reader that they actually do, but for very good reasons: they position themselves differently with regard as to how "exceptional" a policy defence is from the outset and how it therefore can be expected to remain so in the process. In contrast with the others, Anand Menon holds that despite all the nitty gritty of institutional reforms emphasized by other authors as evidence of an increased EU's role, states leave no room for the EU in this field. In other words, while some see changes, he does not (Menon 2013): depending on one's core theoretical assumptions, the CSDP's glass is half-full, or half empty.

This debate cannot and should not have a definite conclusion, for the pros and cons of applying standard public policy approaches may well vary from case to case and over time. As a branch of political science, Public Policy has provided scholars with relevant theoretical frameworks and methodological tools to address questions relating to policymaking, its actors, processes, and consequences. But what are the key areas where public policy can contribute to a better understanding of defence? What does it mean, methodologically, to study defence through a public policy approach? This chapter will first present some of the traditional as well as more recent studies where public policy's approaches have been usefully applied to defence. After that, it will discuss the methodological issues facing researchers in this field, most notably the question of dealing with confidentiality and the researcher's fieldwork.

Public Policy contributions to Defence Studies

Because it is not a homogenous field, Public Policy offers a variety of theoretical and methodological approaches. This variety is reflected in how scholars have investigated defence policy. This section first proposes a reading of Public Policy contributions to Defence Studies organized around the policy cycle's main stages (Jones 1984). Despite the criticism the policy cycle has drawn (Harguindeguy 2014), it is here a heuristic device to cluster questions together. These subsections bring together scholarship that does not originate solely from Public Policy, but that relies on questions and concepts developed by this field. I will then go on considering how Public Policy has contributed to the study of policy internationalization and international cooperation, with a special focus on the European Union and NATO. This section concludes with a focus on certain types of actors beyond national executive branches, such as parliaments or bureaucrats.

Setting the agenda: when does defence matter?

Agenda setting has constituted one of the most advanced research agenda in Public Policy (Baumgartner and Jones 1991; Birkland 2016; Rochefort and Cobb 1994). The aim of this literature is to understand why, i.e. under which conditions, a problem is constructed, emerges and is eventually put on the political agenda. It brings nuances to the conventional wisdom according to which, to put it in a nutshell, governments deal with problems because they just "matter" or matter more than others: the fact that governments deal with certain problems rather than others cannot be captured by functional logics alone. The nature of the problem at stake (more or less appealing to the public, more or less useful to political actors), institutional features (number of veto points, federal v. central government, for instance), as much as various actors' preferences and strategies (the media and media coverage, public opinion, political entrepreneurs) constitute different explanatory factors to analyse why certain problems make it onto the political agenda while others remain unanswered. These questions have been applied to defence policy at both national (McDonald 2013) and international/European (Dijkstra 2012a; Vanhoonacker and Pomorska 2013) levels.

Who governs if not the Commander in Chief?

Dahl's famous "Who governs?" (Dahl 2005) is a core question of Public Policy. Based on sociological accounts of decision-making and of organizations (Allison and Zelikow 1999; Cohen et al. 1972), Public Policy accounts of defence policies have much focused on the institutional logics shaping decisions. Historically this has come as a critique against the conventional wisdom according to which the elite at the top of the executive branch holds a monopoly over this policy (*domaine réservé*) and that they are able to lead rationally. In this respect, studies about the influence of specific politicians have mostly shown that these leaders, while being visible and vocal, appear much less influential than institutional and bureaucratic factors in the shaping of national defence policies (Allison and Zelikow 1999; Missiroli 2007; Williams 2004). Yet, leadership studies are not to be discarded (Beckett and Gooch 1981; Starr 1980); they have seen a revived level of interest, with scholars showing how under comparable conditions leaders' personal characteristics matter (Dyson 2006; Howorth 2011; Irondelle 2011). This literature has mostly been qualitative in nature and focusing on the micro-level of individuals and their behaviour. They rely mostly on interviews, archives, and the press, such as important newspapers (the *New York Times*, the *Financial Times, Le Monde, die Zeit*) or specialized media outlets and blogs (*Defense News, Janes*, etc).

Notwithstanding the importance of these studies, much work has been done to decentre theories from these "grands hommes" for a number of (good) epistemological and theoretical reasons. This shift has also been accompanied by a pluralization of methodologies, with the development of quantitative approaches imported in large parts by comparative politics' input. Disputing the idea that political parties share a consensus over issues related to high politics, many scholars from Public Policy's, Comparative Politics' and IR's ranks have investigated the role of party politics in national and European defence policies (Hofmann 2017, 2013; Wagner et al. 2017). These can be either qualitative (Hofmann) or quantitative (Rathbun and Wagner et al.). Another important question has been the role of public opinion's support to governments' choices in matters of defence, at national and international levels (Brummer 2007; Höse 2007; Schoen 2008). Jason Reifler et al. compare for instance three competing theoretical models to explain British public opinion regarding the use of force in Libya and Afghanistan (Reifler et al. 2014). Catarina P. Thomson analyses the ups and downs of executives' approval, based on public support for economic and military coercion and on executives' (in)consistency (Thomson 2016).

Implementation

Implementation is another important research agenda of Public Policy (Elmore 1979; Pressman and Wildavsky 1984; Sabatier and Mazmanian 1980; Sabatier 1986; Spillane et al. 2002). Implementation studies explain how public policies are implemented, which very often account for explaining why policies profoundly change from their original design up until their application at the local level by "street-level bureaucrats" (Lipsky 1983). These questions can either be theory-driven or policy-oriented (meaning targeting practical action): explaining why and how policies "deviate" in their implementation is a valuable knowledge for policymakers seeking to enhance policy efficiency. Many studies have investigated defence policy from an implementation perspective (Eckhard and Dijkstra 2017; Juncos 2009; Merlingen and Ostrauskaite 2010; Morillas 2011; Smith 2016; Strikwerda 2018; Whitman 1998). Key issues are how military operations are implemented on the ground, to better capture military efficiency and the possible flaws in the decision-making. For instance, the analysis of privatization process of the former Defence Evaluation and Research Agency into Qinetiq gives a better understanding of its implications for the quality of defence R&D.

The internationalization of national defence policies: the case of the European Union

The internationalization of public policies has been an important research agenda since the 1980s. Globalization and regional integration have been two dynamics affecting how policies are made, by whom and with what impact. The development of European integration in defence has first occurred through the institutionalization of cooperation among EU Member States, then through the creation and strengthening of proper EU-institutions (intergovernmental and supranational). These dynamics have constituted an important field of research at the intersection between European integration theories and IR, with contributions of Public Policy and Comparative Politics (Bickerton et al. 2011; Howorth 2014; Howorth and Menon 1997; Hurrell and Menon 1996; Kempin and Mawdsley 2013; Mérand 2008). Debates evolved around the concept of Europeanization, defined as

> the processes of (a) construction (b) diffusion and (c) institutionalization of formal and informal rules, procedures, policy paradigms, styles, 'ways of doing things' and shared beliefs and norms which are first defined and consolidated in the making of the EU public policy and politics and then incorporated in the logic of domestic discourse, identities, political structures and public policies.
>
> (Radaelli 2002, p. 110)

Some scholars have found profound traces of Europeanization of national defence policies (Britz 2010; Dover 2007; Eriksson 2006; Gross 2007; Irondelle 2003; Rieker 2006), whereas others have doubted the importance of such dynamics (Olsen 2011), going sometimes as far as arguing that some policies display a process of de-Europeanization (Hellmann et al. 2005; Wagner 2005).

An emphasis on certain types of actors: beyond national executives

Parallel to these themes, numerous studies focus on the role of specific actors throughout the policy process. In the case of defence, public policy scholarship has emphasized the importance of other actors over the executive branch.

Contrary to conventional wisdom, defence policy is not the monopoly of the head of the executive branch and her advisers. Some have inquired the role of parliaments at national and European levels (Béraud-Sudreau et al. 2015; Cutler and Von Lingen 2003; Deschaux-Dutard 2017; Fonck et al. 2019; Lord 2011; Martin and Rozenberg 2014; Peters et al. 2010; Riddervold and Rosén 2016; Rosén 2015). Other studies have underlined the unexpected influence of bureaucrats over international cooperation and national policies. This is especially clear in the case of the EU and its bureaucracy: Both the Commission (Blauberger and Weiss 2013; Lavallée 2011; Mörth 2000; Riddervold 2016; Riddervold and Rosén 2016) and the European External Action Service (Adler-Nissen 2014; Furness 2013; Vanhoonacker and Pomorska 2013) have proved more influential than state-centred accounts had expected. This influence of EU bureaucrats can run through from agenda setting to implementation phases of CSDP (Dijkstra 2012b, 2012a; Eckhard and Dijkstra 2017). Others have worked on the role of the industry in the shaping of either national or European defence policies (Bitzinger 2008; Oikonomou 2012).

Methodologies and methodological challenges

Public Policy studies focusing on defence policies display a variety of methodologies, which this chapter cannot comprehensively account for. This variety is partly attributable to the heterogeneity of the Public Policy field itself, stretched between its policy-oriented and its more critical poles (and their dedicated methodologies). This chapter first considers the methodological variety in studies dealing with one of the Public Policy's core themes identified above. It then discusses some methodological challenges.

Towards methodological plurality

Much of the scholarship devoted to defence policies has adopted qualitative methods. A great deal of Public Policy scholarship has developed theoretical approaches centred on discourse analysis of some forms (Béland 2009; Schmidt and Radaelli 2004). This also holds true for studies focused on defence policy. This focus on discourse analysis has many roots. First, the fields of IR (Katzenstein 1996; Wendt 1999) and Public Policy (Hall 1993; Jobert and Muller 1987; Sabatier 1998) both went through their ideational turn. Ideational factors (ideas, representations, discourses, etc) are considered to play a distinctive (yet possibly complementary of material ones) role in interpreting or explaining policy changes. But the focus on discourses also finds its origin in the scarcity of "hard" data, which is especially true in the defence realm. Given that there is less quantitative data, less access to fieldwork, the researcher finds him/herself much more dependent on the very discourses produced by the institution itself and its actors. Paradoxically enough, in a policy domain where (national) interests are often taken for granted as the main (if not only) explanatory factor, research is mostly dependent on discourses and sensemaking. This point and the challenges it raises will be discussed later in this section. Discourses are gathered through the analysis of general and specialized media (press, blogs), parliamentary records, official speeches, grey literature (reports, either for dissemination or not) and by semi-structured interviews.

Jolyon Howorth has early on adopted such an approach for his research on CSDP:

Ideas, though not unconnected to interests, can take on a life of their own. The aim of this article is to scrutinize the policy-making process in order to understand the connection between interests, ideas and discourse in the construction of yet another security narrative emerging in 1998/99 – European Security and Defence Policy (ESDP) – which many were led to believe posed a challenge to the apparently triumphal NATO narrative of the mod-1990s. This study concentrates on the role in this process of three countries – Britain, France, and to a lesser extent, Germany – not only because they are the main security players in Europe, but also because they offer strikingly contrasting pictures of the metamorphosis of a policy community, of the seminal role of ideas, and of the importance of appropriate political discourse.

(Howorth 2004, p. 212)

Embedded in the same theoretical framework of discursive institutionalism, Antoine Rayroux shows how military cooperation (in the European Union Force (EUFOR) Chad operation) between two countries with diverging interests (France and Ireland) was made possible by ambiguities in the discourses developed by national defence policies (Rayroux 2014). This author shows how discursive and institutional variables interact to explain the evolution of national defence policies and potential international cooperation. In a comparable direction, many other authors study the framing of defence policies (Blauberger and Weiss 2013; Kurowska 2009; Mörth 2000). Discourses and ideational factors' relevance is yet not to be taken for granted, but to be assessed on a case-by-case basis and can be combined rather than opposed to other factors (Meyer and Strickmann 2011). In some epistemologies and methodologies, discourses constitute an explanatory factor per se. In others, they can be used as a tool to reconstruct processes of policy change and identify factors within them, for instance by using process tracing. Beyond a simple description of events, the method of process tracing allows to identify the mechanisms of change (Bennett and Checkel 2014; Bezes et al. 2018; Mahoney 2012). Bastien Irondelle used process-tracing to explain the French President Chirac's decisive role in the reform that ended conscription in French armed forces (Irondelle 2011). His book was a prime example of excellent inductive research, based on very rich empirical material (Irondelle 2011, pp. 28–29), which allowed him to reconstruct the decision-making process in a very convincing manner.

Beyond the analysis of institutional documents (the "grey literature") and of the press, many studies rely on the conduct of semi-structured interviews (Deschaux-Beaume 2012; Hoeffler 2012; Hofmann 2013). The number of interviews used and/or referred to in published articles in academic journals varies a lot, from a dozen to more than 100. The acceptable number of interviews depends on the status given to the interviews, which is defined by an article's epistemology and theoretical approach and by what journal is targeted. Whereas positivist journals may require a high number of interviews and some data on the interviewees, post-positivist journals may accept interviews as performing an illustrative rather than explanatory function. Other qualitative methods adopted can range from archival work (Cohen 1999; Deschaux-Beaume 2011) to participant observation or even participation as (semi-)insiders (Pajon 2005; Schmitt 2015).

Quantitative methods have a long history in comparative politics and IR when it comes to investigating peace and war dynamics (Doyle and Sambanis 2000; Soeters et al. 2014; Wimmer et al. 2009). They are also on the rise in studies pertaining to defence policies. This is particularly visible in studies that focus on party politics and public opinion's influence on defence policies (Wagner et al 2017). Political parties' manifestos have constituted a fruitful source of data through the Manifesto Project[2] supported by the German Wissenschaftszentrum Berlin für Sozialforschung (WZB) and the Deutsche Foschungsgemeinschaft (DFG) (Volkens et al. 2018). Party manifestos have been used by some quantitative studies analysing the parties' impact on defence policies (Herbel 2017) along with other qualitative studies (Hofmann 2013). Other studies rely on the Chapel Hill Expert Survey[3] (CHES): Wagner et al. use this survey to map political parties' positions on military missions on a left-right axis (Wagner et al. 2017). Regarding public opinion analysis, many studies focusing on Europe make use of the Eurobarometers (Brummer 2007; Schoen 2008) or other national surveys (Mader 2017). Qualitative analysis of media coverage is complemented with quantitative research focusing on social media (Gupta and Brooks 2013; Simon et al. 2014).

Innovative methodologies have also been applied to the analysis of defence policy, with attempts at combining in new ways qualitative and quantitative methodologies. De Vreese et al. use survey-embedded experiments to analyse how the framing the EU's common foreign and security policy on public support, in order to analyse the various frames the elite and media use (De Vreese and Kandyla 2009). A current research project on CSDP led by Harald Schoen (University of Mannheim) focuses on the elite-public opinion nexus in CSDP and involves mixed methodologies, i.e. mass surveys, elite interviews and media analysis.[4]

Specific and not so specific methodological challenges

Doing research on defence policy entails a few methodological challenges. Some have already been discussed elsewhere recently (Carreiras 2006; Soeters et al. 2014; Deschaux-Dutard 2018), which allows me to focus on a few that seem of particular importance. I argue that these challenges are not necessarily unique: they can be compared to the ones encountered by studies focusing on policies with high levels of confidentiality, linked to security concerns and/or big economic interests (think of big business, such as pharmaceuticals and mining industries). Moreover they may epitomize difficulties that research in social sciences is increasingly encountering. As such, they may be interesting to consider for scholars that are not working on defence as well. This subsection considers two sets of questions: first, the various impacts of secrecy and confidentiality at different levels in the research process when studying defence as a public policy; second, the researcher's relationship to her fieldwork and the questions that arise from it.

Confidentiality and research: public policy approaches caught in the crossfire of conflicting methodological demands

Quite a large number of publications deal with the impact of secrecy and confidentiality on doing research in security and defence domains. Many focus on how to access information and how to get and conduct interviews (Boumaza and Campana

2007; Cohen and Arieli 2011; Cohen 1999; Deschaux-Beaume 2012; Garcia and Hoeffler 2015; Lancaster 2017). The difficulty can be of various intensities and natures, considering that it can stem from administrative hurdles or from the dangers of doing research in conflict zones. Obstacles to do "normal" fieldwork can be so important on some topics or in some areas that some scholars interrogate the very limits of research. Ahram explains how the Iraqi regime's opacity has made fieldwork almost impossible, which had led researchers to look for alternatives (Ahram 2013). Difficulties to analyse war "on the ground", from Vietnam to Mali, can be included here. This is crucial because difficulties to access fieldwork define the borders of knowledge production, i.e. what areas, topics, historical periods, etc. scientists do publish about. Needless to say that this has tremendous political consequences too.

Next to the question of access, what is at stake is the nature and quality of the accessible data. Interviewees may give erroneous information, be it because they flat-out lie, because they make unintentional mistakes, or because this is just how they experienced a given situation. These biases could be even stronger in policy domains combining an explosive mix, i.e. being characterised by high stakes (political, economic, symbolic, etc) and by high levels of confidentiality, for formal-institutional reasons (institutional authorizations required) or informal-symbolic (professional cultures of secrecy) ones. This may prevent the researcher from trusting information gathered through interviews. Another methodological issue would lie in the sampling problem. Overall, snowballing strategies' lack of randomness (selection bias) and the low number of interviews lead positivist, mostly quantitative approaches to mistrust interviews as a reliable source of data. In defence, this problem is magnified by the unpredictability of elite interviewing: not only can they be harder to get, but they are few in absolute numbers, they may not be recordable, and information triangulation may not be possible. This does not mean that interviews are useless or to be discarded. They can serve different purposes, from getting information, to triangulating sources and to making sense of processes and "facts" obtained elsewhere (Garcia and Hoeffler 2015; Mosley 2013). Interviews may well be the most appropriate source of empirical material in those very policies marked by formal and informal forms of confidentiality. Methodological challenges may rather arise when it comes to designing and implementing comparative research projects (Deschaux-Beaume 2011; Hoeffler 2013, 2008).

Last, but not least, confidentiality also impacts how to use empirical material, mostly interviews, in writing and publishing research (Kaiser 2009; Lancaster 2017; Lilleker 2003). Researchers have come up with different "technical" solutions to use these sources without compromising in any way their interviewees' identity and thus without harming the trust interviewing relies on and necessitates. While doing interviews in defence used to be seen as very specific given its high(er) confidentiality requirements, it could be argued that this specificity is waning. The emergence or rise (depending on countries) of codes of ethics and stricter procedural rules for interviews, for all advantages they entail, also represent a new administrative hurdle for researchers to overcome, irrelevant from the policy's characteristics at stake. They impact both the authorization process by which the researcher can contact potential interviewees and how data are handled afterwards, for in most cases data storage is now required to be anonymous and safe for "civilian" policies as well.

Qualitative research based on interviews finds itself caught in the crossfire of conflicting demands between increasing replicability requirements and open access on the one hand,[5] and measures pertaining to cyber-criminality and the protection of data privacy: this used to particularly affect security and defence policies but does now touch policies across the board.

A researcher's relationship to fieldwork: power, autonomy and safety

I consider here three questions that seem of particular importance for a public policy researcher. First, one needs to consider how power affects research on defence policy. While it is widely acknowledged that interviewing entails a power relationship (Chamboredon et al. 1994; Cohen 1999; Lancaster 2017), gendering this power relationship is not yet sufficiently achieved in Public Policy approaches to defence, in sharp contrast to other academic fields (Arendell 1997; Enloe 2014; Margaret Fonow and Cook 2005; Mazur and Pollack 2009; Shepherd 2010; Tickner 1992). Thinking and acting upon the gender dimension may be obviously important when female scholars interview male defence-elites, but it is just as important in other situations. However gender cannot be considered in isolation from other characteristics: it should be thought of as working in relation to other dimensions such as race and class (Chowdhry and Nair 2004). Power is performed through gender and gender is (re)produced through power. The knowledge produced by interviews is thus not immune of these gendered, racialized power relations (Carreiras and Alexandre 2013).

Second, the researcher's independence is of paramount importance. This has been captured as the insider/outsider question (Deschaux-Beaume 2011): how to be sufficiently close to the military institution in order to get information, yet not too close so as to not be biased in any way? This is a trade-off between access and independence that many researchers face at some point. This concern is obviously also true for other policies as well. But a difference lies in the fact that in some policies more than in others, state institutions have an interest in (and an historically acknowledged habit of) shaping the academic discourse and/or in using it in self-legitimizing strategies. Shaping the academic discourse does not need to take the ultimate form of censorship: concealing information or cherry picking what information to reveal, selecting the researcher's interlocutors, requiring formal authorization prior to publication, financing only certain research projects (by framing the acceptable concepts, cases, etc.), or demanding a "give and take" exchange of information with defence services, among others, can, voluntarily or not, influence research. Engaging in a more or less institutionalized relationship with the defence establishment has downsides and advantages, which the researcher should be aware of, especially when it entails financial aspects (Monjardet 1997). While becoming an insider may improve fieldwork opportunities, it also increases the risk of being influenced by the institution under scrutiny and of participating in a dilution of the frontier between the academic and military spheres.

Last, and in relation to the second point, doing research on defence policy can entail security risks, for the researcher, her home institution and the interviewees. Fieldwork can be dangerous, especially in dynamic, unstable political contexts of non-democratic regimes: the murder of an Italian PhD student in Egypt, the arrest of some others on suspicion of treason or spying activities are sadly here to remind us of it (Glasius 2018). These cases have triggered more discussion about our research practices and obligations (Knott,2019; Wackenhut 2018), but they have also led to a strengthening of fieldwork rules by many universities, supported by national ministries of Foreign Affairs. While these may improve researchers' safety, they also represent a securitization of research for some (Peter and Strazzari 2017). This latter dimension has potential important methodological consequences for research on defence policies, in non-democratic but also in democratic regimes. The researcher's physical safety becomes dependent on bureaucratic criteria beyond her reach (for instance, the definitions of situations of risk, that may differ), and that can be influenced by other (political) considerations. This is not to say that safety is not a legitimate concern: but researchers should be aware of how bureaucratic safety requirements may influence fieldwork in the future, from the definition of what is feasible up to what is publishable. For instance, in France, the Direction for Military Intelligence signed a partnership with the National Center for Scientific Research (CNRS), the long-standing public state-funded research institution in France in June 2018.[6] This sparked much controversy over the scientific independence's meaning and concrete dimensions: will research be as free when some objects, some concepts and definitions are preferred and encouraged over others by the MoD? How can a researcher be credible and reliable towards her sources when her home organization supports and promotes such transfer of knowledge towards military institutions? Such questions are of paramount importance not only for the quality of research, but also for its very possibility and for the researcher's safety.

Conclusion

Public policy has contributed to Defence Studies by providing scholars tools to analyze defence policies, their actors and processes. This chapter has explored agenda-setting approaches, decision-making theories, and implementation studies, and how they have been applied to defence policy. Moreover, public policy scholars have engaged in exploring international military cooperation through concepts such as policy internationalization or integration. In the case of the European Union, a large literature on the CSDP has brought together scholars from public policy and IR in discussions about the Europeanization of national policies. Methodologically, these contributions are manifold: while many analyses are qualitative and based on interviews, an increasing number of scholars explore national or international defence policies with quantitative or mixed methodologies. Analysing defence through a public policy approach does not go without methodological challenges though. This chapter has engaged with two of them: how confidentiality impacts various stages of research, from getting access to interviewees to publication; the relationship of the researcher to his/her fieldwork in front of new or renewed obstacles.

Notes

1 Public Policy in this chapter designates the field of political science that focuses on the analysis of governments' actions (and absence thereof), including many stages such as agenda-setting, decision-making, implementation, and evaluation (Cairney 2012; Howlett et al. 2009; Kingdon 2011; Sabatier 2007). According to Ribemont et al. 2018, "Studying public policy is essentially a question of how a society tries to solve its own problems. What is called 'public policy' can indeed be described as all the means, formal and informal, that a society develops to deal with the problems that can weaken its coherence and functioning. [...] The 'public' response to these problems means that these problems are dealt with collectively, often through the action of the State: facing difficulty to find solutions, society gradually equips

itself with 'public policies', that is to say, rules, funding, specialized personnel, programs, indicators, always more sophisticated, allowing it to come with ways of dealing with these problems" (Ribemont et al. 2018, p. 5). Public Policy with capital letters refers to the scientific field; without capital letters, it means the object, i.e. a state policy.
2 https://manifesto-project.wzb.eu/ [accessed 31 March 2019].
3 https://www.chesdata.eu/ [accessed 31 March 2019].
4 https://www.mzes.uni-mannheim.de/d7/en/projects/fighting-together-moving-apart-european-common-defence-and-shared-security-in-an-age-of-brexit-and-trump [accessed 31 March 2019].
5 This issue is discussed in the chapter dedicated to secondary analysis of qualitative data in defence studies by Borzillo and Deschaux-Dutard in this volume.
6 See for instance: http://www.opex360.com/2018/06/10/direction-renseignement-militaire-a-signe-convention-de-partenariat-cnrs/ (Consulted on 25 June 2019).

References

Adler-Nissen, R. (2014). Symbolic power in European diplomacy: The struggle between national foreign services and the EU's External Action Service. *Review of International Studies*, 40, 657–681.
Ahram, A. I. (2013). Iraq in the social sciences: Testing the limits of research. *The Journal of the Middle East and Africa*, 4, 251–266.
Allison, G. T., Zelikow, P. (1999). *Essence of Decision: Explaining the Cuban Missile Crisis*, 2nd ed., New York, Longman.
Arendell, T. (1997). Reflections on the researcher-researched relationship: A woman interviewing men. *Qualitative Sociology*, 20, 341–368.
Baumgartner, F., Jones, B. D. (1991). Agenda dynamics and policy subsystems. *The Journal of Politics*, 53, 1044–1074.
Beckett, I. F. W., Gooch, J. (Eds.) (1981). *Politicians and defence: Studies in the formulation of British defence policy, 1845–1970*, Manchester, Manchester University Press.
Béland, D. (2009). Ideas, institutions, and policy change. *Journal of European Public Policy*, 16, 701–718.
Béraud-Sudreau, L., Faure, S. B., Sladeczek, M. (2015). Réguler le commerce des armes par le Parlement et l'opinion publique. *Politique européenne*, (2), 82–121.
Bennett, A., Checkel, J. T. (Eds.) (2014). *Process Tracing: From Metaphor to Analytic Tool*, Cambridge, Cambridge University Press.
Bezes, P., Palier, B., Surel, Y. (2018). Le process tracing: du discours de la méthode aux usages pratiques. *Revue française de science politique*, 68, 961–965.
Bickerton, C. J., Irondelle, B., Menon, A. (2011). Security co-operation beyond the nation-state: The EU's Common Security and Defence Policy. *JCMS: Journal of Common Market Studies*, 49, 1–21.
Birkland, T. A. (2016). *Agenda Setting and the Policy Process: Focusing Events*, Oxford, Oxford University Press.
Bitzinger, R. A. (2008). The revolution in military affairs and the global defence industry: reactions and interactions. *Security Challenges*, 4(4), 1–11.
Blauberger, M., Weiss, M. (2013). 'If you can't beat me, join me!' How the Commission pushed and pulled member states into legislating defence procurement. *Journal of European Public Policy*, 20, 1120–1138.
Boëne, B. (1990). How 'unique' should the military be? A review of representative literature & outline of a synthetic formulation. *European Journal of Sociology*, 31, 3.
Boumaza, M., Campana, A. (2007). Enquêter en milieu « difficile ». Introduction. *Revue française de science politique*, 57, 5–25.
Britz, M. (2010). The role of marketization in the Europeanization of defense industry policy. *Bulletin of Science, Technology & Society*, 30, 176–184.

Brummer, K. (2007). Superficial, not substantial: The ambiguity of public support for Europe's security and defence policy. *European Security*, 16, 183–201.

Cairney, P. (2012). *Understanding Public Policy: Theories and Issues*, Houndmills, New York, Palgrave Macmillan.

Carreiras, H. (2006). *Gender and the Military: Women in the Armed Forces of Western Democracies*, London, Routledge.

Carreiras, H., Alexandre, H. (2013). Research relations in military settings. In: Carreiras, H., Castro, C. (2013). *Qualitative Methods in Military Studies: Research Experiences and Challenges*, London, New York, Routledge.

Carreiras, H., Castro, C. (2014). *Qualitative Methods in Military Studies: Research Experiences and Challenges*, London, New York, Routledge.

Chamboredon, H., Pavis, F., Surdez, M., Willemez, L. (1994). S'imposer aux imposants. A propos de quelques obstacles rencontrés par des sociologues débutants dans la pratique et l'usage de l'entretien. *Genèses*, 16, 114–132.

Chowdhry, G., Nair, S. (2004). *Power, Postcolonialism and International Relations: Reading Race, Gender and Class*, Abingdon, New York, Routledge.

Cohen, M. D., March, J. G., Olsen, J. P. (1972). A garbage can model of organizational choice. *Administrative Science Quarterly*, 17, 1–25.

Cohen, S. (Ed.) (1999). *L'art d'interviewer les dirigeants*, 1st ed. Paris, Presses universitaires de France. Politique d'aujourd'hui.

Cohen, N., Arieli, T. (2011). Field research in conflict environments: Methodological challenges and snowball sampling. *Journal of Peace Research*, 48, 423–435.

Cutler, R., Von Lingen, A. (2003). The European Parliament and European Union security and defence policy. *European Security*, 12, 1–20.

Dahl, R. A. (2005). *Who Governs? Democracy and Power in an American City*, 2nd edn. New Haven, CT, London, Yale University Press.

De Vreese, C.H., Kandyla, A. (2009). News framing and public support for a common foreign and security policy. *JCMS: Journal of Common Market Studies*, 47, 453–481.

Deschaux-Beaume, D. (2011). Studying the military in a comparative perspective: Methodological challenges and issues. The example of French and German officers in European defense and security policy. In: Carreiras, H., Castro, C. (Eds.), *Qualitative Methods in Military Studies: Research Experiences and Challenges*, London, New York, Routledge.

Deschaux-Beaume, D. (2012). Investigating the military field: Qualitative research strategy and interviewing in the defence networks. *Current Sociology*, 60, 101–117.

Deschaux-Dutard, D. (2017). Usage de la force et contrôle démocratique: le rôle des arènes parlementaires en France et en Allemagne. *Revue Internationale de Politique Comparée*, 24(3), 101–131.

Deschaux-Dutard, D. (2018). *Methods in Defence Studies*, 40–55. In: Galbreath, D., Deni, J. (Eds.) (2018). *Routledge Handbook of Defence Studies*, London, Routledge.

Dijkstra, H. (2012a). Agenda-setting in the Common Security and Defence Policy: An institutionalist perspective. *Cooperation and Conflict*, 47, 454–472.

Dijkstra, H. (2012b). The influence of EU officials in European security and defence. *European Security*, 21, 311–327.

Dover, R. (2007). *Europeanization of British Defence Policy*, London, Routledge.

Doyle, M. W., Sambanis, N. (2000). International peacebuilding: A theoretical and quantitative analysis. *American Political Science Review*, 94, 779–801.

Dyson, S. B. (2006). Personality and Foreign Policy: Tony Blair's Iraq decisions. *Foreign Policy Analysis*, 2, 289–306.

Eckhard, S., Dijkstra, H. (2017). Contested implementation: The unilateral influence of member states on peacebuilding policy in Kosovo. *Global Policy*, 8, 102–112.

Elmore, R. F. (1979). Backward mapping: Implementation research and policy decisions. *Political Science Quarterly*, 94, 601–616.

Enloe, C. H. (2014). *Bananas, Beaches and Bases: Making Feminist Sense of International Politics*, 2nd ed., Berkeley, CA, University of California Press.

Eriksson, A. (2006). *Europeanization and Governance in Defence Policy: The Example of Sweden*, Stockholm, Stockholm University, Department of Political Science.

Esping-Andersen, G. (1998). *The Three Worlds of Welfare Capitalism*, Repr. Ed., Princeton, NJ, Princeton University Press.

Fonck, D., Haesebrouck, T., Reykers, Y. (2019). Parliamentary involvement, party ideology and majority-opposition bargaining: Belgian participation in multinational military operations. *Contemporary Security Policy*, 40(1), 85–100.

Furness, M. (2013). Who controls the European external action service? Agent autonomy in EU external policy. *European Foreign Affairs Review*, 103–125.

Garcia, N., Hoeffler, C. (2015). Chapitre 15:L'entretien et la place des acteurs dans la sociologie de l'action publique, 377–404. In: Boussaguet, L., Jacquot, S., Ravinet, P. (2015). *Une French Touch dans l'analyse des politiques publiques?* Paris, Presses de Sciences Po.

Genschel, P., Jachtenfuchs, M. (Eds.) (2013). *Beyond the Regulatory Polity?: The European Integration of Core State Powers*, Oxford, Oxford University Press.

Glasius, M. (2018). *Research, Ethics and Risk in the Authoritarian Field*, Cham, Springer International Publishing, S.l.

Gross, E. (2007). Germany and European security and defence cooperation: The Europeanization of national crisis management policies? *Security Dialogue*, 38, 501–520.

Gupta, R., Brooks, H. (2013). *Using Social Media for Global Security*, 1st ed., Indianapolis, IN, John Wiley & Sons, Inc.

Hall, P. A. (1993). Policy paradigms, social learning, and the State: The case of economic policymaking in Britain. *Comparative Politics*, 25, 275–296.

Harguindeguy, J.-B. (2014). Cycle (Policy cycle), 196–201. In: Boussaguet, L., Jacquot, S., Ravinet, P. (2014). *Dictionnaire des politiques publiques: 4e édition précédée d'un nouvel avant-propos*, Paris, Presses de Sciences po.

Hartley, K. (2003). The future of European defence policy: An economic perspective. *Defence and Peace Economics*, 14(2), 107–115.

Hellmann, G., Baumann, R., Bösche, M., Herborth, B., Wagner, W. (2005). De-Europeanization by default? Germany's EU policy in defense and asylum. *Foreign Policy Analysis*, 1, 143–164.

Herbel, A. (2017). Parliamentary scrutiny of the EU's Common Foreign and Security Policy. *West European Politics*, 40, 161–182.

Hoeffler, C. (2012). European armament co-operation and the renewal of industrial policy motives. *Journal of European Public Policy*, 19, 435–451.

Hoeffler, C. (2013). L'émergence d'une politique industrielle de défense libérale en Europe: Appréhender le changement de la politique d'armement par ses instruments. *Gouvernement et action publique*, 4, 641–665.

Hoeffler, C. (2008). Les réformes des systèmes d'acquisition d'armement en France et en Allemagne: un retour paradoxal des militaires? *Revue internationale de politique comparée*, 15, 133–150.

Hofmann, S. C. (2013). *European Security in NATO's Shadow: Party Ideologies and Institution Building*, Cambridge, Cambridge University Press.

Hofmann, S. C. (2017). Party preferences and institutional transformation: Revisiting France's relationship with NATO (and the common wisdom on Gaullism). *Journal of Strategic Studies*, 40, 505–531.

Höse, A. (2007). Public opinion and the development of the European security and defence policy. *European Foreign Affairs Review*, 12(2), 149–167.

Howlett, M., Ramesh, M., Perl, A. (2009). *Studying Public Policy: Policy Cycles & Policy Subsystems*. 3rd ed., Ontario, New York, Oxford University Press.

Howorth, J. (2004). Discourse, ideas, and epistemic communities in European security and defence policy. *West European Politics*, 27, 211–234.

Howorth, J. (2011). The 'new faces' of Lisbon: Assessing the performance of Catherine Ashton and Herman van Rompuy on the global stage. *European Foreign Affairs Review*, 16(3), 303–323.

Howorth, J. (2014). *Security and Defence Policy in the European Union*, 2nd ed., Basingstoke, Palgrave Macmillan.

Howorth, J., Menon, A. (Eds.) (1997). *The European Union and National Defence Policy*, London, New York, Routledge. The State and the European Union series.

Hudson, V. M. (2005). Foreign policy analysis: Actor-specific theory and the ground of international relations: Foreign policy analysis. *Foreign Policy Analysis*, 1, 1–30.

Hurrell, A., Menon, A. (1996). Politics like any other? Comparative politics, international relations and the study of the EU. *West European Politics*, 19, 386–402.

Irondelle, B. (2003). Europeanization without the European Union? French military reforms 1991–96. *Journal of European Public Policy*, 10, 208–226.

Irondelle, B. (2008). *Chapitre 3: Les politiques de défense, 93–112, in: Politiques publiques 1*. Paris, Presses de Sciences Po.

Irondelle, B. (2011). *La réforme des armées en France. Sociologie de la decision*, Paris, Presses de Sciences Po.

Joana, J. (2012). *Les armées contemporaines*, Paris, Presses de La Fondation nationale des sciences politiques.

Jobert, B., Muller, P. (1987). *L'État en action: politiques publiques et corporatismes*, 1st ed., Paris, Presses universitaires de France. Recherches politiques.

Jones, C. O. (1984). *An Introduction to the Study of Public Policy*, 3rd ed., Monterey, CA, Brooks/Cole Pub. Co.

Juncos, A. (2009). The Lisbon Treaty and the Foreign, Security and Defence Policy: Reforms, implementation and the consequences of (non–) ratification. *European Foreign Affairs Review*, 14(1), 25–46.

Kaarbo, J. (2015). A Foreign Policy Analysis perspective on the domestic politics turn in IR Theory. *International Studies Review*, 17, 189–216.

Kaiser, K. (2009). Protecting respondent confidentiality in qualitative research. *Qualitative Health Research*, 19, 1632–1641.

Katzenstein, P. J. (Ed.) (1996). *The Culture of National Security: Norms and Identity in World Politics, New Directions in World Politics*, New York, Columbia University Press.

Kempin, R., Mawdsley, J. (2013). The Common Security and Defence Policy as an act of American hegemony. *European Security*, 22, 55–73.

Kingdon, J. W. (2011). *Agendas, Alternatives, and Public Policies*, Updated 2nd ed., Boston, Longman. Longman classics in political science.

Knott, E. (2019). Beyond the field: Ethics after fieldwork in politically dynamic contexts. *Perspectives on Politics*, 17, 140–153.

Kurowska, X. (2009). 'Solana Milieu': Framing security policy. *Perspectives on European Politics and Society*, 10, 523–540.

Lancaster, K. (2017). Confidentiality, anonymity and power relations in elite interviewing: Conducting qualitative policy research in a politicised domain. *International Journal of Social Research Methodology*, 20, 93–103.

Lavallée, C. (2011). The European Commission's position in the field of security and defence: An unconventional actor at a meeting point. *Perspectives on European Politics and Society*, 12, 371–389.

Lilleker, D. G. (2003). Interviewing the political elite: Navigating a potential minefield. *Politics*, 23, 207–214.

Lipsky, M. (1983). *Street-level Bureaucracy: Dilemmas of the Individual in Public Services*, New York, Russell Sage Foundation.

Lord, C. (2011). The political theory and practice of parliamentary participation in the Common Security and Defence Policy. *Journal of European Public Policy*, 18, 1133–1150.

Mader, M. (2017). Citizens' perceptions of policy objectives and support for military action: Looking for prudence in Germany. *Journal of Conflict Resolution*, 61, 1290–1314.

Mahoney, J. (2012). The logic of process tracing tests in the social sciences. *Sociological Methods & Research*, 41, 570–597.

Margaret Fonow, M., Cook, J. A. (2005). Feminist methodology: New applications in the academy and public policy. *Signs: Journal of Women in Culture and Society*, 30, 2211–2236.

Martin, S., Rozenberg, O. (2014). *The Roles and Function of Parliamentary Questions*, Hoboken, NJ, Taylor and Francis.

Mazur, A. G., Pollack, M. A. (2009). Gender and public policy in Europe: An introduction. *Comparative European Politics*, 7, 1–11.

McDonald, M. (2013). Foreign and defence policy on Australia's political agenda, 1962–2012: Foreign and defence policy. *Australian Journal of Public Administration*, 72, 171–184.

Menon, A. (2013). Defence Policy and the logic of 'high politics', 66–84. In: Genschel, P., Jachtenfuchs, M. (Eds.), *Beyond the Regulatory Polity?* New York, Oxford University Press.

Mérand, F. (2008). *European Defence Policy: Beyond the Nation State*, New York, Oxford University Press.

Mérand, F., Angers, K. (2013). Military integration in Europe, 46–65. In: Genschel, P., Jachtenfuchs, M. (Eds.), *Beyond the Regulatory Polity?* New York, Oxford University Press.

Merlingen, M., Ostrauskaite, R. (2010). *European Security and Defence Policy. An Implementation Perspective*, London, Routledge.

Meyer, C. O., Strickmann, E. (2011). Solidifying constructivism: How material and ideational factors interact in European Defence. *JCMS: Journal of Common Market Studies*, 49, 61–81.

Missiroli, A. (2007). Italy's security and defence policy: Between EU and US, or just Prodi and Berlusconi? *Journal of Southern Europe and the Balkans*, 9, 149–168.

Monjardet, D. (1997). Le chercheur et le policier. L'expérience des recherches commanditées par le ministère de l'Intérieur. *Revue française de science politique*, 47, 211–225.

Morel, N., Palier, B., Palme, J. (Eds.) (2012). *Towards a Social Investment Welfare State? Ideas, Policies and Challenges*, Bristol, Policy Press.

Morillas, P. (2011). Institutionalization or intergovernmental decision-taking in foreign policy: The implementation of the Lisbon Treaty. *European Foreign Affairs Review*, 16(2), 243–257.

Mörth, U. (2000). Competing frames in the European Commission – the case of the defence industry and equipment issue. *Journal of European Public Policy*, 7, 173–189.

Mosley, L. (Ed.) (2013). *Interview Research in Political Science*, Ithaca, Cornell University Press.

Oikonomou, I. (2012). The political economy of EU space policy militarization: the case of the global monitoring for environment and security, 151–164. In: Stavrianakis, A., Selby, J. (2012). *Militarism and International Relations in the Twenty-first Century*, London, Routledge.

Olsen, G. R. (2011). How strong is Europeanisation, really? The Danish defence administration and the opt-out from the European security and defence policy. *Perspectives on European Politics and Society*, 12, 13–28.

Pajon, C. (2005). Le sociologue enrégimenté: méthodes et techniques d'enquête en milieu militaire, 45–57. In: Gresle, F., Delfolie, D. (Eds.), *Sociologie Du Milieu Militaire: Les Conséquences de La Professionnalisation Sur Les Armées et l'identité Militaire*, Paris, Harmattan. Logiques Sociales.

Peter, M., Strazzari, F. (2017). Securitisation of research: Fieldwork under new restrictions in Darfur and Mali. *Third World Quarterly*, 38, 1531–1550.

Peters, D., Wagner, W. M., Deitelhoff, N. (2010). *Parliaments and European Security Policy. Mapping the Parliamentary Field*, Austria, ECSA.

Pierson, P. (1996). *Dismantling the Welfare State?: Reagan, Thatcher, and the Politics of Retrenchment*, Cambridge, Cambridge University Press.

Pressman, J. L., Wildavsky, A. B. (1984). *Implementation: How Great Expectations in Washington are Dashed in Oakland*, Berkeley, CA, University of California Press. Oakland Project series.

Radaelli, C. M. (2002). The domestic impact of European Union public policy: Notes on concepts, methods, and the challenge of empirical research. *Politique européenne*, 5, 105–136.
Rathbun, B. C. (2007). Hierarchy and community at home and abroad: Evidence of a common structure of domestic and foreign policy beliefs in American elites. *Journal of Conflict Resolution* 51, 379–407.
Rayroux, A. (2014). Speaking EU defence at home: Contentious discourses and constructive ambiguity. *Cooperation and Conflict*, 49, 386–405.
Reifler, J., Clarke, H. D., Scotto, T. J., Sanders, D., Stewart, M. C., Whiteley, P. (2014). Prudence, principle and minimal heuristics: British public opinion toward the use of military force in Afghanistan and Libya. *The British Journal of Politics and International Relations*, 16(1), 28–55.
Ribemont, T., Bossy, T., Evrard, A., Gourgues, G., Hoeffler, C. (2018). *Introduction à la sociologie de l'action publique*, Bruxelles, De Boeck.
Riddervold, M. (2016). (Not) in the hands of the Member States: How the European Commission influences EU security and defence policies. *JCMS: Journal of Common Market Studies*, 54, 353–369.
Riddervold, M., Rosén, G. (2016). Trick and treat: how the Commission and the European Parliament exert influence in EU foreign and security policies. *Journal of European Integration*, 38, 687–702.
Rieker, P. (2006). From common defence to comprehensive security: Towards the Europeanization of French foreign and security policy? *Security Dialogue*, 37, 509–528.
Rochefort, D. A., Cobb, R. W. (Eds.) (1994). *The Politics of Problem Definition: Shaping the Policy Agenda, Studies in Government and Public Policy*, Lawrence, KS, University Press of Kansas.
Rosén, G. (2015). EU confidential: The European Parliament's involvement in EU Security and Defence Policy: EU confidential. *JCMS: Journal of Common Market Studies*, 53, 383–398.
Sabatier, P., Mazmanian, D. (1980). The implementation of public policy: A framework of analysis. *Policy Studies Journal*, 8, 538–560.
Sabatier, P. A. (1986). Top-down and bottom-up approaches to implementation research: A critical analysis and suggested synthesis. *Journal of Public Policy*, 6, 21.
Sabatier, P. A. (1998). The advocacy coalition framework: Revisions and relevance for Europe. *Journal of European Public Policy*, 5, 98–130.
Sabatier, P. A. (Ed.) (2007). *Theories of the Policy Process*, 2nd ed., Boulder, CO, Westview Press.
Schmidt, V.A., Radaelli, C.M. (2004). Policy change and discourse in Europe: Conceptual and methodological issues. *West European Politics*, 27, 183–210.
Schmitt, O. (2015). L'accès aux données confidentielles en milieu militaire: problèmes méthodologiques et éthiques d'un positionnement intermédiaire, *Champs de Mars*, 26, 50–58.
Schoen, H. (2008). Identity, instrumental self-interest and institutional evaluations: Explaining public opinion on common European policies in foreign affairs and defence. *European Union Politics*, 9, 5–29.
Shepherd, L. J. (Ed.) (2010). *Gender Matters in Global Politics: A Feminist Introduction to International Relations*, New York, Routledge.
Simon, T., Goldberg, A., Aharonson-Daniel, L., Leykin, D., Adini, B. (2014). Twitter in the Cross Fire—The Use of Social Media in the Westgate Mall Terror Attack in Kenya. *PLoS ONE* 9, e104136.
Smith, M. E. (2016). Implementing the global strategy where it matters most: the EU's credibility deficit and the European neighbourhood. *Contemporary Security Policy*, 37, 446–460.
Soeters, J. L., Shields, P. M., Rietjens, S. J. H. (Eds.) (2014). *Routledge Handbook of Research Methods in Military Studies*, Abingdon, Routledge.
Spillane, J. P., Reiser, B. J., Reimer, T. (2002). Policy implementation and cognition: Reframing and refocusing implementation research. *Review of Educational Research*, 72, 387–431.
Starr, H. (1980). The Kissinger Years: Studying individuals and foreign policy. *International Studies Quarterly*, 24, 465.

Strikwerda, J. (2018). Unexpected compliance? The implementation of the Defence and Security Procurement Directive. *Journal of European Integration*, 40, 889–904.

Thelen, K. A. (2014). *Varieties of Liberalization and the New Politics of Social Solidarity, Cambridge Studies in Comparative Politics*, Cambridge, New York, Cambridge University Press.

Thomson, C. P. (2016). Public support for economic and military coercion and audience costs. *The British Journal of Politics and International Relations*, 18(2), 407–421.

Tickner, J. A. (1992). *Gender in International Relations: Feminist Perspectives on Achieving Global Security, New Directions in World Politics*, New York, Columbia University Press.

Vanhoonacker, S., Pomorska, K. (2013). The European external action service and agenda-setting in European foreign policy. *Journal of European Public Policy*, 20, 1316–1331.

Vennesson, P. (Ed.) (2000). *Politiques de défense: institutions, innovations, européanisation*, Paris, Harmattan. Collection Logiques politiques.

Volkens, A., Lehmann, P., Matthiess, T., Merz, N., Regel, S., Wessels, B. (2018). *The Manifesto Data Collection: Manifesto Project (MRG/CMP/MARPOR)*. Version 2018a. Berlin, Wissenschaftszentrum Berlin fur Sozialforschung (WZB).

Wackenhut, A. F. (2018). Ethical considerations and dilemmas before, during and after fieldwork in less-democratic contexts: Some reflections from post-uprising Egypt. *The American Sociologist*, 49, 242–257.

Wagner, W. (2005). From vanguard to laggard: Germany in European security and defence policy. *German Politics*, 14, 455–469.

Wagner, W., Herranz-Surrallés, A., Kaarbo, J., Ostermann, F. (2017). The party politics of legislative–executive relations in security and defence policy. *West European Politics*, 40, 20–41.

Weiss, M. (2013). Integrating the acquisition of Leviathan's swords? The emerging regulation of defence procurement within the EU, 26–45. In: Genschel, P., Jachtenfuchs, M. (Eds.), *Beyond the Regulatory Polity?* Oxford, Oxford University Press.

Wendt, A. (1999). *Social Theory of International Politics, Cambridge Studies in International Relations*, Cambridge, New York, Cambridge University Press.

Whitman, R. G. (1998). Creating a foreign policy for Europe? Implementing the common foreign and security policy from Maastricht to Amsterdam. *Australian Journal of International Affairs*, 52, 165–183.

Williams, P. (2004). Who's making UK foreign policy? *International Affairs* (Royal Institute of International Affairs), 80, 911–929.

Wimmer, A., Cederman, L.-E., Min, B. (2009). Ethnic politics and armed conflict: A configurational analysis of a new global data set. *American Sociological Review*, 74, 316–337.

6 Sociological Methods in defence studies

Gregor Richter

Introduction

Almost all classics of sociology have expressed their view on the subject of war, military and society in monographs or longer statements. Hans Joas and Wolfgang Knöbl (2013) presented a comprehensive review of the scholarly literature and chose the starting point of their analysis in the 17th century beginning with Thomas Hobbes. The considerations in sociology in this field after the end of the Cold War, however, the two authors see and deplore the prevalence of a "monothematic approach" (Joas and Knöbl 2013: 252) in most of the outlines of theory. For instance, the debates over the "new wars" are shortened to marketization and privatization: "It is always *one particular* macrosocial process that has guided the analysis of wars and their possible cessation" (Joas and Knöbl 2013: 252, emphasis in original). The assessment according to different sociological thought about war, military and society is often narrowed in a specific way and is insufficiently supported by social theory. What the two authors do not pronounce, is the fact that sociology too often confronts this topic in the form of macro-sociological theory with the emphasis on macro-sociological processes. At least since Robert K. Merton's criticism of "grand theories" (Parsons) one should be familiar with the weaknesses of such theoretical conceptions: Either the conclusions have a high degree of generality and lead to trivial statements, or hypotheses cannot be tested empirically due to their high level of abstraction.

The reference point for an overview of *sociological methods in defence studies* are therefore reasonably micro-sociological theory concepts in the 1940s, more specifically, the entry of the US into World War II in 1941 and the launch of the *Research Branch of the US War Department* under the direction of Samuel A. Stouffer one year later. The result of this three-year mammoth project was over 200 reports based on hundreds of thousands of interviews with soldiers. The studies on "The American Soldier" (Stouffer 1949; Merton and Lazarsfeld 1950) not only fertilized military-sociological research for years to come, but they were also trendsetting the development of methods in the social sciences in general. This initial phase can be characterized by a high degree of practical relevance – the research should increase the knowledge base on the motivational foundations of US soldiers – and from today's perspective by an astonishing high level of transparency in dealing with the research results. A newsletter with selected survey results titled "What the Soldier Thinks" was issued by the *Morale Service Division in the US War Department* monthly and distributed to overseas military executives from December 1943 shortly until the end of the war.

"The American Soldier" showed impressively the potential "for examining the interplay of social theory and applied social research" (Merton and Kitt 1950: 40). The well-known theory of reference groups, for example, was developed in dealing with the data of the *Research Branch of the US War Department* and is considered a prime example of the division of labour and the fruitful interplay of theory and empirical evidence until today. Sociologist Robert K. Merton, himself a member of the working group around Stouffer, was able to work out his conception of "theories of the middle range" with the theory of reference groups. Likewise, the core of the theory of relative deprivation may be well explained using the example of soldiers. Dissatisfaction with one's own situation, for example the current career, is not merely the reflection of objective circumstances, but relative, and depends on the standards of comparison used by the individual, i.e. the reference group chosen by him or her. Provided with the survey data only, it was not easy to interpret, at first glance, that in US military units, where promotions were relatively more frequent than in peer groups, subjective satisfaction with career opportunities among respondents was relatively low.

Merton extended the theory of relative deprivation to a general theory of reference groups, in which non-membership groups become the reference point for the assessment of living conditions and career development. In this context, the notion of anticipatory socialization was formulated, which has meanwhile found its way into everyday usage. Claims to research and methodology in the sense of an incremental understanding of the progress in science and practice should therefore be to develop military-sociological theories step by step:

> Systematic empirical materials help advance social theory by imposing the task and affording the opportunity for interpretation along lines often unpremeditated, and social theory, in turn, defines the scope and enlarges the predictive value of empirical findings by indicating the conditions under which they hold.
> (Merton and Kitt 1950: 40)

How such empirical material is systematically collected is part of the methodology that forms the starting point for the following remarks on sociological methods in defence studies. Before that, it is necessary to delimit the field of research:

> Defence studies is a multi-disciplinary field examining how agents, predominately states, prepare for, prevent, avoid and/or engage in armed conflict.
> (Galbreath and Deni 2018: 1, Introduction)

This definition, taken from a recent textbook on the topic, should also be the reference point for the chapter at hand. Defence studies are difficult to define from a neighbouring branch of research, i.e. military studies (Soeters et al. 2014; Soeters 2018). Even if the research topics and especially the traditions of military studies differ from the here examined research field, there is no reason to conjure boundaries at the level of methods and research techniques. According to Soeters (2018) military studies can be found in the works of classics of sociology such as Marx, Durkheim, Weber, Simmel, Elias, and Goffman. The research field of the defence studies, on the other hand, has fewer classics, but can be characterized with its very interdisciplinary orientation:

[...] defence studies is naturally an inter-disciplinary area of scholarship that touches on political science, sociology, economics, international relations, social anthropology, human geography and organisational studies.

(Galbreth and Deni 2018: 1, Introduction)

Following earlier work (Richter 2017) I assume, that defence organizations and civil organizations must not be treated fundamentally different. In the case of military research, the repertoire of sociological methods and research techniques should not deviate from that of research on other types of organizations, such as corporations, churches or universities. According to my present knowledge, the opposite position had not yet been formulated. For example, if you look in the relevant anthologies (Soeters et al. 2014; Carreiras and Castro 2013; Carreiras et al. 2016), you encounter the major social science standard methods and research techniques. In the field of military psychology an analogous situation can be observed (Laurence and Matthews 2012). Regardless of this, a position in military sociology is advocated that advises us to take into account the respective "state of aggregation" of the organization, i.e. empirical results found in so-called *in-extremis* situations are not transferable to the routine area under peace conditions and *vice versa* (see Kolditz 2006). As with any sociological research, the same applies to defence studies. The choice of the appropriate method should be made against the background of the specific research problem and environmental parameters.

In what follows does not deal with sociological methods and research techniques in detail, such as survey research, experimental designs, qualitative interviews, etc. There are numerous textbooks available for this purpose (for instance Babbie 2016; Bryman 2016; Marsden and Wright 2010; and with a focus on organization research: Liebig et al. 2017). Nor will I recommend which method is best suited for researching a particular topic. Rather, the focus is on the particular institutional framework of defence studies.[1] This includes, as we will demonstrate in the second part of this chapter, the dominant organizational integration of research facilities, the generation of research issues, the access to the field, specific requirements for the researcher and the handling of the research results. Some of these specifics can be explained by specifics of the military organization in our first part.

Characteristic features of the organization type military

The characteristic features of military organizations include distinctive forms of recruitment and socialization, a high importance of symbols and rituals in everyday military life, military-specific camaraderie, the principle of command and obedience, and the attribution of the military as a "total institution" in the sense of Erving Goffman (1961). All attempts, however, to want to award the military a *sui generis* status, run dispassionately into the void. Even the danger to life and limb that soldiers may have to face can't be claimed as a unique proposition when one considers the often life-threatening conditions in organizations such as a fire brigade or the police. In this sense, the military and other organizations that operate under high risk and live-threatening circumstances constitute a special type of organization and a new research field known as "High-Reliability-Organizations" (Weick and Sutcliffe 2007). Instead, defence organizations are to be characterized by some contingent features which are relevant according to sociological research.

On the one hand, this contingency is to be understood in a military-historical way; for example, if one looks at the different structure of early-modern mercenary troops and the barracked mass armies of the 19th and 20th centuries. It can be understood cross-sectionally to note the gradual differences between defence organizations and other types of organizations on the other hand. Although economic objectives (budget compliance, efficient use of material resources, profit, etc.) play a role in defence organizations they are not, as is the case with private companies, the top organizational goals.

Four of such contingent features of defence organizations must be highlighted. *Firstly*, the special relationship of military organizations and their environment can admirably be described by the notion of "dilute feedback":

> Numerous features of the military organization are explained by the fact that it has fewer possibilities of success control compared to economic enterprises and fewer possibilities to objectively check the functional adequacy of its structure, its equipment, its training methods, and its action programs.
>
> (Geser 1983: 145, translation by the author)

Whether structures and patterns of action make sense usually only turns out in serious or warlike conditions, which are objectively the rather seldom state the organization is in. This is different for example in businesses organizations, which are continuously receiving feedback from the environment as result of sales and customer reactions.

Closely related to the diluted feedback, *secondly*, is the particular uncertainty for military organizations: even the best peacetime planning and the most realistic manoeuvres can only conditionally anticipate future uncertainties of war or other endangering scenarios. The Prussian officer and military intellectual Carl von Clausewitz puts this fact in a nutshell in his famous metaphor of the "fog of war". The high degree of formalization and ritualization of actions compared to most other organizations and the pronounced hierarchical centralization may be interpreted as a compensation attempt for such uncertainty.

Peculiarities of force-related organizational research, ranging from methodological problems, questions of access to the field, the appropriate time of collection of data, and research-ethical considerations, *thirdly*, result from the "Janus-face" of the military. It is most of the time in the so-called cold state of aggregation, in which the daily work in military staffs and departments hardly differs from other governmental or private organizations. Then administrative issues, the billing of business travel, and budget planning are in the foreground. On the other hand, in the so-called hot state of aggregation, that is under conditions of combat for example, organizational communication and decision-making processes can radically shift. Hardly any other type of organization unites two such different states of aggregation, which are activated according to changes in environmental factors.

A *fourth* peculiarity of military organizations concerns the relationship between individual and organization. Upon joining most organizations, as Chester Barnard (1938) depicts it, a momentous "indifference-zone" is created, which can be interpreted as a blanket agreement of the new member of the organization to obey to commands, accept regulations and instructions from superiors. It is a peculiarity of military organizations that this initially unspecified general obedience can in due course receive a broad interpretation, ranging in extreme cases to the use of one's own life in pursuit of organizational goals.

Institutional framework of defence studies

The organizational embedding of research institutions

Defence organizations and the military are among the best studied organizations worldwide. This has less to do with a fixed anchorage of military-sociological research in civilian universities, but with the many research institutions that are either part of the armed forces or financed by those at least. The *Social Science Institute of the Federal Armed Forces (SOWI)* in Germany, for example, was founded in 1974 as part of a general academization of the armed forces by the social-liberal federal government. It originally had the task to develop the curricula for the two newly established universities of the German Armed Forces, where military cadets should undergo an undergraduate academic study (Langer and Pietsch 2013: 33). Later the SOWI was converted into an in-house research facility and should contribute to the democratic control of armed forces as part of society. In the USA the armed forces were forced to build their own research facilities, as the academic world distanced itself from the US Armed Forces in reaction to the Vietnam War (see Ben-Ari 2016: 24). The initial close cooperation between the military and independent social science research, as it was practiced in the context of "The American Soldier", became increased brittle. Although nation-specific trajectories can be found in today's military-sociological landscape, so is the trend towards insourcing of defence studies owed to the special conditions of research on the military:

> In fact, given the potential risks represented by external academic actors it is not surprising that armed forces around the world are typified by the establishment of 'in-house' research arms and at times a wariness of publishing their findings outside of it.
>
> (Ben-Ari and Levy 2014: 13)

Scientific standards of the armed forces research institutes are primarily embedded in international contexts, i.e. in the *International Sociological Association, Research Committee 01* (ISA RCO 01), the *European Research Group on Military and Society* (ERGOMAS) and the *Inter-University Seminar on Armed Forces & Society* (IUS). For example in the case of Germany one hardly finds an exchange between established research in military institutions and academic sociology in universities. This can be recognized in the fact that the national sociological association in Germany (*Deutsche Gesellschaft für Soziologie – DGS*) still does not have an independent platform for military sociology.

The institutional embedding of social science research in the military organizational structures must be assessed ambivalently. From the perspective of the researchers, it would be advantageous if their work is funded basically, i.e. resources are available regardless of specific project financing. In the case of the SOWI, respective its successor organization in the *Center for Military History and Social Sciences of the German Armed Forces*, a remarkable part of the scientists is working as civil servants. Funding and organizational integration may cast doubt on the independence of research institutions. The dependence of in-house research institutions may have the result that the Ministry of Defense (MoD) has influence on the research question, the methods used, and even on item formulations in questionnaires. On the other hand, intervention options are just as present when a contractor of a research project, for example an independent polling firm, is forced to accept a research contract for economic reasons even if its own scientific standards are threatened. In reality, the level of intervention via contract control is likely to be even higher than via researchers, who do not have to fear great sanctions by the MoD and therefore experience more freedom in their professional decisions. Moreover, in addition to academic and military-bureaucratic mechanisms, modern societies are media societies and the public sphere thwarts encroachments of political and non-scientific interests into research activities. In the case of the Federal Republic of Germany, Article 5 of the Basic Law guarantees freedom of scholarship. The article can be invoked if the coordination between research institution and the ministerial client about the design of a scientific study turns into an exertion of influence on the theoretical work and the use of methods.

In many cases, the commissioning of social science research projects serves legitimacy purposes. Typically, internal employee surveys, on topics such as job satisfaction, management culture and working environments also reflect the efforts of an employer to take care of employee concerns. This is also the case in defence organizations. Much undisguised interference with the freedom of scientific research of in-house institutes undermines the credibility of research results, especially when inconceivable positive values are reported to the public. A behaviour like this defeats the purpose and misses the legitimacy function of social science studies for military leaders and defence politicians.

Generation of research questions

Which research questions are pursued and which topics do not receive any attention, have a variety of reasons that are to be found in the interests of the researchers, in the interests of decision-makers or in academic considerations. Sociological research, for example, had in the 1960s and 1970s (in the spirit of a social-technical understanding of science) its starting point often in social problems (material poverty, lack of education, etc.). If one ignores the social and political causes for the research project for the time being and focuses on the scientific reasons, in the field of defence studies two triggers are identified, each based on a specific handling of existing theoretical knowledge.

First, general sociological theories can be applied to the specific case of the military. The aim of this strategy is to broaden the scope of application and thus the informational content of general theories or to obtain new insight into the military or defence organizations with the new theoretical views. One can find both, for example, in Soeters (1997) and his study of military academies in 13 countries. In his empirical survey he applies the cultural concept developed by Hofstede and notes that national cultural differences – along the four cultural dimensions "power distance", "individualism", "masculinity", and "uncertainty avoidance" – can be identified in defence organizations as well. Nevertheless, he identified areas of a general military culture, which also can be detected in all 13 academies and are overlaying the national cultures. Soeters succeeds in this way to produce scientific evidence of the existence of an international military culture. Likewise, research in the military context may lead to irritation of previously accepted theories. This is the case, for example, in Richter (2018), where a leadership study in a multinational headquarters shows that the level of participation of followers in decision-making processes had no effect on central military-relevant variables, such as organizational commitment.

Second, research questions may arise from theories that had been developed specifically for the case of the military and to some degree are validly applicable only in this field. A prime example is Charles Moskos' well-known I/O-model. In his seminal work, he conceptualized the theory of military identity on a continuum ranging from institutional to occupational orientations:

> An institution is legitimated in terms of values and norms, that is, a purpose transcending individual self-interest in favor of a presumed higher good. […] An occupation is legitimated in terms of the marketplace. Supply and demand, rather than normative considerations, are paramount.
> (Moskos 1988: 16)

His original focus was to provide a theoretical framework for the analysis of changes in the US military under an all-volunteer force. The model, originally formulated in the 1970s for the case of the US military, is still proving to be fruitful in analysing dynamics of defence organizations (see Richter 2020).

The systematic reasons why research projects emerge may be the same in other sociological research fields. More specific is the special interplay between the interests of the researchers and the interests of decision-makers (in the MoD). The above-average intensive research on military organizations compared to other types of organizations can be explained by the consequences of specific features of the organization itself, namely the high level of uncertainty, the need for special knowledge in politics, and by the need to demonstrate the effectiveness and efficiency of the organization:

> […] government-based research to the military (as governmental organization) can be understood as a manifestation of a will to constantly rationalize political decisions, make political leadership processes more effective and extend institutional attempts for order and control.
> (Langer and Pietsch 2013: 40)

This also has implications for the choice of research methods. The following assertion has a certain charm: The preference for "numbers, data, and facts" expressed in technical reports based on opinion and survey research is a reaction to the specific uncertainty to which the military – in a volatile organizational environment – is continuously is exposed. This uncertainty can be at least partially compensated the rationality of "hard" measurements. This may explain the methodological preference for survey research in the defence sector:

> Surveys are ever-present and expanding in their use in society. So too, the military has increasingly used surveys to gather information from soldiers […] for purposes of informing the development and implementation of policies.
> (Griffith 2014: 191)

Experience shows that it is the search for the appropriate sociological method for a defence study that sometimes evokes different positions. Clients prefer quantitative methods, and the social researchers often prefer to use qualitative methods. For instance, nearly all social research projects launched by Germany's MoD in the last 20 years were questionnaire-based studies. An almost inflationary use of survey studies conducted in the armed forces on all sorts of issues must be assessed critically (Richter 2017: 667). This has negative consequences for sociological research in defence organizations, for example, if declining response rates are to be complained of:

> For example, in the U.S. Navy, the top three reasons for non-response were a belief that surveys have no impact, general apathy towards surveys and survey length. Studies have also indicated the following reasons as pertinent: over surveying; the size and formal structure of the organization, high work demands; and lack of perceived benefit to respondents.
>
> (Davis et al. 2013: 161)

Interview fatigue as a result of ritually conducted employee surveys without defined follow-up processes and without concrete recommendations can not only be found in the defence sector, but in many other areas, too. For instance, a considerable internal questionnaire-based study on leadership behaviour and its perception by soldiers and civilian employees was conducted by the *Center for Military History and Social Sciences of the German Armed Forces* in 2016. The report had not been published until 2019, and if any consequences were drawn from the research results by the MoD at all, they were not communicated to the participants of the survey in a systematic follow-up process.

Access to the field

Reasonably two aspects of access to the field are to be distinguished:

> Gaining access to the field of military studies implies two types of entrées: the organizational or institutional kind that involves being admitted into a large-scale bureaucracy and the epistemological one of encountering a certain field of knowledge.
>
> (Ben-Ari, Levy 2014: 10)

In the case of the German Armed Forces, for example, the organizational type of entrées is clearly regulated by law and includes all types of empirical surveys, in particular interviewing in the cold and the hot state of defence organizations. The central service regulation (*Zentrale Dienstvorschrift – ZDv*) on "Empirical Studies on Attitude, Opinion and Behavior Research in the Bundeswehr" (A-2710/1) regulates the conditions under which personnel interviewing can take place. For example, the prescriptions stipulate that an official empirical study may only be carried out if it has received a registration number from the responsible branch in the MoD after the consultation with the respective military command units that are involved in the study. This number must be shown on the survey documents. The approval process often leads to revised study designs and survey instruments according to ministerial guidelines.

Private individuals and external research institutions may also be allowed to conduct surveys for research purposes. They undergo the same approval process as federal researchers. Applicants are obliged to submit the results of the investigation to the MoD before publication. In special cases, the MoD reserves the right not to agree to publication of the results, or only in part. From an academic point of view such restrictions are to be regretted, especially if political rationality criteria do not allow the pursuit of a certain military-sociological research question. In general, however, field access in practice is, despite the formal approval process, not a particular hurdle in relation to the usual research obstacles in other public and private organizations. The barriers for surveys, for the access to the field and for the publication of results are, according to my experience, dependent on the political leadership of the defence ministry currently in office. Nevertheless, it is true that the "gatekeeping problem" characterizes the research field "defence organizations" in relation to civilian organizations as at best contingent if one disregards the fact that in the case of surveys in civil organizations often alternative possibilities exist if a requested enterprise denies field access. The research question then may be examined in another organization of the same branch. Military organizations, on the other hand, are monopolies; alternatives to surveys among soldiers do not exist if the MoD refuses the conduct of interviews or the distribution of questionnaires.

The epistemological aspect of field access is closely linked to the researchers' specific roles and their disciplinary backgrounds; this will be discussed in the next paragraph.

Specific requirements for the researchers

The challenge that researchers face in the area of defence studies can best be summed up in "Gaining entry while maintaining distance" (Ben-Ari and Levy 2014: 16). Any social science research is not just a collection of information about social reality, but an interaction process between researcher and researched subjects and requires a high degree of reflexivity (see Carreiras and Caetano 2016). Claude Weber (2016: 132) analytically distinguishes four types of interaction relationships: "complete participant, complete observer, observer as participant, and participant as observer". The possibilities to keep aloof and objectively confront the subject of research are as good as none existent in the case of the "complete participant". In practice, this case can occur, for example, when military cadets carry out their own empirical surveys in the circle of comrades within courses in sociology at military academies. At the other extreme on the continuum, the role of "complete observer", interaction does not take place in the true sense. One could think of document analysing, for example of protocols from missions abroad. In particular, the two hybrid forms, i.e. "observer as participant" and "participant as observer", are more typical and theoretically more relevant at this point.

Because of a relatively high degree of embedding of social science research in the defence organizations, the hybrid forms are relatively common. The role of an observer as participant is similar to that of a researcher who has received his education at a civilian university and conducts sociological studies in and about the military without having a military rank him/herself. The role of the participant as observer corresponds to a social science-educated staff officer, who goes through an assignment as a researcher in an in-house research institute. This role requires a high level of self-reflexivity to avoid the pitfalls of "going native". In any case, experience shows that the hybrid types are not only common but also adequate for conducting defence studies: "The very position of dual membership in military and civilian organizations carries great potential for research" (Ben-Ari 2016: 30). Claude Weber highlights the advantages of one of the two hybrid types, too: "To be a participant observer is a very attractive position [...] because it allows the researcher to be in a direct and 'official' contact with the studied group" (Weber 2016: 135). Overcoming access barriers to the field is then easier and stakeholders can more easily be convinced of the meaningfulness (and even the sincerity) of a study – especially if the research is based on an order from the MoD.

Firstly, a researcher in the area of defence studies must therefore be particularly sensitive to his/her understanding of one's role and to the interaction process with the research subject. He or she is therefore confronted with what is discussed as the "insider/outsider dilemma" (Deschaux-Dutard 2018: 42). *Secondly*, a particular sensitivity for the point of time of the collection of data, for both qualitative and quantitative studies, should be emphasized. Here is an example from the literature. Particularly in the case of military-specific research questions such as combat motivation and morale, the method and especially the timing of a survey is to be chosen with particular care. In the leading academic journal *Armed Forces & Society* (AF&S), a critical debate was conducted on a field study on the morale of Iraqi and American soldiers during Operation "Iraqi Freedom" in 2003 (Wong et al. 2003; MacCoun et al. 2006). In addition to the debate over the suitability of quantitative or qualitative research methods it was critically questioned to what extent self-information from Iraqi prisoners of war allow valid statements about their mission motivation. The problem of socially desirable responses is certainly particularly explosive in *in-extremis* situations: the researchers were promptly told by the interviewed Iraqis in American war captivity that they had only fought under duress on the part of the Iraqi army and by no means shared the war aims of dictator Saddam Hussein. The debate in the AF&S has led the military-sociological community once again to be aware that military-related surveys have to reflect point-of-time of data collection, the very condition of its object, especially the mentioned above "state of aggregation" (cold or hot?). The starting point is the debate in the classic essay by Shils and Janowitz (1948), which referred to a survey of Wehrmacht soldiers in British war captivity. Understandable from the specific situation, the soldiers stated that their motivation to endure to the last was not based on being convinced of the mission and the goals of Hitler's war. Rather, the morale was based on a sense of attachment and social cohesion to the comrades they did not want to abandon.

Dealing with the research results

> Social Science research in the defence field raises an inherent dilemma for the researcher in the profound aim of his research: accessing military discourse, which is traditionally supposed to remain confidential and surrounded by secret, comes up against the purpose of research: disclosure and publishing of the collected data.
>
> (Deschaux-Dutard 2018: 45)

For many cases, this assessment is unequivocally correct. Nevertheless, a differentiation is necessary. The interests of the scholars are rather uniform. The scientific community is interested in the research results in order to expand the theoretical and empirical knowledge of military sociology; for scholars, the publication of their work is indispensable for professional and financial reasons ("publish or perish"), because the academic reputation is normally linked to a long list of own publications. In practice, results from defence studies are prepared for two different addressees. The technical reports drawn up for the client from military and politics are rather practice-oriented and recommendations are added. In addition, the results of defence studies are often prepared for publications in scientific journals, which are theoretically better founded. It goes without saying that the style and wording of the two publication formats often differ.

Often less uniform are the interests of military and politics, which should not be thought of as a monolithic block with regard to dealing with research results. My own experience with several applied contract research projects shows that, for example, critical results from internal surveys on satisfaction with working conditions and accoutrement are pressured to be published as quickly as possible by the military side, while politicians in the MoD are blocking the release of research reports. With still other topics, the positions can be exactly opposite. The publication of most defence studies, including those of in-house research agencies, is in the end guaranteed, albeit with an often-not inconsiderable delay.

The assertion that military-related contract research has no effect on politicians and military leaders is rather a prejudice among the interviewed soldiers and civilian members of the armed forces, as a volume with an overview of research in the now defunct SOWI showed (see Dörfler-Dierken and Kümmel 2016). The contributions from politicians, representatives of the armed forces and researchers represent a picture according to which the scientific results have not seldom influenced political and military decision-making processes. For instance, a former member of the defence committee of the German parliament, Winfried Nachtwei, reflects on SOWI-research reports and how they were utilized in the meetings of the committee. As is known, the impact of social science research is more hidden and indirectly conveyed through awareness-raising processes and thus not always directly attributable to a specific study, its results and its specific recommendations. Positive attitudes towards surveys and interviewing and a consequently higher willingness to respond arise when the respondents receive feedback and see the consequences from the research results (see Foster Thompson and Surface 2009).

Conclusion

Conceptions of defence and defence policies have been changing during the last decades. Defence and security politicians as well as military practitioners whose task it is to adopt military organizations to new economic, social, political, and cultural conditions are facing diverse and unknown challenges. Sociological and social science research in general, especially quantitative research like surveys among soldiers or public opinion research, are getting increasingly an indispensable resource for shaping the adoption process and decision-making processes in the military field, for instance in the area of recruitment and retention of service personnel. Since the classical studies on "The American Soldier" in the end of World War II, the military and defence organizations are – compared to other social institutions – often an object of social research and are quite well investigated. The reasons therefore have been shown up in this chapter. While sociological research methods in the military field in a narrower sense do not substantially differ from research methods in general and in other social fields (like for instance organization and military studies), defence research of course has some peculiarities concerning access to the field, collaboration between principals and agents in research projects, and last, but not least, the application of the results.

Note

1 Another limitation is the focus on the "internal" perspective, that is, methods of defence studies that are applied primarily within the organization, for example research on recruitment and retention, soldiers in general (including veterans, see Schulker 2017) and internal organizational structures. For the "external" perspective, for instance public attitudes about defense and security or strategic cultures, see Biehl et al. (2013), Giegerich (2018), and the chapter by Steinbrecher and Biehl in this volume.

References

Babbie, E. (2016). *The Practice of Social Research*, 14th ed., Boston, MA, Cengage Learning.
Barnard, C. (1938). *The Functions of the Executive*, Cambridge, MA, Harvard University Press.
Ben-Ari, E., Levy, Y. (2014). Getting access to the field. Insider/outsider perspectives, 9–18. In: Soeters, J. et al. (Eds.) (2014) *Routledge Handbook of Research Methods in Military Studies*, London, New York: Routledge.
Ben-Ari, E. (2016). What is worthy of study about the military? The sociology of military-in-use in current-day conflicts, 23–35. In: Carreiras, H., Castro, C., Frederic, S. (Eds.) (2016). *Researching the Military*, London, New York: Routledge.
Biehl, H.et al. (Eds.) (2013). *Strategic Cultures in Europe. Security and Defence Policies across the Continent*, Wiesbaden: Springer VS.
Bryman, A. (2016). *Social Research Methods*. 5th ed., Oxford, Oxford University Press.
Carreiras, H., Castro, C. (Eds.) (2013). *Qualitative Methods in Military Studies. Research Experiences and Challenges*, London, New York: Routledge.
Carreiras, H.et al. (Eds.) (2016). *Researching the Military*, London, New York: Routledge.
Carreiras, H., Caetano, A. (2016). Reflexivity and the sociological study of the military, 8–22. In: Carreiras, H.et al. (Eds.) (2016). *Researching the Military*, London, New York: Routledge.
Davis, E.et al. (2013). Surveys: Understanding the measurements that inform decision-making, 157–164. In: Johnston, P. J., Farley, K. M. (Eds.) (2013) *Military Human Resource Issues. A Multinational View*, Kingston, Ontario, Canadian Defence Academy Press.
Deschaux-Dutard, D. (2018). Methods in defence studies, 40–52. In: Galbreath, D., Deni, J. R. (Eds.) (2018). *Routledge Handbook of Defence Studies*, London, New York: Routledge.
Dörfler-Dierken, A., Kümmel, G. (Eds.) (2016). *Am Puls der Bundeswehr. Militärsoziologie in Deutschland zwischen Wissenschaft, Politik, Bundeswehr und Gesellschaft*, Wiesbaden, Springer VS.
Foster Thompson, L., Surface, E. (2009). Promoting favorable attitudes toward personnel surveys: The role of follow-up. *Military Psychology* (21), 139–161.
Galbreath, D., Deni, J. R. (Eds.) (2018). *Routledge Handbook of Defence Studies*, London, New York, Routledge.
Geser, H. (1983). Soziologische Aspekte der Organisationsformen in der Armee und in der Wirtschaft, 140–164. In: Wachtler, G. (Ed.) (1983). *Militär, Krieg, Gesellschaft – Texte zur Militärsoziologie*, Frankfurt, New York, Campus.
Giegerich, B. (2018). Public opinion and defence, 291–301. In: Galbreath, D., Deni, J. R. (Eds.) (2018). *Routledge Handbook of Defence Studies*, London, New York, Routledge.
Goffman, E. (1961). *Asylums: Essays on the Social Situation of Mental Patient and Other Inmates*, New York, Anchor Books.
Griffith, J. (2014). Surveys in military settings, 179–193. In Soeters, J.et al. (Eds.) (2014). *Routledge Handbook of Research Methods in Military Studies*, London, New York, Routledge.
Joas, H., Knöbl, W. (2013). *War in Social Thought. Hobbes to the Present*, Princeton, Oxford, Princeton University Press.
Kolditz, T. (2006). Research in extremis settings. Expanding the critique of 'why they fight'. *Armed Forces & Society*, 32(4), 655–658.

Langer, P., Pietsch, C. (2013). Studying cross-cultural competence in the military. Methodological considerations of applied contract research for the German Armed Forces, 31–49. In: Carreiras, H., Castro, C. (Eds.) (2013). *Qualitative Methods in Military Studies. Research Experiences and Challenges*, London, New York, Routledge.

Laurence, J., Matthews, M. (Eds.) (2012). *The Oxford Handbook of Military Psychology*, Oxford, New York, Oxford University Press.

Liebig, S.*et al.* (2017) (Eds.). *Handbuch empirische Organisationsforschung*, Wiesbaden, Springer Gabler.

MacCoun, R.*et al.* (2006). Does social cohesion determine motivation in combat? An old question with an old answer. *Armed Forces & Society*, 32(4), 646–654.

Marsden, P., Wright, J. (Eds.) (2010). *Handbook of Survey Research*. 2nd ed. Bingley, Emerald.

Merton, R., Kitt, A. (1950). Contributions to the theory of reference group behavior, 40–105. In: Merton, R., Lazarsfeld, P. (Eds.) (1950). *Continuities in social Research. Studies in the scope and method of "The American Soldier"*. Glencoe, IL, Free Press.

Merton, R., Lazarsfeld, P. (Eds.) (1950). *Continuities in Social Research. Studies in the Scope and Method of "The American Soldier"*, Glencoe, IL, Free Press.

Moskos, C. C. (1988). Institutional and occupational trends in armed forces, 15–26. In: Moskos, C. C., Wood, F. R. (Eds.) (1988). *The Military. More than Just a Job?* Washington, Pergamon-Brassey's.

Richter, G. (2017). Methoden und Daten zur Erforschung spezieller Organisationen: Bundeswehr, 657–674. In: Liebig, S.*et al.* (Eds.) (2017). *Handbuch empirische Organisationsforschung*. Wiesbaden, Springer Gabler.

Richter, G. (2018). Antecedents and consequences of leadership styles. Findings from research in multinational headquarters. *Armed Forces & Society*, 44 (1), 72–91.

Richter, G. (2020). Explaining retention of medical officers: A comparison of person-organization fit and the I/O model. In: Kümmel, G., Elbe, M. (Eds.) (2020). *Was es (heute) heißt Soldat zu sein*, Band 50 der Reihe Militär und Sozialwissenschaften, hrsg. vom AMS. Baden-Baden: Nomos-Verlag [in press].

Schulker, D. (2017). The recent occupation and industry employment of American veterans. *Armed Forces & Society*, 43(4), 695–710.

Shils, E., Janowitz, M. (1948). Cohesion and disintegration in the Wehrmacht in World War II. *Public Opinion Quarterly*, 12(2), 280–315.

Soeters, J. (1997). Value orientations in military academies: A thirteen country study. *Armed Forces & Society*, 24(1), 7–32.

Soeters, J.et al. (Eds.) (2014). *Routledge Handbook of Research Methods in Military Studies*, London, New York, Routledge.

Soeters, J. (2018). *Sociology and Military Studies. Classical and Current Foundations*, London, New York, Routledge.

Stouffer, S. (1949). *The American Soldier. Studies in Social Psychology in World War II*. 2 vol., Princeton, NJ, Princeton University Press.

Weber, C. (2016). Immersion experiences within military organizations, 131–141. In: Carreiras, H., Castro, C., Frederic, S. (Eds.) (2016). *Researching the Military*, London, New York, Routledge.

Weick, K. E., Sutcliffe, K. M. (2007). *Managing the Unexpected. Resilient Performance in an Age of Uncertainty*, 2nd ed. San Francisco, Jossey-Bass.

Wong, L.*et al.* (2003). *Why they Fight. Combat Motivation in the Iraq War*, Carlisle Barracks, PA, Strategic Studies Institute, U.S. Army War College.

Part II
Quantitative methods and defence studies

7 Quantitative analyses in defence studies

Mayeul Kauffmann

Introduction

Defence and security studies must deal with a wide variety of information (often in large quantities) and, to achieve this effectively, may use quantitative methods. Purely descriptive (textual) analyses and literary case studies are useful but can result in the use of an inductive scientific method; however, modern epistemology teaches us the effectiveness of the hypothetico-deductive method, and the importance of collecting sufficient quantities of high-quality empirical data necessary for the falsifiability of the theories. A brief overview of these methods illustrates their usefulness. A historical look at the evolution of the discipline, compared to that of economics, teaches us a lot. Then we study the epistemological foundations of the use of statistics in defence and security studies, and focus on the central concept of operationalization. These quantitative analyses are based on datasets that are generally stored in databases; discussion on related issues is provided in Chapter 8 (written by the same author) in this edited volume.

Why use quantitative methods in defence studies?

Quantitative methods applied to defence studies can provide useful information and are used by defence policymakers, strategists, command and control staffs, and other defence professionals, such as those of the defence industrial base.

Overview of quantitative methods in defence and security

Risk analysis is the basis for defence strategy planning (Halkia et al. 2017). It requires estimating the probability and impact of the various threats. Theoretical models combined with statistical methods highlight the relative importance of threats and their interaction. These methods help develop scenarios and allocate resources. They are used in the study of numerous questions, such as:

- the risk of terrorist attack (Perl 2007)
- some factors of conflict such as natural resources (Kauffmann et al. 2011; Kucera et al. 2011) or famine (Kauffmann 2011)
- the political stability of neighbouring or partner countries (Kauffmann 2017; Kemper et al. 2011)
- the initiation and escalation of civil wars and international conflicts (Kauffmann 2006a, 2008a)

- war simulation
- defence economics
- the supply of strategic goods ....

Comparative evolution with respect to quantitative methods

With respect to both quantitative methods and to training in these tools, strategic analysis lags behind other social sciences. If we compare defence studies with economics, several findings emerge.

First, the construction of concepts and their translation into quantitative measures is a long process. If Plato and Aristotle had already identified some of the concepts used by economists today, it was not until 1758 that Quesnay developed a draft macroeconomic model. The beginnings of modern econometrics date back to the 19th century, with the work of Cournot. It was not until 1930 that the Econometric Society structured these efforts, thanks to the progress of the League of Nations (Roser 2012), then the IMF and the World Bank in data collection, allowing econometric models to be calibrated and improved. A similar but faster evolution can be observed in defence analyses. While it took more than a century between Quesnay's work and the development of global economic databases, the work of Richardson (1948, 1960) and Wright (1942), pioneers in the quantitative study of conflicts in the 1940s, was quickly followed by conflict datasets.

Second, it is economics which mainly fostered the development of quantitative approaches in defence studies. Many of the illustrious directors of the Econometric Society made forays into the economics of peace and security, beginning with Keynes (1919). However, the Cold War led the international financial institutions (especially the IMF) to act with a more cautious attitude (Kauffmann 2006b), separating more strictly quantitative economics and strategic issues, including the measurement of military spending, the study of its determinants or the diversion of international aid to finance military expenditure or arms imports (Kauffmann 1998, 1999, 2000).

The end of the Cold War allowed a partial catching up, thanks to the foundation of the association "Economists Against the Arms Race" (ECAAR) in 1989, which became "Economists for Peace and Security" (EPS) in 2005. Among the directors of EPS, 17 are Nobel Prize winners in economics, and 10 of them are former directors of the Econometric Society.[1] However, if the evolution has been rapid in the Anglo-Saxon and Scandinavian countries, Latin Europe (including France) is lagging behind. According to Beauguitte (2011: 23), "Unlike some of their English-speaking colleagues, French political scientists seem to have little sensitivity to quantification. It was not until 2009 that the first manual presenting these methods was published" (this manual, Kauffmann [2009], is partly summarized in the next section).

Defence studies borrowed a lot from other disciplines, for instance economics, geography or medicine, to help assess the variety of defence issues with quantitative methods.[2] In effect, the reality of these interactions is often too complex to be studied systematically using only human language. In practice, statistical methods are a useful complement to other methods to study international issues.

Methodology of statistics applied to defence issues

We now carry out a review with a description of the most frequent methods and practices in defence studies, and an epistemological evaluation of the legitimacy of these methods and practices. We will describe the different steps of the hypothetico-deductive method, by comparing it with empirical and inductive approaches. Statistics can be useful in all cases, as well as for the dissemination of scientific results.

This leads to an observation: The notion of operationalization is at the crossroads of questions that defence experts must resolve. This centrality leads to recommendations in terms of the tools to be used, so that security and defence studies coherently implement epistemological precepts often proclaimed but not always respected.

The hypothetico-deductive method

The hypothetico-deductive method begins with hypotheses, from which propositions concerning observable phenomena are deduced, allowing a theory to be tested.

Definition of hypotheses

The first step is therefore to define a coherent set of hypotheses concerning a system of actors and their environment, for which we propose to construct a theory. So-called "rational" approaches assume that actors maximize something (an "objective function"), for example their capacity to defend or attack ("bang for a buck") for a given budget (Christiansson 2017). States can maximize their "security" vis-à-vis their rivals.

There are also hypotheses concerning the constraints imposed on these actors. Game theories define the "players", their objectives, the information and means at their disposal as well as the "rules of the game".

Deductive reasoning

The second step is to use the logical rules of deduction to infer propositions from the hypotheses.

These logical rules are sometimes expressed in mathematical form. For simple models, the two types of reasoning (literary deduction, with words, against mathematical deduction) can be strictly identical.

However, when a model is complex, mathematics is essential and its interest is two-fold.

On the one hand, the approach is absolutely rigorous. The entire mathematical processing is itself subject to clearly defined assumptions and logical rules (theorems …) and uses perfectly known objects (real numbers, functions, sets …). If mathematical rules are respected, the logical link between hypotheses and propositions is certain (internal coherence of the theory).

On the other hand, mathematics makes it possible to establish deductions that are sometimes counter-intuitive. For example, in the absence of an adequate coordination mechanism, two countries may have a mutual interest in having an international policy of mutual cooperation, but, in the uncertainty of each other's policy, their own interest could push them towards a non-cooperative solution that is harmful to both. A simple table shows this in the case of the famous two-player "prisoner's dilemma" game; mathematics is very useful when one wants to make this game more complex, with a large number of players (for example, all UN Member States), by playing repeatedly (over several years) … while maintaining the certainty of the logical link between the hypotheses and the propositions.

Predictions and falsifiability

Some of the propositions deduced from the hypotheses concern observable phenomena. This is referred to as predictions (even if the theory in question was constructed to explain long-past events).

These predictions are used to test a theory. For example, some models of the nuclear arms race predict that an increase in a country's nuclear warhead count will encourage its opponent to develop its nuclear arsenal as well. By observing the evolution of the nuclear weapons of the USSR and the United States during the Cold War, it can be said whether it is in line with this prediction. If this is the case, we will say that the facts tend to confirm the theory. Otherwise, the facts irrevocably reject the theory; since there is a clear logical connection between hypotheses and predictions, this means that at least one of the hypotheses must be rejected.

For Popper (1934), it is this very approach that is at the heart of scientificity. For him, a theory is not scientific if it cannot be "falsified", that is, if it is impossible to design a test that has at least a chance to reject the theory. An unfalsifiable theory is a theory that cannot be confronted with the facts, or for which there is conceptually no fact that could falsify it.

The falsifiability of a theory does not imply that a theory is false, but that it is possible to construct an experiment, or to compare a prediction with observations from the real world. It must be *possible* to establish a test showing that the theory is either false (it produces at least one prediction in contradiction with the facts), or not yet falsified.

Let us take the example of a theory that studies the relationship between economic development, the level of inequality and the risk of civil war (the example is intentionally simplistic). We propose to build a theory based on the following hypotheses 1 to 4:

Hypothesis 1: The State levies taxes on the economy that increase according to the wealth created on its territory.
Hypothesis 2: A certain proportion of the resources collected by the State is allocated to "social expenditure" aimed at reducing inequalities.
Hypothesis 3: The perceived level of inequality is only related to the level of social spending.
Hypothesis 4: When perceived inequalities are too high, disadvantaged population groups violently challenge the legitimacy of the state, leading to civil war.

By combining hypotheses 1 and 2, we can deduce the following proposition:
Proposition 1: The state of a poor country has lower social spending than the state of a rich country.
By combining Proposition 1 with Hypothesis 3, we deduce:
Proposition 2: The level of perceived inequality in a poor country is higher than in a rich country.
By combining Proposition 2 with Hypothesis 4, we finally obtain Proposition 3:
Proposition 3: Poverty leads to civil war.

Our theory is based on hypotheses, some of which are difficult or even impossible to verify: for example, Hypothesis 3 refers to perceptions, a concept that is difficult to define and measure. This does not prevent our theory from being scientific. It is the falsifiability of the propositions that allows a possible refutation of the theory; if one or more predictions of the model are not verified, the theory is falsified and at least one of the hypotheses is to be rejected.

Falsifiability and statistical modelling

However, the procedure for verifying whether or not a prediction has been fulfilled must be as rigorous as the rest of the method; this can be done with a statistical model.

A) FORMAL MODELLING

In an attempt to falsify our theory (based on Hypotheses 1 to 4), let us try to rewrite Proposition 3 in another form, that of a formalized model. It is a question of implementing this proposition. We can (simplistically) define a variable p (poverty in a given country) which is 1 (one) if that country is in poverty, and 0 (zero) if not. We will also define a variable w (civil war) which will be worth 1 (one) if this country is in a civil war situation the following year and will be worth 0 (zero) otherwise.

A first analysis of a selection of countries could lead to the data set in Table 7.1. A poor country is defined as a country whose GDP per capita in PPP dollars (purchasing power parity) is less than 4,000 PPP dollars per year.

The data in Table 7.1 seem to confirm Proposition 3. The two poor countries in the sample (Pakistan and Rwanda) entered civil war in 1994, while the two developed countries (United States and France) did not enter civil war. However, Table 7.1 does not allow us to say that Proposition 3 is true, but only that, in view of the available, it has not been contradicted by the facts. The theory underlying this proposition is therefore not falsified by the data in Table 7.1 (it could have been, which contributes to making it a scientific theory). This theory can therefore be considered as effective here: it allows correct predictions to be made.

However, as new data become available on a subject, a successful theory may suddenly be refuted by the facts, as shown in Table 7.2. Three poor countries in 1993 did not enter civil war in 1994. Only one of these observations would have been sufficient to invalidate Proposition 3.

Table 7.1 Poverty and civil war (1993–1994, 4 countries)

Row of the dataset	Country	GDP per cap. ($ PPP) 1993	Poverty in 1993	Civil war in 1994
1	United States	24,680	0	0
2	France	19,140	0	0
3	Pakistan	2,160	1	1
4	Rwanda	740	1	1

Sources: PNUD (1996), 157–159 for the GDP pc PPP; Sarkees (2000) for civil wars.

Table 7.2 Poverty and civil war (1993–1994, 4 other countries)

Row of the dataset	Country	GDP per cap. ($ PPP) 1993	Poverty in 1993	Civil war in 1994
5	Congo	2750	1	0
6	Mali	530	1	0
7	Uganda	910	1	0
8	Russia Fed.	4,760*	0	1

* Preliminary data (UNDP Note). Same sources as previous table.

B) FALSIFICATION, DETERMINISM AND PROBABILISTIC CAUSALITY

Note that line 8 of the dataset (Russian Federation, see Table 7.2) does not contradict Proposition 3: factors other than poverty can lead to civil war. On the other hand, this line 8 falsifies (contradicts) the following proposition:

Proposition 4: Only poor countries enter civil war.

Lines 5, 6 and 7 falsify Proposition 4. All the lines in Table 7.2 contradict the following proposition:

Proposition 5: All poor countries (and only they) enter into civil war.

To be falsifiable, a proposition must be precise. But the precise propositions above (Proposition 3, 4 and 5) have been flawed at least once by our observations, and are therefore to be rejected. These propositions are deterministic: a given cause must always have the same effects. Building a deterministic proposition, testing it and then rejecting the theory from which it is derived corresponds to an epistemology more appropriate to the physical sciences than to the social sciences.

In the social sciences, it is impossible to take all the factors into account; experimentation is more difficult than in the physical sciences: trivially speaking, one cannot "manufacture" several copies of the same country and see if each of the "samples" enters a civil war.

However, the refutability of a social science theory still requires a criteria for refutation and non-refutation. In this context, testing deterministic propositions is of little use, as very few social phenomena are deterministic. On the other hand, the following proposition is useful:

Proposition 6: Civil wars are more likely in poor countries than in developed countries.

This proposition is not deterministic: even if this proposition were true, given a country's level of economic development, it is impossible to determine with certainty whether or not it is about to enter a civil war civil war. Nevertheless, it is possible to construct statistical tests to verify that the available observations do confirm that civil wars are more likely in poor countries than in developed countries. If this is the case, indicators can even be developed to quantify the influence of income level on the risk of civil war.

However, even if Proposition 6 passed all the statistical tests performed, it would not allow for infallible predictions. Proposition 6 introduces the notion of probability in the search for scientific truth. This epistemological approach, common in the social sciences, also exists in hard sciences, for example in physics (quantum physics) or biology (Darwinian evolutionary biology). In all these examples, observing a set of causes does not always make it possible to predict the consequences. The causal relationship is not deterministic but probabilistic.

To falsify a proposition referring to a deterministic causal relationship, a single observation is sufficient. On the other hand, with probabilistic causality, the attempt to falsify requires the use of a statistical model. To illustrate the difference between the deterministic and probabilistic models, we use the example of poverty as a cause of civil wars. We have a variable $p_{i,t}$ (poverty in country i in year t) which is 1 (one) if this country is in poverty, and 0 (zero) if not. We also have a variable $w_{i,t+1}$ (civil war in country i in year t+1) that will be equal to 1 (one) if this country is in a civil war situation the following year and will equal to 0 (zero) otherwise. The deterministic model is represented by Equation 1.

$$w = f(p) \qquad \text{(Equation 1)}$$

This model reads "w equals f of p", i.e. w is a function of p. In fact, we will use the following more precise notation:

$$w_{i,t+1} = f(p_{i,t}) \qquad \text{(Equation 2)}$$

Equation 2 means that $w_{i,t+1}$ is a function of $p_{i,t}$.
In other words, the state of civil peace or civil war (w) in a given country i for year t+1 depends directly on the state of poverty (p) measured the previous year (t), and on nothing else. We now need to specify the form of function f (Equation 3).

$$\begin{array}{rcl} f : \{0,1\} & \to & \{0,1\} \\ x & \mapsto & x \end{array} \qquad \text{(Equation 3)}$$

The first line of Equation 3 means that function f must receive 0 or 1 as an argument and that it will return the value 0 or 1. The second line indicates (left) that if f receives the value x, then f returns a value that is equal to x (right). (This is the identity function.) The combination of Equations 2 and 3 is simply a mathematical writing of Proposition 7 (close to Proposition 5, but more precise), which is deterministic:

Proposition 7: Countries that are poor in one year are still in civil war the following year, while countries that are not poor in one year are never in civil war the following year.

Let us write a statistical model that attempts to translate Proposition 6 into mathematical terms. The statistical model corresponds to a probabilistic (and not deterministic) view of the world and the causal relationships between the phenomena observed in defence studies. It has an additional element compared to Equation 2:

$$w_{i,t+1} = f(p_{i,t}) + \varepsilon_{i,t} \qquad \text{(Equation 4)}$$

The random variable $\varepsilon_{i,t}$ (read "epsilon sub i, t") represents the hazard, the chance, what we do not control or what we do not know. Interpretations are diverse as to its exact meaning. These may include unknown variables, measurement errors, unsuspected causal relationships ... Anyway, if $\varepsilon_{i,t}$ was perfectly known and predictable, it could be integrated into f, so we would use the deterministic Equation 2 (we could then predict all civil wars with certainty). The error $\varepsilon_{i,t}$ does exist. If predictions are made with the model from Equation 4, Equation 5 is obtained.

$$\hat{w}_{i,t+1} = f(p_{i,t}) \qquad \text{(Equation 5)}$$

The value $\hat{w}_{i,t}$ ("w hat") is the value predicted by the model. It differs from the observed $w_{i,t}$ so there is a residual. The residual $\varepsilon_{i,t}$ is the observed variable $w_{i,t}$ minus the predicted value $\hat{w}_{i,t}$ of this variable. This residual is zero for all rows in Table 7.1. For example, if we take the first line of Table 7.1, we have i=USA and t=1993. The residual for this country and this year is given by Equation 6.

$$\begin{aligned}\varepsilon_{usa,1993} &= w_{usa,1994} - \hat{w}_{usa,1994} \\ &= w_{usa,1994} - f(p_{usa,1993}) \\ &= 0 - f(0) = 0 - 0 = 0\end{aligned} \qquad \text{(Equation 6)}$$

On the other hand, the model leads to a poor prediction in the case of Mali, a poor country in 1993 but at peace in 1994 (see Table 7.2), which gives a non-zero residual (Equation 7).

$$\begin{aligned}\varepsilon_{mali,1993} &= w_{mali,1994} - \hat{w}_{mali,1994} \\ &= w_{mali,1994} - f(p_{mali,1993}) \\ &= 0 - f(1) = 0 - 1 = -1\end{aligned} \qquad \text{(Equation 7)}$$

Statistical methods make it possible to construct useful criteria to assess this type of situation. They help assess the value of a theory even when a few observations tend to falsify it. Indeed, in social sciences, there are many "borderline" cases and exceptions, which can lead to a probabilistic vision of truth. In this context, statistical work on defence studies consists of operationalizing a theoretical model in order to construct a statistical model and to research the characteristics of this model. A statistical test with a well-established decision rule then normally makes it possible to know whether the theory is falsified by the facts or not (see the following sections).

However, the wide variety of statistical models means that progress in scientific consensus is slow. For example, a researcher observing Table 7.2 could argue that countries temporarily at peace may be on the verge of entering civil war. It could build a model allowing for lagged causal effects, and use the data in Table 7.3.

When a theory remains unfalsified despite many empirical attempts at falsification, then confidence in it generally grows: it is a powerful theory (however, it can never be

Table 7.3 Civil wars after 1993 (2 countries)

Row of the dataset	Country	Civil war in 1994	Start year of the next civil war (starting after 1993)
5	Congo	0	1997
7	Uganda	0	1996

Source: Sarkees (2000).

proven with certainty that it is "true"). On the contrary, a theory falsified at least once should be rejected. Experience shows that it often takes several falsifications, with several different methods, for a theory to be effectively rejected, especially if it belongs to a dominant paradigm in a discipline.

Inductive method and empirical approaches

The method that is most opposed to the hypothetico-deductive method is the inductive method. In practice, a significant part of a researcher's research time in international relations is devoted to empirical heuristic practices. These are generally closer to the inductive method than the hypothetico-deductive method, at least in appearance. By detailing the main empirical heuristic practices, we will see how they can also be used to support the hypothetico-deductive approach and how they can be complementary to statistical methods in this context.

Induction

Induction is the logical operation which consists, on the basis of observed facts, in inferring propositions concerning objects considered similar but which cannot be directly observed. Inductive reasoning often proceeds by generalization. By observing a number of similar objects, we can find a common point for these objects, and we infer (we "conclude") that all the objects in this family of objects necessarily have this common point.

This generalization can be made in space or time. For example, observing the data in Table 7.1, one could infer by inductive reasoning that all the countries in the world that were poor in 1993 entered civil war in 1994, and that none of the developed countries entered civil war in 1994 (generalization in space). By also generalizing over time, one could infer that this is always true, in the past, present and future.

Obviously, in this case, this spatio-temporal generalization is abusive, as shown in Table 7.2.

Popper (1934) gave a famous example challenging the common wisdom that "all swans were white". At the end of the 17th century, an explorer observed black swans in Australia. Popper concludes that inductive reasoning is unsustainable: accumulating many observations of white swans proves nothing; observing a single black swan helps to advance science by refuting a false theory. Similarly, extending the list of data in Table 7.1 that appear to confirm Proposition 3 is not very useful; it is better to establish a theory based on assumptions, deduce Proposition 5 from it, then look for at least one observation that contradicts this proposition and falsifies the underlying theory.

Case studies

A case study is a detailed analysis of a particular observation, based on description of the events, the phenomenon and the particular context of a unique, dated and localized case. This approach is denigrated by some advocates of the hypothetico-deductive method (based on Popperian falsificationism, see Flyvbjerg 2006), because it can be used inductively. Nevertheless, while the hypothetico-deductive approach prohibits inductive generalization aimed at confirming theories, it recognizes the value of a case study falsifying a theory. For example, studying Mali in the 1990s can demonstrate that poverty does not always lead to civil war. This case may also help refine the quantitative methodology for measuring the different observed variables (e.g. poverty). It can also identify unsuspected variables or causal relationships that play a decisive role in triggering wars, helping hypothesis development. Finally, this is true that case studies are particularly suitable for qualitative studies (e.g. on the motivations of actors); however, this does not mean that quantitative methods cannot take into account qualitative variables (e.g. political system from the Polity IV database), nor that the motivations of actors are ignored in statistical methods: in economics for example (including defence economics), the dominant paradigm is based on assumptions about the motivations of actors (utility maximization). Hence, case studies are useful for studying qualitative variables and can "enlighten" many statistical analyses.

Comparative studies

A comparative study can be seen as a case study involving several cases. By studying two relatively similar countries, their similarities and differences can be highlighted. Additionally, as Lijphart (1971: 684) puts it:

> The comparative method resembles the statistical method in all respects, except one. The crucial difference is that the number of cases it deals with is too small to permit systematic control by means of partial correlations. (…) The comparative method should be resorted to when the number of cases available for analysis is so small that cross-tabulating them further in order to establish credible controls is not feasible. There is, consequently, no clear dividing line between the statistical and comparative methods; the difference depends entirely on the number of cases.

Since several variables vary at the same time when switching from one case to another, it is difficult to know which variables have a decisive influence on the observed phenomenon. To illustrate this limitation of comparative studies, let us use our model of civil wars by enriching Equation 4. The risk of civil war w still depends on the variable p, but also on another variable q, for example an indicator of the ethnolinguistic composition of the country observed:[3]

$$w_{i,t+1} = f(p_{i,t}) + h(q_{i,t}) + \varepsilon_{i,t} \quad \text{(Equation 8)}$$

Imagine that we have two countries in our comparative study, with the data in Table 7.4 (dummy data). The two countries are ethno-linguistically comparable; the poor country enters civil war, not the other. A comparative study will suggest that it is the level of poverty that is the cause of the civil war in the country 2. Country 1 can be seen as a control country.

Now, let us suppose that, thanks to the empirical research carried out as part of a comparative study, we realize that countries 1 and 2 are very different from each other in terms of their political systems. We add a variable r, an indicator of the political regime of the country observed, and a function $l(.)$ which measures the contribution of r to w.

$$w_{i,t+1} = f(p_{i,t}) + h(q_{i,t}) + l(r_{it}) + \varepsilon_{i,t} \quad \text{(Equation 9)}$$

It is then necessary to have observations for a larger number of countries. Table 7.6 shows that country 3 can act as a control case here. Comparing countries 2 and 3, it can be seen that the political system does not seem to matter. It is therefore only the level of poverty that would explain why country 2 is going into civil war and not country 1.[4]

Table 7.4 Comparative study (two countries, two explanatory variables)

Country (i)	Poverty ($p_{i,t}$)	Ethnolinguistic composition ($q_{i,t}$)	Civil war ($w_{i,t+1}$)
Country 1	0	0	0
Country 2	1	0	1

Table 7.5 Comparative study (two countries, three explanatory variables)

Country (i)	Poverty ($p_{i,t}$)	Ethnolinguistic composition ($q_{i,t}$)	Political regime ($r_{i,t}$)	Civil war ($w_{i,t+1}$)
Country 1	0	0	0	0
Country 2	1	0	1	1

Table 7.6 Comparative study (three countries, three explanatory variables)

Country (i)	Poverty ($p_{i,t}$)	Ethnolinguistic composition ($q_{i,t}$)	Political regime ($r_{i,t}$)	Civil war ($w_{i,t+1}$)
Country 1	0	0	0	0
Country 2	1	0	1	1
Country 3	1	0	0	1

In practice, examples such as Table 7.6 are extremely rare (with this table it is possible to build a model whose estimation leads to residuals ε_i equal to zero). As the residuals are, in reality, not nil, more cases are needed to carry out a statistical study (for example, several dozen countries). This is where the statistical study shows its advantage over the comparative study: it is possible to take into account simultaneously a large number of variables and to measure with some precision the influence of each of them; this is possible even if these variables vary simultaneously so that the type of inference we have made from Table 7.4 is excluded.

However, comparative studies are useful. First, they often reveal variables to add to a statistical model. Secondly, collecting data suitable for statistical processing is a very time-consuming and sometimes impossible task. (What was the GDP per capita in PPP at the time of the Pharaohs?). Finally, even for the researcher wishing to conduct a statistical study, a comparative study (as well as a case study) will provide him/her with knowledge of the subject as well as research experience and skills that will be useful in his/her statistical study.

Descriptive statistics

A third group of heuristic practices often associated with descriptive or inductive methods is the use of descriptive statistics.

Its methods belong to three groups:

- First, the construction of single statistics, summarizing data series into a single number (for example, the average of a series).

- Then, the development of organized series of statistics (for example, the quartiles of a series, i.e., first quartile, median and third quartile).
- Finally, the design of statistical charts, possibly combined by statistics summarizing the data.

Descriptive statistics provide an organized overview of a large amount of data, make it possible to identify regularities (trends) and irregularities. Finally, graphic representations transmit a large amount of information in a way that is easy to understand.

Descriptive statistics are often associated with the inductive method because they do not directly use the notion of a model (although statistical models are sometimes the basis of indicators). This makes descriptive statistics less useful in the hypothetico-deductive method; still, they help improve operationalization..

Operationalization of concepts for statistical analyses in defence studies

In general, theories cannot be falsified by directly testing their predictions: operationalization is an essential step to obtain testable predictions. We will study it in theory and practice, and see that the choice of software tools matters.

Operationalization in security analysis

We define operationalization on the basis of Bridgman's work and apply this definition to an example. Then, we describe the main stages of a scientific dispute related to the operationalization of a variable frequently used in defence studies.

DEFINITION

In most cases, theories cannot be falsified directly by testing their predictions. The predictions of a theory are generally of a high level of abstraction and cannot be directly tested. This is particularly true in social sciences, let alone in defence studies: highly aggregated categories ("countries" …) are far from consensual. This is also true in "hard sciences", according to Physics' Nobel Prize winner Percy Bridgman. According to Bridgman (1927), even a physical concept as obvious as "length" requires a more precise definition to be useful in the process of testing a theory:

> What do we mean by the length of an object? We evidently know what we mean by length if we can tell what the length of any and every object is, and for the physicist nothing more is required. To find the length of an object, we have to perform certain physical operations. The concept of length is therefore fixed when the operations by which length is measured are fixed.

The operationalization of a concept involves listing the operations required to measure the corresponding quantity. With respect to length, the Académie des Sciences defined in 1791 the metre as a fraction of the circumference of the earth; field measurements were made to determine the standard metre; by dividing this metre by 1,000, a ruler graduated in millimetres was created, allowing to measure the length of any object.

This way of defining a concept is closely linked to Popperian epistemology. According to Bridgman's approach, physical concepts have no meaning if you are unable to observe them. Similarly, for Popper, a theory is not scientific if it cannot be confronted with observable facts. According to these approaches, a theory in defence studies is not falsifiable (and therefore not scientific) if it only uses abstract, non-operationalized concepts, as shown by Proposition 3 mentioned above (Proposition 3: Poverty leads to civil war).

Testing this proposition requires the researcher to operationalize "poverty" and "civil war". Poverty could be defined based on GDP per capita in PPP. For example, a country can be said to be in poverty if its GDP per capita is less than 3,650 PPP dollars (or any other threshold) per year, or less than 10 dollars per day.

It is also necessary to define what GDP is, determine the method for counting inhabitants (how to count short-term migrants, frontier workers, etc.), define what a PPP exchange rate is and then calculate this rate … A civil war could be defined as a period of at least one year during which the number of deaths directly related to fighting in that country is equal to or greater than 1,000 for each year. The complete procedure for measuring these quantities must be explained.

Once the operational concepts have been operationalized and the quantities measured (observation of facts), an empirical model can be created. The experience shows that operationalizing concepts used in defence studies is difficult, as exemplified by the notions of "terrorism" (next section), "conflict-induced internal displacement" (IDMC 2016), or "active diamond mining areas" in the context of the fight against blood diamonds (Kauffmann 2012; Kauffmann et al. 2013).

THE OPERATIONALIZATION OF TERRORISM

Schmid et al. (1988) found 109 different research definitions of terrorism. Sheehan (2012) selected five of the most used event databases of terrorism. He found that, together, their definitions involved 12 elements, only 2 of them were common to all databases. With those 12 definitional elements, assuming we always keep two of them (1. perpetrators are sub-state groups or clandestine agents; 2. legitimate warfare or coup d'état are excluded), we can still choose 0 to 10 of the remaining 10 definitional elements … which gives us 1,024 different possible forms of operationalization of "terrorism"![5] If we acknowledge that each definitional element could have several variants, we get to the conclusion that allowing for nuances would enable the creation of millions of definitions of "terrorism" (see also LaFree 2018; Perl 2007).

To better see in practice how the operationalization process works, we study the Global Terrorism Database (GTD), which consists of coded data for 170,000 terrorist incidents (START 2017), used to build the Global Terrorism Index (GTI).

The GTI defines terrorism as "the threatened or actual use of illegal force and violence by a non-state actor to attain a political, economic, religious, or social goal through fear, coercion, or intimidation". Hence, an incident has to meet three criteria in order for it to be counted as a terrorist incident:

1   The incident must be intentional – the result of a conscious calculation on the part of a perpetrator.
2   The incident must entail some level of violence or threat of violence – including property damage as well as violence against people.
3   The perpetrators of the incidents must be sub-national actors. GTD does not include acts of state terrorism.

In addition to this baseline definition, two of the following three criteria have to be met in order to be included in the START database from 1997:

1   The violent act was aimed at attaining a political, economic, religious or social goal.
2   The violent act included evidence of an intention to coerce, intimidate or convey some other message to a larger audience other than to the immediate victims.
3   The violent act was outside the precepts of international humanitarian law.

This is just a short extract of the rules operationalizing the concept of "terrorism" (the codebook has 65 pages).

Open Source software in support of operationalization in defence studies

The consequence is that operationalization is a crucial part of the scientific process, as it can have a considerable influence both on the results and on whether or not some rules of the scientific method are respected, in particular the accuracy, transparency and reproducibility of research. The software used during data processing can have a significant impact on compliance with these rules.

OPEN SOFTWARE

The data used to address defence issues are often complex. Time series can be irregular; variables are generally of heterogeneous types; individuals (in the statistical sense) are often poorly defined (e.g. state boundaries are changing). This makes data management and processing more difficult than in other social sciences (in economics, for example, managing data such as GDP per quarter is comparatively much simpler). Thus, relatively sophisticated tools are needed.

However, epistemological "grand discourses" and attention to methodological issues must not stop when the data management work begins, i.e. when the tools for storing and processing the collected data are chosen. Data storage and processing is an integral part of the operationalization process (Bridgman 1927), for at least two reasons.

First, the task of software is to implement a method in an efficient, accurate and transparent manner. It must not hide this method from the user. The hypothetical-deductive method requires that the rules of logic be respected from start to finish, including during the data storage and processing procedures.

Secondly, scientific data and research are intended to be shared among researchers, analysts, decision-makers and operational actors. The software should not hinder sharing but should facilitate it, and serve the objectives of transparency of methods, replicability of research and debate, which are important values of the community of experts in defence studies.

In looking for ways to achieve these objectives, it seems that FLOS (Free, Libre and Open Source) software have a number of advantages over proprietary software. The R statistical software, used by many authors of scientific articles in the field of quantitative security studies, is a quality FLOS software that meets these criteria (Kauffmann 2008b).

Its features will allow us to illustrate some of the advantages of FLOS software. They explain why the US DoD[6] and other defence ministries or related entities[7] use the R software.

TRANSPARENCY, PRECISION AND RELIABILITY

Transparency of methods, algorithms and tools is the key to accuracy and reliability. A researcher cannot be sure that a statistical analysis has been carried out rigorously if the tools used are not transparent. Since software tools allow new data and information to be created from raw data, these tools deserve as much as the data to be thoroughly inspected. Only open source software allows this inspection.

The source code of FLOS software is freely available and can be consulted and modified. This allows users to check the algorithms used, discover bugs and fix them, which is not the case with software whose source code is secret. For example, there are many episodes of late bug discoveries in Microsoft Excel® (Altman and McDonald 2001), which should be avoided for statistics. Despite modest progress, according to Mélard (2014),

> Microsoft did not make an attempt to fix all the errors in Excel, and this point needs to be made strongly. Microsoft continues to market a product that contains known statistical errors, some of them going back to Excel 4, released in 1994. This should be contrasted with what is found on some open source or free software packages.

Some of these Excel bugs were discovered by chance, by doing simple calculations that are easy to check with a calculator. Proprietary software is a "black box", whereas with open source software it is easy to check what each function does (with R, by simply entering the name of a function), and improve it if needed.

INTERTEMPORAL REPLICABILITY

The transparency of software is an essential criterion to guarantee the intertemporal replicability of the data processing. For example, to create a conflict indicator from raw data, proprietary software should not be used, as the manufacturer can change algorithms without notice. If this type of software is used, the result may be different depending on the version of the software being used, without being predictable in advance. On the other hand, when one studies an estimated conflict model with R and the version number of R is specified in the scientific article in question, one is protected from this risk. If any of R's features should change in the coming years, this code change will be documented (at http://cran.r-project.org/src/base/NEWS); the ultimate documentation being the source code, all versions of which are archived online.

In short, it is safe to say that the statistical algorithms and functions used in scientific articles developing armed conflict models with R will still be feasible with R in a many years' time, even on computers using electronic components and operating systems that do not yet exist. On the other hand, the old versions of Excel no longer work on the latest versions of Windows.

With two different versions of Microsoft Excel®, it is not possible to be sure that the results of the calculation of a standard deviation will be the same. With R, the replicability of calculations across time and space is guaranteed.

INTERPERSONAL REPLICABILITY

All R users can always have the latest version of the software. Upgrading the software to the latest version involves no software costs. Hence, it is not necessary to maintain several versions of an application based on this software: all users can use the latest version (easing communication between researchers), all benefit from the latest software improvements. On the contrary, when two administrations of a country (for example: Ministry of Defence and Ministry of Foreign Affairs), or the Ministries of Defence of two allied countries, use proprietary software, they can only collaborate effectively if they all have the same version of the software, which requires synchronizing procurement.

The wide availability of FLOS software contribute to the reliability of the data and research: the more researchers can use a given tool or reproduce a given calculation, the greater the chance that bugs and errors will be discovered, discussed and corrected.

OPEN SOURCE SOFTWARE AT THE DEFENCE MINISTRIES

The above are some of the reasons why the American DoD promotes the use of Open Source software, as well as the publication in Open Source of the code developed by its employees.

Several studies mention the use of numerous FLOS software at the DoD for at least two decades (the earliest comprehensive study was published in 2002). The fields that are of concern for this chapter are those of statistics (R), spreadsheet (OpenOffice/LibreOffice Calc), calculus (Octave), machine learning (Weka), interactive data visualization (Ggobi), scientific visualization (gnuplot), relational databases (Mysql, PostgreSQL), operating systems (contributing to Linux, see Loscocco and Smalley 2000; Vaughan-Nichols 2011; OpenBSD), web servers (Apache) ....[8] More recently, the US Congress required the DoD to focus more on open source software in acquisition procedures.[9]

With respect to statistics in a narrow sense, the DoD Quantitative Methods Directorate uses the R software (US DoD Inspector General 2009). The Air Force Flight Test Center gives a course whose purpose is to make engineers and flight test practitioners better "consumers" of statistics, using R (US DoD (2012), 35). The R software is also considered by the DoD as one of the "Best Packages for Statistical Analysis" (US DoD (2012) "APPENDIX C Software options", p. 39).[10]

The French Gendarmerie (a military component for civil law enforcement) also choose to switch to OpenOffice/LibreOffice Calc (a spreadsheet application allowing simple to intermediate statistical analysis) in 2005 (Guillemin 2005) and to Linux between 2007 and 2009 (Feugey 2010).

Conclusion

Surely, none of the statistical methods and systems we mentioned is perfect; human experts remain essential to improve them, and to analyse the results. However, it is very difficult to find people with dual skills in international security on the one hand, and in information systems and quantitative analysis on the other. In front of the French Defence Committee, General Ferlet (2018) mentioned the recruitment difficulties of the Directorate of Military Intelligence. As seen in this chapter with the notion of operationalization, there is a real need to train analysts having both quantitative and qualitative skills applied to defence studies.

Notes

1 Amartya Sen, Lawrence Klein, Kenneth Arrow, Daniel McFadden, Roger Myerson, Robert Solow, Franco Modigliani, Wassily Leontief, Jan Tinbergen, James Tobin.

2 For example, Seiglie and Kauffmann (2004) in economics. Medical survival models have been applied to the causes of war, see Kauffmann (2004, 2006c, 2007) and Barnier et al. (2019: 597–622). Geostatistics helps estimate data in emergencies and detect houses from satellite imagery to assess war damages (Corban et al. 2010; Florczyk et al. 2014).
3 For the purposes of this explanation, it does not matter what the exact definition of this variable is.
4 It is this type of observation that Lijphart (1971) refers to when he mentions the observation of partial correlations: we look at the correlation between the explanatory variables and the explained one in the case that only one of the explanatory variables varies.
5 In addition to the two elements common to all definitions of terrorism, we need to choose 0, or 1, or 2, ... or 10 additional definitional elements.
6 See Kitto (2012); Knopp et al. (2012); Brown and White (2017). See discussion about approval of the use of R at the DoD, 5 June 2012, http://r.789695.n4.nabble.com/regis try-vulnerabilities-in-R-tp4619217p4632431.html where the reliability of R in Regulated Clinical Trial Environments was considered as a reason to use R at the DoD.
7 Greek Defence Ministry: Lappas and Bozoudis (2018); European Commission's JRC: Halkia et al. (2017).
8 All these examples (but two) from: MITRE Corporation (2003). PostgreSQL and Open-Office.org (now superseded by LibreOffice) mentioned in: DoD Chief Information Officer (2019).
9 Schwartz and Peters (2018); under FY2018 (P.L. 115–91, Sec. 875. "Pilot program for open source software"), during a three-year pilot program, federal agencies are also required to release at least 20 percent of their custom-developed code to the public as open source software.
10 The DoD High Performance Computing Modernization Program also acknowledges the use of R (https://centers.hpc.mil/software/).

References

Altman, M., McDonald, M. P. (2001). Choosing reliable statistical software. *PS: Political Science & Politics* 34 (3): 681–687.

Barnier, J., Biaudet, J., Briatte, F., Bouchet-Valat, M., Gallic, E., Giraud, F., Gombin, J. et al. (2019). *Analyse-R. Introduction à l'analyse d'enquêtes avec R et Rstudio*. Joseph Larmarange (Ed.), available online: https://www.researchgate.net/publication/334400593_analyse-R_Intro duction_a_l'analyse_d'enquetes_avec_R_et_Rstudio (Consulted in 2019).

Beauguitte, L. (2011). *L'Assemblée Générale de l'ONU de 1985 à nos Jours: Acteur et Reflet du Système-Monde. Essai de Géographie Politique Quantitative*. Paris, Université Paris-Diderot, VII, available online: https://tel.archives-ouvertes.fr/tel-00634403 (Consulted in 2019).

Bridgman, P. (1927). *The Logic of Modern Physics*, London, Macmillan.

Brown, G., White, E. (2017). An investigation of nonparametric data mining techniques for acquisition cost estimating. *Defence Acquisition Research Journal*, 42(2), 302–332.

Christiansson, M. (2017). Defence planning beyond rationalism: The third offset strategy as a case of metagovernance. *Defence Studies* 18(1), 1–17.

Corban, C., Lemoine, G., Kauffmann, M. (2010). Can real-time crisis sms messages help in diagnosing the spatial distribution of structural damage? Analysis of the relationship between the distribution of damage and the location of SMS messages sent during the Haiti crisis, 117–125. In: *Proceedings of the 2nd International Workshop on Validation of Geo- Information Products for Crisis Management - VALgEO 2010*, European Commission.

DoD Chief Information Officer. (2019). *Frequently Asked Questions Regarding Open Source Software (OSS) and the Department of Defence (DoD)*, available online: https://dodcio. defence.gov/Open-Source-Software-FAQ/ (Consulted in 2019).

Ferlet, J.-F. (2018). *Commission de la Défense Nationale et des Forces Armées*. Compte rendu n° 52. Paris, available online: http://www.assemblee-nationale.fr/15/cr-cdef/17-18/c1718052.asp (Consulted in 2019).

Feugey, D. (2010). *La Gendarmerie Poursuit sa Migration Vers Linux*, available online: https://www.silicon.fr/la-gendarmerie-poursuit-sa-migration-vers-linux-42777.html (Consulted in 2019).

Florczyk, A., Kemper, Th., Kauffmann, M., Soille, P. (2014). VGI in automatic information retrieval from big RS data. In: *GIScience 2014 Workshop "Role of Volunteered Geographic Information in Advancing Science: Effective Utilization*. Vienna, Austria, available online: https://pdfs.semanticscholar.org/9930/11c12b82c837b0fb459f10a5b6e62e419317.pdf (Consulted in 2019).

Flyvbjerg, B. (2006). Five misunderstandings about case-study research. *Qualitative Research Practice*, 12(2), 219–245.

Guillemin, C. (2005). *La Gendarmerie Nationale Passe à OpenOffice*, available online: https://www.zdnet.fr/actualites/la-gendarmerie-nationale-passe-a-openoffice-39203431.htm (Consulted on 2019).

Halkia, S., Ferri, S., Joubert-Boitat, I., Saporiti, F., Kauffmann, M. (2017). *The Global Conflict Risk Index (GCRI) Regression Model: Data Ingestion, Processing, and Output Methods*. JRC technical report JRC108767, European Commission, JRC.

IDMC. (2016). *Global Report on Internal Displacement – GRID 2016*, Geneva, Internal Displacement Monitoring Centre, available online: http://www.internal-displacement.org/assets/publications/2016/2016-global-report-internal-displacement- IDMC.pdf (Consulted on 24 June 2019).

Kauffmann, M. (1998). Armements, Sous-Développement, Conflits: Des Relations Dangereuses, 63–82. In: *Ventes d'armes de la France*, Rapport 1998. Lyon, France, Observatoire des transferts d'armements.

Kauffmann, M. (1999). Le Fonds Monétaire International et les Dépenses Militaires. *Damoclès, Observatoire des transferts d'armements*, 83, 13–18.

Kauffmann, M. (2000). La Conditionnalité du Fonds Monétaire International et les Dépenses Militaires. *Pax Economica* 3, 13–38.

Kauffmann, M. (2004). *Les Organisations Économiques Internationales Face aux Dépenses et à la Sécurité Militaires: Banque Mondiale, FMI et GATT/OMC*. Doctoral Dissertation, Université Pierre Mendès France.

Kauffmann, M. (2006a). Les Couples dans l'étude Empirique du Modèle Libéral Néo-Kantien. *Arès* 22(57), 87–104.

Kauffmann, M. (2006b). Les Actions du FMI, de la Banque Mondiale et de l'OMC, Facteurs de Réduction des Conflits Internes ou Internationaux? *Annuaire Français des Relations Internationales*, 7(15), available online: http://www.afri-ct.org/article/les-actions-du-fmi-de-la-banque/.

Kauffmann, M. (2006c). *Gouvernance Économique Mondiale et Conflits Armés: Banque Mondiale, FMI et GATT-OMC*, Paris, L'Harmattan.

Kauffmann, M. (2007). Short term and event interdependence matter: A political economy continuous model of civil war. *Peace Economics, Peace Science and Public Policy*, 13(1).

Kauffmann, M. (ed.) (2008a). *Building and Using Datasets on Armed Conflicts*, Amsterdam, IOS Press/NATO.

Kauffmann, M. (2008b). Enhancing openness and reliability in conflict dataset creation, 107–132. In: Kauffmann, M. (Ed.) (2008). *Building and Using Datasets on Armed Conflicts*, Amsterdam, IOS Press.

Kauffmann, M. (2009). *Méthodes Statistiques Appliquées aux Questions Internationales*, Paris, L'Harmattan.

Kauffmann, M. (2011). "La Fame Accende le Guerre? Un Sito Dice Dove. E Perché. (Interview)". *ItaliaOggi*, 233: 22.

Kauffmann, M. (2012). *The Scientific Contribution of the European Commission to the Kimberley Process Certification Scheme*, European Commission.

Kauffmann, Mayeul (2017). Resilience to oppression and to violent conflict escalation through nonviolent action, 82–91. In: *The 2nd International Workshop on Modelling of Physical, Economic and Social Systems for Resilience Assessment*, European Commission.

Kauffmann, M., Jennings, M., Wcislo, M.et al. (2011). *Research and Innovation: New Modelling Results Link Natural Resources and Armed Conflicts*, Press Release Ip-11-1090, European Commission.

Kauffmann, M., Al-Khudhairy, D., Louvrier, C., Chirico, P., Malpeli, K. (2013). *Joint EU-US Methodology for Monitoring Alluvial Diamond Mining Activities in Cote d'Ivoire*. EC-JRC/ 84711. A European Commission (JRC) and United States Geological Survey (USGS) report.

Kemper, T., Kauffmann, M., Sebahara, P., Kayitakire, F. (2011). Conflicts and political crises. In: *GMES and Africa - Summary of the Baseline Action Plan 29*. Global Monitoring for Environment and Security, European Commission.

Keynes, J. M. (2017 [1919]). *The Economic Consequences of the Peace*, London, Routledge.

Kitto, W. (2012). Air Force Flight Test Center (AFFTC) Courses. In: *DoD Scientific Test and Analysis Techniques in Test and Evaluation Implementation Plan*, 36, available online: https://www.dote.osd.mil/docs/TempGuide3/STAT_TE_Implementation_Plan_30Jan2012.pdf (Consulted in 2019).

Knopp, J., Grandhi, R., Zeng, L., and Aldrin, J. (2012). Considerations for statistical analysis of non-destructive evaluation data: Hit/miss analysis. *E-Journal of Advanced Maintenance*, 4(3), 105–115.

Kucera, J., Kauffmann, M., Duta, A.-M., Tarrida Soler, I., Tenerelli, P., Trianni, G., Hale, C., Rizzo, L., Ferri, S. (2011). *Armed Conflicts and Natural Resources*, Brussels, European Commission.

LaFree, G. (2018). *Conceptualizing and Measuring Terrorism*, 22–33. In: Silke, A. (Ed.) (2018). *Routledge Handbook of Terrorism and Counterterrorism*, London, Routledge.

Lappas, I., Bozoudis, M. (2018). The development of an ordinary least squares parametric model to estimate the cost per flying hour of 'unknown' aircraft types and a comparative application. *Aerospace*, 5(4), 104.

Lijphart, A. (1971). Comparative politics and the comparative method. *The American Political Science Review*, 65(3): 682–693.

Loscocco, P., Smalley, S. (2000). *Integrating Flexible Support for Security Policies into the Linux Operating System*. National Security Agency, available online: https://www.nsa.gov/Portals/70/images/resources/everyone/digital-media-center/publications/research-papers/flexible-support-for-security-policies-into-linux-feb2001- report.pdf. (Consulted in 2019).

Mélard, G. (2014). On the accuracy of statistical procedures in Microsoft Excel 2010. *Computational Statistics*, 29(5), 1095–1128.

MITRE Corporation. (2003). *Use of Free and Open Source Software (FOSS) in the U.S. Department of Defence*. version 1.2.04, available online: https://dodcio.defence.gov/Portals/0/Documents/OSSFAQ/dodfoss_pdf.pdf (Consulted on 2019).

Perl, R. (2007). *Combating Terrorism: The Challenge of Measuring Effectiveness*, CRS report to the Congress.

PNUD. (1996). *Rapport Mondial Sur le Développement Humain 1996*, Paris, Economica, available online: http://hdr.undp.org/en/global-reports.

Popper, K. (1934). *Logik der Forschung*, Germany, Mohr Siebeck.

Richardson, L. (1948). Variation of the frequency of fatal quarrels with magnitude. *Journal of the American Statistical Association*, 244: 523–546.

Richardson, L. (1960). *Arms and Insecurity: A Mathematical Study of the Causes and Origins of War*, London, Stevens and Sons Publishers.

Roser, C. (2012). L'activité Statistique de l'Organisation Économique et Financière de la Société des Nations. Un Nouveau Lien Entre Pouvoir et Quantification. *Histoire & Mesure* XXVII-2.

Sarkees, M. (2000). The Correlates of War Data on War: An Update to 1997. *Conflict Management and Peace Science*, 18(1), 123–144.

Schmid, A., Jongman, A. J., Stohl, M. (1988). *Political Terrorism: A New Guide to Actors, Authors, Concepts, Data Bases, Theories, and Literature*, Amsterdam, Transaction Books.

Schwartz, M., Peters, H. (2018). *Acquisition Reform in the FY2016-FY2018 National Defence Authorization Acts (NDAAs)*. R45068. Congressional Research Service, available online: https://fas.org/sgp/crs/natsec/R45068.pdf.

Seiglie, C., Kauffmann, M. (2004). *The Economics of Chemical and Biological Weapons. In: Encyclopedia of Life Support Systems (EOLSS)*. Oxford, UNESCO, EOLSS Publishers, available online: https://www.eolss.net/Sample-Chapters/C13/E6-28A-04-02.pdf.

Sheehan, I. (2012). Assessing and comparing data sources for terrorism research, 13–40. In: Lim, C., Kennedy, L. (Eds.) (2012). *Evidence-Based Counterterrorism Policy*, New York, Springer.

START. (2017). *GTD Global Terrorism Database Codebook: Inclusion Criteria and Variables.* College Park, MD: University of Maryland, National Consortium for the Study of Terrorism and Responses to Terrorism (START). https://www.start.umd.edu/gtd/downloads/Codebook.pdf.

US DoD. (2012). *Scientific Test and Analysis Techniques in Test and Evaluation - Implementation Plan*, available online: https://www.dote.osd.mil/docs/TempGuide3/STAT_TE_Implementation_Plan_30Jan2012.pdf.

US DoD Inspector General. (2009) *Testing Requirements for Body Armor.* D-2009–2047, available online: https://media.defence.gov/2009/Jan/29/2001712184/-1/-1/1/09-047.pdf.

Vaughan-Nichols, S. (2011). *The Air Force's Secure Linux Distribution*, available online: https://www.zdnet.com/article/the-air-forces-secure-linux-distribution/ (Consulted in 2019).

Wright, Q. (1942). *A Study of War*, Chicago, University of Chicago Press.

8 Databases for defence studies

Mayeul Kauffmann

Introduction

Among the first to collect and analyse statistical data on conflicts were Sorokin (1937), Wright (1942), and Richardson (1948), who modelled the arms race and the risk of war (Richardson 1960). These pioneers were followed by Singer and Small (1966) and many other researchers (Suzuki et al. 2002). Today, there are research centres, university departments or institutes that are largely, if not entirely, dedicated to studying defence issues using quantitative methods. A few examples in the United States include the Correlates of War Consortium, the Center for Systemic Peace (CSP), the Center for International Development and Conflict Management (CIDCM), the Interuniversity Consortium for Political and Social Research (ICPSR). In Sweden, the Stockholm International Peace Research Institute (SIPRI) and the Uppsala Conflict Data Program of Uppsala University are noteworthy; in Norway the International Peace Research Institute in Oslo (PRIO); in Germany, the Bundeswehr Academy for Information and Communication (AKUF) group (Hamburg) and Heidelberger Institut für Internationale Konfliktforschung (HIIK) (Heidelberg).

In this chapter, we first introduce existing databases in defence and security studies, then show the interest of relatively novel approaches in the field using Big Data and Natural Language Processing, and end up with guidelines for the creation (or improvement) of databases in defence and security studies.

Existing databases in defence studies

After a brief overview of some of the databases in the field, we focus on the sub-field of data on armed conflicts, provide explanations of the proliferation of such databases, of the lack of interoperability in strategic databases, as well as some solutions.

Overview

There exist many event datasets (especially on armed conflicts); these are either coded by analysts (ACLED, IBC ...) or by robots using NLP methods (ICEWS, GDELT, UTD Phoenix, UCDP ...).

Some of the main other areas are:

- data in defence economics, especially military spending, of official nature (World Bank, Eurostat ...) or private nature (SIPRI, COW, GRIP ...)

- arms transfers (SIPRI, SAS, Ruestungsexport.info, GRIP)
- collective civilian action and resistance (GNAD, MV&R, MAR, NAVCO)
- minority at risk and internal displacement related to armed conflicts (MAR, IDMCs GIDD …)
- political regime, elections and votes (Polity, CREV, PDVP …)
- terrorism (GTD)
- contentious issues (ICOW).

In many cases, data are hard to get or to process, so accessibility to data is in itself a subject of study (Small Arms Trade Transparency Barometer of the Small Arms Survey); in this respect, open data repositories and combination of indicators also play an import role (CYBIS, COW, GCRI, Ruestungsexport.info, ICPSR, PRIO …).

A single research project often requires the researcher to work with heterogeneous datasets, which can be a difficult task. To this end, some meta-databases try to tightly combine several datasets (such as the Correlates of War), sometimes producing a single dataset and building composite indicators like in Halkia et al. (2017). Table 8.1 summarizes some of these databases.

The proliferation of databases on armed conflicts

The number of databases on armed conflict is high. In a non-exhaustive review of these databases, Eck (2005) counted 59; Eck (2008) suggested a typology. There are about as many definitions of what a conflict is as there are different databases (see Kauffmann 2008a). Of all the criteria used to define and classify, the one related to a threshold in the level of violence is the most common, so we will begin with this one. The other criteria will then be discussed.

The diversity of databases on armed conflict is mainly due to multiple classifications according to the level of violence. The absence of a commonly accepted theoretical concept is also an important explanatory factor. Multiple classifications according to the level of violence

The most common criterion used to determine whether a given time period is a period of armed conflict is the level of violence, measured by a threshold on the number of victims. A dozen of the 59 databases mentioned by Eck (2005) only take into account events that resulted in at least 1,000 victims. This criterion of the number of victims is, of all the possible criteria, probably the most objective one and the easiest to define and measure. However, this is a much more complex criterion than it seems.

Each period of armed conflict can be seen as an aggregation of many one-off events, including the death of each of the victims of the conflict. A first difficulty concerns the type of one-time event to be posted. Does the figure of 1,000 victims refer to 1,000 dead or 1,000 dead or injured? In addition, some people may be victims of rape, theft, forced expropriation or forced displacement.

Another difficulty may concern the delay between a belligerent act and its consequences. A person may die as a result of his or her injuries several weeks after being injured, or even several years later. Indeed, some weapons have immediate effects and others are delayed in time: in addition to the Hiroshima and Nagasaki nuclear bombings, this is the case, for example, for so-called conventional weapons such as bullets whose tips are hardened with depleted uranium. The difficulty in defining the exact causes of the health problems of some Gulf War veterans illustrates this issue. The same is true of anti-personnel mines, which can cause casualties decades after the end of a conflict.

Table 8.1 Sample databases in defence studies

Acronym	Name	Website	Notes
ACLED	Armed Conflict Location and Event Data Project	https://www.acleddata.com/	Disaggregated conflict event data, with geolocation coded by human analysts
COW	Correlates of war	http://www.correlatesofwar.org/	Data on State System Membership, wars and disputes, national capability, religion, IGOs, diplomatic exchange …
CREV	Countries at Risk of Electoral Violence	http://www.electoralviolenceproject.com/datasetviolence/countries-risk-electoral-violence-dataset/	Data on electoral violence measured in a ten-month window around each election
CSP	left for Systemic Peace; Polity 4	http://www.systemicpeace.org	Data on political regime/polity, State Fragility …
CYBIS	Cyber and International Security	http://cybis.univ-grenoble-alpes.fr/	Open data platform focusing on international security and cyber governance, with integrated analytics and sharing tools
Eurostat	Eurostat	https://ec.europa.eu/eurostat/statistics-explained/index.php/Government_expenditure_on_defence	Official disaggregated data on military expenditures for EU countries
GCRI	Global Conflict Risk Index	http://conflictrisk.jrc.ec.europa.eu	Conflict risk index and background database of the European Commission
GDELT	Global Database of Events, Language, and Tone	https://www.gdeltproject.org/	Disaggregated conflict event data, coded by robots using sources from 1979 in over 100 languages
GNAD	Global Nonviolent Action Database	https://nvdatabase.swarthmore.edu/	More than 1,200 campaigns of non-violent action, segmented in sequences
GRIP	Group for Research and Information on Peace and Security	https://www.grip.org/fr/databases	Embargo on arm transfers …
GTD	Global Terrorism Database	https://www.start.umd.edu/gtd	Data on terrorist events

Another difficulty concerns the context of these events and the motivations of their authors. Crime is a cause of death by firearm (for example, robbery). If there are more than a thousand crimes resulting in death in a given country in a given year, should we conclude that this country is in a civil war? Conversely, in a civil war situation, a deceased victim will not be able to say whether he/she was killed because of his/her identity or for his/her wallet; moreover, a civil war probably tends to make armed robberies more frequent because the disorganization of the police creates a sense of impunity.

Another difficulty concerns the exact cause of events. Should we only count people killed with a weapon? Some counts include indirect victims, such as those related to famines caused by wars, which is challenged by Kreutz (2008). A problem with this approach is that it leads to confusion between the measurement of conflict and the consequences of conflict.

However, famines are not necessarily indirect consequences of conflict. For example, raids, looting and burning of homes or crops can be acts of war deliberately aimed at causing many "indirect" victims.

Another difficulty relates to the status of victims: should we count only military victims or only civilians, or both? In the so-called classic international wars, the primary military objective was the surrender of the adversary ensuring the conquest of part of its territory; in this context, most of the victims were military. This is not the case for genocides or other massacres that primarily affect civilians.

Other causes of diversity in conflict data

There is no homogeneity in the general concept used in conflict databases: about one-third of these 59 databases deal with "wars", another third with "conflicts" and another third with various concepts.

In many cases, adjectives are used to describe these categories. Some of these adjectives refer to the nature of the actors involved in the event, which may be "international", "civil", "intra-state", "extra-state", "non-state". Eleven of the 59 databases mention the term "violent" or "violence" in their description or definition; there are 22 of them if we consider the description of the different types of conflicts in the same database, often categorized according to the degree of intensity of violence. One database refers to "mass violence", another to "violent mass conflict", others to "unilateral violence" or "violent conflict". The term "massacre" appears in the definitions of six databases, "genocide" in two databases.

Sometimes violence is not the central concept, as in the following typologies: "disagreement issues", "crises", "disputes", "rivalries". Other categories included in these 59 databases include "major wars", "insurrections", "interventions" (by States or international organizations).

A small part of this diversity is related to the fact that some of these databases do not focus on conflicts but on related topics, such as military expenditures, failed states, regime changes, territorial changes or armed interventions by international organizations.

Constructing a "conflict" using disaggregated event data

All the difficulties we have mentioned add to each other, but disaggregated data collection and semi-automated coding can solve some of them.

Currently, given the diversity of the criteria cited in the previous section, different researchers may take different decisions about the preferred solution: for instance, there is no theoretical reason to set the threshold at 1,000 rather than 900 or 1,100 deaths per year. By combining the different ways of responding to each of these difficulties, we obtain a very large number of possible operationalizations.

The method we propose in order to solve many of the problems associated with the operationalization of the concept of armed conflict is to store data as disaggregated as possible and organized in such a way as to allow the automation of part of the conflict coding process. As far as possible, data are coded at a level of disaggregation close to the individual level (individuals who are victims of armed violence) and additional information is stored to allow aggregation according to a large number of different typologies.

As an example, we will take data from the Iraq Body Count project, a project that systematically documents and counts violent civilian deaths related to the 2003 military intervention in Iraq and its aftermath. The database mainly contains lists of civilians (non-combatants) killed by fighting. The main sources are reports from the media, as well as official figures or those from hospitals, morgues and NGOs. The methods for collecting and processing information are clearly defined and the database is available online (http://www.iraqbodycount.org).

For each incident identified, the following information is recorded:

1. A code to uniquely identify the incident (the code consists of a letter, which indicates which encoder recorded the information,[1] followed by a serial number).
2. The type of incident (bombing, stray bullets, car bomb…).
3. The number of deaths recorded, or a range of two numbers (low and high estimates).
4. The target (targeted or hit).
5. The location of the incident.
6. The date of the incident.
7. The name and date of each source: press articles, press releases, official figures, or direct sources (direct visual witnesses, relatives of victims, journalists, first aiders, etc.).

Another table records information about victims, with for each victim:

1. The code of the incident to which it corresponds.
2. Identification information (name if known, or any other information that helps to identify the victim).
3. Age or age range.
4. The sex.
5. The profession or function (political, religious, tribal …).
6. Nationality.
7. Marital status.
8. Parental status.

In general, some of this information remains unknown.

By combining this disaggregated information in different ways, it is possible to obtain different datasets on "the war in Iraq", each referring to different operationalizations of the notion of armed conflict (Figure 8.1).

134 *Mayeul Kauffmann*

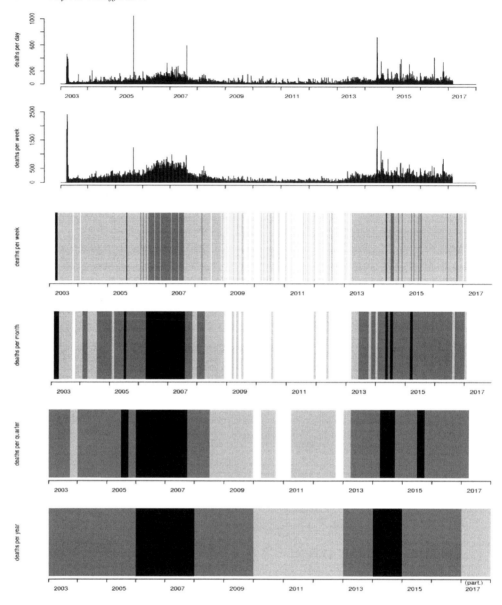

Figure 8.1 Various classifications of conflict based on the Iraq Body Count event data
Note: Darker areas indicate more victims per unit of time.

While the above shows the interest of a database such as the Iraq Body Count, it should be mentioned that this database has many shortcomings, including the limitations of the number of sources used, the time lag between news sources and consolidated data, and the geographic coverage, among others; these are discussed by IBC (2010) and Kleinfeld (2017). Big Data and Natural Language Processing seem to offer promising answers to some of these questions (see the next section).

Lack of interoperability in strategic databases compared to economic databases

There is still a delay in strategic statistical databases compared to economic databases. The strict separation of the two disciplines in many cases has made it more difficult to analyse international data today, as illustrated by the study of institutional web-mapping platforms. We have identified a dozen web platforms capable of displaying indicators on a world map (with a cursor on a timeline allowing the user to choose the displayed year), most of them created by major international institutions (International Monetary Fund (IMF), World Bank, Organisation for Economic Co-operation and Development (OECD), World Health Organisation (WHO) …): none of them displays border changes, the most significant being the World Bank's, which, besides a Germany shown as united since 1970, literally chose not to represent Western Sahara (which appears as water – not as land – as part of the Atlantic Ocean!). This makes scientific or operational research more difficult, for example for studies in defence economics based on military industry production indicators and public defence finance (IMF, World Bank, OECD data); or support by military forces for emergency humanitarian operations (WHO data).[2]

Another of these issues refers to the most common unit of analysis, namely the definition of the members of the international system (states or "countries"). In its population statistics yearbooks, the United Nations lists 233 countries and territories, which does not include the Republic of Kosovo. UNDP (2018) collects data

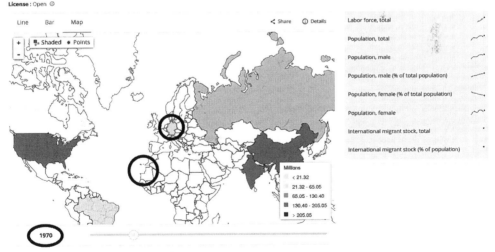

Figure 8.2 World Bank Data platform (circles added by the author).
Notes: Post-Cold War map shown for 1970 (sic). The data extract and chart display tools show that the population of both German states during the Cold War are already merged at the data storage level, so the information on the population of the GDR and pre-1990 FRG is lost. Western Sahara is absent (shown as part of Atlantic Ocean). Population and land shape of Western Sahara are ignored.
Source: https://data.worldbank.org/indicator/SP.POP.TOTL?locations=DE&view=map&year=1970

from 171 countries for its HDI (Human Development Index). The Correlates of War project lists 243 countries and territories, the CIA World Factbook lists 267 entities, while the list of independent states of Gleditsch and Ward (1999) contains 216 states (version 6: July 2018), with a minimum population criterion of 250,000 inhabitants, but exceptions (Belize in 1998 has a population of 230,160 inhabitants, but is included) and a draft list of 23 microstates. Due to political obstacles from their Member States, international organizations have not been able to disentangle this mess: the International Organization for Standardization (ISO) has not defined an ISO-3 code for Kosovo, so public actors (including the EU) or private actors have done so; at least four different three-letter codes are used for Kosovo (XKX, KOS, KVA, RKS). While weeks of data management and hundreds of lines of codes were needed to merge several databases in defence studies in the early 2000s (Kauffmann 2004; Kauffmann 2006), little has changed: using data created by different agencies together is still a headache.

Big Data and Natural Language Processing

While statistical methods were traditionally applied to numbers, such methods can now process a large amount of textual data through Natural Language Processing. Open Source Intelligence (OSINT) applies Natural Language Processing (NLP) to publicly available data (web pages, tweets…). We will focus on three of these projects: ICEWS, GDELT and Phoenix (other projects exist, such as the European Commission's Europe Media Monitor). Such projects help create highly disaggregated event datasets, which are necessary to take into account short-term effect and event interdependence (Kauffmann 2007).

ICEWS

ICEWS (the Integrated Conflict Early Warning System) is a database of political events, describing who did what to whom, when, and where, using the CAMEO (Conflict and Mediation Event Observations) classification of events (ontology). The project was launched in 2008 by the US Defence Advanced Research Projects Agency (DARPA). The database was created and is maintained by the Lockheed Martin Advanced Technology Laboratories (ATL). ICEWS uses an NLP engine to analyse texts from the news. This engine being a closed source, we use Stanford's open source equivalent to illustrate its functioning. We take this sentence: "Iran's elite Revolutionary Guards have shot down a US 'spy' drone in the southern province of Hormozgan" (sixth sentence of Baghishov (2019), referenced by ICEWS); we feed it to Stanford CoreNLP (http://corenlp.run/), which recognizes the parts-of-speech (nouns (NN …), verbs (VB …), adjectives (JJ), prepositions (IN), determiners (DT) …). The recognition is based on grammatical rules rather than on simple lists of words (US is not confused with the plural pronoun "us", even when both are in upper case). The engine also finds named entities (countries, places …) and relations (dependencies) between words or group of words (Figure 8.3).

Finally, the engine allows an Information Extraction (IE) algorithm to extract data from it: who (the subject: Iran's elite Revolutionary Guards), what (the verb: shot down), to whom (the object: a US "spy" drone), where (the location: the province of Hormozgan). A similar process allowed the generation of ICEWS data. Figure 8.4 shows the standard way to interact with relational databases, using the standardized SQL language. The "SELECT" statement is followed by the names of the fields (columns) to display;

Databases for defence studies 137

Part-of-Speech:

Named Entity Recognition:

Basic Dependencies:

Open IE:

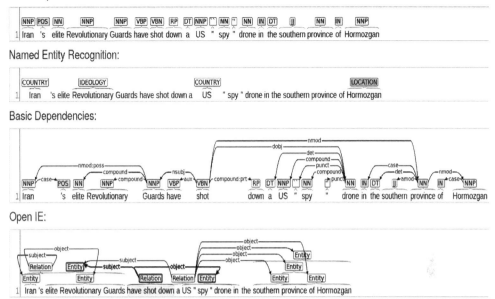

Figure 8.3 Automatic analysis of conflict event by NLP

"FROM" is followed by the name of the table from which the data is retrieved; the "WHERE" clause is followed by conditions (when "like" is used, "%" will match any character(s)); the results are ordered according to the criteria of "ORDER BY".

The SQL language is used by a large majority of the database systems,[3] and the field of defence studies is no exception (see last section of chapter 7). There are other types of database systems, for instance document databases (MongoDB …), search engines (Elasticsearch …), graph databases (Neo4j, PostgreSQL's AgensGraph …), with specific applications.

Figure 8.4 Sample query and result from the ICEWS database

A similar process can be done to extract a large amount of data from huge datasets. Let's say we want to know which countries have used intensively conventional military force in fighting since 1995. We operationalize this question by saying "we want countries that, for at least one month, are the source of at least 300 monthly events of type 190 according to ICEWS", about 10 per day (190 is the CAMEO code (Conflict and Mediation Event Observations) for "use conventional military force"). In SQL, we create a table "countries_at_war" which contains the answer to this question:

```
CREATE TABLE countries_at_war AS SELECT country_at_war FROM
(SELECT source_country AS country_at_war, yearmonth,
count(*) as count_event FROM EVENTS
WHERE cameo_code=190 AND source_country IS NOT NULL
GROUP BY source_country, yearmonth HAVING count_event>299)
GROUP BY country_at_war;
```

Now, we would like to display the monthly intensity of events for each of these countries. We select the data with:

```
SELECT source_country, yearmonth, count(*) as count_event
FROM EVENTS
WHERE source_country IN (SELECT country_at_war FROM countries_at_war)
AND cameo_code=190
GROUP BY source_country, yearmonth;
```

We can display the resulting dataset on a graph, with darker rectangles showing more fight-intensive months. It summarizes 4,649 events extracted from a database of 18 million events (Figure 8.5).

GDELT

GDELT (Global Database of Events, Language, and Tone) is another well-known database of events, created in the early 2010s, in which disaggregated conflict event data is coded by robots, using sources from 1979 in 65 languages (relying extensively on machine translation). It uses a similar methodology as ICEWS, described in Schrodt (2011), to produce more than 2.5 terabytes of synthetic data each year (about 4,000 CD-ROMs).

In addition to its huge size, GDELT has one major advantage over ICEWS for analysts: it does provide the URL of the source for each coded event; ICEWS cannot provide such URL as news stories are received by ICEWS systems through a specific, paid subscription (they are not downloaded from the Internet). This allows analysts to double-check the initial coding done by robots (as long as the original source stays online). GDELT (2015) also provides a full-text search API allowing a search of the full text of all monitored coverage from the last 24 hours.

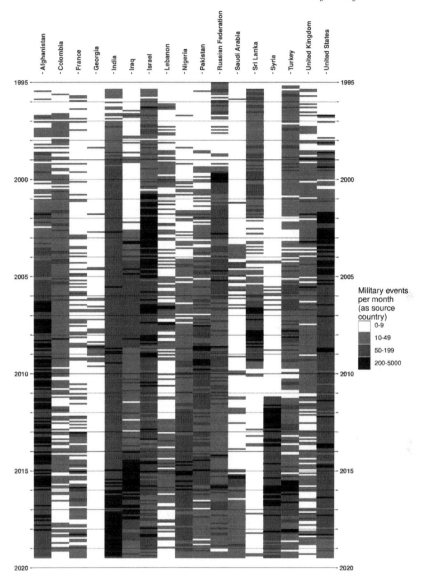

Figure 8.5 Military events per month based on ICEWS
Source: author's computations based on ICEWS data.

Still, Ward (2013) and Steinert-Threlkeld (2013) find that there are many false positives in GDELT, while ICEWS has more false negatives. As summarized by Ward (2013), "GDELT over-states the number of events by a substantial margin, but ICEWS misses some events as well". In other words, GDELT seems to have a high sensitivity (a high proportion of actual positives are correctly identified as such), and ICEWS a high specificity (a high proportion of actual negatives that are correctly identified as such); this could be related to the sponsorship of the two projects (partly commercial for GDELT with Yahoo! and Google; military for ICEWS).

Another shortcoming of GDELT is the high number of duplicates, which results in very large datasets that are partly redundant. A consequence is that it might not be as easy to work with GDELT data as with other event datasets.

Phoenix

Phoenix is the newest of the major event databases. It is the only one whose software and data processing workflow is fully open source. It is maintained by the Open Event Data Alliance (OEDA), a US-based non-profit organization (which consists of several US academics, among other contributors).

Several OEDA's archive files for the period 1945–2015 include millions of events extracted from 14 million news stories; the archive data was produced using NLP software to analyse content from the *New York Times* (1945–2005), the BBC Monitoring's Summary of World Broadcasts (1979–2015) and the CIA's Foreign Broadcast Information Service (1995–2004). The more recent "Real-time" (Phoenix_RT) dataset is updated every day since October 2017. Table 8.2 shows a sample event which occurred in June 2019; the first row "code" refers to CAMEO code 190: "Use conventional military force, not specified below".

Table 8.2 Sample violent event from Phoenix database

code	190
src_actor	IRN
tgt_actor	USA
country_code	IRN
year	2019
month	06
day	20
date8_val	2019-06-20
date8	20190620
id	5d0b0a1a230d874052550a14_1
source	IRNMIL
src_agent	MIL
latitude	35.69439
longitude	5.42151
src_other_agent	
geoname	Tehran
quad_class	4
source_text	australia_smh_world
root_code	19
tgt_other_agent	
target	USASPY
goldstein	-10
tgt_agent	SPY
url	http://www.smh.com.au/world/iran-claims-to-have-shot-down-a-spy-us-drone-20190620-p51zmf.html

Databases for defence studies 141

Given the complexity of maintaining a system to store and access big data, the Phoenix database provides a way to directly access a subset of events.[4]

We now look at subsets of this large dataset. There are 218,000 events with the US as an actor for the 18 months starting January 2018 and ending June 2019. The following chart displays a subset of these data, showing only events for which the US are the actor and Iran the target of the action. For each month, an histogram shows the number of events, summarized by their Goldstein score (from -10, the most conflictive types of events; to +10, most cooperative type).

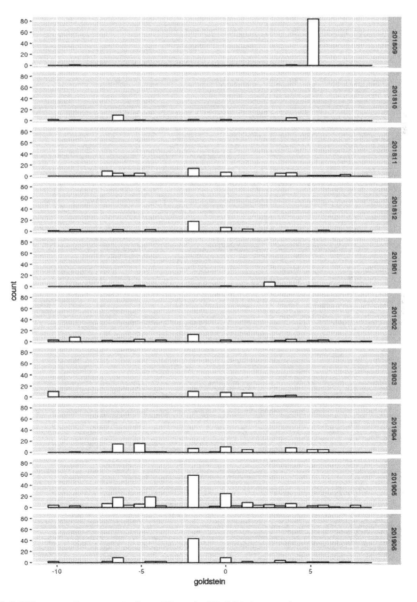

Figure 8.6 US versus Iran events from Phoenix (Goldstein score)

We can see from the chart that the US authored many cooperative events targeted at Iran in September 2018. On the contrary, in June 2019, most US-Iran events were classified with a Goldstein score of -2; these June 2019 events fall into one of the following CAMEO categories: Disapprove (110), Criticize or denounce (111), Accuse (112); an extract of these events (for the second half of June 2019) is listed in Table 8.3 (only actors, dates and URLs are shown here; the full list of fields can be seen in Table 8.2).

Limitations of Big Data and NLP

While apparently appealing, Big Data (and methods that can generate or process those data, such as NLP) have their limitations. The human languages are still not fully understood by robots; workflows often start by machine-translating texts into English, which adds to the imprecision. For instance, surprisingly, the ICEWS database says

Table 8.3 US/Iran event with Goldstein score of -2, second half of June 2019

src_actor	tgt_actor	date8	url
USA	IRN	20190619	https://www.nytimes.com/2019/06/19/world/middleeast/navy-tanker-iran-evidence.html?emc=rss&partner=rss
USA	IRN	20190619	https://www.bangkokpost.com/world/1698064/iran-categorically-rejects-us-tanker-attack-allegations
USA	IRN	20190619	https://www.bangkokpost.com/news/world/1696616/pompeo-vows-us-will-guarantee-passage-through-strait-of-hormuz
USA	IRN	20190619	https://www.dw.com/en/germany-says-there-is-strong-evidence-iran-behind-tanker-attacks/a-49248524?maca=en-rss-en-all-1573-rdf
USA	IRN	20190619	http://www.smh.com.au/world/iran-and-us-move-closer-to-a-flashpoint-as-tensions-spike-20190618-p51yux.html
USA	IRN	20190619	https://www.telegraph.co.uk/news/2019/06/17/iran-gives-europe-10-days-save-nuclear-deal/
USA	IRN	20190619	https://www.telegraph.co.uk/news/2019/06/17/iran-gives-europe-10-days-save-nuclear-deal/
USA	IRN	20190619	https://www.telegraph.co.uk/news/2019/06/17/iran-gives-europe-10-days-save-nuclear-deal/
USA	IRN	20190620	https://www.bbc.co.uk/news/world-middle-east-48700965
USA	IRN	20190620	https://www.nation.co.ke/news/world/Iran-says-has-shot-down-US-drone-over-its-territory–state-TV/1068–5164236-g3tjkaz/index.html
USA	IRN	20190620	http://www.rte.ie/news/world/2019/0620/1056415-iran-us-drone/
USA	IRN	20190620	https://www.theeastafrican.co.ke/news/world/Iran-shot-down-US-drone/4552918–5164276-qcg84x/index.html
USA	IRN	20190620	https://www.nytimes.com/2019/06/20/world/middleeast/iran-drone-united-states.html?emc=rss&partner=rss
USA	IRN	20190620	http://www.hurriyetdailynews.com/iran-says-has-shot-down-us-drone-over-its-territory-state-tv-144335

Source: Extracted by the author from ICEWS (Althaus et al. (2017a), retrieved 8 July 2019).

```sql
SELECT event_date, source_name, cameo_code, event_text, target_name, publisher, country FROM events
WHERE event_date > 20190515 AND source_name like "%Le Pen%";
```

event_date	source_name	cameo_code	event_text	target_name	publisher	country
20190518	Marine Le Pen	042	Make a visit	Estonia	Baltic Daily	Estonia
20190518	Marine Le Pen	051	Praise or endorse	Russia	Baltic Daily	Estonia
20190518	Marine Le Pen	051	Praise or endorse	Crimea	Baltic Daily	Estonia
20190518	Marine Le Pen	010	Make statement	Matteo Salvini	Deutsche Welle	Belgium
20190524	Marine Le Pen	010	Make statement	France	Associated Press Newswires	France
20190526	Marine Le Pen	190	Use conventional military force	Emmanuel Macron	Agence France-Presse	France
20190526	Marine Le Pen	190	Use conventional military force	Emmanuel Macron	Daily Star	France
20190526	Marine Le Pen	190	Use conventional military force	Emmanuel Macron	Agence France-Presse	France
20190526	Marine Le Pen	172	Impose administrative sanctions	Legislature (France)	Agence France-Presse	France
20190527	Marine Le Pen	010	Make statement	Emmanuel Macron	Irish Times	France
20190607	Marine Le Pen	121	Reject material cooperation	Lawmaker (France)	Agence France-Presse	France

Figure 8.7 Sample query and result from the ICEWS database
Source: SQL code (top part) by the author; data (lower part) from ICEWS.

that French nationalist political leader Marine Le Pen "used conventional military force" against the French President (Figure 8.7).

ICEWS does not provide the full text of sources used (for copyright reasons); reading the news for that day allowed us to strongly suspect the following, which is just the most likely explanation of this erroneous classifications. Marine Le Pen was reported several times by the French newspapers to "tirer à boulet rouge". The French wording "tirer à boulet rouge" (literally "to fire red hot cannon balls") refers to a warfare technique used between the 16th and 19th centuries; nowadays, it is a colloquial expression which generally means "to launch a verbal attack" or "to severely criticize". Examples like this one are numerous in the three databases mentioned here, as well as the large number of duplicates in this type of databases.

There are other limitations, for instance: the sensitivity to fake news and to rumours; the selection bias (more sources are available for countries whose official language is English, as well as for developed countries with well-established press and media entities); the quality bias (sources in English will be better analysed by the robots). Geolocation is often the data with the worst quality (often, the location coded is not the location of the event, but that of the news agency). Hence, depending on the application, it might be wise to rely on human analysts to double-check the events classified by these platforms ... noting that the mere purpose of these projects are to save on time by human analysts. In some cases, data from crowd-sourcing can get early data in emergency situations (Corban et al. 2010) or help train robots (Florczyk et al. 2014). Yet, creating databases based on human analysis is often necessary; we present some guidelines in the next section.

Guidelines for the creation of databases in defence studies

Most of the advice given here also apply to contributing to existing databases, or improving them (in scope or details).

Collaboration

Expanding an existing database

In some cases, a careful review of existing databases allows not the creation of a new database, but instead expand or improve an existing one. With the increasing popularity of the principles of open data, a database whose objectives are close to those required for a given project might already exist and be publicly available. If not, it could be useful to ask partner organizations about relevant projects; for instance, a defence ministry needing a new database could ask defence ministries of allied countries whether they already have such a database. In some cases, the allies or partners might not be in a position to share the data they own at the time of request, but may share the database specifications (definitions of concepts, codebook, data collection procedures, technical specifications ...). Hence, in Kucera et al. (2011), we built and expanded ACLED's codebook, which in turn took advantage of our previous work (Kauffmann 2008a).

The challenge of intersubjectivity

Intersubjectivity can be defined as "the ability to replicate the same data set by using the same coding rules and to replicate the identical hypothesis using that data or another comparable data set" (Eberwein 2008: 15). A robust way to get intersubjectivity of complex data related to security and defence is to go through a collaborative data collection and validation process.

By definition, many databases related to international security contain data on several countries. Due to the degree of specialization required and to linguistic barriers, the data collection task can rarely be done by a single investigator. Collaborative methods must be used. Horizontal split involves asking each investigator to work on only one or a few countries, based on their regional areas of expertise. For instance, the ACLED (2019a) team includes about 50 researchers located in a dozen countries, including 6 regional or national research managers, and a dozen research coordinators/directors with no regional focus. The creation of the Resource Governance Index (RGI) 2017, showing inter alia whether natural resources are diverted by military dictatorships, is a more extreme example of massive division of labor: 150 local experts based in 81 individual countries, plus more than a dozen global staff (Bailey (2017)).

Workflows

Many teams doing research or building composite indicators on general international issues fully publish background materials, including answers to questionnaires made by national experts. The case of defence and security databases is often different: even when some output aims at being published, the background/raw material is often kept private for security reasons (for instance for the safety of the researchers, or to keep the raw data private). Online platforms have several advantages over simpler workflows based on sending email:

- It is easier to encrypt a single database on a single server than all the files on the computers of all the contributors.

- It is easier to encrypt the communication of all contributors, between their web browser and the server (using standard https protocol), than encrypting all the emails sent (because various contributors may use email accounts from various domains, accessed from various email clients, the latter storing locally their data in various ways).
- It is easier to get a centralized data backup that is secure (resilient to hardware or software failure and to malicious attacks), than tens or hundreds of decentralized backups.

Hence, when no validation is required, online forms (e.g. LimeSurvey) suffice. Some of these systems can be fine-tuned, configured or extended to enable functionalities resembling those of a BPM system, for instance with plug-ins and/or a token system (as in Kauffmann et al, 2014). However, those solutions lack the power of dedicated systems such as Business Process Management (BPM). Nafie (2016) shows that several open source Workflow Management Systems (BonitaBPM, Joget) are on par or superior to proprietary software. Figure 8.8 shows the three-stage process of a data collection system (two validators) built at the Université Grenoble Alpes with BonitaBPM to translate a database on nonviolent actions.

Facilitating traceability

Facilitating traceability necessitates to write a detailed codebook and, where possible, to give access to primary or secondary data used (see below). We developed elsewhere other methods that are useful in related matters, to ensure the compatibility with other datasets, methods and software, the transparency of procedures, the automatic versioning of data, and the ways to facilitate alternate ways to process the raw data (Kauffmann 2008b; Barnier 2018: 63–67, 257–280).

Codebook content

Creating a codebook necessitates a review of the existing databases and a careful reading of existing codebooks, for instance ACLED (2019b) or Althaus et al. (2017b). Then, creating a draft codebook is advised. It is good practice to test the draft codebook on a limited sample, with several analysts studying the same events or cases, and compare the results. For instance, if the new database is a terrorism event data based on OSINT with three types of terrorist acts, the research supervisor(s) should select six events (two of each types), 12 news sources or more (at least 2 per event), and give this material to at least 2 analysts, working independently. Once the analysts have finished their work, comparing the results and discussing them should help refine the codebook.

The codebook should clearly define any concept, and all codes and abbreviation used. When there are corner cases or situations where difficult interpretation could be involved, it is advised to give clear guidelines and decision rules, as in ACLED (2019a: 11):

> Violence against civilians
>
> ACLED defines 'Violence against civilians' as violent events where an organized armed group deliberately inflicts violence upon unarmed non-combatants. By definition, civilians are unarmed and cannot engage in political violence. The perpetrators of such acts include state forces and their affiliates, rebels, militias, and external/other forces.

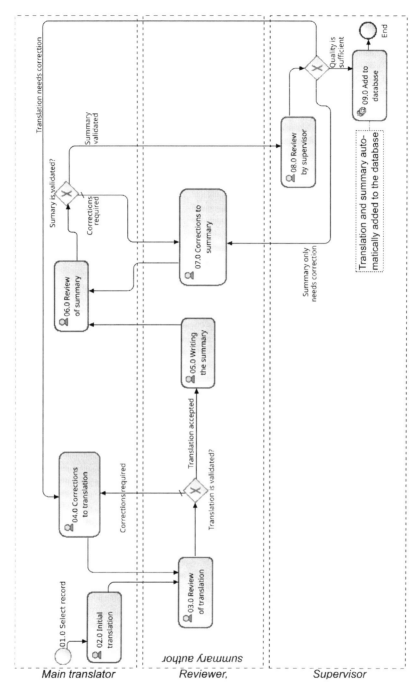

Figure 8.8 Collaborative validation workflow for a database in defence studies
Source: Author's diagram made in BonitaBPM.

In cases where the identity and actions of the victims are in question (e.g. the target may be employed as a police officer), ACLED determines that if a person is harmed or killed while unarmed and unable to either act defensively or counter-attack, this is an act of 'Violence against civilians'.

By definition, some of these guidelines are arbitrary. A precise, detailed decision rule (which may sometimes seem inappropriate in particular cases) is always better than a vague definition which would leave too much appreciation freedom to the analyst.

The concept of "intersubjectivity" is related to the acknowledgement that "objectivity" is a relative concept since "full objectivity" cannot be attained. The following guidelines is useful: imagine you ask the following people to record a given violent event: a relative of the victim, the perpetrator or one of their ally, a local journalist, a soldier of an international peacekeeping operation. They have access to the same pieces of information; how is it likely that they would all record the event in the same way? If the guidelines are good, then they should have little to no interpretation freedom and all coders would end up with the same result (provided they follow the guidelines).

Access to sources

Wherever possible, primary sources should be rendered accessible. For copyright reasons, it is usually not possible to redistribute entire news articles. However, the following can generally be done:

- Provide a summary of news articles used.
- Provide a short extract of news articles used. This exception to the law of copyright is known as "fair use" in the United States, "fair dealing" in many other countries. For instance, in most countries and cases, it would probably be authorized to provide the sentence that served to code each event in ICEWS, GDELT, Phoenix and the Iraq Body Count.
- Make an online backup of all online resources found (pages, reports, videos etc.), using the Internet Archive service (https://archive.org/).

Database security

Database systems hosting large amounts of data or multiple interrelated data sets can be complex or impossible to setup, populate and maintain for a single user. Hence, such database systems are most commonly hosted on centralized servers, with data transiting to multiple users through a local network or the Internet.

This makes such systems vulnerable to cybersecurity breaches. In 2003, the SQL Slammer worm affected 75,000 Microsoft database servers in 10 minutes, including at Microsoft's premises (Schwartz 2003), caused air flights cancellation and rendered inoperant many ATMs, one 911 call centre and one nuclear power plant control system (Erbschloe 2004).

Many of these attacks can be avoided by following two pieces of advice: update database software (a patch to the Slammer vulnerability had been released six months before); change the default database password with a complex one.

Conclusion

Progress is under way: the 2007 NATO Advanced Research Workshop on methodologies for building conflict databases began to list a number of good practices (Kauffmann 2008a), which were gradually applied in several databases over the next decade. However, when comparing defence studies with other fields, it must be noted that significant progress is still needed in terms of concept definition, data collection and standardization; verifiability, transparency and documentation of classification procedures; interoperability of storage and analysis tools; and creation of efficient data visualization tools. This is true in a wide range of areas, for example: victims of armed conflict (including deaths, internal displacement (IDMC 2016), sexual abuse, etc.), the arms trade, international sanctions, cyber security regulations, etc.

While examples in this chapter were largely taken from the academic field, military departments suffer from similar issues. According to a report to the US Congress, the "lack of reliable data hampered decision-making in Afghanistan: DOD did not have the right information systems or data architecture, existing data was not always sufficiently reliable; existing data was not always used by decision makers" (Schwartz 2016).

For improvements to occur, "the search of innovative approaches for conflict prevention and management of the conflicts should take into account the development of the new technologies that have proved to be efficient for data collection and processing" (Kemper et al. 2011). Remote sensing, Big Data and NLP are relatively new in the field of defence studies, and could help build databases in fields where they are almost absent, for instance that of massive nonviolent actions in conflict resolution (Kauffmann 2017).

Notes

1 Source: e-mail exchange between the author of this chapter and the Iraq Body Count team, January 2008.
2 To overcome this problem, our research team, thanks to a partnership between the University of Grenoble and an NGO (the School of Peace), launched the Peace PRISM system in 2009; it is to our knowledge the only web platform of its kind that correctly manages fluctuating borders; open-source, it has been actively improved since September 2018 as part of the Cybis project.
3 In June 2019, out of the top 10 database systems (according to https://db-engines.com/en/ranking, 6 are relational databases management systems (RDBMS) that use SQL; they represent 84% of the usage of the top-10 systems.
4 In our experience, this proved to be easier to use and more efficient than working with ICEWS and GDELT. For instance, to get all June 2019 US events from the Phoenix database using the UTDEventData R package, the following R code is enough (a free API key is required):
subset_US_June2019 <- pullData(utd_api_key="your_API_key", table_name="Phoenix_rt", country=list('USA'), start='20190601', end='20190630', citation=F)

References

ACLED (2019a). *About ACLED*, available online: https://www.acleddata.com/about-acled/; https://www.linkedin.com/company/acleddata/people/.
ACLED (2019b). *Armed Conflict Location & Event Data Project (ACLED) Codebook*, available online: https://www.acleddata.com/wp-content/uploads/dlm_uploads/2017/10/ACLED_Codebook_2019FINAL_pbl.pdf.
Althaus, S., Bajjalieh, J., Carter, J., Peyton, B., Shalmon, D. (2017a). *Cline Center Historical Phoenix Event Data. v.1.0.0.* Cline Center for Advanced Social Research, available online: http://www.clinecenter.illinois.edu/data/event/phoenix/.

Althaus, S., Bajjalieh, J., Carter, J., Peyton, B., Shalmon, D. (2017b). *Cline Center Historical Phoenix Event Data Variable Descriptions. v.1.0.0.* Cline Center for Advanced Social Research, available online: http://www.clinecenter.illinois.edu/data/event/phoenix/.

Baghishov, E. (2019). Foreign Ministry: Iran warns those who intend to attack country's territory. *Trend News Agency (Azerbaijan)*, 20 June, available online: https://en.trend.az/iran/politics/3078966.html.

Bailey, L. (2017). *Sixty-Six Countries Struggling with Oil, Gas and Mining Governance - Resource Governance Index.* Press Release. London, Natural Resource Governance Institute, available online: https://resourcegovernance.org/news/sixty-six-countries-struggling-oil-gas-and-mining-governance-resource-governance-index.

Barnier, J. (2018). *Introduction à R et au Tidyverse,* available online: https://halshs.archives-ouvertes.fr/halshs-01925234.

Corban, C., Lemoine, G., Kauffmann, M. (2010). Can real-time crisis SMS messages help in diagnosing the spatial distribution of structural damage? Analysis of the relationship between the distribution of damage and the location of SMS messages sent during the Haiti crisis, 117–125. In: *Proceedings of the 2nd International Workshop on Validation of Geo-Information Products for Crisis Management - VALgEO 2010*, European Commission.

Eberwein, W.-D. (2008). The creation and use of data: Scientific requirements and political utility, 13–27. In: Kauffmann, M. (Ed.). (2008). *Building and Using Datasets on Armed Conflicts*, Amsterdam, IOS Press.

Eck, K. (2005). *A Beginner's Guide to Conflict Data: Finding and Using the Right Dataset.* UCDP Paper1. University of Uppsala, available online: http://www.pcr.uu.se/publications/UCDP_pub/UCDP_paper1.pdf.

Eck, K. (2008). An overview and typology of conflict data: The advantages of data diversity, 29–40. In: Kauffmann, M. (Ed.) (2008). *Building and Using Datasets on Armed Conflicts*, Amsterdam, IOS Press.

Erbschloe, M. (2004). *Trojans, Worms, and Spyware: A Computer Security Professional's Guide to Malicious Code*, Oxford, Elsevier.

Florczyk, A., Kemper, T., Kauffmann, M., Soille, P. (2014). VGI in automatic information retrieval from Big RS Data. In: *GIScience 2014 Workshop "Role of Volunteered Geographic Information in Advancing Science: Effective Utilization"*, Vienna, Austria, available online: https://pdfs.semanticscholar.org/9930/11c12b82c837b0fb459f10a5b6e62e419317.pdf.

GDELT (2015). *Announcing The GDELT Full Text Search API*, available online: https://blog.gdeltproject.org/announcing-the-gdelt-full-text-search-api/.

Gleditsch, K., Ward, M. (1999). A revised list of independent states since the Congress of Vienna. *International Interactions*, 25, (4), 393–413.

Halkia, S., Ferri, S., Joubert-Boitat, I., Saporiti, F., Kauffmann, M. (2017). *The Global Conflict Risk Index (GCRI) Regression Model: Data Ingestion, Processing, and Output Methods.* JRC technical report JRC108767, European Commission, JRC.

IBC (2010). *Iraq War Logs: What the Numbers Reveal*, available online: https://www.iraqbodycount.org/analysis/numbers/warlogs/.

IDMC (2016). *Global Report on Internal Displacement – GRID 2016*, Geneva, Internal Displacement Monitoring Centre, available online: http://www.internal-displacement.org/assets/publications/2016/2016-global-report-internal-displacement- IDMC.pdf.

Kauffmann, M. (2004). *Les Organisations Économiques Internationales face aux Dépenses et à la Sécurité Militaires: Banque Mondiale, FMI et GATT/OMC.* Doctoral dissertation, Université Pierre Mendès France, available online: http://www.theses.fr/2004GRE21010.

Kauffmann, M. (2006). *Gouvernance Économique Mondiale et Conflits Armés: Banque Mondiale, FMI et GATT-OMC.* La Librairie des Humanités. Editions L'Harmattan.

Kauffmann, M. (2007). Short term and event interdependence matter: A political economy continuous model of civil war. *Peace Economics, Peace Science and Public Policy*, 13(1), 19.

Kauffmann, M. (Ed.). (2008a). *Building and Using Datasets on Armed Conflicts*. NATO Science for Peace and Security Series - E: Human and Societal Dynamics, Amsterdam, IOS Press/NATO, available online: http://ebooks.iospress.nl/volume/building-and-using-datasets-on-armed-conflicts.

Kauffmann, M. (2008b). Enhancing openness and reliability in conflict dataset creation, 107–132. In: Kauffmann, M. (Ed) (2008). *Building and Using Datasets on Armed Conflicts*, Amsterdam, IOS Press.

Kauffmann, M. (2017). Resilience to oppression and to violent conflict escalation through nonviolent action, 82–91. In: *The 2nd International Workshop on Modelling of Physical, Economic and Social Systems for Resilience Assessment*, European Commission, 2. Ispra, available online: https://www.researchgate.net/publication/334400567_Resilience_to_oppression_and_to_violent_conflict_escalation_through_nonviolent_action.

Kauffmann, M., Chenu, D., Tokarski, G. (2014). *LimeSurvey-Workflow. A Set of Tools to Help Using LimeSurvey to Design Surveys Collaboratively Answered by Several People*, available online: https://github.com/mayeulk/LimeSurvey-workflow.

Kemper, T., Kauffmann, M., Sebahara, P., Kayitakire, F. (2011). Conflicts and political crises. In: *GMES and Africa - Summary of the Baseline Action Plan*, 29. Global Monitoring for Environment and Security, European Commission, available online: https://www.researchgate.net/publication/318184591_Conflicts_and_political_crises.

Kleinfeld, R. (2017). Why is it so difficult to count dead people? *BBC News*, available online https://www.bbc.com/news/world-41038987.

Kreutz, J. (2008). Calling a conflict a conflict: Violence and other aspects of war, 49–61. In: Kauffmann, M. (Ed.). (2008). *Building and Using Datasets on Armed Conflicts*, Amsterdam, IOS Press.

Kucera, J., Kauffmann, M., Duta, A.-M., Tarrida Soler, I., Tenerelli, P., Trianni, G., Hale, G., Rizzo, L., Ferri, S. (2011). *Armed Conflicts and Natural Resources*, Brussels, European Commission.

Nafie, F. M. (2016). The comparison of the workflow management systems Bizagi, Arabdox, Bonita and Joget. *International Journal of Engineering Science Invention*, 5(5), 26–31.

Richardson, L. (1948). Variation of the frequency of fatal quarrels with magnitude. *Journal of the American Statistical Association*, 244, 523–546.

Richardson, L. (1960). *Arms and Insecurity: A Mathematical Study of the Causes and Origins of War*, London, Stevens and Sons Publishers.

Schrodt, Ph. (2011). *Automated Production of High-Volume, Near-Real-Time Political Event Data*. Pennsylvania State University, available online: https://pdfs.semanticscholar.org/2231/7c1fb2e0339771cb6f263e58c31ea421054c.pdf.

Schwartz, J. (2003). Worm hits Microsoft, which ignored own advice. *The New York Times*, 28 January, available online: https://www.nytimes.com/2003/01/28/business/technology-worm-hits-microsoft-which-ignored-own-advice.html.

Schwartz, M. (2016). *Using Data to Improve Defence Acquisitions: Background, Analysis, and Questions for Congress*. R44329, Congressional Research Service.

Singer, D., Small, M. (1966). Formal alliances, 1815–1939: A quantitative description. *Journal of Peace Research*, 3(1), 1–31.

Sorokin, P. (1937). *Social and Cultural Dynamics*. 4 vols., New York, American Book.

Steinert-Threlkeld, Z. (2013). *The Arab Spring and GDELT*, available at: http://zacharyst.com/2013/09/27/the-arab-spring-and-gdelt/.

Suzuki, S., Krause, V., Singer, D. (2002). The correlates of war project: A bibliographic history of the scientific study of war and peace, 1964–2000. *Conflict Management and Peace Science*, 19(2), 69–107.

UNDP (2018). *Human Development Report 2018*, available online: http://hdr.undp.org/en/year/2018.

Ward, M. (2013). GDELT and ICEWS, a short comparison. *Predictive Heuristics*, available online: https://blog.predictiveheuristics.com/2013/10/17/gdelt-and-icews-a-short-comparison/.

Wright, Q. (1942). *A Study of War*, Chicago, University of Chicago Press.

9 Economics methods for defence studies

Julien Malizard

Introduction

According to the latest figures published by the think tank, Stockholm International Peace Research Institute (SIPRI), world defence spending (DS) was USD 1,750 billion in 2018, which is the highest level in history, surpassing the levels previously observed during the Cold War. On average, the share of DS is close to 2% and seems rather small compared to previous periods (Sandler and George 2016). There are microeconomic figures corresponding to these macroeconomic figures and, in particular, those related to the equipment market. From SIPRI figures on the defence industry, the total turnover of the top 100 is close to USD 450 billion. Flows of trade are difficult to measure but a recent estimation indicates that arms exports are less than USD 100 billion.

Given the economic importance of the defence sector, economic evaluation of defence matters a great deal. Of course, the main goal of defence is to provide security, and economic factors should play a limited role. However, given the importance of DS at the macroeconomic and microeconomic levels, the relationship between economics and strategy is of interest.[1] Economic literature provides useful information on many aspects of defence policy, such as the armament industry, defence budget or economic impact of defence activities. The aim of this chapter is to discuss the economic approach of defence studies and to review briefly the main themes of the academic literature in economics.

Following Robbins, "Economics is the science which studies human behavior as a relationship between ends and scarce means which have alternative uses" (1935, p. 16). Defence economics should not be different than economics: an economic approach requires a comparison of ends and means. However, the key issue is to convert military ends and means into economic ends and means. Strategic means are obviously difficult to evaluate and, thus, economists often rely on defence policy in order to investigate military ends. Military means are more easily converted into economic means because there is a price tag for each item.

The relationship between military ends and means has been investigated by Malizard (2019). He stresses the importance of "strategic autonomy" for the French defence policy that provides the framework for strategic ends. Strategic autonomy is barely defined, but refers to nuclear deterrence, the choice to conduct (alone or in a coalition) a large spectrum of military operations, and the necessity to rely on French equipment; the French interests include not only its national territory, but also overseas departments. Given these ends, France armed forces require a large spectrum of equipment. The military means (in terms of soldiers and equipment) are then converted into economic means: a large defence budget compared to other European countries, and an independent defence and industrial base (DIB). These economic means are more easily analysed by economists as they refer to the budget (macroeconomics) or industry (microeconomics), which constitute the two main areas in economics.

Standard economic evaluation is based on "cost-benefit approach" (CBA). For each alternative, CBA requires data on what is paid (cost) and what is gained (benefit). The net result provides an economic rationale for each alternative and one may rank all the alternatives to get the best solution, which is called "an optimum" in economics. In macroeconomics, such a method is difficult to apply because there is no data on each alternative; in such a case, the solution is to directly analyse the effect of one variable on another, possibly by directly comparing the two alternatives.

Unfortunately, CBA cannot be used for defence economics. The main reason is that the benefits are not measurable. Consider a rise in DS by USD 1. How will this rise affect security? Does this dollar translate into something more than, less than, or equal to one dollar in terms of security? These questions remain unsolved as security does not have (monetary) proxies.

This chapter is about the main economic approaches applied to the defence sector. By doing so, I follow closely the Intrilligator's definition (1990, p. 3):

> Defence economics is concerned with that part of the overall economy involving defence-related issues, including the level of defence spending, both in total and as a fraction of the overall economy; the impact of defence expenditure, both domestically for output and employment and internationally for impacts on other nations; the reasons for the existence and size of the defence sector; the relation of defence spending to technological change; and the implications of defence spending and the defence sector for international stability and instability.

As Smith (2009, p. 2) points out "Defence and peace economics, like much of the rest of economics, uses a mathematical and statistical language that makes it incomprehensive to many who might be interested but do not have a quantitative training". This chapter is written in a manner so that it can be fully comprehended by all researchers, whatever their level of competence in mathematics.

Economic reasoning is well established in, at least, what is called "mainstream economics": markets provide a useful framework to investigate economic behaviour because this is the best way to achieve "optimality", except in certain cases, such as externality, asymmetry of information, or public goods. Economic modelling relies on theoretical models that use the concept of markets; then, the model is confronted with data. One issue is to know what should come first between data and model. Data are not neutral per se and reflect theoretical considerations. This point is worth remembering as many economists do not wonder how data are built. With these remarks in mind, I first discuss economic modelling applied to the defence sector and, second, data related to defence economics.

The chapter is organized as follows. The first section provides an insight on "how much is enough", which, as already discussed, is the key issue for economists. The second section presents the main theoretical approaches and the third section the main empirical analysis. As the scope of economics is vast, a selection of the most investigated topics in defence economics are presented in the fourth section. The final section concludes this chapter with a discussion of the future of defence economics.

The main issue: how much is enough?

A lot of actions can be analysed through economic thinking. The decision to do something is related to its costs and benefits. As long as the costs are smaller than the benefits, the action is called profitable. Difficulties arise when the researcher must consider all the direct and indirect costs and benefits and translate them into a single measure, such as a monetary one.

Markets are among one of the most useful concepts used by economists. Markets help in determining both the supply and demand for a single good. The interaction of supply and demand may lead to an equilibrium, with an "optimal" quantity of the good supplied and bought at a certain price. Markets allow economists to measure the monetary relationships between two agents. Defence industry and labour forces constitute the supply side of the market as they provide inputs for defence. Governments represent the demand side of the market as they provide security.

Economists evaluate complex consequences. These consequences can be either positive or negative and one has to take into account all these elements in an economic evaluation. Some consequences are easier to capture than others. In the case of defence, the consequences are mostly non-economic. In particular, the primary aim in defence is to ensure security. However, the links between defence, which can be measured from a macroeconomic perspective with a defence budget, and security cannot be measured precisely. Following Smith (2009), defence activities rely on inputs, such as soldiers, equipment, experience, or trainings. Defence inputs[2] are "bought" by governments by utilizing their defence budget. These inputs are known, but the defence output is unknown. One cannot measure, in economic terms, defence capabilities except by estimating the inputs required for creating the said capability. Security can, thus, be considered the sum of all the capabilities needed, given a defence policy that is supposedly representative of citizens' preferences. From this point of view, security is the sum of goods and services provided by the "public planner" expressed in monetary terms.

In the case of defence, defence production remains unknown. For example, consider an increase of EUR 1 of the defence budget in France. What are the consequences for defence output? Are the inhabitants of France safer by EUR 1? For economists, there is no simple relationship between the amount of money spent on defence and security gained. If security is accurately provided, one empirical possibility is to measure the economic gain by comparing it to a hypothetical situation of conflict. This is difficult, given the methodological assumptions required to compute a situation that does not exist.

If security is not measurable, one may investigate the benefits of defence. According to Hartley (2012), the benefits of security are both economic and non-economic. Defence economics is mainly interested in economic benefits of defence, such as the defence sector's impact. Non-economic benefits are difficult to measure and, therefore, rarely evaluated.

The problem of measuring the benefits has a straightforward, but rather unsatisfying solution. Economists consider output to be equal to the sum of inputs. This solution is also applied to public spending in other sectors, particularly health and education; in these sectors, there is a "private" counterpart, whose effectiveness can be computed and compared with that of public spending. In defence, there are few private counterparts; these are mainly private military companies that are relevant for specific defence missions.

Finally, note that the problem implies flaws not only in macroeconomics, but also in microeconomics. On the macroeconomic side, the key issue is to investigate whether the size of the defence sector is appropriate, with respect to both budgetary and strategic constraints. On the microeconomic side, one major problem is to identify defence firms, which is quite difficult in the case of dual-use firms. More specifically, their inputs are potentially developed for military products, civil products, or both.

Building theoretical models

Economics relies on theoretical models to simplify social interactions between economic actors. The main goal of the models is to disentangle the main economic channels of interaction between these actors and, then, evaluate the best public policy, if required. Thus, economists have to identify the actors, how they are involved with each other, and the result of their interactions. By comparing the model's equilibrium with an optimal situation, one may gauge the pertinence of public interventions.

Markets are among the main formal approaches to discuss economic interactions and the way to reach an equilibrium. Markets aggregate both supply and demand and the interactions between generate an equilibrium of both price and quantity. If this equilibrium has undesirable properties, such as idle capacity, public policy intervention is needed.

Even if the defence sector is quite special, markets offer an interesting perspective for both macroeconomics and microeconomics. For instance, the demand for defence arises from government and is measured by DS; the supply side of defence is composed of all the sectors that provide inputs.

This section discusses how defence economists analyse the defence sector in terms of theoretical models. I assume that markets are useful in synthesizing this literature because they offer the possibility of discussing some general economic features. The concept of markets can be "aggregated" to analyse both the microeconomic and macroeconomic aspects.

Microeconomics

Microeconomics is the branch of economics that studies the interactions of individuals and firms within markets by choosing the optimal composition of scare resources that maximize utility (individuals) or profit (firms). It is widely accepted among economists that optimality and desirable outcomes may be reached through markets, but sometimes market failures arise, and then, public authorities must intervene to change individual behaviour.

Conceptually, individual behaviours are determined by a maximization problem. An economic agent seeks to maximize its utility or profit under budget or costs constraints. Optimal behaviour is determined thanks to this problem and leads to a situation where marginal cost is equal to marginal benefit.

Several assumptions ("perfect competition") are made, such as symmetry of information or multiplicity of actors (on both demand and supply sides), so that they do not influence the optimal price. Within this framework, markets are the best way to achieve optimal outcomes. In this context, prices reflect incentives. However, there are several cases of market failure, such as externalities, public goods or asymmetry of information, that require public intervention.

DS is considered a public good. Because of its features of non-rivalry and non-excludability, this is a special type of good in economics. Non-rivalry implies that the consumption of this good by an economic agent is not at the expense of the consumption of the same good by some other economic agent. The property of non-excludability indicates that the consumption of this good does not require the consumer to pay for it (or no one can be excluded from its consumption). Rivalry and excludability define private goods. Common goods are a mixture of rivalry and non-excludability and club goods a mixture of non-rivalry and excludability.

Public goods cannot be provided by private players as they have no incentive to enter the market; given both non-excludability and non-rivalry, a firm is not able to make a profit. Public interventions are, then, required because governments may levy taxes to finance public goods. However, the features of public goods may also imply free riding, so that some countries in an alliance have an incentive to not provide the optimal level of DS.

The concept of public good implies that defence is provided collectively. This may involve the defence being provided directly by the public sector, by the private sector or by a mix of the two (Macdonald 2010). Defence remains a "final" public good, but one that requires a sum of private goods (e.g. military equipment for which there is both rivalry and exclusion) and human capital. From a practical point of view, it is a question of determining for the Ministry of Defense how much should be achieved "in-house" and which missions can be delegated to private sector companies (outsourcing). Traditionally, the private sector provides equipment, but since the end of the Cold War, many services have been carried out by external suppliers (i.e. clothing, catering). As Bellais et al. (2014) point out, the US and the UK practice outsourcing with a mixed record. Finally, some companies known as "private military companies" participate in defence missions, either alongside or replacing the regular forces. Singer (2001) recalls that they are used for operational activities, consulting (strategy and training) or operational and logistical support. The rise of these companies has led to a blurring of the line between regal and private activities (Markusen 2003) and hence justifies the need to regulate them.

A microeconomics-based approach is useful to analyse markets related to the provision of equipment or labour. In these markets, one has to identify the economic agents. In the case of equipment, a government is the buyer and the defence firms are the sellers. As explained by Sandler and Hartley (1995), this situation leads to a "monopsony" where there is only one buyer, but several sellers. Moreover, economics generally seeks to identify the best alternative from a set of different ones. In the case of defence, in many situations, there is only one choice. As argued by Hartley (2012), lack of incentives is likely to lead to inefficiencies.

Microeconomics theory fails to fully encompass security issues related to defence. Governments' goals are linked to not only the economy, but also strategic preferences. For instance, the equipment market in Europe exhibits low concentration, with national champions enjoying monopoly in their own country, but harsh competition in other markets. Economic theory indicates that this situation would require concentration to reduce production costs through economies of scale. As discussed by Belin et al. (2017), this situation is not likely to occur, given countries' preferences in terms of equipment. For example, strategic autonomy is the French's defence policy pillar; industrial nations, such as Germany, Italy, and the UK, use the defence sector as a way to do industrial policy, whereas other countries prefer American supplies. Moreover, in terms of use of equipment, individual choices are not identical, as shown by the multiple versions of the aircraft A400M.

Macroeconomics

As stressed in the introduction, the size of the defence sector is significant in terms of macroeconomic measures (GDP, public spending, and trade, to name a few), but some countries bear a greater "burden" than others. For example, in 2018, Oman spent 8.2% of its GDP on defence; this accounted for 19% of its public spending. Thus, it seems reasonable to question the influence of DS on the economy.

From a macroeconomic point of view, economists evaluate all the channels through which defence affects the global economy. Obviously, there are many channels – some are direct (such as the multiplier), whereas others are indirect ones. Summing up all the effects of the different channels may provide a measure of defence's influence. However, quantifying all the channels is difficult because it requires a vast amount of information. As a consequence, the economic literature focuses mainly on one channel. This subsection is based on the surveys by Dunne et al. (2005) and Malizard (2011). Three main channels have been identified.

The first channel is the "demand channel." It mainly relates to Keynesian theory. The basic idea is that an increase of DS implies an increase in GDP by a number called the multiplier. The existence and the size of this multiplier has been widely discussed by economists since the 2008 economic crisis; the key issue is to know whether the multiplier is below, equal to, or above 1. As part of public spending, DS may play a role. There is also a negative indirect impact to DS. As discussed by Smith (1980), DS and private investment compete for a fixed share of the savings, so that an increase in DS leads to less resources for investment because of the increase in the interest rate. This situation is called crowding-out and may reduce the final effect of DS from the demand side.

The second channel is the "supply channel". Rather than focusing on the quantity of DS, as in the demand channel, this channel analyses the quality of DS: does DS increase the quality of inputs? As discussed by Ruttan (2006), American DS led to several technological breakthroughs that have been reused in a civilian context. Others, such as Schumpeter (1934), consider that DS is unproductive. The final impact, then, depends on the quality of the final expense: defence R&D expenditure is more likely to generate a positive influence than defence compensation. Ram (1993) discusses at length the positive and negative supply-side impacts of DS and, in particular, the debate on technological spillovers and inefficiency of defence industries.

The last channel is called the "security channel" and relies mainly on the primary purpose of defence: ensuring security. Two opposite effects have been identified. In the first, a country may gain greater security when DS is increased because rule of law, especially property laws, is enforced. The second one is related to arms race because an increase in a neighbour's DS can be perceived as a threat to national security that requires an increase in DS by the country under threat; consequently, the level of DS can be above the optimal level, leading to major inefficiencies. The final effect is the sum of these two effects, but given the absence of data for measuring security, this issue remains unresolved.

The way these channels are modelled is crucial. Focusing on a specific channel may imply an incomprehensive approach. Depending on the preferences of the researcher, this can lead to biased results. In this vein, Malizard (2011) shows that within the inconclusive macroeconomic literature, regularities in terms of results arise when papers are classified according to the underlying theoretical model. Modelling choices are not neutral.

For the purpose of interpretation, economic models tend to distinguish between short- and long-run effects. The former is mainly related to the demand-side channel, whereas the supply-side channel witnesses the latter. The basic idea behind this interpretation is the following: a DS shock may affect the economy in the short run because of extra public spending flowing into the economy – this is particularly useful when unemployment prevails. In the long run, the effect is more likely to arise because of changes in productivity or technological spillovers.

Empirical issues

Having described the theoretical models in the previous section, the next step is to check whether the conclusions of these models are in line with data. Since the end of World War II, national accounts have gained credibility and data are available to the scientific community. Notably, this allows economists to publish more papers based on empirical analysis (Angrist et al. 2017) and provide more insightful recommendations on public policy. Moreover, the development of econometric theory provides reliable tools to identify the causal relationship between two variables.

However, in defence studies, there still exist major gaps in measuring defence activities. For instance, there is no "defence sector" in national accounts. As mentioned in the first section, defence production is not measurable. Because the defence sector is characterized by secrecy, many of the measures used do not provide an accurate econometric analysis. Data exist but are subject to criticism. This section is about how data are used by defence economists despite the various limitations.

Two types of data are available. From a macroeconomic point of view, the main figures are defence budget and arms trade. From a microeconomic point of view, the key issue is to determine the turnover associated with defence activities in a company.

This section first discusses some relevant sources. Then, I briefly present the main problems associated with these data: perimeter, accuracy and econometric issues due to data limitations.

Data

Economists enjoy providing and using economic data. This is a language which also requires strong academic backgrounds to be comfortable with. However, there is little discussion among them on the appropriateness of these data because most papers are "technical", rather than being theory oriented. As stressed by Smith (1998, p. 423), "many articles give the impression that the authors have applied the statistical procedures without looking at the data". In this subsection, I review some main data sources.

Macroeconomic data

Quantitative measures of the defence sector rely mainly on defence budget or the size of the army, both in terms of personnel and equipment, and provide researchers the opportunity to discuss defence policy. Two main sources are worth mentioning. The first, SIPRI, has gained much of its visibility because of its long-lasting evaluation of defence budget, as well as that of arms transfers and defence industry. The International Institute for Strategic Studies (IISS) provides useful information with respect to the size of armed forces and defence budgets. Other sources, such as data published by national authorities in charge of DS, can also be mentioned.

Defining a defence budget, at least theoretically, seems easy, but there are numerous practical difficulties. One definition is commonly used by international organizations and is based on the NATO definition that includes operating costs (personnel and pensions), procurement, construction, and R&D. Statistics from the Ministry of Defense and other ministries can be used, as long as their budgets are aligned with those of military forces. Even if the definition appears clear, many problems arise when it comes to evaluating the budget, such as inclusion of paramilitary forces, direct funding of the defence industry through other public expenditures, peacekeeping operations, and so on. Malizard and Richter (2018) discuss the different sources of these problems in France and the UK and show major gaps between them that ultimately lead to different empirical estimates. It appears that, for France, DS is overestimated by SIPRI, but the NATO figures suffer from major breaks.

One major drawback of DS is that it is an imperfect measure of power and security. DS does not reflect the military capabilities of one country and the capabilities are subject to depreciation, which is not considered in official publications. The size of the armed forces is, then, a complement of DS because it provides useful information regarding the ratio of troops to equipment and, ultimately, military capacity.

Trade data are used to gauge the intensity of the arms trade between two nations. This kind of data requires information regarding the quantity of equipment (including all the intangibles, such as training, technological offsets, etc.), the price, whether the equipment is new or refurbished, and the time between order and delivery. It is crucial to get a single measure that encompasses all the production costs from different countries, with different production systems, as was the case in USA and USSR during the Cold War.

SIPRI is the international standard in arms trade data and serves as a primary source for the World Bank database. The database is rich enough to analyse trade flows between countries since 1950. SIPRI develops its own measures, such as trend indicator value (TIV), to compute trade. TIV does not measure the monetary value of the arms trade; rather, it relies on production costs for comparable features of specific arms. Other data sources, such as Arms Control and Disarmament Agency (ACDA) or national data, are not used in the literature given their lack of transparency and comparability (Malizard 2018).

Microeconomic data

It is worth remembering that DS has a microeconomic counterpart because public spending generates economic activities for firms or workers, both in the private and public sectors. In the case of defence, microeconomic data rely mainly, on defence firms.

Given its production volume and turnover, the defence industry is subject to numerous debates. These potential controversies require the most transparent and reliable data to perform an accurate empirical analysis. Two mains sources regarding the defence industry have been used in the economic literature. The first one is provided by SIPRI, which cover the top 100 defence firms, and discusses some parameters related to their performances; these include the turnover, the share of turnover because of military activities (which is, in a sense, one measure of the duality of a firm), and the number of employees. This database is easily downloadable from the SIPRI website and covers the period 2002–2017; older data are available in print in the form of SIPRI Yearbooks. The publications from *Defense News* are another source.

Although these data may be useful for quantitative analysis, they suffer from some limitations. First, the sample may be limited. Often, the time period covered is quite short and does not include the period of transition following the end of the Cold War that shaped the defence industry in terms of its concentration (Bellais et al. 2014). Besides, the ranking only includes 100 firms and, thus, neglects smaller firms, which could be potentially crucial for procurement. Second, the activities of firms are not decomposed into domestic turnover and external turnover; this, in turn, complicates the firm-level analysis of arms trade. Finally, for dual-product firms, the number of employees, R&D, and capital (i.e. the inputs) are not separated into civil and military outputs. This is a frustrating issue as economists cannot discuss the performance of firms by comparing inputs and outputs. One solution is to assume that the share of inputs is equal to the share of outputs. This solution is simple to implement but does not fully capture the process of production, especially the potential cross dependencies between civilian and military productions.

Problem with data

For empirical analysis, it is crucial to measure precisely the same economic phenomenon. Thus, cross-countries studies require a single measure of defence activities to avoid any bias of over- or under-estimation. Countries do not have the same interpretation of DS and, as already stressed earlier, international institutions such as SIPRI may lead to a bias. Moreover, for a single country, one may observe a break in the definition; for example, France's 2009 exclusion of its paramilitary forces (*gendarmerie*) from the defence category has not yet been corrected by NATO in its official statistics.

Different sources are used to compute DS. SIPRI lists three categories. Primary sources consist of budgetary documents provided by the government. Secondary sources are quotes from primary sources, such as NATO or IMF; other secondary sources are less reliable. According to Perlo-Freeman and Ferguson (2015), primary sources have increased since 1988 and constitute almost 80% of data in the most recent period; this gives confidence in the reliability of data. However, the authors warn the recent increasing trend of absence of data for numerous countries.

Cross-country comparisons are also complicated due to the purchasing parity conversion. A dollar bill may have different purchasing power in each country and standard market exchange rate does not adequately address this problem. One solution is to consider the purchasing power parity (PPP) exchange rate. As noted by Smith (2009, p. 91), the difference on converting Chinese DS from the market exchange rate to the PPP exchange rate is huge – the value of the latter is almost four times that of the former.

The last difficulty with data is comparison over time. Macroeconomic data are subject to major quantity and price changes over time. Thus, it is necessary to control for the change in price, captured by the GDP deflator, to give real values of the measured economic variable. In the case of defence, there is no "military deflator" and the common solution consists of using GDP deflator as a proxy for the military deflator. This solution is unsatisfactory because defence inflation appears to be higher than that indicated by the GDP deflator (Hartley 2016).

Opportunity costs are widely used by economists to discuss all available alternatives in making an economic decision. In the case of defence, one major issue is the impossibility to quantify all the alternatives: we observe DS or wars but there is no real situation in which there is no DS or the absence of conflict,[3] even if one can calculate counterfactuals to compare the alternatives.

Transparency is a key issue in DS. Many data are subject to classification because they are related to national security issues. The economic literature uses open source data when they exist; since the beginning of the 2010s, SIPRI does not provide any information on many Middle Eastern countries. Developing countries may either lack statistical institutions or, given the nature of their political regimes, lack the incentives to provide an accurate measure.

Trade data also suffer from severe limitations. Even if a large number of countries ratify the arms trade treaty, it seems that data still lack transparency. According to Malizard (2018), SIPRI data are a kind of "black box" offering few insights on the way data are computed. Further, because SIPRI uses TIV measures, rather than monetary ones, data are not comparable.

Econometrics is a useful tool as it relies on statistical routines to evaluate the significance of the relationship between different variables that are based on theoretical models. The development of new econometric approaches allows the researcher to apply more effective routines by improving the precision of the estimates. Given the power of the econometric methods, one can distinguish between correlation and causality, except in a case of theoretical misspecification.

Two types of econometric problems may arise: the consequences of measurement error due to data limitations and reverse causality. According to Smith (1998), empirical studies are more interested in "using cooking tricks" instead of amending the model to fit data. These tricks potentially lead researchers to use the best empirical results in terms of statistical significance given the potential publication bias with "star wars",[4] as stressed by Brodeur et al. (2016).

The data limitations that have been discussed above may have potentially huge consequences on econometric results. Greene (2003) shows that the estimates may suffer from a severe bias. There is no good solution to avoid this problem but checking the collected database and investigating sources to ensure that there are no breaks, is one of the obvious steps in any empirical analysis. Malizard and Richter (2018) indicate that different measures of DS lead to different conclusions about its economic impact.

Econometric analysis allows the researcher to investigate the causal influence in a given relationship by distinguishing endogenous (dependent) and exogenous (independent) variables. For instance, growth theory indicates that GDP is "explained" by investment and DS; however, it is as likely that GDP explains investment or DS, so that the variables considered exogenous variables prove to be endogenous. This is called "reverse causality". This problem is very serious in empirical economics and requires specific remedies. One of them is to consider whether the system formed by all the variables is endogenous (each variable is explained by all the others), but this solution needs many observations. Instrumental variables have been also used by econometricians; this involves a two-stage model in which one has to find an "instrument" that is related to exogenous variables, but not to the endogenous ones. In practice, finding a suitable instrument is difficult.

The defence economic literature, a critical survey

The defence economics literature embraces many different subjects incorporating economics tools relevant to the defence sector. I decided to focus on subjects that have been widely examined by numerous authors and correspond with the central features explained above: how do we deal with security issues without taking them accurately into account?

The outline of this section is the following. First, I discuss the literature on alliance with a specific focus on burden sharing. Second, I analyse arms trading and compare the causes and consequences. Third, I review the main results of the literature on the defence industry and R&D. Finally, I assess the economic impact of DS.

Alliance and burden sharing

Defence spending is considered a public good. Given its nature, public economic theory emphasizes that the government is the only agent that has the ability to pay for defence. The share of national wealth that is allocated to defence is subject to numerous factors (Smith 1989). One such factor is alliance membership.

Olson and Zeckhauser (1966) offered the first formal analysis of alliance using economic theory. The authors discussed the production of security from NATO and concluded that it is a pure public good. This good is produced at the expense of richer economies that bear a disproportionate share of the burden while smaller economics have a tendency to free-ride. Empirically, the authors show a significant correlation between the share of DS to GDP and gross national product (GNP) for each ally. This result is called the exploitation hypothesis.

However, after 1970, NATO changed its doctrine, and more recent contributions do not support the conclusion of Olson and Zeckhauser (see, for instance, the survey from Sandler and Hartley 2001). The change in doctrine led to different benefits for alliance members (deterrence, but also more local defence activities). Therefore, the costs of membership alliance are more aligned with the benefits, and the exploitation hypothesis no longer holds. For many scholars, the key issue now is to evaluate the degree of publicness of international security provided by an alliance (see Gates and Terasawa 2003).

From an empirical point of view, many researchers have addressed burden sharing within NATO. For instance, Khanna and Sandler (2002) computed a benefit function that includes GDP, population, and area and compare it with cost (which is simply the relative share of an ally's DS to the sum of all individual defence budgets). Until recently, these papers showed that benefits and costs are in line so that the exploitation hypothesis is rejected. However, a recent paper by Shimuzu and Sandler (2012) indicated that, since 2004, NATO has exhibited divergence between costs and benefits, and the authors conclude that there is a risk that NATO could become a two-tier alliance. The costs-benefits approach is simple and flexible enough to be extended to other alliances such as the EU (Kollias 2008).

Nonetheless, this approach suffers many drawbacks. Costs are mainly proxied by defence budgets, which do not have qualitative effects: France spends less than 2% of its GDP on defence, but its military capabilities are probably greater than Estonia, which respects the 2% criteria. Benefits are also subjective and subject to criticism: they mainly include what a country wants to protect (its population, its wealth, and its area), but do not reflect any preference in terms of defence policy such as interventions in military operations or contributions to international organizations.

Trade

Arms trade is controversial among economists; there is an obvious ethical concern given the nature of arms. Arms trade is related to the industrial organization of a country's defence sector but also to attitudes toward international security and international treaties. A critical question regarding arms trade is the following: what are the drivers that explain the export and import of arms? It is important to distinguish between economic and security factors. Another subject of debate among economists and social scientists, is related to the use of arms and whether arms trade has a stabilizing effect (i.e. deterring aggression) or a destabilizing effect (i.e. fuelling conflict).

Initially, it is appealing to analyse global arms trade as a market. One feature of arms exports relies on its extreme concentration. Only a few countries export arms: according to the SIPRI database, the top 10 countries exported 96% of global arms during the Cold War and 90% after the Cold War. The United States and the Union of Soviet Socialist Republics (USSR) (later, Russia) are the market leaders followed by some European countries. Emerging countries are still marginal (China ranked sixth after the Cold War), but their influence is growing. Turning to the demand side, arms imports are less concentrated: during the Cold War, the top 10 countries accounted for less than a third of arms imports and, after the Cold War, the top 10 countries' share was close to 50%. Given these statistics, standard economic theory indicates that the supply side should have substantial market power. However, economic factors play a minimal role in the explanation of the global arms trade while political and strategic factors emerge as crucial factors.

The analysis of arms trade as a standard market has been a focus of researchers. Anderton (1995) summarized this literature, which is mainly theoretical. As emphasized by Levine et al. (1994), two opposite drivers may lead to arms exports: economic profit and external security. Arms exports provide insecurity for the seller when the buyer is a rival or security when the buyer is a friend. Arms exports show that depending on the quality of the buyer, the level of exchange is different from a pure economic model. These results explain some features of the global arms trade, but standard economic theory does not fully capture the frictions arising from the peculiarities of arms.

Following new political economic theory, some researchers analyse arms trade using political factors such as proxy of democracy, political orientation, or security factors such as alliances, conflict, and neighbours engaged in conflict.

Some papers evaluate the decision to export arms (proxied by a dummy that takes the value of one if one export is observed or zero otherwise) and the quantity of exports. From an econometric point of view, this type of model is known as the Heckman model. Blanton (2005) provided an example of this model and showed that in the selection stage, democracy is a key positive determinant of US exports; that is, the more democratic the country, the more likely the United States is to export arms to that country. Comola (2012) insisted on the importance of political factors as an explanatory variable for arms exports. More recently, Martinez-Zarzoro and Johannsen (2019) show that alongside economic factors, both political and security factors play a significant role based on a sample of 104 exporting countries over the period 1950 to 2007. The authors also note major shifts due to the end of the Cold War. These papers offer interesting insights on arms exports, but they fail to circumvent endogeneity: the papers use conflicts as explanatory variables, but they do control for the fact that trade may have consequences regarding conflicts. This type of circularity could potentially cause reverse causality.

Arms trade generates effects beyond commercial operations because of the nature of arms, their effects in terms of security, and their influence on economic structures. As acknowledged by SIPRI (1971, p. 73), "perhaps the most important question about arms supplies is ... what effect they have on the development of wars – on the likelihood of wars breaking out, on the course of wars and their general severity". In this vein, several papers cast doubt on the destabilization hypothesis as they do not conclude any significant impacts concerning arms trade on conflicts (Moore 2012). Fauconnet et al. (2019) indicate that French arms trade does not exhibit any significant role on intrastate conflicts, whereas arms trade in the rest of the world fuels conflicts. Unfortunately, these papers cannot address the endogeneity issue and may imply reverse causality.

Industry and R&D

Among all the studies on defence economics, those that discuss the defence industry are most closely related to microeconomic theory and, in particular, industrial organization. Standard economic theory provides a useful framework within which to investigate the defence industry, but the specificities of the defence sector such as sovereignty technology, the importance of fixed costs, and barriers to entry, among others, must be considered. These features imply that the equipment market is somewhat unique: there are only a few firms and one buyer (the government), and these entities form a monopsony. In some cases, the context is called a bilateral monopoly if there is only one firm.

Defence industries represent the "supply side of the market for defense equipment" (Sandler and Hartley 1995, p. 177). All firms included in the defence industries define the defence industrial base (DIB). Defining the DIB requires a perimeter which is, unfortunately, difficult to operationalize. For instance, should housing services be included in the perimeter? Dunne (1995, p. 402) had a clear definition by distinguishing three types of products: lethal large or small weapons systems, non-lethal strategic products (fuel), and other products consumed by the military (food). Reliable DIB perimeters are crucial for public policy as they may shed light on the efficiency of a country in providing arms. For example, should a country rely on its own capacity? The notions of self-sufficiency and security of supply are crucial determinants in constructing a DIB because arms can be produced domestically or through international trade with partners. In this vein, the procurement choices of the Ministry of Defence are multiple and correspond to a trade-off between national sovereignty, cost of equipment and existence of industrial capacity. Not all countries have the same strategic ambitions and needs, so acquisition policies are diverse (Hartley and Belin 2019).

As the survey by Hartley (2007) noted, the literature is mainly composed of papers on R&D issues such as defence financing and its impact on the economy, procurement, and industrial cooperation. This subsection briefly follows this outline.

Many Western armed forces rely on technological superiority for their missions. Consequently, defence equipment is considered highly advanced in terms of complexity (Mowery 2010). The innovation concept is complex and widely analysed through the lens of R&D (a measure of inputs) or patents (a measure of outputs). The means of innovation are crucial, and some papers follow their evolution (Mowery 2010): the defence sector absorbed a large share of budgetary and financial means during the Cold War, but these shares declined after 1990. Nonetheless, for many Western countries, the defence sector is at the core of their national system of innovation given the architectural knowledge; that is, the way that knowledge is applied to optimize production by assembling parts from different subcontractors.

Relative to innovation output, patents are used by economists, and there is a need to control the quality (rather than the quantity) of innovation. Patents are identified in technological classes, but defence is not one of them. Therefore, the identification of defence patents is complicated and requires industrial expertise. Some indicators measure the influence of a patent, and papers show that the economic impact is significant due to their effect on productivity (Moretti et al. 2017).

Data measurement is the crucial issue for this subfield: patent behaviour is supposedly the same among civilian and military sectors, which is not the case given the secrecy associated with the military sector. For example, Acosta et al. (2017) showed that defence firms patent less than civil firms. Moreover, the statistical approaches used by economists acknowledge that a firm with 1% of its turnover accounted for by the military sector is a firm of the defence industrial base. There is obviously a limit because given the different defence submarkets and their industrial organization, the gradient must range between 0% and 100% (and cannot be a binary measure).

The procurement issue is crucial because it allows us to analyse the industrial choices of states in terms of armaments. Given the importance of R&D, the price of weapons systems is rising faster than civilian inflation (Hartley 2016). From this point of view, it is necessary to arbitrate between the cost over the entire life cycle (procurement, maintenance, dismantling) and the need to master technologies crucial to sovereignty (Rogerson 1995). Contractual mechanisms (fixed-price contracts or cost-plus contracts) are used to assess the risk sharing inherent in the production process (Hartley 2007). In order to avoid cost overruns, fixed-price contracts are the standard choice in many developed countries (Bellais et al. 2014).

Industrial cooperation is a popular subject in Europe. There are many firms and programmes, and duplication is well-established (Hartley 1995) compared to the integrated American equipment market. Economic theory shows that cooperation is economically optimal given the costs savings (Sandler and Hartley 1995). However, as reviewed by Hartley and Braddon (2014), both the demand and supply sides generate inefficiencies, particularly the complexities that cause partners to collaborate. These inefficiencies are likely to increase costs and delays.

Economic impacts

A main subject in the defence economics literature is the economic impact of military activities. As DS is a component of public spending, many papers address the influence of DS on macroeconomic performance such as GDP, unemployment, or investment. However, as defence activities are also localized in a few areas (for historical or geographical reasons), another arm of the literature examines the impact of DS on regional activities. From this huge literature body, little consensus emerges on the macroeconomic effect of DS. On average, based on a sample of estimates in the literature, Yesilyurt and Yesilyurt (2019) indicated that DS has no significant effect on growth. DS is not a crucial determinant of growth (Sala-i-Martin et al. 2004), and its effect is minimal compared to other factors such investment.

There are two explanations for the impact of DS. The first is related to Keynesian theory: an increase (or decrease) in DS positively (or negatively) affects economic activities; a multiplier effect. The second reason is linked to the quality of defence inputs: defence activities are widely technological, and the technologies conceived and used for the military generate spillovers to the civilian sector. Ruttan (2006) provided many examples of such military technologies: nuclear, semi-conductor etc.

Direct economic impacts have received much attention from economists. This is because the impacts are easier to assess from an econometric point of view. The simplest way to model a direct relationship is to use only two variables, DS and GDP, in level form or defence burden and growth rate of GPD in a relative form. This approach has been widely used because of a lack of global theory encompassing all the channels through which defence affects the economy. This type of model is close to the one chosen by Benoit (1972) in his seminal publication. Another advantage is the fact that the endogeneity issue can easily be controlled using proper econometric tools. These atheoretical approaches lead to interesting results, notably, the existence of a multiplier effect. However, there are several significant limitations. The approach neglects opportunity costs: What would have been the effect if public spending had been included? Finally, as mentioned by or Dunne and Smith (2010), the results are sensitive to the econometric specification.

Many economists use a theoretical model given the limits of the atheoretical approach. Growth theory provides a useful framework to investigate the influence of public spending, and the theory has been popularized among defence economists for its solid foundations (Dunne et al. 2005). Many empirical analyses focus on both defence and non-defence spending and compare their respective effect on GDP growth among other determinants such as private investment or population growth. This approach tends to show a negative impact of DS.

Some indirect models have been used. These models evaluate the existence of a drain of resources that, ultimately, reduce economic performance. Smith (1980) popularized a model where the crowding-out effect is estimated considering that private investment and public spending compete for the same pool of resources. An increase in DS implies less resources for private investment and a higher interest rate. DS has a strong negative impact on private investment, which is the key determinant for economic growth (Sala-i-Martin 1997). However, DS composition matters as shown by Malizard (2015) French DS implies crowding-out, but French defence equipment spending fosters private investment.

Finally, some models rely on multiple equations that encompass direct effect, indirect impact, and endogeneity of DS (Deger and Smith 1983). The system of equations is based on a growth equation to quantify the direct effect, an investment equation to model the indirect effect, and a DS equation to circumvent endogeneity. Many papers show that DS has a positive direct impact that is surpassed by a negative indirect impact leading to a global negative impact.

As explained by Malizard (2011), some regularities emerge from the global picture of the results. Some models are well-designed to exhibit a positive effect of DS, whereas others lead to the opposite conclusion. A comparison of models may lead to proper evaluations relative to DS impact. Additionally, the defence economics literature is somewhat original in the global literature: except for growth estimates, the results are based on specific models without points of comparison with other macroeconomic papers.

To summarize the economics of DS, the primary purpose of defence is not to foster economic activity but to ensure security. Economists are unable to discuss the effect of security. If DS exhibits a positive effect, it could be a type of double dividend in a sense that both security and economic activities are stimulated. However, as Smith (2009) noted, a high macroeconomic impact cannot be expected given the relatively weak influence of DS in terms of its percentage of GDP.

Conclusion: What is the future of defence economics?

In their introduction to the second volume of the *Handbook of Defense Economics*, Hartley and Sandler (2007) acknowledged that defence economics has changed. From a semantics point of view, a prominent journal in the defence economics field changed its name from *Defense Economics* to *Defense and Peace Economics*. This change is a recognition that defence economics is interested in economic means but also strategic ends such as security, peace, war, and conflicts.

Peace and conflicts economics are not, by far, the core of defence economics from a historical point of view. Conflicts economics is mainly interested in the causes, consequences, and costs of all forms of violence (interstate conflicts, civil wars, and terrorism, among others). The modelling perspective is reversed: defence economics considers conflict as exogenous whereas conflict economics uses defence as exogenous. There is a kind of simultaneity between defence and conflict. However, the literature is now intertwined as economic factors are crucial in the explanation of conflicts (Collier and Hoeffler 2007) and conflicts have huge consequences on economies (Abadie and Gardeazabal 2003). Besides, the concept of security web has been popularized by Dunne et al. (2003) by gathering data on both conflict and defence sources.

The crucial issue for defence economics is to measure output: security is a multidimensional concept that cannot be summarized in a single index. The absence of conflicts is one item that can be included as a means of defence. From a statistical point of view, a conflict is coded as 1 so that 0 has different meanings (Fauconnet et al. 2019): the durable absence of conflict or a peaceful period between two periods of conflict. Statistical measures must be cautiously evaluated as peace (i.e. 0) is the absence of conflict in this approach. However, these data are used by many economists and social scientists to discuss conflict but also development issues.

From an economic perspective, there is still a missing link: translating defence means into monetary measures. In my opinion, "How much is enough?" would be a question without answer. Therefore, defence economics is then a complement to other disciplines, notably strategy and international relations. However, it helps policymakers to formulate better informed description and prescription when economics tools are relevant.

Notes

1 Smith (2009) discusses the notion of "military value chain" and shows how economics is original among social sciences, especially because of the analysis of means in economic terms.
2 See the first subsection of our second part for a discussion on how governments source its national defence. Note that these inputs are private goods, despite the fact they are collectively procured.
3 Abadie and Gardeazabal (2003) investigate the costs of terrorism for the Basque region by considering a counterfactual region in which there are no terrorist attacks.
4 Statistical significance is labelled in table thanks to " * ".

References

Abadie, A., Gardeazabal, J. (2003). The economic costs of conflict: A case study of the Basque Country. *American Economic Review*, 93(1), 113–132.

Acosta, M., Coronado, D., Ferrandiz, E., Marin, M. R., Moreno P. J. (2017). Patents and dual-use technology: An empirical study of the world's largest defence companies. *Defence and Peace Economics*, 29(7), 821–839.

Anderton, C. H. (1995). Economics of arms trade, 523–561. In: Hartley, K., Sandler, T. (Eds.) (1995). *Handbook of Defence Economics. Defense in a Globalized World*, Amsterdam, Elsevier.

Angrist, J., Azoulay, P., Ellison, G., Hill, R., Lu, S. F. (2017). Economic research evolves: Fields and styles. *American Economic Review*, 107(5), 293–297.

Bellais R., Foucault, M., Oudot, J.-M. (2014). *Economie de la défense*, Paris, La Découverte.

Belin J., Droff, J., Malizard, J. (2017). The economics of European defence: Some additional insights, *ARES – Comment*, 15, available online: https://www.iris-france.org/wp-content/uploads/2017/04/Ares-Group-Comment-avril-2017-.pdf.

Benoit, E. (1972). *Defence and Economic Growth in Developing Countries*, Lexington, MA, Lexington Books.

Blanton, S. L. (2005). Foreign policy in transition? Human rights, democracy and U.S. arms exports. *International Studies Quarterly*, 49, 647–667.

Brodeur, A., Lé, M., Sangnier, M., Zylberberg, Y. (2016). Star wars: The empirics strike back. *American Economic Journal: Applied Economics*, 8(1), 1–32.

Collier, P., Hoeffler, A. (2004). Greed and grievance in civil war. *Oxford Economic Papers*, 56, 563–595.

Comola, M. (2012). Democracies, politics and arms supply: A bilateral trade equation. *Review of International Economics*, 20(1), 150–163.

Deger, S., Sen, S. (1983). Military expenditure, spin-off and economic development. *Journal of Development Economics*, 13(1–2), 67–83.

Dunne, J. P. (1995). The defence industrial base, 399–430. In: Hartley, K., Sandler, T. (Eds.) (1995). *Handbook of Defence Economics: Defense in a Globalized World*, Amsterdam, Elsevier.

Dunne, J. P., Perlo-Freeman, S. (2003). The demand for military spending in developing countries: A dynamic panel analysis. *Defence and Peace Economics*, 14(6), 461–474.

Dunne, J. P., Smith, R., Willenbockel, D. (2005). Models of military expenditure and growth: A critical review. *Defence and Peace Economics*, 16(6), 449–461.

Dunne, P., Smith, R. (2010). Military expenditure and granger causality: A critical review. *Defence and Peace Economics*, 21(5–6), 427–441.

Fauconnet, C., Malizard, J., Pietri, A. (2019). French arms exports and intrastate conflicts: An Empirical investigation. *Defence and Peace Economics*, 30(2), 176–196.

Gates, W. R., Terasawa, K. L. (2003), Reconsidering publicness in alliance defence expenditures: NATO expansion and burden sharing. *Defence and Peace Economics*, 14(5), 369–383.

Greene, W. (2003). *Econometric Analysis*, 5th ed., Upper Saddle River, NJ, Prentice Hall.

Hartley, K. (1995). Industrial policies in the defence sector, 459–490. In: Hartley, K., Sandler, T. (Eds.) (1995). *Handbook of Defence Economics: Defense in a Globalized World*, Amsterdam, Elsevier.

Hartley, K. (2007). The arms industry, procurement and industrial policies, 1139–1176. In: Hartley, K., Sandler, T. (Eds.) (1995). *Handbook of Defence Economics. Defense in a Globalized World*, Amsterdam, Elsevier.

Hartley, K. (2012). Conflict and defence output: An economic perspective. *Revue d'Economie Politique*, 122(2), 171–195.

Hartley, K. (2016). UK defence inflation and cost escalation. *Defence and Peace Economics*, 27(2), 184–207.

Hartley, K., Braddon, D. (2014). Collaborative projects and the number of partner nations. *Defence and Peace Economics*, 25(6), 535–548.

Hartley, K., Belin, J. (2019). *The Economics of the Global Defence Industry*, London, Routledge.
Hartley, K., Sandler, T. (Eds.) (1995). *Handbook of Defense Economics: Defense in a Globalized World*, Amsterdam, Elsevier.
Intrilligator, M. D. (1990). On the nature and scope of defence economics. *Defence Economics*, 1(1), 3–11.
Khanna, J., Sandler, T. (1996). NATO burden sharing: 1960–1992. *Defence and Peace Economics*, 7(2), 115–133.
Kollias, C. (2008). A preliminary investigation of the burden sharing aspects of a European Union common defence policy. *Defence and Peace Economics*, 19(4), 256–293.
Levine, P., Sen, S., Smith, R. (1994). A model of international arms market. *Defence and Peace Economics*, 5(1), 1–18.
MacDonald, P. (2010), *The Economics of Military Outsourcing*. PhD thesis, University of York.
Malizard, J. (2011), *Dépenses militaires et croissance économique*. Ph.D. thesis manuscript, University of Montpellier 1.
Malizard, J. (2015). Does military expenditure crowd-out private investment? A disaggregated perspective for the case of France, *Economic Modelling*, 46(1), 44–52.
Malizard, J. (2018). Taking stock on the measure of arms trade: The case of France, *unpublished mimeo*.
Malizard, J. (2019). Introduction to the special issue on France. *Defence and Peace Economics*, 30(2), 129–132.
Malizard, J., Richter, F. (2018). *Comparing defence output: a methodological nightmare?* Conference paper presented at the 22nd International Conference on Economics and Security at Güzelyurt (Morphou).
Markusen, A. (2003). The case against privatizing national security. *Governance*, 16(4), 471–501.
Martinez-Zarzoso, I., Johannsen, J. (2019). The gravity of arms. *Defence and Peace Economics*, 30(1), 2–26.
Moore, M. (2012). Selling to both sides: The effects of major conventional weapons transfers on civil war severity and duration. *International Interactions*, 38(3), 325–347.
Moretti, E., Steinwender, C., Van Reenen, J. (2014, July). *The intellectual spoils of war?* Defense R&D, productivity and spillovers. Conference paper presented at the 2016 American Economic Association Annual Meeting.
Mowery, D. C. (2010). Military R&D and innovation, 1219–1256. In: Hall, B. H., Rosenberg, N. (Eds.) (2010). *Handbook of the Economics of Innovation*, Vol. 2, Amsterdam, London, Elsevier.
Olson, M., Zeckhauser, R. (1966). An economic theory of alliances. *Review of Economics and Statistics*, 48(3), 266–279.
Perlo-Freeman, S., Ferguson, N. (2015). *Capacity and openness: the determinants of the availability and quality of military expenditure data*. Conference paper presented at the 19th International conference on economics and security, Grenoble.
Ram, R. (1993). Conceptual linkages between defence spending and economic growth, 19–39. In: Payne, J. E., Sahu, A. P. (Eds.) (1993). *Defence Spending & Economic Growth*, Boulder, CO, Westview Press.
Robbins, L. (2007 [1935]). *An Essay on the Nature and Significance of Economic Science*, London, Macmillan.
Rogerson, W. P. (1995), Incentive models of the defense procurement process, 309–346. In: Hartley, K., Sandler, T. (Eds.) (1995). *Handbook of Defense Economics: Defense in a Globalized World*, Amsterdam, Elsevier.
Ruttan, V. W. (2006). *Is War Necessary for Economic Growth? Military Procurement and Technology Development*, Oxford, Oxford University Press.
Sala-i-Martin, X. (1997). I just ran two million regressions. *American Economic Review P&P*, 87(2), 178–183.
Sala-i-Martin, X., Doppelhoffer, G., and Miller, R. I. (2004). Determinants of long-term growth: A Bayesian averaging of classical estimated (BACE) approach. *American Economic Review*, 94(4), 813–835.

Sandler, T., Hartley, K. (1995). *The Economics of Defence*, Cambridge, Cambridge University Press.
Sandler, T., Hartley, K. (2001). Economics of alliances: The lessons for collective action. *Journal of Economic Literature*, 39, 869–896.
Sandler T., George, J. (2016). Military expenditure trends for 1960–2014 and what they reveal. *Global Policy*, 7(2), 174–185.
Sandler, T., Shimizu, H. (2012). NATO burden sharing 1999–2010: An altered alliance. *Foreign Policy Analysis*, 1–18.
Schumpeter, J. A. (1934). *The Theory of Economic Development: An Inquiry into Profits, Capital, Credit, Interest and the Business Cycle*, Harvard, CA, Harvard University Press.
Singer, P. W. (2001). Corporate warriors: The rise of the privatized military industry and its ramifications for international security, *International Security*, 26(3), 186–220.
Stockholm International Peace Research Institute (SIPRI) (1971). *The Arms Trade with the Third World*, Solna, Paul Elek.
Smith, R. (1980). Military expenditure and investment in OECD countries, 1957–1973. *Journal of Comparative Economics*, 4(1), 19–32.
Smith, R. (1989). Models of military expenditure. *Journal of Applied Econometrics*, 4(4), 345–359.
Smith, R. (1998). Quantitative methods in peace research. *Journal of Peace Research*, 34(4), 419–427.
Smith, R. (2009). *Military Economics, the Interaction of Power and Money*, London, Palgrave Macmillan.
Yesilyurt, F., Yesilyurt, M. E. (2019). Meta-analysis, military expenditures and growth. *Journal of Peace Research*, 56(3), 352–363.

10 Voting on the use of armed force*

Challenges of data indexing, classification, and the value of a comparative agenda

*Falk Ostermann, Florian Böller,
Flemming J. Christiansen, Fabrizio Coticchia,
Daan Fonck, Anna Herranz-Surrallés, Juliet Kaarbo,
Kryštof Kučmáš, Michal Onderco, Rasmus B. Pedersen,
Tapio Raunio, Yf Reykers, Michal Smetana,
Valerio Vignoli and Wolfgang Wagner*

Introduction

Contemporary politics is characterized by an increasing *politicization* (Zürn 2014), be it in the realm of domestic, international, or regional politics, such as within the European Union (Hooghe and Marks 2009). In European states, as well as in Canada and the United States, the aftermath of the financial crisis, the fight against Islamic terrorism, the inflow of refugees from Syria and elsewhere, and the (related) rise of populist movements and politicians (Mudde 2004; Müller 2016; Poier et al. 2017) have generated political climates that challenge both the domestic foundations of economic and cultural liberalism and the acceptance of globalization (Hooghe et al. 2019). On the international level, the global liberal order, its institutions, and multilateral diplomacy are subjected to severe stress, unilateralist temptation, and decay (Kagan 2018; Posen 2018). Although some might call these developments systemic, they represent the aggregated result of states' foreign policies whose governments are subject to the aforementioned processes of politicization. Our general argument is, quite simply, that this politicization matters and that we should examine it more deeply with regard to foreign policy.

The field of Foreign Policy Analysis (FPA) has long rejected the idea that *politics stops at the water's edge*. FPA scholars investigate the impact of domestic politics on foreign policies from a variety of theoretical perspectives (for an overview see Kaarbo et al. 2013). Yet, with the exception of Rathbun (2004), attention has only recently turned toward an analysis of the role of ideology and party-positions on foreign policy (Ecker-Ehrhardt 2014; Plagemann and Destradi 2019; Verbeek and Zaslove 2017), particularly in the field of defence and security. When it comes to military deployments, large parts of existing scholarship adopt a single-case perspective that highlights national particularities (e.g. Böller and Müller 2018; Fonck and Reykers 2018; Kaarbo and Kenealy 2016; Mello 2017) rather than engaging with the topic in a comparative manner. Recent work by Mello (2014), Mello and Peters (2018) or Wagner et al. (2017, 2018) has started, however, to look at broader and comparative patterns of contestation of foreign policy among parties. This work breaks with the ideas that foreign policy imposes consensus across parties and that security threats necessarily create a *rally around the flag* effect (Eichenberg et al. 2006; Mueller 1970). Against the backdrop of contemporary politicization both inside and outside political institutions, we can expect that contestation of security policies will also increase in parliament and parties. This means that we build on the parliamentary research agenda that is already well developed (overview in Raunio 2014; Raunio and Wagner 2017) and also further develop the party-political research agenda. From a methodological point of view, this predicament also means that we need to strengthen our analytical tools in order to better capture politicization in our research on parties and foreign, security, and defence policy. This chapter aims at making such a contribution by presenting a new database, by measuring agreement/dissent with an index, and by looking at contestation comparatively based on party families and cabinets.

This chapter contributes to this research area in two ways. First, we present new data on voting on military missions from the *Parliamentary Deployment Votes Database's* (PDVD)[1] version #2 dataset now encompassing 514 deployment votes between 1990 and 2017 from eleven countries: Belgium, the Czech Republic, Denmark, Finland, France, Germany, Italy, Slovakia, Spain, the United Kingdom, and the United States. In an effort at including more countries, the current version of the dataset covers not only major and middle powers (US, France, Germany, UK), but also countries with varying cultures of national security (Britz 2016; Katzenstein 1996). These cultures reach from interventionist ones (France, UK, US) to states reticent toward the use of force (Germany); states with strongly parliamentary, semi-presidential (France), or presidential (US) constitutional systems; and countries with older or younger democratic legacies and patterns of authoritarianism in the 20th century. The recorded votes in these states reflect the trend of increasing liberal-democratic interventionism since the 1990s. Thus, they provide "an opportunity to observe the revealed preferences of elites" (Milner and Tingley, 2015, p. 129), and, by virtue of the central role of parties in liberal-democratic politics, an inroad into understanding the party politics of foreign policy. The dataset provides raw data on voting practices on three levels: plenary-vote data for parliament as a whole, party-vote data, and family-cabinet data. These three sources will be used to show patterns and drivers of contestation across the eleven countries, their ideological spread, and government-opposition dynamics. Second, the chapter discusses the methodological and methodical challenges involved in constructing the dataset, reflecting on several issues, including cultures of national security and parliaments' role therein, existing record and its accessibility, and party, mission, and vote classifications. We also explain our idea behind the transfer of Hix et al.'s (2005) *Agreement Index* from the European Parliament to our data.

The chapter proceeds as follows: the first section discusses challenges to a comparative agenda when researching party politics and foreign policy, especially military missions, while proposing and discussing the *Agreement Index* as a measurement of contestation in parliaments. The chapter then puts issues of data availability into perspective and suggests practical steps to set up a comparative research agenda. After these methods and methodology-focused sections, the chapter presents insights from comparative research into deployment votes on the level of parties, party families, and government-opposition dynamics, with continued attention to methodological issues throughout the empirical analyses. Ultimately, the chapter argues that a comparative research agenda on the party politics of foreign (and here more precisely defence) policy is promising despite challenges on the methods and data side, and it argues that a scholarly consensus is emerging around evidence for party politics in the field of military deployment votes.

Parliaments in security and defence policy: challenges to a comparative agenda and the measurement of contestation

Researching parliament's role in security and defence policies comparatively, yet establishing a voting database as PDVD does, is difficult because parliament's role in foreign policy varies considerably. Traditionally, foreign policy – and security and defence even more so – belong to the realm of executive prerogatives that endow governments with a lot of room for manoeuvre in conducting diplomacy and coercive action. Except for a formal declaration of war, which is usually parliament's right but rendered futile in the face of contemporary conflict politics, some parliaments, such as in Australia, Belgium, Greece, or the UK, hardly ever get the chance to vote on deployments. In these cases, the constitutions vest chief executives both with the right to send forces abroad whenever they deem fit and the freedom to search parliamentary approval, or not, for this action (Fonck and Reykers 2018; Mello 2017; Strong 2018). At an intermediate level of influence, through the 1973 *War Powers Resolution*, the U.S. Congress has formal information rights. It votes on deployments after 60 to 90 days, and it can withhold funding for missions through its *power of the purse*. The law suffers, however, from vague formulations and does not fundamentally constrain the executive (e.g. Howell and Pevehouse 2007). A similar case is the French one, where the president has full authority to send troops abroad but according to Article 35 of the French Constitution, presidents must ask both chambers of parliament to approve the mission when it exceeds four months (Ostermann 2017). The Czech government also has to seek parliamentary approval for every deployment that exceeds 60 days.[2] The Italian parliament's competences are extremely ambiguous (Mello 2014, p. 78; Peters and Wagner 2011). Formally, it enjoys very strong powers (Dieterich et al. 2010) but in practice the executive has often bypassed the constitutional veto on military operations abroad, deploying troops without its consent.

Going much further, other states endow parliament with far-reaching rights as to defence issues. Thus, parliaments in Denmark, Germany, or Spain must approve missions prior to deployment (in Spain only since 2002). The German case, for instance, is deeply affected by the country's historical legacy of war-proneness and dictatorship, resulting in a culture of military self-restraint and substantial parliamentary involvement (e.g. Duffield 1998). These differences notwithstanding, as Figure 10.1 shows, deployment votes have proliferated since the end of the Cold War across the countries under study to produce a vast body of data than can be used to tap into party-voting, procedural aspects, and executive-legislative relations more broadly speaking (Mello 2014; Saideman and Auerswald 2012). The votes reflect the trend of increasing liberal-democratic interventionism since the 1990s with several votes on the high-intensity interventions in Bosnia and Kosovo and many votes on Afghanistan and Iraq, but also low-intensity security management missions in Lebanon (UNIFIL), Darfur (UNAMID), Mali (MINUSMA and European Force Training Mission (EUTM)) and others in the 2000s and 2010s.

Different constitutional dispositions and role-distributions also lead to vastly different ways parliaments deal with security and defence issues once they are up for a vote. The French National Assembly and Senate, for instance, simply vote on a mission-specific declaration of government. In the German case, the *Bundestag* and its committees are involved in all aspects of foreign policy strategy and action through a Parliamentary Participation Law (*Parlamentsbeteiligungsgesetz*). When it votes on missions, the Bundestag approves a concrete mandate, changes, or extends it, usually

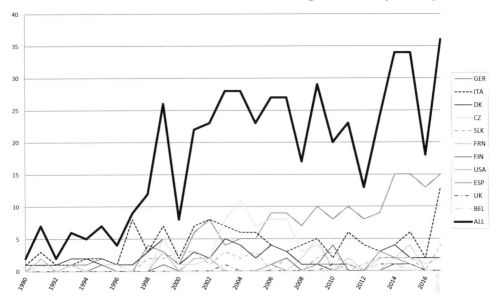

Figure 10.1 Number of deployment votes over time (all chambers), 1990–2017
Note: The authors themselves produced all figures and tables. They are based on data from the *Parliamentary Deployment Votes Database*, as found on www.deploymentvotewatch.eu.

every twelve months (Wagner 2017). Slovakia's National Council votes in a similar fashion, but debate about deployments is often located outside the chamber. The Czech Chamber of Deputies and the Senate often hold bundle-votes on several missions that make it hard for lawmakers or parties to raise substantial concerns on one mission only. In Italy, additional refinancing votes used to be passed for specific or multiple missions, sometimes occurring several times a year. The Comprehensive Law no. 145 2016, however, changed this practice to yearly refinancing votes that bundle specific missions in a package. The Spanish *Cortes* increasingly votes in committee, particularly in case of renewal of an existing operation.[3] Thus, parliamentary involvement not only relies on different constitutional dispositions and traditions, but it also varies in ways parliaments and parties (can) deal with a mission once it is up for a vote.

It is our belief that these differences and peculiarities should not hinder a comparative agenda. Although deployment votes might be of a different nature and number across countries, a comparative agenda strengthens our understanding of foreign, security, and defence policy in several ways. First, it allows for creating a knowledge base on types and patterns of parliamentary involvement in security and defence issues – i.e. hot military action – that reveals both common features and differences. Second, by virtue of this, deployment-vote research contributes to the investigation of legislative-executive relations in defence policies broadly speaking. Third, such study enables us to disentangle culture-specific factors from ideology-driven/related explanations that cut across cases. In doing so, a comparative agenda contributes to causal analysis in Elster's sense of *explaining interaction* (Elster 1983, pp. 25ff., 84) while transcending the accumulation of – valid and equally relevant – case-level knowledge. Further below, we will also make the point that cabinet-averages enable us to compare divergent situations across countries.

Grasping contestation: calculating an agreement index

The fact that parliaments vote on missions and, therefore, that parties must position themselves on mission-related issues, a mission as a whole, or a precise mandate means that the decisions are principally open to party-political contestation. Although common wisdom holds that citizens are not that interested in foreign policy as they are, for instance, in domestic issues (Boix 2007; Lipset and Rokkan 1967), there are numerous votes on military deployments that have become salient to the public and strongly politicized. This happened, for example, in US politicians' voting behaviour on the Iraq War (Böller 2017), in British House of Commons debates about Syria (Kaarbo and Kenealy 2016), and in the German participation in the Kosovo War in 1999. Danish participation in Kosovo, Afghanistan, and the Iraq War have also been debated vividly in public and, as a result of parliamentary pressure, led to extensive scrutiny (Mariager and Wivel, 2019). The decision to conduct a mission generates public attention, especially with the spectre of *hot* action and casualties rising. Therefore, it induces the executive and lawmakers to ponder arguments in favour or against operations carefully.[4] Furthermore, as previous work has revealed and the below analysis demonstrates, these situations are characterized by genuine, party-political and ideological arguments and dissent.

Although parliaments have typically endorsed government proposals to send troops (with a few notable exceptions),[5] party contestation often underlies this approval. One way to grasp contestation over deployment is to measure agreement levels. Hix et al. (2005) developed a similar approach to gauge party cohesion in roll-call votes in the European Parliament, with their *Agreement Index* (AI).

The precise formula is:

$$AI_i = \frac{\max\{Y_i, N_i, A_i\} - \frac{1}{2}[(Y_i + N_i + A_i) - \max\{Y_i, N_i, A_i\}]}{(Y_i + N_i + A_i)}$$

The AI equals 1 when all MPs vote together and it equals 0 when they are equally divided between the voting options. This index has become an established measure to assess the unity of groups within legislatures – these groups are mostly political parties, but in studies of the European Parliament, groups can be MEPs from the same country. With the exception of some previous work (Wagner et al. 2018), the AI has not been used to measure degrees of consensus within a parliament as a whole,[6] most likely because the recording of individual votes already is a sign of contestation; uncontroversial parliamentary decisions are often adopted without the time-consuming recording of individual votes. Moreover, parliaments differ enormously in the ways they vote, with some often recording votes and others doing so only rarely (Saalfeld 1995). Hence, recorded votes may be a very unrepresentative sample of all votes in a parliament (Carrubba et al. 2008). Conversely, as mentioned above, constitutional dispositions in many countries (most countries in our dataset) today simply force governments to hold deployment votes no matter whether they are contested or not, even in so strongly executive-centred ones like France. For the purposes of this project, therefore, the AI allows assessment of the degree of dissent on mission votes. From a methodological point of view, the AI provides a good way to compare agreement/dissent on deployment votes across countries that allows as to overcome the aforementioned issues in comparison. Additionally, it can serve as a proxy for measuring contestation in parliaments where party-based voting data on deployments is not available.

Figure 10.2 shows the average degree of contestation of all deployment votes, as captured by the AI, per country. The figure demonstrates that contestation varies across the countries in the PDVD dataset: it is highest in the US and lowest in Spain. The high degree of contestation in the US seems in line with traditional expectations of low party discipline and high levels of independence of individual members of Congress. A closer look at our data reveals, however, that the opposition party in Congress casts most dissenting votes. This observation confirms more recent studies on the increasing partisan division in Congress, which also extends to votes on military interventions (see Hildebrandt et al. 2013, p. 245). Differences among European countries are more difficult to explain by institutional features of the political system. Instead, they seem to reflect differences in political culture, which in some cases include a strong commitment to cross-party consensus in defence policy[7] and a much weaker commitment in others.[8]

Defining missions and units of analysis

In addition to measuring (dis)agreement, a comparative methodology must also deal with the predicament that missions are of very different type. Some deployments in our dataset are high-intensity combat missions, such as the wars in Kosovo, Iraq, or Libya, while others are low-intensity, civil-military EU security management missions (EUPOL, EUTM) or UN peacekeeping deployments. Yet others rather focus on combatting terrorism. Accordingly, some missions are mandated by the UN Security Council while others are not or do not need such mandates. One can reasonably argue that these various mission-types influence the way parties position themselves. At the same time, classification of a mission may itself be political. Critics of a specific mission, for example, may be driven by an

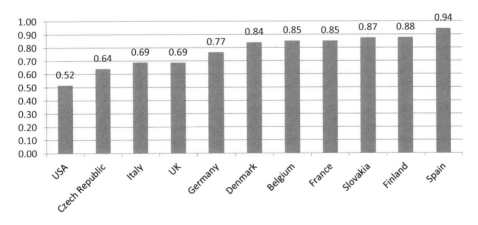

Figure 10.2 Average Agreement Index (AI) of deployment votes

alternative worldview that they bring to the political process. Any classification would therefore necessarily privilege a worldview – i.e. the one where the researcher classifying a mission as humanitarian or offensive – that might clash with and obscure (conflicting) perceptions in politics. While we agree that researchers usually do and must make these calls for research purposes and for structuring reality, we argue that these choices must be made consciously while pondering implications for the research of party politics and ideology. Our data show that party-political contestation occurs across mission-types (see also Wagner et al. 2018, pp. 546, 557). For future research, the advantage of disaggregating these votes further increases with the number of votes and countries covered, allowing for larger-n analyses. At the end of the day, we posit that disaggregating mission-types further depends on the particular research question and the specific methodological choices any scholar must make when designing research.

Cabinets as appropriate unit for gauging and comparing contestation

Another issue to consider concerns units of analysis and disciplinary standards. When setting up the project and using the database for a first time, some of us originally worked with legislatures' tenures as temporal delimiter. While this worked well for understanding the general pattern of party-political contestation on both the party and parliamentary level, we realized that with the increasing number of countries and votes joining the database, using cabinets as unit of analysis was the better choice. Whereas it is possible that legislature, cabinet duration, and the term of a specific chief executive are the same, problems of data presentation and interpretation emerge when they are not. For instance, in Belgium, there can be a considerable gap between legislatures and cabinets because of long periods of government formation due to Belgium's linguistic-administrative federalism; thus, aggregating votes from caretaker and normal cabinet-periods could be misleading. Slovakia's *Direction* party changed partisan positions after moving to the government for the first time, and remained consistently pro-deployment since. Hence, moving in and out of government potentially changes the party politics of foreign and defence policy. On the contrary, it is reasonable to assume that parties behave the same way during a cabinet's term as cabinets clearly define government-opposition roles and dynamics. Therefore, in this project, we follow the *Parliaments and governments database* (ParlGov, see Döring and Manow, 2018) cabinet coding to achieve more consistency and validity in the data.[9] ParlGov presents the most encompassing data collection on elections, cabinet duration, and governing parties, covering 37 EU and OECD countries. In the case of the US, we rely on presidential terms instead as more valid measurement unit.

Cabinets are also a useful unit for normalizing data. One consequence of the vastly differing voting practices described above is a highly uneven distribution of deployment votes across countries in our dataset. As Figure 10.3 shows, Germany alone accounts for 33% of all votes (n_{all}=514), and five of eleven countries account for 88% of all deployment votes in our dataset. At the other extreme, Belgium and the UK account for about 1% of the votes each. These numbers demonstrate that some sort of normalization between countries is necessary to compare data, and cabinets are a useful unit for this.

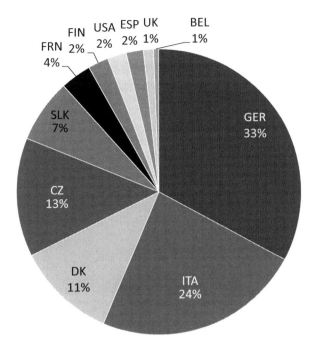

Figure 10.3 Number of Cases [votes] (all chambers)

Crossing the boundaries of parliamentary systems and collecting data

We made a final pragmatic choice about how to analyse parliamentary votes in differing parliamentary systems. Our dataset combines both unicameral and bicameral parliamentary systems.[10] Yet although states may have bicameral systems, in Belgium, Germany, and Spain, for instance, the upper chambers have no say in military deployments. The Czech, Italian, and French Senates, however, do vote on missions.[11] In France, in case of dissenting opinions between the two chambers, the lower chamber can overrule the higher chamber's vote. Against this background, we follow disciplinary standards and use lower-chamber votes only when calculating cabinet or cabinet-party family averages for avoiding distortion. We collected data on the date of each vote:

- parties in government at the time of the vote;
- cabinet in office;
- chamber in which the vote took place;
- mission in question;
- total number of votes cast/in favour/against/abstaining;
- yes and no-vote shares (all on vote, party, and cabinet level);
- Agreement Index (AI, family level); and
- government-opposition status of parties and party families during cabinets.[12]

Whenever possible, we collected data on specific votes by party and party family, with almost complete data availability from the 2000s onward.[13]

In the remainder of this chapter, we introduce the PDVD version #2 dataset in more depth and present some basic descriptive statistics of its two further levels of aggregation (beyond the parliament level): individual parties and party families. These different levels of aggregation are useful for different research questions. Some scholars will be more interested in the disaggregation of data on the level of individual parties, whereas others might take an interest in the level of party families in order to compare developments across countries with divergent party systems and, for instance, more than one party per family presenting itself to the electorate. In any case, the PDVD database's main added value is the inclusion of data from eleven liberal democracies, which will facilitate and stimulate the comparative study of military missions. For the purpose of this book's methodological purposes, we will discuss methods and methodological issues throughout our empirical analyses.

The level of individual parties: water's edge *but*...

The PDVD *party-votes* dataset provides data on the voting behaviour of 138 political parties in individual votes. The party-vote, i.e. the voting behaviour of a particular party in a particular vote, is the unit of analysis. The dataset provides data for 2,672 cases (i.e. combinations of a party and a vote). The party-votes dataset also provides the basis for the *party-family-cabinet* dataset (see next section). The number of parties is distributed very unevenly across the countries under study, ranging from two in the US to 22 in Italy. Occasionally, political parties merge, split or rename, raising the question whether the new party should be treated as a distinct case or as a continuation of its predecessor. Our dataset follows the coding of the *Comparative Manifesto Project* (CMP), i.e. we treat a party as a distinct entry when the CMP assigns a new ID to it and otherwise consider it a continuation of its predecessor. In all coding issues across the project, however, final coding decisions were made by country experts (in dialogue with the project leaders) who are best qualified to judge parties' developments, and, for instance, their ideological leaning when it comes to family categorization. For parties not included in the CMP, the country experts involved in this project made the necessary classifications.

The party-vote level of the dataset will be most useful for future studies of party politics and military deployments in individual countries.[14] The histogram in Figure 10.4 shows that the most-frequent voting behaviour of the 138 parties is unanimous (46%) or close-to-unanimous support, and the second-most common voting behaviour is total absence of support (22%), either by voting against or by abstaining. Notably, in less than a third of the 2,672 cases members of the same party did not vote the same way. This indicates a high degree of party discipline, as expected in parliamentary systems.[15] Nevertheless, the considerable number of (near to) absolute opposition to deployments shows clearly, too, that politics is involved when voting on military missions. Thus, the data qualifies the concept of a *water's edge*-effect: parties vote highly consistently in favour of missions but contestation clearly exists. What drives this contestation? We turn next to examining the ideological dimension of these results and introduce the aggregate level of party families and cabinets.

Studying the clear and present relevance of ideology: average voting by party families per cabinet

PDVD also provides average data on the level of party families per cabinet. These data are most useful for comparisons across countries because aggregation into

Voting on the use of armed force 179

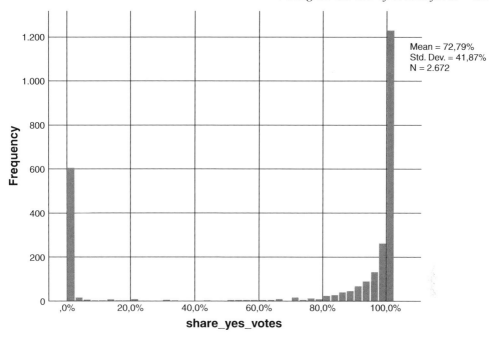

Figure 10.4 Frequencies of Shares of Yes-Votes

cabinet-averages reduces the uneven distribution of cases across countries. Without any doubt, these family-cabinet data are the avenue that can be exploited most for analysing the party politics of deployment votes. We take cabinets as a basic structuring principle because, with the exception of the US, the position of parties in either government or opposition remains stable during such a term. In distinguishing cabinets, we follow ParlGov that records a new cabinet whenever there was (i) a change in the set of parties holding cabinet membership; (ii) a change of the prime minister; (iii) a general election or (iv) any substantively meaningful resignation. The only case that does not entirely fit these criteria is the US, which is not covered by ParlGov. Here, we equal cabinet with presidential term, being well aware of the shifting congressional majorities (including periods of divided government). Again, as mentioned above and in rare instances only, we deviate from ParlGov where country experts advise to do so.[16] In a similar spirit, when merging parties into ideological families, the CMP classification has been our point of departure but country experts were free to amend these classifications as they deem fit either in accordance with their own judgement on the party's ideological leaning, or regarding changes in this leaning over time occurring, for instance, due to party mergers. Additionally, country experts recoded regionalist parties with national representation into one of the other families, based on the identification of their ideological leanings, leading to a more inclusive and ideologically coherent dataset.

At this level, as Figure 10.5 shows, the dataset includes 389 cases (i.e. party families with recorded votes during distinct cabinet terms). For each case, the average number of yes, no and abstention-votes per party family and cabinet has been recorded. To be sure, this dataset is also skewed with Italy accounting for 27% of the cases.

180 *Falk Ostermann et al.*

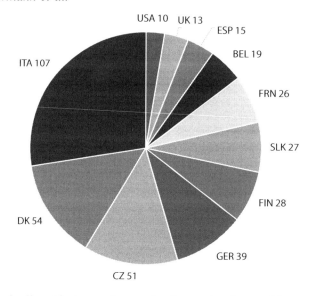

Figure 10.5 Party family-cabinet cases by country (lower chambers only)

However, the five countries with the smallest number of cases together account for approximately 21% – in contrast to approximately 8.5% share of the cases on the votes and party-vote levels. The differences in voting practices across countries make it impossible to overcome this skewedness of the data but the aggregation into averages per party family and cabinet minimizes the skewedness and thus facilitates comparisons across countries.

Figure 10.6 and the corresponding Analysis of Variance in Statistical Models (ANOVA) analysis (Table 10.1) show that the average share of no-votes across party families is U-shaped: no-votes are very common among radical-left parties, still frequent among green parties and not uncommon among social-democratic parties. They are seldom among liberal, Christian-democratic and conservative parties but become more frequent again among radical-right parties. Thus, the larger version #2 of the dataset confirms the results of the smaller sample from the previous version. Parties systematically contest deployment votes in accordance with their ideological leanings. The – upon visual inspection – somewhat considerable number of outliers (n=36, showed with cabinet name*) does not alter this conclusion as they only represent about 9% of the overall family-cabinet cases. Many outliers come from the US whose legislative-executive dynamics are not entirely captured by our cabinet-unit of analysis. During the Clinton and Obama presidencies, contestation against military missions stemmed from the Republican Party (which accounts for the outliers on the conservative party family), while Democrats opposed military interventions of Republican presidents – for example, the Iraq intervention in 1991 (see outliers in the socialist party family). Another bunch of deviating family/cabinet-averages stems from Italy, where the party system is highly polarized and majorities are often unstable. Different parties may belong to the same family but find themselves in alternative coalitions. In Finland, the Christian Democrats during the Vanhanen I and II cabinets voted against the missions for a mixture of reasons, whereas the

Table 10.1 ANOVA analysis of no-votes per party family and cabinet

	N	Mean %	Std. Deviation %	Minimum %	Maximum %
Radical Left	58	68.3	36.2	0.0	100.0
Greens	40	30.5	37.5	0.0	100.0
Socialists	75	12.3	22.8	0.0	96.7
Liberals	62	5.4	16.7	0.0	100.0
Christian Democrats	47	5.3	15.8	0.0	100.0
Conservatives	63	6.3	20.1	0.0	98.3
Radical Right	44	21.1	29.7	0.0	100.0

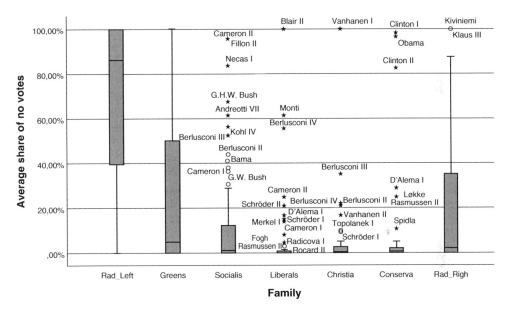

Figure 10.6 Average number of no-votes per party family with outliers
Notes: Labels refer to cabinets. For instance, Blair II refers to the exceptionally high number of no-votes of MPs from the Liberal Party in the British House of Commons during Blair's second cabinet.

radical-right True Finns party mostly voted against missions because it wants to better use the money for territorial defence. Finally, UK deployment votes are often highly controversial because prime ministers tend to only submit deployments to parliament when there is some expressed parliamentary or public opposition to the mission. Altogether though, the dataset shows clear differences among party families. Wagner et al. (2018) theorize that these differences can be explained with genuine ideological differences that can be best understood as a classical left-right division of the political spectrum. Thus, parties on the political left, centre, or right do not only differ substantially on their positioning on the welfare-state aspect of politics but show similar differences when it comes to foreign and defence policy i.e. its high-politics component, which is military deployments and the related question of the use of armed force.

Uncovering the clear and present relevance of government: other drivers of deployment votes

The ANOVA analysis in Table 10.1 also shows that all party families have sometimes voted unanimously in favour (0% no-votes) and at other times almost unanimously against deployments (96.7% to 100%). The U-shaped differences between party families that we have seen above can be clearly identified when looking at standard deviations: they are strongest on the Radical Left and somewhat reigned in among Socialists; they flatten considerably toward the ideological centre while deviations increase again when reaching the Radical Right, although to a lesser degree than on the opposite extreme.

Figure 10.7 shows that – unsurprisingly – this voting behaviour is heavily influenced by a party family being in government or in opposition, with limited family/cabinet-outliers from five countries only. The average share of no-votes for party families in the opposition is 36% whereas for parties in government it is 1.8%. However, being in government does not rule out voting against (a government proposal for) a military mission. The radical-left and green parties during Prodi I, for example, voted against deployments to Bosnia and Albania. Backbench dissent from governing parties can also be found in the USA, the UK, Denmark, and Germany. Thus, being in opposition or government is certainly an important driver of political position-taking on deployment votes but it is far from being the only driver of votes. Taken together, a party's ideology (as captured by its affiliation with a family) and its position in or out of government are the two main driving forces of its voting behaviour. Of course, they may also interact in the sense that parties that have continuously voted against military missions are less likely to become part of a governing coalition whereas parties that have supported deployments even when in opposition are more likely to do so.

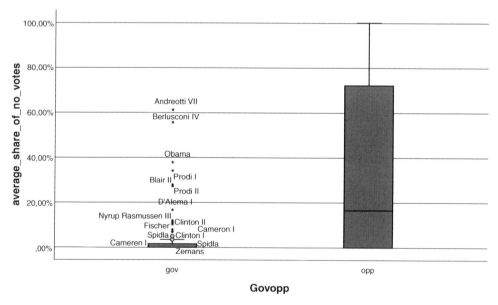

Figure 10.7 Average number of no-votes for party families in government or in opposition with outliers during specific cabinets

Conclusions

The *Parliamentary Deployment Votes Database* (PDVD) is an ongoing project with the ambition to provide regular updates on the countries already covered and to include data from additional countries whenever possible. On the one hand, it contributes data that is useful for students of foreign policy and defence studies who are interested in the democratic politics of foreign and defence policy decision-making and legislative-executive relations more generally. On the other hand, the project also aims at driving further the methodical discussion on using a comparative approach for investigating the party politics of foreign and defence policy, with a special emphasis on security and defence issues. The broader idea is also that proving the existence of party politics in the highly sensitive field of military deployment is an argument for expecting party politics to also matter in less sensitive foreign policy areas, such as in diplomacy, trade, or development aid.

As discussed above, the compilation of deployment votes has demonstrated that there is no such thing as ready-made data, or at least not always. First of all, different cultures of national security, deriving constitutional/legal dispositions, and jurisprudence determine *how often* parliaments vote on military missions – if they vote *at all* – *when* they do that (ex-ante/ex-post), and *what* exactly they are voting on (declarations of government, precise mandates, funding, or extensions). Second, voting practices, record-keeping and data-availability differ considerably across countries and parliaments. Data availability and format have considerable consequences for retrieval work and the workload required to process the data; this also affects the attainable depth of analysis. In some cases, for example, we may only be able to measure contestation on the level of parliament as a whole if individual or at least group-voting data are unavailable. This chapter has shown, however, that constructing an agreement index can help us estimate the degree of contestation on deployments, especially when comparing it to other parliamentary business (see Wagner et al. 2018). Finally, another aspect and – at the same time – resolve is the use of existing datasets' expertise, such as the Comparative Manifesto Project's party classifications or ParlGov's cabinet data but also the Chapel Hill Expert Survey (beginning with Steenbergen and Marks 2007). These datasets help settle cross-national classification issues but also give country experts' crucial discretion to decide differently in order to maintain validity. We are convinced that rigorous data collection and experts' informed judgement go hand in hand; we cannot – and should not – avoid the latter.

It is our belief that despite the challenges discussed in this chapter, it is worthwhile and promising to construct datasets on military deployments that help us investigate party politics. Against the background of country-specific predicaments as, for instance, executive stability or the degree of political fragmentation of a party system, which will differ the more the database grows, we suggest that aggregating votes on the level of party families and cabinets is a reliable and valid avenue to achieve normalization and meaningful comparability. Further research might also tap into comparing patterns of contestation across different time periods or distinguish mission-types and contextual aspects for analysis. This becomes methodologically easier the larger the dataset is but also has trade-offs in terms of imposing meaning. We think, however, that disentangling the votes further along these lines and examining the relevance of a Security Council mandate, differences between first and later mission votes, or differences in intensity levels are promising avenues for future research.

The analyses presented in this chapter are made possible by the *Parliamentary Deployment Votes Database* and corroborate recent results that military deployments are subject to party-political contestation and politicization. On the one hand, the votes-data can be used as a measure of politicization of military missions over time and across countries. On the other hand, the party-votes-data can be used to map the policy space in security and defence policy for individual countries while putting the party politics of military interventions in an individual country in a comparative perspective. Although voting behaviour may change when parties move in and out of government, the data clearly show the relevance of ideological leanings and are hence a valuable indicator of a country's likely future deployment practice. At the time of writing this chapter, this is particularly relevant with a view to radical-left and radical-right parties, some of which have gained in strength and entered government. Their past voting record indicates what citizens and allies can expect from these parties in government. Finally, the party-votes and the party-family-cabinet data are useful for studying the party politics of military interventions (Kaarbo 2012; Mello 2012; Rathbun 2004). Although comparative politics scholars remind us that "democracy is unthinkable save in terms of parties" (Schattschneider 1942, p. 1), political parties have been the "neglected element" (Alden and Aran 2012, p. 60) in the study of democratic politics and foreign affairs. Therefore, the datasets introduced in this chapter can stimulate comparative studies of political parties and military interventions.

Notes

* This chapter was presented prior to publication at the ECPR General Conference 2018 in Hamburg. We are grateful for Patrick Mello's valuable remarks as discussant. Further thanks go to the Giessen Graduate Centre Social Sciences, Economics and Law section on Norms and Change in World Politics for hosting a colloquium discussing the draft chapter, and especially to Helmut Breitmeier, Julia Drubel, Jacob B. Manderbach, and Sandra Schwindenhammer. Additionally, we would like to thank Joen Magieres for his competent work collecting data for the Danish case. We are also grateful for the anonymous reviewers' valuable comments.
1 All datasets and accompanying information can be obtained from www.deploymentvotewatch.eu. See also Wagner et al. (2018).
2 The law further stipulates that those short-term decided by the government without prior approval by parliament must result from treaty obligations or be part of peacekeeping, rescue, or disaster relief missions decided upon by international organizations.
3 Of course, the aggregate number of deployment votes for all countries in our dataset is driven by the high number of votes in Germany and Italy. The many extension votes that take place in the *Bundestag* have been a main driver of the aggregate number of votes. It should be noted, however, that the upward trend also holds if Germany (or Germany and Italy) are excluded. The introduction of deployment votes by law in Spain in 2004 and by constitutional reform in France in 2008 as well as the decisions by British and Belgian governments to have their parliaments vote on deployments in the 2000s account for this upward trend.
4 Other examples of high politicization of military missions without votes are, for instance, the refusal of many European states to engage in the Iraq War causing vivid political debate on foreign policy issues.
5 The most prominent parliamentary decision to reject a government proposal is of course the 2013 UK House of Common Vote on Syria (Kaarbo and Kenealy, 2016). In addition, the Italian Senate vote against a re-financing of International Security Assistance Force in Afghanistan (ISAF) in 2007 (Coticchia and Vignoli, 2018, online first) and the US House of Representatives voted against a resolution expressing support for the use of force in Libya (Böller, 2017). In December 2008, the Czech parliament voted against the continuation of the deployment of Czech troops in Iraq. However, the decision was reversed by another vote at the beginning of 2009 and troops stayed.

6 Research on the US Congress uses a similar measurement (Kupchan and Trubowitz, 2007) but we deem the AI to be more precise.
7 In the case of Spain, the consensus culture applies only to the two main parties, but agreement will most likely decrease with the recent erosion of the bipartisan system.
8 For the four countries included in the first version of this dataset, Wagner et al. (2018, p. 546f.) have also calculated the AI for votes on business other than military deployments. The data shows that military deployments are usually less contested than other parliamentary business.
9 Country experts also largely followed ParlGov classifications of parties in government, with some exceptions for Belgium, France, and Italy that can be retrieved from the codebook version #2 on www.deploymentvotewatch.eu.
10 In our dataset, Belgium, the Czech Republic, France, Germany, Italy, Spain, and the US have bicameral systems.
11 In the US, the Senate is considered to be more influential in foreign policy than the House of Representatives due to the longer term of senators and more legislative responsibilities (treaty power, appointments).
12 In the British House of Commons, MPs cannot abstain. However, they can cast a vote in favour and a vote against, which is a functional equivalent of an abstention, and we record it as such.
13 Whether or when parliament started to provide disaggregated voting data varies between countries. Most votes since the 2000s are recorded nominally or at least group-wise, allowing for analysis by party/party families.
14 See, e.g. Fonck et al. (2019); Pedersen and Christiansen (2017); Coticchia and Vignoli (2018, online first), or Wagner (2017).
15 In the presidential system of the US, scholars observe an increasing partisan polarization in foreign policy (see Jeong and Quirk 2019).
16 The only deviations from ParlGov in this version of the dataset relate to parties being out of/in government in Belgium, France, and Italy on some occasions.

References

Alden, C., Aran, A. (2012). *Foreign Policy Analysis. New Approaches*, Oxon, Routledge.
Boix, C. (2007). The emergence of parties and party systems, 499–521. In: Boix, C., Stokes, S. C. (Eds.), *Handbook of Comparative Politics*, Oxford, Oxford University Press.
Böller, F. (2017). Debating war and peace: US Congress and the domestic legitimization of military interventions. *Democracy and Security*, 13(3), 196–219. doi:10.1080/17419166.2017.1326309.
Böller, F., Müller, M. (2018). Unleashing the watchdogs: Explaining congressional assertiveness in the politics of US military interventions. *European Political Science Review*, 10(4), 637–662. doi:10.1017/S1755773918000152.
Britz, M. (2016). *European Participation in International Operations. The Role of Strategic Culture*, London, Palgrave Macmillan.
Carrubba, C., Gabel, M., Hug, S. (2008). Legislative voting behavior, seen and unseen: A theory of roll-call vote selection. *Legislative Studies Quarterly*, 33(4), 543–572. doi:doi:10.3162/036298008786403079.
Coticchia, F., Vignoli, V. (2018, online first). Italian political parties and military operations: An empirical analysis on voting patterns. *Government and Opposition*, 1–18. doi:10.1017/gov.2018.35.
Dieterich, S., Hummel, H., Marschall, S. (2010). *Parliamentary War Powers: A Survey of 25 European Parliaments*, Geneva, available from: https://www.files.ethz.ch/isn/122963/OP21_FINAL.pdf.
Döring, H., Manow, P. (2018). *Parliaments and Governments Database (ParlGov)*. Development version, available from: http://www.parlgov.org/.
Duffield, J. S. (1998). *World Power Forsaken: Political Culture, International Institutions, and German Security Policy After Unification*, Stanford, CA, Stanford University Press.

Ecker-Ehrhardt, M. (2014). Why parties politicise international institutions: On globalisation backlash and authority contestation. *Review of International Political Economy*, 21(6), 1275–1312.

Eichenberg, R. C., Stoll, R. J., Lebo, M. (2006). War president: The approval ratings of George W. Bush. *Journal of Conflict Resolution*, 50(6), 783–808. doi:10.1177/0022002706293671.

Elster, J. (1983). *Explaining Technical Change. A Case Study in the Philosophy of Science*, Cambridge, London et al., Cambridge University Press.

Fonck, D., Reykers, Y. (2018). Parliamentarisation as a two-way process: Explaining prior parliamentary consultation for military interventions. *Parliamentary Affairs*, 71(3), 674–696. doi:10.1093/pa/gsx081.

Fonck, D., Haesebrouck, T., Reykers, Y. (2019). Parliamentary involvement, party ideology and majority-opposition bargaining: Belgian participation in multinational military operations. *Contemporary Security Policy*, 40(1), 85–100. doi:10.1080/13523260.2018.1500819.

Hildebrandt, T., Hillebrecht, C., Holm, P. M., Pevehouse, J. (2013). The domestic politics of humanitarian intervention: Public opinion, partisanship, and ideology. *Foreign Policy Analysis*, 9(3), 243–266. doi:10.1111/j.1743-8594.2012.00189.x.

Hix, S., Noury, A., Roland, G. (2005). Power to the parties: Cohesion and competition in the European parliament, 1979–2001. *British Journal of Political Science*, 35(2), 209–234. doi:10.1017/S0007123405000128.

Hooghe, L., Marks, G. (2009). A postfunctionalist theory of European integration: From permissive consensus to constraining dissensus. *British Journal of Political Science*, 39(1), 1–23. doi:10.1017/S0007123408000409.

Hooghe, L., Lenz, T., Marks, G. (2019). Contested world order: The delegitimation of international governance. *The Review of International Organizations*, 14(4), 731–743. doi:10.1007/s11558-018-9334-3.

Howell, W. G., Pevehouse, J. C. (2007). *While Dangers Gather: Congressional Checks on Presidential War Powers*, Princeton, NJ, Woodstock, Princeton University Press.

Jeong, G.-H., and Quirk, P. J. (2019). Division at the water's edge: The polarization of foreign policy. *American Politics Research*, 47(1), 58–87. doi:10.1177/1532673x17719721.

Kaarbo, J. (2012). *Coalition Politics and Cabinet Decision Making. A Comparative Analysis of Foreign Policy Choices*. Ann Arbor, MI, University of Michigan Press.

Kaarbo, J., Lantis, J. S., Beasley, R. K. (2013). The analysis of foreign policy in Comparative Perspective, 1–26. In: R. K. Beasley, J. Kaarbo, J. S. Lantis, and M. T. Snarr (Eds.), *Foreign Policy in Comparative Perspective. Domestic and International Influences on State Behavior*, Thousand Oaks, CA, CQ Press.

Kaarbo, J., Kenealy, D. (2016). No, Prime Minister: Explaining the House of Commons vote on intervention in Syria. *European Security*, 25 (1), 28–48, available from http://dx.doi.org/10.1080/09662839.2015.1067615.

Kagan, R. (2018, 12 July). Things will not be okay. *The Washington Post*, available from from https://www.washingtonpost.com/opinions/everything-will-not-be-okay/2018/07/12/c5900550-85e9-11e8-9e80-403a221946a7_story.html?noredirect=on&utm_term=.727b588af959.

Katzenstein, P. J. (Ed.) (1996). *The Culture of National Security. Norms and Identity in World Politics*, New York, Columbia University Press.

Kupchan, C. A., Trubowitz, P. L. (2007). Dead center. The demise of liberal internationalism in the United States. *International Security*, 32(2), 7–44.

Lipset, S. M., Rokkan, S. (1967). Cleavage structures, party systems and voter alignments: An introduction, 1–64. In: Lipset, S. M., Rokkan, S. (Eds.), *Party Systems and Voter Alignments*, New York, Free Press.

Mariager, R., Wivel, A. (2019). *Hvorfor gik Danmark i krig? Uvildig udredning af baggrunden for Danmark militære engagement i Kosovo, Afghanistan og Irak*, Copenhagen, available from: https://krigsudredning.ku.dk/.

Mello, P. A. (2012). Parliamentary peace or partisan politics? Democracies' participation in the Iraq War. *Journal of International Relations and Development*, 15(3), 420–453.

Mello, P. A. (2014). *Democratic Participation in Armed Conflict: Military Involvement in Kosovo, Afghanistan and Iraq*, Basingstoke, Palgrave Macmillan.

Mello, P. A. (2017). Curbing the royal prerogative to use military force: the British House of Commons and the conflicts in Libya and Syria AU - Mello, Patrick A. *West European Politics*, 40(1), 80–100. doi:10.1080/01402382.2016.1240410.

Mello, P. A., Peters, D. (2018). Parliaments in security policy: Involvement, politicisation, and influence. *The British Journal of Politics and International Relations*, 20(1), 3–18. doi:10.1177/1369148117745684.

Milner, H. V., Tingley, D. (2015). *Sailing the Water's Edge: The Domestic Politics of American Foreign Policy*, Princeton, NJ, Princeton University Press.

Mudde, C. (2004). The populist zeitgeist. *Government and Opposition*, 39(4), 541–563. doi: doi:10.1111/j.1477-7053.2004.00135.x.

Mueller, J. E. (1970). Presidential popularity from Truman to Johnson. *The American Political Science Review*, 64(1), 18–34.

Müller, J.-W. (2016). How to think – and not to think – about populism. *Comparative Politics Newsletter*, 26(2), 58–62.

Ostermann, F. (2017). France's reluctant parliamentarisation of military deployments: The 2008 constitutional reform in practice. *West European Politics*, 40(1), 101–118.

Pedersen, R. B., Christiansen, F. J. (2017). *Informal Institutions and the Domestic Roots for Parliamentary Control Mechanisms: The Case of Denmark*. Paper presented at the Dutch-Flemish Political Science Conference, Leiden.

Peters, D., Wagner, W. (2011). Between military efficiency and democratic legitimacy: Mapping parliamentary war powers in contemporary democracies, 1989–2004. *Parliamentary Affairs*, 64 (1), 175–192. doi:10.1093/pa/gsq041.

Plagemann, J., Destradi, S. (2019). Populism and foreign policy: The case of India. *Foreign Policy Analysis*, 15(2), 283–301. doi: https://doi.org/10.1093/fpa/ory010.

Poier, K., Saywald-Wedl, S., Unger, H. (2017). *Die Themen der "Populisten": Mit einer Medienanalyse von Wahlkämpfen in Österreich, Deutschland, der Schweiz, Dänemark und Polen* (first ed. Vol. 5), Baden-Baden, Nomos.

Posen, B. R. (2018). The rise of illiberal hegemony. *Foreign Affairs*, 97(2), 20–27.

Rathbun, B. C. (2004). *Partisan Interventions. European Party Politics and Peace Enforcement in the Balkans*, Ithaca, NY, London, Cornell University Press.

Raunio, T. (2014). Legislatures and foreign policy, 543–566. In: S. Martin, T. Saalfeld, K. W. Strøm (Eds.), *The Oxford Handbook of Legislative Studies*, Oxford, Oxford University Press.

Raunio, T., Wagner, W. (2017). Towards parliamentarization of foreign and security policy? *West European Politics*, 40(1), 1–19.

Saalfeld, T. (1995). On dogs and whips: Recorded votes, 528–565. In: H. Döring (Ed.), *Parliaments and Majority Rule in Western Europe*, Frankfurt am Main, New York, Campus, St. Martin's Press.

Saideman, S. M., Auerswald, D. P. (2012). Comparing caveats: Understanding the sources of national restrictions upon NATO's mission in Afghanistan. *International Studies Quarterly*, 56 (1), 67–84. doi:10.1111/j.1468-2478.2011.00700.x.

Schattschneider, E. E. (1942). *Party Government*, New York, Rinehart.

Steenbergen, M. R., Marks, G. (2007). Evaluating expert judgments. *European Journal of Political Research*, 46(3), 347–366. doi:doi:10.1111/j.1475-6765.2006.00694.x.

Strong, J. (2018). The war powers of the British parliament: What has been established and what remains unclear? *The British Journal of Politics and International Relations*, 20(1), 19–34. doi:10.1177/1369148117745767.

Verbeek, B., Zaslove, A. (2017). Populism and foreign policy, 384–405. In: C. R. Kaltwasser, P. Taggart, P. Ochoa Espejo, P. Ostiguy (Eds.) *The Oxford Handbook of Populism*, Oxford, New York, Oxford University Press.

Wagner, W. (2017). The Bundestag as a champion of parliamentary control of military missions. *S&F Sicherheit und Frieden*, 35(2), 60–65. doi:10.5771/0175-274X-2017-2-60.

Wagner, W., Herranz-Surrallés, A., Kaarbo, J., Ostermann, F. (2017). The party politics of legislative-executive relations in security and defence policy. *West European Politics*, 40(1), 20–41.

Wagner, W., Herranz-Surrallés, A., Kaarbo, J., Ostermann, F. (2018). Party politics at the water's edge. Contestation of military operations in Europe. *European Political Science Review*, 10(4), 537–563.

Zürn, M. (2014). The politicization of world politics and its effects: Eight propositions. *European Political Science Review*, 6(1), 47–71. doi:10.1017/S1755773912000276.

11 The other civil-military gap
Researching public opinion on security and defence policy

Markus Steinbrecher and Heiko Biehl

Introduction

What people think about security policy, defence issues, and military affairs is an important factor for political decision-makers, military leaders and the armed forces in Western democracies: politicians have public opinion in mind when deciding to send their military on missions abroad. Soldiers gain part of their professional motivation from support by civil society. Therefore, public opinion polls on attitudes towards security and defence policy are a well-established instrument for political background information, public debates in media, society, and politics as well as academic research. This chapter provides an overview – with a focus on Germany – on the methodological and conceptual challenges in this research field.

Quantitative, standardized surveys have been an established instrument for collecting and measuring public opinion – the opinion of citizens as measured by polls – since the 1930s in the US and since the late 1940s in Germany and other European countries.[1] Armed forces and ministries of defence have also regularly commissioned surveys and used their results as a base for political decisions and policymaking (Kohr 1989). An independent and continuous debate has developed in military sociology and also in political science by using these polls and the instruments of research on political attitudes. For this part of military sociology, the repeated reproach of an empirical surplus without theoretical ambition does not apply (Kümmel and Biehl 2015: 15). On the contrary, the questions, problems and results of military-related polls discussed in this article overlap in many ways with research fields and lines of discussion that are theoretically and empirically well developed. These include, e.g. public opinion research as part of political sociology, research on individual information processing in communication science and political psychology, respectively, and studies on the behaviour of political actors and institutions in international relations and comparative politics.

Based on this rich literature, we will look at the situation and the peculiarities of military-related public opinion polls with a specific focus on Germany. In addition, we will present and discuss selected empirical results from the early 2000s until the present day, usually by comparing Germany, France, and the United Kingdom. The chapter is structured as follows. The first part presents the two main research strands – the discussion about public opinion on security and defence policy in military sociology on the one hand and in political science on the other. The second part describes various types of military-related population surveys and discusses motives for carrying out surveys related to the armed forces before addressing some selected issues which are relevant for survey research in general and military-related surveys in particular. The third part discusses selected results of opinion polls, including attitudes towards the armed forces and security issues in Germany, France, and the United Kingdom. The conclusive section summarizes the key issues and aspects and highlights the gaps and potential perspectives of future research in this field.

Public opinion research on security and defence policy – traditions, results, and controversies

Research on public opinion on security and defence policy can be linked both to (military) sociology as well as to political science – with slightly different interests and goals between the two disciplines. In military sociology, the findings of population surveys are of particular relevance as an indicator of civil-military relations. The attitudes of the public indicate the social integration of the armed forces (e.g. Biehl 2018a). On the one hand, high approval ratings for the military represent a close link between the military and civil society. Disinterest, criticism and rejection, on the other hand, indicate a crisis in civil-military relations. The relationship between the citizens and the armed forces accordingly is in the main focus of military sociology research with public opinion data. Political science pursues a somewhat different route. Here, public opinion is of particular interest due to its relation to decisions in security policy. Survey results serve as an indicator for the societal legitimacy of political decisions, e.g. whether citizens approve of or reject a military mission and how political actors deal with it. From a theoretical perspective, public attitudes towards the armed forces and security policy constitute an element of a country's strategic culture. Studies which analyse the structures and determinants of public opinion on security and defence affairs from a socio-psychological perspective are represented in both, military sociology and political science. Subsequently, we will discuss the sociological and political science research debates in more detail and will outline their essential approaches and positions.

Security and defence policy attitudes in military sociology: social integration and military motivation

The question of the involvement of armed forces in society is a core theme for military sociology. The classics of Samuel Huntington and Morris Janowitz, presented in the 1950s and 1960s, shape the debate on the relations between armed forces and civil society up to this day. On the one hand, this research tradition deals with "the effects of society on the role, mission, structure and culture of the military, including its operational effectiveness", and, on the other hand, with "the consequences of the behaviour of armed services as coercive, warfighting organizations for society in terms of their power and prestige and legitimacy" (Dandeker 2001: 4). Huntington (1957) argues in his work *The Soldier and the State* for a segregation of the armed forces and society, so that the civilian and military sphere are strictly separated. According to Huntington, this is necessary to preserve the effectiveness of the armed forces and to guarantee their functionality. For him, the military stands out with features such as sacrifice, collectivism, hierarchy, command, and obedience, valour, honour, cohesion, patriotism, and conservatism. These values, in turn, are in conflict with societal developments that Huntington observes in American society and describes as individualization, liberalism, and egalitarianism. Huntington fears for the functioning of American and other Western militaries as they converge too closely with the values and practices of their societies. This inevitable closeness leads to a diffusion of social trends into the armed forces, which, for Huntington, go hand in hand with a loss of military functions, operational readiness, fighting power, defence readiness, and national security. In addition to commitment to a professional vision and a military ethos, Huntington therefore advises that societal influences on the armed forces should be prevented. Janowitz (1960) represents the opposite position in his work *The Professional Soldier*, which is a reaction to Huntington. He emphatically supports the integration of armed forces into society. Against Huntington, he argues that the idea of a segregation of the military and civilian spheres is simply unrealistic, since there are always lively relationships with society through the exchange of personnel (new soldiers joining and long-term soldiers leaving the army). Young recruits transport their beliefs and values from the civilian world into the military. Conversely, active soldiers in their roles as family members, members of social groups, associations and unions, and even retired soldiers, impart their military experience to their civilian environment. For Janowitz, the attempt to isolate the military sphere seems to be dysfunctional, since the armed forces, like any other organization, depend on social legitimacy and support. The armed forces distancing themselves from society would jeopardize the necessary social acceptance and could lead to a loss of reputation, autonomy, and meaning.

We have outlined the contributions of Huntington and Janowitz in more detail, as they have paradigmatic significance for military sociology. Important theoretical conceptions based on Huntington and Janowitz include publications by, e.g. Rebecca Schiff (2008) who developed a concordance theory of civil-military relations, Peter Feaver (2005) who has conceptualized the question of the political influence of soldiers, Wolfgang R. Vogt (1986) who took up the 19th-century incompatibility theorem and sharpened it with a view on the nuclear age, or Martin Shaw (1991) who outlined a post-military society. However, the positions of Huntington and Janowitz continue to form the conceptual framework in which the debate in military sociology develops when it examines citizens' attitudes towards defence issues. Especially since the question of integration or isolation of the armed forces into or from civil society is not only of scientific, but also of some political and social relevance. We will show this by providing examples for studies on social support for the military.

A pioneer study of the recent discussion is the study by Peter Feaver and Richard Kohn (2001) who have identified a "civil-military gap" for the United States. According to them, relations between the military and civilian worlds are dwindling, the importance of the military is falling and social support for the armed forces is in decline. Despite the subsequent events of September 11, 2001, as well as the Afghanistan and Iraq wars, the diagnosis of Feaver and Kohn received great academic and public attention and sparked a series of follow-up studies for other nations, as well as for selected sections of the population (Caforio 2007; Collmer and Kümmel 2007). It is noteworthy that the diagnosis of a civil-military gap got approval in almost all Western armed forces, regardless of the extent of societal popularity (Bacevich 2013; Duradin 2013). Meanwhile, the debate has become so established and advanced that, based on a contribution to the journal *Armed Forces and Society*, four dimensions of the civil-military gap can be differentiated (Rahbek-Clemmensen et al. 2012). From a cultural perspective, the attitudes and values of civilians and soldiers differ (Rahbek-

Clemmensen et al. 2012: 671f; even more nuanced: Franke 2012). Military virtues like sacrifice, bravery and discipline clash with social norms of individuality, consumerism and self-interest – this perspective follows Huntington's reflections. The apparent transnational end of conscription has also fuelled fears that volunteer armies would only recruit from narrowly defined social groups, with the military burden increasingly resting on the shoulders of socially disadvantaged and poorer people (Rahbek-Clemmensen et al. 2012: 672f.). Other dimensions of the civil-military gap which are rarely related to public attitudes on security policy identify differences in the policy preferences of military and civilian elites as well as divergences of interest between the armed forces and other public institutions (Rahbek-Clemmensen et al. 2012: 673f.).

The emergence of a civil-military gap is problematic for the armed forces, as soldiers derive a significant portion of their motivation and legitimacy from support by their compatriots. Studies on soldiers in wars and missions have shown the connection between perceived social support and soldiers' motivation (Biehl 2012; Moskos 1970). This means that soldiers identify more closely with their mission and tasks assigned to them, if they know that their commitment receives social approval. For the armed forces in general, the importance of public opinion goes beyond the professional motivation of soldiers. Studies have shown that the reputation of the armed forces influences, in addition to other factors, the interest in the military as an employer. (e.g. Höfig 2017; Manigart 2005; Moskos 1977). Accordingly, it is easier for armed forces to find qualified recruits if they enjoy the trust and support of the population than if they encounter indifference or open rejection. These explanations show that public opinion is an essential link between the armed forces and society. The attitudes of citizens are both an indicator and a determinant of civil-military relations. In contrast, political science's view on these attitudes focuses more on their relevance for political decisions (and decision-makers).

Political science research on security and defence policy attitudes: social legitimacy and political culture

Public opinion provides information about the social legitimacy of political decisions. A certain degree of support for political actions is a prerequisite for legitimacy and acceptance of policies by citizens in democratic states, as stated by participatory (e.g. Bachrach and Botwinick 1992) and elite-oriented democracy theorists (e.g. Schumpeter 2008). Public opinion polls can be a key tool to find out whether the population supports or rejects certain measures or not. Thus, citizens' attitudes and opinions are an essential benchmark for security policy decisions and define the scope of security and defence policy, even if different security measures such as military operations or armaments procurement have been enforced against resistance and rejection in the population (Kümmel and Biehl 2015: 25f.).

In order to analyse the influence of public opinion on security policy, political science research must, first, clarify whether sufficient information and knowledge exist on the matter: are people able to provide reliable and valid statements about their attitudes? For a long time, political science used the assumptions of the so-called Almond-Lippmann consensus (Almond 1950; Lippmann 1922) to describe citizens' attitudes on foreign and security policy as well as military issues. This catchword summarizes that many citizens are not interested in politics in general and in security policy and the military in particular as well, and that they have little knowledge of these issues. Therefore, their attitudes on these topics are unstable, unstructured and easy to influence. Consequently, public opinion could and should not play a major role for policymaking on these issues (Endres et al. 2015; Holsti 1992). Meanwhile, the Almond-Lippmann consensus in this strict interpretation is outdated and has been displaced by revisionist approaches with different theoretical and substantive emphases. Thus, a branch of the literature was able to show that public opinion at the aggregate level reacts rationally and comprehensibly to political events and decisions ("rational public", e.g. Isernia et al. 2002; Page and Shapiro 1992; Shapiro and Page 1988). In addition, there is extensive evidence demonstrating that citizens carry out cost-benefit evaluations when assessing security policy issues. These assessments are the base for their attitudes, e.g. in the form of economic self-interest (e.g. Carrubba and Singh 2004; Schoen 2008) or military losses (e.g. Gelpi et al. 2005, 2009). Another line of revisionist research shows that citizens derive their specific attitudes to security policy issues from basic attitudes to general aspects of international politics (e.g. Hurwitz and Peffley 1987). These so-called postures include the dichotomies of internationalism – isolationism, militarism – non-militarism, unilateralism – multilateralism, and, in European countries, anti-Atlanticism – Atlanticism (see Mader 2015 for a more detailed account). Other generalized orientations, so-called heuristics, may also facilitate citizens' attitude formation and information processing. There are several suggestions for heuristics and related empirical findings in the literature, e.g. value orientations (e.g. Pötzschke et al. 2012), assessments of political actors and elites (e.g. Balmas 2018), group membership and identity (e.g. Schoen 2008), or party ties and elite signals transmitted by mass media (e.g. Mader and Fiebig 2015, Rattinger et al. 2016). Furthermore, the knowledge on security policy (in Germany) is not below the level of knowledge on other policies or general political knowledge (Steinbrecher and Biehl 2018, 2019). However, all the approaches listed above cannot solve the fundamental problem of low information and interest levels in foreign and security policy in many countries and, thus, one of the premises of the Almond-Lippmann consensus continues to apply. On the one hand, this is reflected in possible problems with the reliability and validity of respondents' responses in surveys when they provide non-attitudes (Converse 1970) or derive their answers based on the mechanisms mentioned above. On the other hand, most foreign, defence and security policy issues are of little salience to the majority of citizens. According to the saying "All Politics is local", election campaigns are more oriented towards domestic economic and social issues. In Germany, the Bundestag election in 2002 was an exception in this regard, when Gerhard Schröder and the SPD could benefit from their categorical rejection of German participation in the US-led military intervention in Iraq (Fuchs and Rohrschneider 2005; Schoen 2004). For the US, the empirical evidence is clearer in this regard: foreign and security policy issues were relevant for the outcome of several elections (e.g. Aldrich et al. 2006, Rattinger 1990).

These interactions between public opinion and political decisions already point to another discussion in political science in which security policy attitudes play a key role. In the field of international relations, the concept of strategic culture increasingly combines an elite-centred perspective and a societal dimension that treats public attitudes as an essential component of political culture. Strategic culture encompasses the widely shared societal values, norms and beliefs that influence security preferences and decisions of a state (Giegerich 2006; Gray 1998; Johnston 1998; Longhurst 2000; Snyder 1977). In their security policy, states not only pursue interests, but also ideas. In other words, strategic culture sets the framework within which specific security policy decisions are taken. The (security) political elites as well as the population are both carriers of the strategic culture of a country. The older literature had mainly focused on the security policy elites: ministers, parliamentarians, administrative leaders, diplomats, generals, correspondents, think tanks, etc. Meanwhile, the influence of the public is largely undisputed. The omnipresent public opinion influences security policy decisions. Civic engagement – in the form of associations, lobby groups, petitions, etc. – also impacts the political process. Political decisions in democracies arise through the interaction of elites and citizens. Opinions and attitudes of the citizens constitute an essential benchmark for decisions on security policy and define the choices in this field. This does not mean that politics solely follows the will of the electorate. In this way, security policy measures with sufficient political support can be enforced against massive public mobilization. With regard to (West) Germany historical examples are the redeployment of German forces after the World War II, the implementation of the NATO double-track decision in the late 1970s and early 1980s, or the Bundeswehr's deployment in Afghanistan. In the long-run, however, it is difficult to act against the explicit will of the electorate – especially since security policy decisions deal eventually with the questions of war and peace.

Especially for the US, there is some research that shows the influence of public opinion on political decisions and vice versa (e.g. Burstein 2003; Wlezien and Soroka 2016). Thus, the meta-analysis by Burstein (2003: 36) demonstrates that citizens' positions have an influence on politics and political decisions in 75% of the cases examined. The strength of this effect is influenced by salience, which is the relevance and public presence of a topic. The more important a topic, the more likely it is that political decision-makers take into account or even follows citizens' attitudes when drafting a policy (Wlezien and Soroka 2016). The relevance of public opinion is not reduced in Burstein's analyses (2003) if the activities of interest groups, parties or elites are taken into account as additional explanatory variables. Burstein (2003) shows that there is a higher responsiveness of political decisions to the attitudes of the population in defence policy than in other policies. This is particularly evident with respect to the attitude towards defence expenditures and the level of defence spending (e.g. Eichenberg and Stoll 2003; Hartley and Russett 1992; Wlezien 1995), which seem to react to each other like a thermostat. These findings provide additional evidence against the assumptions of the Almond-Lippmann consensus. However, Burstein (2003) points to the partly relatively thin research situation in this area.

From an international comparative perspective, Viehrig (2010) has pointed out with regard to the current military deployments of Western countries that public opinion in the home country determines not so much "whether" to participate in international missions, but rather "how" to participate. This refers to the scope, equipment, and focus of the military contribution. As a result, states that face reservations of their citizens do not avoid military deployments, but provide smaller contingents that will be deployed to areas that are more peaceful and are less often involved in hostilities.

In Germany, research on this area is still in its infancy, especially with regard to defence policy. Substantial analyses on the impact of public opinion polls on political decisions are only available to a very limited extent for Germany. Exceptions are a study by Shell (1965) on West Berlin's politics after the construction of the wall and a comparative study by Risse-Kappen (1991), which shows that the influence of public opinion on foreign policy in Germany has increased over time. Instead, there are either normative and theoretical considerations (e.g. Wiesendahl 2016) or anecdotal evidence, like the use of results of the SOWI (Bundeswehr Institute of Social Sciences) surveys in the Defence Committee of the German Bundestag (Nachtwei 2016: 156f.). The political leadership of the German Ministry of Defence (MoD) uses the results of surveys in political discussions, such as in parliamentary debates on the defence budget (Deutscher Bundestag 2015: 13672). Other actors incorporate the results of public opinion surveys into the political and public security debate (Thießen 2016: 63), too.

Military-related public opinion surveys: types, motives, and problems

The subsequent remarks describe various types of military-related population surveys and discuss motives for carrying out surveys related to the armed forces before addressing selected problems for this particular kind of opinion polls.

Types of military-related surveys

We differentiate between several types of military-related opinion surveys. The military or the MoD itself may commission a study. However, other institutions such as think tanks, political foundations, the media, research institutions or individual scientists are also interested in the attitudes of citizens towards the military or foreign and security policy issues. Examples for such studies or survey programmes with an international comparative approach are the Transatlantic Trends studies, by the German Marshall Fund of the United States (and partly the Chicago Council on Foreign Relations) between 2002 and 2015 (The German Marshall Fund of the United States 2018; Inter-University Consortium for Political and Social Research 2018), the Eurobarometer surveys for the European Commission (European Commission 2018) or the regular polls conducted by the Pew Foundation (e.g. Pew Research Center 2017). In addition, there are surveys by commercial providers who frequently ask questions related to the military or foreign and security policy on behalf of newspapers and television broadcasters, or include entire thematic blocks on these issues in their surveys. From a historical point of view, the studies by the United States Information Agency (USIA) or the Office of the Military Government of the US (OMGUS) or other Allied agencies between the end of World War II and the 1990s in (West-) Germany and other European countries are academically relevant. In addition to these large-scale and long-term survey programmes, there are numerous individual studies. To mention just some of them: the study on strategic cultures in selected European countries (Biehl et al. 2011) or studies on foreign and security policy attitudes in individual countries (Berndtsson et al. 2015; Gribble et al. 2015; Holst 1993; Tiargan-Orr and Eran-Jona 2016).

A large part of the studies on public opinion on security policy in Germany has been carried out on behalf of the German MoD since the beginning of the 1960s.[2] Examples are the series of studies on the "Wehrpolitische/Sicherheitspolitische Lage" (Military/Security Condition) between 1981 and 2006, the annual surveys of the SOWI and the Bundeswehr Center for Military History and Social Sciences (ZMSBw) since 1996 and the surveys conducted by the Bundeswehr Center for Public Relations (ZInfoABw) or, previously, the Bundeswehr Academy for Information and Communication (AIK) since 1990 (e.g. Hoffmann 1993). In addition, there are surveys on subgroups of the population, such as the youth studies of the SOWI, conducted between 1993 and 2011 and now conducted by the Bundeswehr Helmut Schmidt University in Hamburg. A special feature of studies on behalf of defence ministries is that a large proportion of the project is developed by military researchers, which, from a ministerial point of view, provides benefits such as loyalty, reliability, and the possibility to exert influence on the researchers (Barlösius 2008: 14ff.).

All studies mentioned so far focus on the public opinion of one's own citizenry. Likewise, the MoD has an interest in the attitudes of the population in the countries in which their armed forces are stationed or deployed. The surveys commissioned by the USIA are an example of US interest in German attitudes on foreign and security policy during the Cold War. However, NATO and its Member States also conduct surveys in the countries of deployment as part of operational communications, e.g. in Afghanistan on a quarterly basis as part of the Afghanistan Nationwide Quarterly Assessment Research survey (ANQAR; D3 Systems 2017, Resolute Support 2018).

Motivation for military-related opinion polls

As already indicated, public opinion polls deliver information, but may also help to legitimize political demands and decisions. Ultimately, survey-based research should contribute to the solution of practical problems (Wiesendahl 2016: 85). For the conceptual integration of military-related surveys into policymaking, we can use the model of the ideal policy-cycle by Hesse and Ellwein (2012: 410): (1) Problem perception, (2) Information acquisition, (3) Programme development, (4) Government decision, (5) Implementation, (6) Impact control, (7) Program evaluation. These steps are independent from each other theoretically, but in the empirical reality merge smoothly into one another. It might even happen that some steps are skipped. Surveys are usually an instrument for steps 1, 2 and 7.

Beyond the general need of state bureaucracies for information, one of the central motives of the armed forces or the MoD for carrying out public opinion polls is the evaluation of civil-military relations. As stated earlier, the armed forces are dependent on societal support. In Germany, this claim is even defined as a goal of the Bundeswehr in a service regulation. Inner Leadership (Innere Führung) is about

> preserving and promoting the involvement of the Bundeswehr in state and society, gaining an understanding of the Bundeswehr's mission within the framework of German security and defence policy among its citizens, and actively engaging the soldiers in the constant change of the armed forces (integration).
> (Bundesministerium der Verteidigung 2008: Number 401; translation by the authors)

It is impossible to achieve this goal without information on citizens' attitudes towards the military and on security and defence policy. Accordingly, in its research regulations, the German MoD strives for "obtaining and providing scientifically based findings on the relevance and functional change of armed forces, their acceptance and attractiveness within the Bundeswehr and in the population, the state of the armed forces and socio-cultural developments in society" (Bundesministerium der Verteidigung 2015: 30). Attitude research and opinion polls are to be carried out by "dealing with key questions of military sociology on civil-military relations" (Bundesministerium der Verteidigung 2014: Number 205). Thus, the justification for ministerial survey research in Germany is, on the one hand, sufficiently precise, but, on the other hand, leaves enough room for a wide range of specific research topics. Of course, similar definitions in the form of research programmes or agendas are also available in other countries, e.g. in the United Kingdom (Ministry of Defence 2017a, 2017b) or Australia (Australian Government 2018a, 2018b). Population surveys in countries of deployment such as Afghanistan are part of a comprehensive intelligence overview for strategic and operational planning and are also available to regional commanders (Resolute Support 2017).

Problems of military-related opinion polls

There are two groups of problems in military-related opinion surveys. On the one hand, we find different methodological problems which are summarized by the construct of the Total Survey Error (Weisberg 2005). The Total Survey Error approach divides errors in surveys into the two general categories of representation errors and measurement errors. The first category combines errors that arise during the sampling and the selection of the target persons while the latter occur, e.g. due to the lack of validity and reliability of the measurement instruments as well as because of processing errors and problems of understanding on the part of the respondents. On the other hand, there are problems that arise from the conflicting goals between the scientific claims of the researchers and the interests of the principal of a study. While social science research is primarily designed to use theories and test hypotheses, the (political) client is interested in the rapid provision of information for political practice, which captures the empirical reality descriptively without much theoretical background (e.g. Streeck 2009: 8). We will discuss both problem categories in more detail below.

Focusing on survey errors first, aspects which are related to the respondents themselves are of primary relevance. To mention just one example, there are sometimes massive problems with access to the field and the accessibility of respondents when conducting surveys in countries of military operations, e.g. due to the security situation or cultural norms. Such aspects can be ignored in surveys in Western countries, even though the response rate has been decreasing for years over different survey modes (e.g. Blohm 2013; Schnell 1997), making it harder to get a representative sample of the population. An additional problem when conducting population surveys, as already mentioned, is the respondents' level of knowledge and information. Only based on sufficient information and basic awareness citizens can make reliable and valid statements about their attitudes. Accordingly, policy-related knowledge, the structure of attitudes and the reliability of information levels are important subjects of research (e.g. Hurwitz and Peffley 1987; Hurwitz et al. 1993; Peffley and Hurwitz 1993; Steinbrecher and Biehl 2018, 2019).

With regard to the second category of problems of military-related opinion polls, the conflict between an academic and a political logic can only be resolved to a limited extent, especially when armed forces or the MoD commission studies. Scientific principles such as truthfulness, objectivity, and scrutiny may clash with principles like military security, protectiveness, and secrecy interests (Wiesendahl 2016: 88f.). However, this antagonism should be significantly less important with respect to population surveys than for surveys within the armed forces. The main reason is the multitude of surveys by other clients on the same topic (see above). Of course, this also applies to issues considered potentially critical or politically sensitive by the ministerial client. There can be divergent interests between scientists and clients not only with regard to the publication of research results, but also with respect to thematic breadth and methodical elaboration of the survey data. There may be demands from the armed forces or the MoD (e.g. a narrow thematic focus or the concentration on descriptive statistics), which contradict or limit scientific standards or do not exhaust the potential of the data. Again, this appears to be a smaller problem for publications based on public opinion surveys than for internal surveys among soldiers (Richter forthcoming). In addition, data from public opinion surveys are often available for further use after reporting to the ministry, thus allowing in-depth analysis according to academic criteria and rules (e.g. Biehl and Schoen 2015; Mader 2017; Steinbrecher et al. 2018).

Another problem for the MoD's interest in clear-cut and explicit information is that, from a scientific point of view, no deterministic predictions are possible. Political players look for clear if-then statements, as well as unambiguous causal mechanisms, including the precise localization of the variables or factors that trigger certain effects or changes. However, social scientists can, at most, make probability statements. Due to different theoretical and deviant interpretive approaches, findings of a specific study may even contradict those related to other surveys and analyses (Wiesendahl 2016: 90ff.). In addition, due to the prevailing principle of falsification, empirical truth can be revoked by research (Streeck 2009), so findings usually do not have a lasting validity.

A final critical point with regard to the model of the ideal policy cycle presented above is the lack of feedback from the client. Consequently, it is often unclear what happens to the results of surveys in the ministerial process and the military evaluation documented in reports. Thus, it is questionable whether the results presented influence policy-making or the evaluation of programmes or measures. Systematic studies on the influence of studies on security attitudes, or on social science investigations, on MoD or armed forces do, to our knowledge, not exist. A rare feedback is the demand for further evaluations. In other cases, there is anecdotal evidence for the use of such research in public debates (see above). It is therefore largely unclear to what extent and how the findings of survey research affect political and military practice.

Topics and selected results of military-related public opinion surveys

Public opinion surveys cover a wide range of topics. The spectrum varies between attitudes on basic issues of security policy such as the legitimacy of military force (militarism vs. non-militarism), cooperation with other countries in international politics (unilateralism vs. multilateralism) or evaluations of the security situation, attitudes towards the armed forces, compulsory military service or the level of defence spending up to specific questions, like the evaluation of a military mission. In view of the variety of topics, we highlight selected aspects below. For the thematic selection, we use the categories of Kümmel and Biehl (2015: 25). We consider the citizens' attitudes to security policy, military tasks and missions and their attitude to the armed forces as an organization or institution. Comparisons between selected Western European countries (Germany, France, United Kingdom (UK), possibly EU average) and detailed analyses of Germany complement each other, depending on data availability.

Foreign and security policy postures

The postures introduced above cover core aspects of international politics and are central parts of individual attitudes and belief systems on foreign and security policy (e.g. Mader 2015). From an aggregate or country perspective the postures are used to operationalize the concept of strategic cultures (e.g. Biehl et al. 2011, 2013).

Figure 11.1 displays average levels of support on two indicators (in percent) in France, Germany, and the United Kingdom from the Transatlantics Trends surveys. One of the questions covers the militarism-non-militarism posture and asks whether war is, under some conditions, necessary to obtain justice. The second indicator is related to the unilateralism-multilateralism posture. The item asks whether NATO is still essential to the respective country's security or not. Unfortunately, comparative data on the postures is only available for the period between 2003/2004 and 2013.

However, the results in Figure 11.1 clearly show that opposition to military violence as an instrument of foreign policy and international politics dominates German strategic culture (Junk and Daase 2013). Support levels are usually around or below 30 percentage points on this question. The only exception is 2003, with a support rate of 38 percent. However, there seems to be a rise in support for the necessity of war after 2009. If we go beyond Figure 11.1 and look at data for the period after 2013, we find a much stronger rise in support for the use of military violence in Germany. In 2015, 50% think that war is necessary under some conditions. The reasons behind this climax are likely to be severe changes in the security policy context like the Civil War in Ukraine or the rise of ISIS (Islamic State in Iraq and Syria). This explanation particularly makes sense if we consider the sharp decline in support for the necessity of war below 30% in the subsequent years (Steinbrecher forthcoming).

We also see a clear multilateral orientation in Germany, in this case towards NATO (Junk and Daase 2013). Except for 2004, between 55 and 63% of the German population think that NATO is essential for the country's security. The graph does

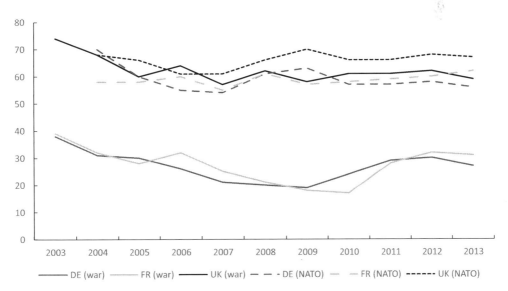

Figure 11.1 Support for postures in France, Germany, and the United Kingdom 2003–2013
Source: 2001–2010, 2014–2018 Eurobarometer surveys; 2011–2013: no data available.

not show a clear development over time. However, surveys on German public opinion after 2013 see a move towards more positive attitudes on NATO (Steinbrecher forthcoming). Accordingly, changes in the security policy context seem to have an impact on citizens' postures.

French public opinion is very similar to public opinion in Germany on both postures. With the exception of 2003, between 17 and 32% of the French public think that war is necessary to obtain justice. After the lowest level of support in 2010, there seems to be a rise in support subsequently. Support for NATO is also at a similar level in France when compared with Germany. This finding is rather surprising considering the long absence of French troops from NATO military structures from 1966 until 2009.

Compared to the two other countries, the UK clearly stands out. Most British citizens see war as a legitimate mean of international politics and prefer to work together with the UK's allies. After the climax of support for the necessity of war to obtain justice in 2003, the level of support for the militarism-posture varies between 57 and 68 percentage points in subsequent years. The UK also takes the lead in terms of support for NATO: between 61 and 70% of British citizens think that NATO is still essential between 2004 and 2013.

Attitudes towards the armed forces

Attitudes towards the armed forces like institutional trust are one core element of citizens' perspective on civil-military relations. Figure 11.2 displays results on institutional trust in

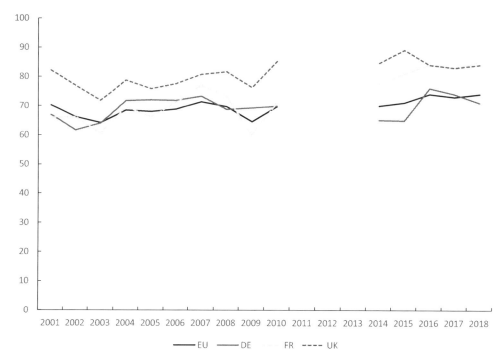

Figure 11.2 Trust in the Armed Forces in the EU, France, Germany, and the United Kingdom 2001–2018
Source: 2001–2010, 2014–2018 Eurobarometer surveys; 2011–2013: no data available.

the armed forces from the Eurobarometer surveys in the United Kingdom, France, and Germany between 2001 and 2018. In addition, we display the mean value of institutional trust in the whole EU as a general benchmark. The Eurobarometer surveys just offer two response options: respondents can either say that they tend to trust the armed forces or that they tend not to trust. The average level of trust between 2001 and 2018 is 69% in Germany, 73% in France, 81% in the United Kingdom, and 70% in all countries of the EU. Trust is rather stable in the EU (difference between the minimum and maximum level of trust: 10 percentage points, standard deviation (sd): 3.2 percentage points), Germany (difference: 14 percentage points, sd: 5.1 percentage points), and Great Britain (difference: 17 percentage points, sd: 5.1 percentage points). The fluctuation is strongest in France (difference: 25 percentage points, sd: 8.0 percentage points). The development in this country can be divided into two periods. While trust in the Armed Forces is lower and varies to a stronger degree between 2001 and 2011, the French people put more trust in their military after 2014. In addition, the over-time variation in trust is much smaller for this period. The trust level is always highest in the United Kingdom with the exception of 2018 when France takes the lead. Trust in Germany usually varies around the EU average and shows a similar stability like other indicators that measure the general attitude towards the military (Biehl 2018a). Obviously, institutional trust is less sensitive to events and media reports in Germany than in France where several terrorist attacks since 2015 likely have changed the perception of the military among citizens.

Attitudes on defence spending

Another central topic for civil-military relations is the amount of economic resources, which is or should be dedicated to the armed forces. Figure 11.3 shows the development of support for increased or more defence spending in percent in the United Kingdom, France, and Germany between 2002 and 2016 from the Transatlantic Trends and Pew Global

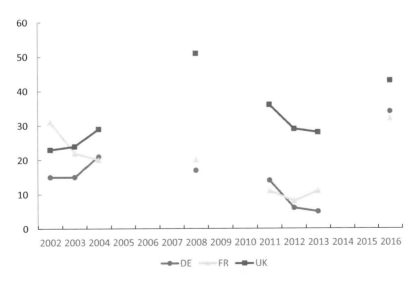

Figure 11.3 Support for increase of/higher defence spending in France, Germany, and the United Kingdom 2002–2016
Source: 2002–2004, 2008, 2011–2013: Transatlantic Trends, 2016: Pew Global Attitudes Survey.

Attitudes surveys.. Question wording and response options vary between different years and surveys, but are comparable for the entire period. Respondents have to indicate whether they want to increase or decrease defence spending or keep the expenditures for this policy at the same level. For the sake of clarity, Figure 11.3 does only display the relative frequencies for the group of those people who prefer increased spending on defence matters.

The support for a rise in defence expenditures in Germany varies between 15 and 20 percentage points between 2002 and 2011. It drops below the 10% mark in 2012 and 2013 and rises to its highest value (34%) in 2016. The largest group of respondents usually either favours keeping defence spending at the same level or cutting expenditures for defence. Compared to the two other countries, support for more defence spending is lowest in Germany. However, other surveys for Germany show a similar development over time, but display higher levels of support for increased defence spending in general, eventually leading to a relative majority of citizens being in favour of a higher defence budget since 2015 (e.g. Steinbrecher 2018).

France shows a higher level of support in 2002 compared to the two other countries. However, support drops very much subsequently and usually is at a similar level as in Germany after 2004. Like in Germany, support for higher defence spending in France reaches its highest level in 2016 (32%). With the exception of 2002 citizens in the United Kingdom show most support for higher defence expenditures compared to the French and Germans. Support levels vary between 23 and 36 percentage points in most of the years, but reach very high levels in 2008 (51%) and 2016 (43%).

Accordingly, the attitude towards defence spending is rather volatile over time in all three countries and seems to be influenced by changes in the security context. Main drivers of increased support for higher defence expenditures in recent years could be the civil war in Ukraine, Russia's annexation of the Crimean peninsula, and the rise and fall of ISIS and its consequences, to name just a few. The likely reaction of public opinion in different countries to these events and developments is clear evidence for the validity of the concept of the "rational public" described above.

Attitudes towards missions and deployments

While France and the United Kingdom have a long tradition of foreign deployments, sending troops in regions out of the NATO and EU area was something new for Germans after their unification in 1990. However, even Germany can look back at a history of almost 30 years of international deployments nowadays. The perceptions of these missions by the citizens at home are not only relevant for the reasons mentioned in the introduction and in our second part, but soldiers on deployment are expecting a high level of support for their military missions (e.g. Biehl 2012; Würich and Scheffer 2014).

As it is rather difficult to find comparative survey data on the same military missions, we are only able to have a look at almost historic data for the ISAF-mission in Afghanistan for which Germany, France, and the United Kingdom contributed troops. The results displayed in Figure 11.4 provide information on the level of combined support for increasing and keeping the number of troops of the respective country at the same level. This question was asked during the years between 2009 and 2012 in the Transatlantic Trends surveys. Figure 11.4 shows that public opinion on this issue was very similar among Germans and Britons: support for increasing and keeping the number of troops at the same level dropped from 42 and 37%, respectively, in 2009 to about 20% in 2012. The decline of support in France over the respective period is also

The other civil-military gap 203

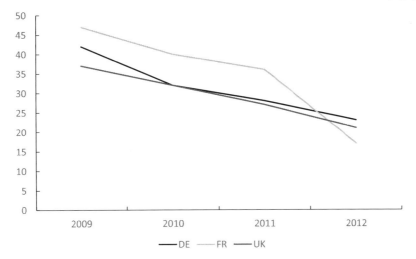

Figure 11.4 Support for increase and keeping the number of troops at the same level combined in France, Germany, and the United Kingdom 2009–2012
Source: Transatlantic Trends.

visible, but very severe from 2011 to 2012 when support dropped by more than 20 percentage points. The similar development in all three countries reflects the lack of success of ISAF and shows a rather rational reaction by public opinion.

However, the large decline in support might be strongly related to the wording and the focus of this particular question. Empirical studies on the attitudes of the German population towards foreign deployments usually show benevolent scepticism towards international engagements of the Bundeswehr, especially if the missions have a robust character and include the use of military force (e.g. Biehl 2018b; Mader 2017; Rattinger et al. 2016).

Conclusion

This chapter has aimed to present the situation, the peculiarities and problems as well as selected results of public opinion surveys on defence and security issues. The presented theories, findings and arguments show that this is an area which is well-developed both theoretically and methodologically, and which is well connected to discourses in political science and sociology. In addition, it is subject to fewer restrictions from the armed forces or the MoD than the research directed at the armed forces and the soldiers, which is in the focus of several other contributions of this volume. Furthermore, the comprehensive availability of quantitative empirical data from various sources offers great potential for further empirical analysis in this area. Research gaps are particularly evident with regard to the relevance of surveys for political decision-making, so that it is often unclear to what extent the attitudes of the population or the respondents in general influence political action.

The results from population surveys exemplified here show that, on the one hand, interruptions in survey continuity lead to knowledge gaps which cannot be closed retrospectively. On the other hand, a partial standardization of the survey instruments over time is necessary to ensure the comparability of the results. Comparability also poses a problem in the analysis of different studies, as they usually use different question wordings and response scales, some of which lead to divergent or even contradictory results. Here, it would make sense to reach an agreement between different research institutions to the effect that normed scales are used, however, this appears to be rather unrealistic, especially for reasons of continuity of time series and the diverging interests of the different clients.

In military sociology surveys on public opinion are an established indicator of the state of civil-military relations. The findings on public opinion are partly opposed to some of the public's, the armed forces' and some of the literature's ideas and expectations. First, there are differences in the attitudes of Western societies. However, German public opinion is by no means an outlier. Rather, the attitude of the German public corresponds to a continental European standard from which an Anglo-Saxon position can be distinguished (Biehl et al. 2011). Second, contrary to the civil-military gap thesis, public support for the armed forces is consistently high. Third, the population's position towards the armed forces is less a question of whether one needs military forces, but for which goals they are used and deployed. Especially military interventions always give rise to political and social strife and protest. On the one hand, these findings underscore the need for a stronger and more systematic examination of the influence of public opinion on security policy decisions. On the other hand, there is a lack of studies that compare (political) attitudes of citizens and soldiers. However, it is especially important for the armed forces in Western democracies to know how representative their soldiers are for society as a whole. For them, both the citizens' and the soldiers' voice are relevant.

Notes

1 For a detailed overview on the development of survey research in Germany on foreign, security and military attitudes, please refer to Rattinger et al. (1995).
2 The earliest survey is probably from 1962 (Eichenberg 1989: 43–46, 59). Rattinger et al. (1995: 43) already point out in 1995 that data and materials on MoD studies before 1981 have been lost. Heinemann dates the beginning of social science research for the Bundeswehr to the beginning of the 1960s (Heinemann 2016: 42f.), this also seems to apply to population surveys.

References

Aldrich, J., Gelpi, C., Feaver, P., Reifler, J., and Sharp, K. (2006). Foreign policy and the electoral connection. *Annual Review of Political Science*, 9, 477–502.
Almond, G. (1950). *The American People and Foreign Policy*, New York, Harcourt, Brace.
Australian Government (2018a). *National Security Science and Technology: Policy and Priorities*, Canberra.
Australian Government (2018b). *Defence Science and Technology Capability Portfolio*, Canberra.
Bacevich, A. (2013). *Breach of Trust: How Americans Failed Their Soldiers and Their Country*, New York, Metropolitan Books.
Bachrach, P., Botwinick, A. (1992). *Power and Empowerment. A Radical Theory of Participatory Democracy*, Philadelphia, Temple University Press.
Balmas, M. (2018). Tell me who is your leader, and I will tell you who you are: Foreign leaders' perceived personality and public attitudes toward their countries and citizenry. *American Journal of Political Science*, 62(2), 499–514.

Barlösius, E. (2008). *Zwischen Wissenschaft und Staat? Die Verortung der Ressortforschung*, Berlin, Wissenschaftszentrum Berlin für Sozialforschung.

Berndtsson, J., Dandeker, C., Yden, K. (2015). Swedish and British public opinion of the armed forces after a decade of war. *Armed Forces & Society*, 41(2), 307–328.

Biehl, H., Fiebig, R., Giegerich, B., Jacobs, J., Jonas, A. (2011). *Strategische Kulturen in Europa. Die Bürger Europas uns ihre Streitkräfte*, Strausberg, Sozialwissenschaftliches Institut der Bundeswehr.

Biehl, H. (2012). Einsatzmotivation und Kampfmoral, 447–474. In: Leonhard, N., Werkner, I.-J. (Eds.) (2012). *Militärsoziologie – eine Einführung*, 2nd updated and supplemented edition, Wiesbaden, Springer VS.

Biehl, H., Giegerich, B., Jonas, A. (Eds.) (2013). *Strategic Cultures in Europe: Security and Defence Policies Across the Continent*, Wiesbaden, Springer VS.

Biehl, H., Schoen, H. (Eds.) (2015). *Sicherheitspolitik und Streitkräfte im Urteil der Bürger. Theorien, Methoden, Befunde*, Wiesbaden, Springer VS.

Biehl, H. (2018a). Haltungen der Bürgerinnen und Bürger zur Bundeswehr, 72–93. In: Steinbrecher, M., Biehl, H., Graf, T. (2018). *Sicherheits- und verteidigungspolitisches Meinungsbild in der Bundesrepublik Deutschland. Ergebnisse und Analysen der Bevölkerungsbefragung 2018*. Forschungsbericht 118, Potsdam, ZMSBw.

Biehl, H. (2018b). Einstellungen zu den Auslandseinsätzen der Bundeswehr, 177–187. In: Steinbrecher, M., Biehl, H., Graf, T. (2018). *Sicherheits- und verteidigungspolitisches Meinungsbild in der Bundesrepublik Deutschland. Ergebnisse und Analysen der Bevölkerungsbefragung 2018*. Forschungsbericht 118, Potsdam, ZMSBw.

Blohm, M. (2013). *Ausschöpfungsquoten und Stichprobenqualität. Erkenntnisse aus dem ALLBUS*. Presentation at the workshop Methoden der empirischen Sozialforschung in amtlichen Haushaltsstatistiken, Wiesbaden.

Bundesministerium der Verteidigung (2008). *Zentrale Dienstvorschrift A-2600/1. Innere Führung. Selbstverständnis und Führungskultur*, Berlin.

Bundesministerium der Verteidigung (2014). *Zentrale Dienstvorschrift A-2713/2. Wissenschaftliche Arbeit des Zentrums für Militärgeschichte und Sozialwissenschaften der Bundeswehr*, Berlin.

Bundesministerium der Verteidigung (2015). *Ressortforschungsplan des Bundesministeriums der Verteidigung für 2016ff*, Berlin.

Burstein, P. (2003). The impact of public opinion on public policy: A review and an agenda. *Political Research Quarterly*, 56(1), 29–40.

Caforio, G. (Ed.) (2007). *Cultural Differences between the Military and Parent Society in Democratic Countries*, Amsterdam, Elsevier.

Carrubba, C., Singh, A. (2004). A decision theoretic model of public opinion: Guns, butter, and European common defence. *American Journal of Political Science*, 48(2), 218–231.

Collmer, S., Kümmel, G. (2007). The civil-military gap among German future elites, 255–259. In: Caforio, G. (Ed.) (2007). *Cultural Differences between the Military and Parent Society in Democratic Countries*, Amsterdam, Elsevier.

Converse, P. (1970). Attitudes and non-attitudes: Continuation of a dialogue, 168–189. In: Tufte, E. (Ed.) (1970). *The Quantitative Analysis of Social Problems*, Reading, MA, Addison-Wesley.

Dandeker, C. (2001). On the need to be different: Military uniqueness and civil-military relations in modern society. *RUSI Journal*, 146(3), 4–9.

Deutscher Bundestag (2015). *Rede von Verteidigungsministerin Ursula von der Leyen in der Debatte über den Verteidigungshaushalt. Plenarprotokoll 18/139, Stenografischer Bericht*, 139. Sitzung, 25. 11. 2015. Berlin, S. 13670–13672, available online: http://dipbt.bundestag.de/dip21/btp/18/18139.pdf#P.13669 (Consulted on 5 March 2019).

D3 Systems (2017). *Methods Report. ANQAR Wave 38*, Tysons Corner, VA.

Duradin, C. (2013). *Le déclin de l'armée française*, Paris, François Bourin Editeur.

Eichenberg, R. (1989). *Public Opinion and National Security in Western Europe: Consensus Lost?* Ithaca, NY, Cornell University Press.

Eichenberg, R., Stoll, R. (2003). Representing defence: Democratic control of the defence budget in the United States and Western Europe. *The Journal of Conflict Resolution*, 47(4), 399–422.

Endres, F., Schoen, H., Rattinger, H. (2015). Außen- und Sicherheitspolitik aus Sicht der Bürger. Theoretische Perspektiven und ein Überblick über den Forschungsstand, 39–65. In: Biehl, H., Schoen, H. (Eds.) (2015). *Sicherheitspolitik und Streitkräfte im Urteil der Bürger. Theorien, Methoden, Befunde*, Wiesbaden: Springer VS.

European Commission (2018). *Public Opinion*, available from: http://ec.europa.eu/commfrontoffice/publicopinion/index.cfm (Consulted on 30 July 2018).

Feaver, P. D., Kohn, R. H. (Eds.) (2001). *Soldiers and Civilians. The Civil-Military Gap and American National Security*, Cambridge, MIT Press.

Feaver, P. D. (2005). *Armed Servants: Agency, Oversight, and Civil-Military Relations*, Cambridge, MA: Harvard University Press.

Franke, J. (2012). *Wie integriert ist die Bundeswehr? Eine Untersuchung zur Integrationssituation der Bundeswehr als Verteidigungs- und Einsatzarmee*, Baden-Baden, Nomos.

Fuchs, D., Rohrschneider, R. (2005). War es dieses Mal nicht die Ökonomie? Der Einfluss von Sachfragenorientierungen auf die Wählerentscheidung bei der Bundestagswahl 2002, 339–356. In: Falter, J., Gabriel, O., Weßels, B. (Eds.) (2005). *Wahlen und Wähler. Analysen aus Anlass der Bundestagswahl 2002*, Wiesbaden, VS Verlag für Sozialwissenschaften.

Gelpi, C., Feaver, P., Reifler, J. (2005). Success matters. Casualty sensitivity and the war in Iraq. *International Security*, 30(3), 7–46.

Gelpi, C., Feaver, P., Reifler, J. (2009). *Paying the Human Costs of War. American Public Opinion and Casualties in Military Conflicts*, Princeton, NJ, Princeton University Press.

The German Marshall Fund of the United States (2018). *Transatlantic Trends – Public Opinion*, available from, http://www.gmfus.org/initiatives/transatlantic-trends---public-opinion/ (Consulted on 30 July 2018).

Giegerich, B. (2006). *European Security and Strategic Culture. National Responses to the EU's Security and Defence Policy*, Baden-Baden, Nomos.

Gray, C. S. (1999). Strategic culture as context. The first generation of theory strikes back. *Review of International Studies*, 25(1), 49–69.

Hartley, T., Russett, B. (1992). Public opinion and the common defence: Who governs military spending in the United States? *American Political Science Review*, 86(4), 905–915.

Heinemann, W. (2016). Das SOWI im Lichte der Akten, 35–50. In: Dörfler-Dierken, A., Kümmel, G. (Eds.) (2016). *Am Puls der Bundeswehr. Militärsoziologie in Deutschland zwischen Wissenschaft, Politik, Bundeswehr und Gesellschaft*, Wiesbaden, Springer VS.

Hesse, Joachim J., Ellwein, Thomas (2012). *Das Regierungssystem der Bundesrepublik Deutschland*. 10th comprehensively revised edition, Baden-Baden, Nomos.

Hines, L., Gribble, A., Wessely, R., et al. (2015). Are the armed forces understood and supported by the public? A wiew from the United Kingdom. *Armed Forces & Society*, 41(4), 688–713.

Höfig, C. (2017). 'Man shall not live by bread alone': Occupational needs of military personnel and their significance for the attractiveness of the German armed forces as an employer. *Res Militaris* 4, "Recruitment and Retention, Part 1".

Hoffmann, H. (1993). *Demoskopisches Meinungsbild in Deutschland zur Sicherheits- und Verteidigungspolitik 1992*, Waldbröl, AIK.

Holsti, O. (1992). Public opinion and foreign policy: Challenges to the Almond-Lippmann consensus. *International Studies Quarterly*, 36, 439–466.

Holst, C. (1993). *Sicherheitsorientierung und status quo – Einstellungen zur Bundeswehr in der Bevölkerung in Ost- und Westdeutschland 1992 bis 1993*. DFG-project "Struktur und Determinanten außen- und sicherheitspolitischer Einstellungen in der Bundesrepublik Deutschland", Research report no. 6, Bamberg, Universität Bamberg.

Huntington, S. P. (1957). *The Soldier and the State: The Theory and Politics of Civil-Military Relations*, Cambridge, MA, Belknap Press.

Hurwitz, J., Peffley, M. (1987). How are foreign policy attitudes structured? A hierarchical model. *American Political Science Review*, 81(4), 1099–1120.

Hurwitz, J., Peffley, M., Seligson, M. (1993). Foreign policy belief systems in comparative perspective: The United States and Costa Rica. *International Studies Quarterly*, 37(3), 245–270.

Inter-University Consortium for Political and Social Research (2018). *Transatlantic Trends Survey Series*, available from: https://www.icpsr.umich.edu/icpsrweb/ICPSR/series/235 (Consulted on 30 July 2018).

Isernia, P., Juhász, Z., Rattinger, H. (2002). Foreign policy and the rational public in comparative perspective. *The Journal of Conflict Resolution*, 46(2), 201–224.

Janowitz, M. (1960). *The Professional Soldier. A Social and Political Portrait*, New York, The Free Press.

Johnston, A. (1998). *Cultural Realism: Strategic Culture and Grand Strategy in Chinese History*, Princeton, NJ, Princeton University Press.

Junk, J., Daase, C. (2013). Germany, 139–152. In: Biehl, H., Giegerich, B., Jonas, A. (Eds.) (2013). *Strategic Cultures in Europe. Security and Defence Policies Across the Continent*, Wiesbaden, Springer VS.

Kohr, H.-U. (1989). *Public Opinion Surveys on Security Policy and the Armed Forces: Policy Polling or Scientific Research?* SOWI-working paper no. 25, München, Sozialwissenschaftliches Institut der Bundeswehr.

Kümmel, G., Biehl, H. (2015). Gradmesser der zivil-militärischen Beziehungen. Der Beitrag von Umfragen und Einstellungsforschung zur Militärsoziologie, 13–38. In: Biehl, H., Schoen, H. (Eds.) (2015). *Sicherheitspolitik und Streitkräfte im Urteil der Bürger. Theorien, Methoden, Befunde*, Wiesbaden, Springer VS.

Lippmann, W. (1922). *Public Opinion*, New York, Macmillan.

Longhurst, K. (2000). The concept of strategic culture, 301–310. In: Kümmel, G., Prüfert, A. (Eds.), *Military Sociology. The Richness of a Discipline*, Baden-Baden, Nomos,.

Mader, M. (2015). Grundhaltungen zur Außen- und Sicherheitspolitik in Deutschland, 69–96. In: Biehl, H., Schoen, H. (Eds.) (2015). *Sicherheitspolitik und Streitkräfte im Urteil der Bürger. Theorien, Methoden, Befunde*, Wiesbaden, Springer VS.

Mader, M., Fiebig, R. (2015). Determinanten der Bevölkerungseinstellungen zum Afghanistaneinsatz. Prädispositionen, Erfolgswahrnehmungen und die moderierende Wirkung individueller Mediennutzung, 97–121. In: Biehl, H., Schoen, H. (Eds.) (2015). *Sicherheitspolitik und Streitkräfte im Urteil der Bürger. Theorien, Methoden, Befunde*, Wiesbaden: Springer VS.

Mader, M. (2017). *Öffentliche Meinung zu Auslandseinsätzen der Bundeswehr. Zwischen Antimilitarismus und transatlantischer Orientierung*, Wiesbaden, Springer VS.

Manigart, P. (2005). Risks and recruitment in postmodern armed forces: The case of Belgium. *Armed Forces & Society*, 31(4), 559–582.

Ministry of Defence (2017a). *Science and Technology Strategy 2017*, London.

Ministry of Defence (2017b). *MOD Area of Research Interest*, London.

Moskos, C. (1970). *The American Enlisted Man*, New York, Russell Sage Foundation.

Moskos, C. (1977). From institution to occupation: Trends in military organization. *Armed Forces & Society*, 4(1), 41–50.

Nachtwei, W. (2016). Sicherheitspolitische Entscheidungsprozesse und Ergebnisse militärsoziologischer Forschungen, 151–165. In: Dörfler-Dierken, A., Kümmel, G. (Eds.) (2016). *Am Puls der Bundeswehr. Militärsoziologie in Deutschland zwischen Wissenschaft, Politik, Bundeswehr und Gesellschaft*, Wiesbaden: Springer VS.

Page, B., Shapiro, R. (1992). *The Rational Public: Fifty Years of Trends in Americans' Policy Preferences*, Chicago, University of Chicago Press.

Peffley, M., Hurwitz, J. (1993). Models of attitude constraint in foreign affairs. *Political Behavior*, 15(1), 61–90.

Pew Research Center (2017). *NATO's Image Improves on Both Sides of the Atlantic. European Faith in American Military Support Largely Unchanged*, Washington, D.C.

Pötzschke, J., Rattinger, H., Schoen, H. (2012). Persönlichkeit, Wertorientierungen und Einstellungen zu Außen- und Sicherheitspolitik in den Vereinigten Staaten. *Politische Psychologie*, 2, 4–29.

Rahbek-Clemmensen, J., Archer, E. M., Barr, J., *et al.* (2012). Conceptualizing the civil–military gap: A research note. *Armed Forces & Society*, 38(4), 669–678.

Rattinger, H. (1990). Bestimmungsfaktoren des Wahlverhaltens bei der amerikanischen Präsidentschaftswahl 1988 unter besonderer Berücksichtigung politischer Sachfragen. *Politische Vierteljahresschrift*, 31(1), 54–78.

Rattinger, H., Behnke, J., Holst, C. (1995). *Außenpolitik und öffentliche Meinung in der Bundesrepublik: Ein Datenhandbuch zu Umfragen seit 1954*, Frankfurt am Main et al., Peter Lang.

Rattinger, H., Schoen, H., Endres, F., *et al.* (2016). *Old Friends in Troubled Waters. Policy Principles, Elites, and U.S.-German Relations at the Citizen Level After the Cold War*, Baden-Baden, Nomos.

Resolute Support (2017). *ANQAR Wave 38. Regional Look, TAAC – C.* November 2017. Präsentation. Kabul.

Resolute Support (2018). *ANQAR Wave 38. National Look.* Jan 2018. FINAL Version 2.0. Präsentation. Kabul.

Richter, G. (forthcoming). Ganz normale Organisationsforschung. Empirische Befragungen in der Bundeswehr. In: Elbe, M., Biehl, H., Steinbrecher, M. (Eds.) (forthcoming). *Empirische Sozialforschung in den Streitkräften. Positionen, Erfahrungen, Kontroversen*, Berlin, Berliner Wissenschaftsverlag.

Risse-Kappen, T. (1991). Public opinion, domestic structure, and foreign policy in liberal democracies. *World Politics*, 43(4), 479–512.

Schiff, R. L. (2008). *The Military and Domestic Politics: A Concordance Theory of Civil-Military Relations*, Abingdon, Routledge.

Schnell, R. (1997). *Nonresponse in Bevölkerungsumfragen. Ausmaß, Entwicklung und Ursachen*, Opladen, Leske + Budrich.

Schoen, H. (2004). Winning by priming? Campaign strategies, changing determinants of voting intention, and the outcome of the 2002 German Federal Election. *German Politics and Society*, 72, 65–82.

Schoen, H. (2008). Identity, instrumental self-interest and institutional evaluations. explaining public opinion on common European policies in foreign affairs and defence. *European Union Politics*, 9(1), 5–29.

Schumpeter, J. (2008 [1942]). *Capitalism, Socialism, and Democracy*, New York, Harper Perennial.

Shapiro, R., Page, B. (1988). Foreign policy and the rational public. *Journal of Conflict Resolution*, 32(2), 211–247.

Shaw, M. (1991). *Post-military Society: Militarism, Demilitarization and War at the End of the Twentieth Century*, Philadelphia, PA, Temple University Press.

Shell, K. (1965). *Bedrohung und Bewährung. Führung und Bevölkerung in der Berlin-Krise*, Köln, Opladen, Westdeutscher Verlag.

Snyder, J. L. (1977). *The Soviet Strategic Culture. Implications for Limited Nuclear Operations*, Santa Monica, Rand Corporation.

Steinbrecher, M. (2018). Einstellungen zur Höhe der Verteidigungsausgaben sowie zum Personalumfang der Bundeswehr, 139–157. In: Steinbrecher, M., Biehl, H., Graf, T. (2018). *Sicherheits- und verteidigungspolitisches Meinungsbild in der Bundesrepublik Deutschland. Ergebnisse und Analysen der Bevölkerungsbefragung 2018*. Forschungsbericht 118, Potsdam, ZMSBw..

Steinbrecher, M. (forthcoming). Im Urteil der Bürger: militärbezogene Bevölkerungsbefragungen. In: Elbe, M., Biehl, He., Steinbrecher, M. (Eds.) (forthcoming). *Empirische Sozialforschung in den Streitkräften. Positionen, Erfahrungen, Kontroversen*, Berlin, Berliner Wissenschaftsverlag.

Steinbrecher, M., Biehl, H. (2020). Military Know-Nothings or (At Least) Military Know-Somethings? Knowledge of Defence Policy in Germany and Its Determinants. *Armed Forces & Society*. doi:10.1177/0095327X18811384.

Steinbrecher, M., Biehl, H. (2019). Nur "freundliches Desinteresse"? Ausmaß und Determinanten verteidigungspolitischen Wissens in Deutschland, 145–175. In: Westle, Bettina, Tausendpfund, Markus (Eds.) (2019). *Politisches Wissen. Relevanz, Messung und Befunde*, Wiesbaden, Springer VS.

Steinbrecher, M., Biehl, H., Bytzek, E., Rosar, U. (Eds.) (2018). *Freiheit oder Sicherheit? Ein Spannungsverhältnis aus Sicht der Bürgerinnen und Bürger*, Wiesbaden, Springer VS.

Streeck, W. (2009). *Man weiß es nicht genau: Vom Nutzen der Sozialwissenschaften für die Politik*, Köln, Max-Planck-Institut für Gesellschaftsforschung.

Thießen, J. (2016). *True love? Neue Herausforderungen für die Militärsoziologie nach der Wende*, 57–66. In: Dörfler-Dierken, A., Kümmel, G. (Eds.) (2016). *Am Puls der Bundeswehr. Militärsoziologie in Deutschland zwischen Wissenschaft, Politik, Bundeswehr und Gesellschaft*, Wiesbaden: Springer VS.

Tiargan-Orr, R., Eran-Jona, M. (2016). The Israeli Public's Perception of the IDF: Stability and Change. *Armed Forces & Society*, 42(2), 324–343.

Viehrig, H. (2010). *Militärische Auslandseinsätze. Die Entscheidungen europäischer Staaten zwischen 2000 und 2006*, Wiesbaden, VS Verlag für Sozialwissenschaften.

Vogt, W. R. (1986). Militärische Gewalt und Gesellschaftsentwicklung. Zur Inkompatibilitätsproblematik und Friedenssicherung im Nuklearzeitalter—ein soziologischer Entwurf, 37–87. In: Vogt, W. R. (1986). *Militär als Gegenkultur. Streitkräfte im Wandel der Gesellschaft*, Wiesbaden, VS Verlag für Sozialwissenschaften.

Weisberg, H. (2005). *The Total Survey Error Approach: A Guide to the New Science of Survey Research*, Chicago, University of Chicago Press.

Wiesendahl, E. (2016). Vom Nutzen und Nachteil sozialwissenschaftlicher Forschung für die Bundeswehr, 85–103. In: Dörfler-Dierken, A., Kümmel, G. (Eds.) (2016). *Am Puls der Bundeswehr. Militärsoziologie in Deutschland zwischen Wissenschaft, Politik, Bundeswehr und Gesellschaft*, Wiesbaden, Springer VS.

Wlezien, C. (1995). The public as thermostat: Dynamics of preferences for spending. *American Journal of Political Science*, 39(4), 981–1000.

Wlezien, C., Soroka, S. (2016). Public opinion and public policy. In: *Oxford Research Encyclopedia of Politics*. doi:10.1093/acrefore/9780190228637.013.74.

Würich, S., Scheffer, U. (2014). *Operation Heimkehr. Bundeswehrsoldaten über ihr Leben nach dem Auslandseinsatz*, Berlin, Christoph Links.

Conclusion

A plea for cross-fertilization of methods in defence studies

Delphine Deschaux-Dutard

This book has presented an overview of methods used in different social sciences (political science, history, geography, public law, and economics) to investigate defence issues. In several contributions, the authors have also interestingly explained the place held by defence issues in their disciplinary field, as it is closely linked with the methodological dimension. To finish the reflection opened in introduction, this conclusion provides a short reflection on the potentialities of mixing methods and cross-fertilizing disciplines in defence studies, so as to better cope with the complexity of defence in the 21st century.

Many defence issues, such as terrorism, defence policies, cyber issues, military effectiveness, and so on, lie at the crossroads of different disciplines and thus could really benefit from cross-fertilization. We will point out a few of these subjects in the first section, as many contributors of this volume underlined the interest of borrowing methods and skills from another discipline to better analyse defence issues. In a second section, the conclusion will come back to a stimulating challenge for the future of defence studies: that of data and digitalization, also raised in several chapters of this volume.

Mixing methods to better comprehend defence topics

As many authors have observed in this volume, numerous defence issues require several methods be borrowed from different close or more distant disciplines. Which defence issues can be better researched by mixing methods? We will more precisely focus on four issues here: two that have been raised in several chapters of this book (terrorism and defence spending), and two that constitute interesting avenues for further research on methodological questions in the future (cyber issues and military effectiveness).

Understanding terrorism and defence spending at methodological crossroads

In the case of terrorism for instance, an important problem immediately arises, as Kauffmann underlines in Chapter 7: there is no unique and accepted definition of terrorism neither at the interstate level nor at the academic level.[1] Thus to grasp the complexity of terrorism, cross-fertilization of methods from different disciplines may be very promising and fruitful. A first possibility is to start with trying to define the scope of terrorism by using statistics from the Global Terrorism Index which codes terrorist incidents in all the countries enlisted in this database. But a question remains: how should we code these incidents? How do we define an incident as a terrorist incident rather than a common law criminal incident? There comes the need for normative elements. As Traversac showed in Chapter 2, through her reflection about the legal codification of the state of emergency in France linked to the way the French President qualified terrorism in 2015, terrorism is also about the legal framework of public law through which each state defines terrorism and translates it into legal measures aimed at preventing and fighting it. It is thus crucial to be able to investigate these legal measures and to know in which parts of public law to look for them. This normative framework also depends on the way terrorism is politically framed by each government and how this framing translates on the political agenda of defence policy as Hoeffler analysed agenda-setting in defence policy in Chapter 5. Borrowing tools from policy analysis indeed contributes to better analysing terrorism by unravelling defence policies, their actors and processes, and how the actors frame defence issues so that they reach the political agenda and then become political solutions implemented by public policies. Terrorism also needs to borrow from economical methods to assess its financial costs (see Frey et al. 2007) and its impact on defence spending for instance (see Malizard's economic analysis of defence spending in Chapter 9). Last but not least terrorism is an issue to take into account when building a survey on public opinion on defence issues (see Biehl and Steinbrecher in Chapter 11) or assessing the parliamentary votes on military deployment (see Ostermann et al. in Chapter 10): how many of these votes validated military operations dedicated to the fight against terrorism for instance? Building an index of parliamentary votes enabling military operations helps identify the operations linked with the fight against terrorism. Analysing terrorism also means analysing its actors, which can be done with sociological tools to understand who they are, what their organization is, what kind of representations they rely on, etc. One could even go further and add the interest of methods borrowed from psychology and social psychology for instance to assess the motivation at work within terrorism and the fight against this phenomenon (see, for instance, De la Corte 2007).

The same kind of observations concerning the interest of mixing methods apply for the analysis of defence spending. Defence spending can be operationalized using quantitative methods and statistics as Malizard shows in Chapter 9 but as he underlines, statistics do not say how much money is enough in the defence field, as it is also linked with political and social representations at work within a society. As Kauffmann underlines in both Chapter 7 about quantitative methods and Chapter 8 about databases in defence studies, quantifying is not enough and the researcher also needs to put defence spending in its legal, social and political thickness. Therefore tools borrowed from political science (and more precisely policy analysis), law, history and sociology can help investigate why defence spending reaches a certain level at different periods in time, how it is legally and politically justified and for what purposes (military deployment, arm procurement, etc.), and how it is socially perceived.

Cyber issues and military effectiveness as two interesting avenues for future cross-fertilization of methods

Two other issues (not tackled as such in a dedicated chapter in this volume) seem to offer stimulating avenues to think further about methodological challenges and increase multidisciplinarity not only between social sciences but also with hard sciences like computing sciences. In the case of cyber issues, we can provide the example of a research project launched at University Grenoble Alpes in September 2018: the Cybersecurity and International Security Databases project (CyBis).[2] This project brings together researchers in international law, political science, economics, geography, computer sciences and statistics so as to build a database on cybersecurity legislations, policies and governance of 30 countries at first (and more in a second phase), an international index of cybersecurity governance, and online maps representing the data collected in the database and completed with qualitative analyses. The project is developed with multiple academic and non-academic partners from different countries, among which several NGOs and the International Telecommunication Union (ITU). Understanding the stakes of cybersecurity and cyberdefence is a good example of a multi-disciplinary topic which can better be comprehended using a mix of methodological tools from different disciplines. For instance, it is important for researchers in social sciences working on cybersecurity to develop knowledge on the technical aspects of this issue (what is a back door, for instance? What does hack back technically mean? etc.) so as to better analyse the legal measures adopted to cope with cyber threats, how cybersecurity is spatialized, the level of defence spending dedicated to cybersecurity and cyberdefence, the financial costs of cyber-attacks, the social practices linked with cybersecurity, the actors governing cybersecurity and cyberdefence, etc. Therefore cyber issues tend to offer an interesting potential for multi-disciplinary research on methodological questions in defence studies.

The same applies to the topic of military effectiveness. Military effectiveness can be measured by statistical tools developed by mathematics so as to assess the level of target-hitting and efficiency of air strikes or bombing, for instance. But military effectiveness is much more than only numbers in databases and may strongly benefit from multi-disciplinary methodological cross-fertilization. Indeed military effectiveness also relates to the political regime of a country (see Biddle and Long (2004) about the link between democracy and military effectiveness), the level of interstate cooperation in military operations (see for instance Schmitt 2018), the history of the studied army and the way soldiers experience fighting (see Chapter 3 written by Lafaye in this volume; see Millett and Murray 2010 for a historical analysis of military effectiveness in World War II), the geographical constraints which could affect military effectiveness (see Chapter 1 written by Cattaruzza in this volume), the economic assessment of this effectiveness and the psychological aspects of the topic (see Britt et al. 2006).

As we have shown in this section, many defence issues benefit from the mixing of methods and research questioning borrowed from several disciplines. Another element appearing in most of the contributions of this book and that we want to conclude with is the question of digitalization and (big) data, and its impact on methods in defence studies.

Data and digitalization: a stimulating challenge for the future of defence studies

Defence issues meet the increasing question of digitalization and generation of a large amount of data. Digitalization and proliferation of data constitute a double challenge regarding the question of methods. On the one hand, as several contributors evoked in this volume, the armies tend to deal with more and more virtual data. This not only uncovers the question of the spatialization of the data and geospatial intelligence (see Chapter 1), but also of the legal protection of the data (see the point made on cybersecurity and public law in Chapter 2 by Traversac), of archiving of the data (see the case of historical data raised by Lafaye in Chapter 3), and also of managing of the data in databases (see Kauffmann in Chapter 8). On the other hand, digitalization and proliferation of data in defence studies also impacts the way researchers produce their own data and require reflexivity. As Borzillo and Deschaux-Dutard underlined in Chapter 4, for instance, using secondary analysis of qualitative data, and more precisely semi-structured interviews, necessarily requires researchers to find an appropriate and secure way of archiving the data and controlling its access by secondary researchers, as qualitative data produced in defence studies may be confidential and subject to specific authorization. The same applies in the case of immediate history, as Lafaye raised the issue in Chapter 3: how should researchers collect virtual archives from soldiers, such as e-mails, photos taken with smartphones, chat with instant messaging applications, online diaries, etc.? The question of data and its digitalization is also present in the chapter on methods used to build an index about parliamentary votes on military deployment for many countries (Chapter 10), and in the chapter about methods required to build an opinion survey (Chapter 10). And once collected, how should we store digitalized data properly? This raises the issue of developing computer skills for social science researchers, and underlines how promising cross-fertilization with computer or mathematic sciences may be in the future. The last question raised by the increasing amount of data is how to process them. In that matter Kauffmann shows in Chapter 7 and 8 that quantitative analysis may be a well-suited method to analyse big amounts of data, but also that this kind of analysis may be more fruitful when mixing it with qualitative analyses to give an in-depth explanation of how the data were produced and for what purposes, and finally what the limits of the data are given the criteria their construction has been based on.

This book has intended to give a non-exhaustive overview of methodological questions in defence studies. As with any comparable initiative, it cannot be expected to cover all the possible methodological questions underlying defence studies. As conceived, this book aims to open avenues much more than closing the case of methods when investigating defence. We assume that it can provide a beneficial addition to the emerging literature on how to produce social science knowledge on defence topics. May these chapters open new doors and help new ideas germinate for further research on methods in defence studies!

Notes

1 For interesting views on the challenges of conceptualizing terrorism, see Weinberg et al. (2004) and Dixit and Stump (2015).
2 This research project is funded by the French Ministry of Defence in 2018–2020. See the website: http://cybis.univ-grenoble-alpes.fr/en (accessed 29 April 2020).

References

Biddle, S., Long, S. (2004). Democracy and Military Effectiveness: A Deeper Look. *Journal of Conflict Resolution*, 48(4), 525–546.
Britt, T. W., Adler, A. B., Castro, C. A. (Eds.). (2006). *Military Life: The Psychology of Serving in Peace and Combat, Volume 1, Military Performance*. ABC-CLIO.
De la Corte, L. (2007). Explaining Terrorism: A Psychosocial Approach. *Perspectives on Terrorism*, 1(2).
Dixit, P., Stump, J. L. (2015). *Critical Methods in Terrorism Studies*. London, Routledge.
Frey, B. S., Luechinger, S., Stutzer, A. (2007). Calculating tragedy: Assessing the costs of terrorism. *Journal of Economic Surveys*, 21(1), 1–24.

Millett, A. R., Murray, W. (Eds.). (2010). *Military Effectiveness* (Vol. 3). Cambridge, Cambridge University Press.

Schmitt, O. (2018). *Allies that Count: Junior Partners in Coalition Warfare*, Washington DC, Georgetown University Press.

Weinberg, L., Pedahzur, A., Hirsch-Hoefler, S. (2004). The Challenges of Conceptualizing Terrorism. *Terrorism and Political Violence*, 16(4), 777–794.

Index

Page numbers in italics refer to figures. Page numbers in bold refer to tables. Page numbers followed by 'n' refer to notes.

Abadie, A. 166n3
access to field 100–101
ACLED *see* Armed Conflict Location and Event Data (ACLED)
administrative regulatory texts 32
administrative Supreme Court 31
Advanced Technology Laboratories (ATL) 136
agenda-setting 76–77, 85n1
Agnew, John 21
agreement index (AI) 171, 174–175, *175*
Ahram, A. I. 83
Air School Research Centre 48–49
Almond-Lippmann consensus 192, 193, 194
American imperialism 15
"American Soldier, The" 93–94
Amoore, Louise 29
amplified analysis 62
analysis of variance in statistical models (ANOVA) analysis 180, *181*, 182
Anderton, C. H. 162
Anglo-Saxon academic literature 36
Annales d'histoire économique et sociale (periodical) 50
anonymization 64, 68–69, 70
Anthropogeographie (Ratzel) 19
anti-Atlanticism 193
anticipatory socialization 94
anti-militarism 50
anti-personnel mines 130
APPENDIX C Software options 124
archives 54–56
area of operations 23
Armed Conflict Location and Event Data (ACLED) 129, **131**, 144, 145, 147
armed conflicts 130; proliferation on 130–132
Arms Control and Disarmament Agency (ACDA) 158
arms trade 162
arms transfers 130

Aron, Raymond 23
Arrow, Kenneth 124n1
Association for War and Strategic Studies (AEGES) 50
assorted analysis 62
Atlanticism 193
attitudes: on defence spending 201–202; towards missions and deployments 202–203; towards the armed forces 200–201
automatic analysis of conflict 137, *137*

Bataclan Theater attack 41
battlefields 23; digitalization 26–27; recorded videos 54
battle history 50, *51*
Beauguitte, L. 110
Belin, J. 155
Bellais, R. 155
Benoit, E. 165
BeQuali catalogue 63, 65, 70, 71, 72n.7
Berlin für Sozialforschung (WZB) 82
Biehl, Heiko 8, 189
Big Data: limitations of, and NLP **142**, 142–143; and natural language processing 134, 136
bipartisan system 185n7
Blanton, S. L. 162
Bloch, Marc 50, 57n14
Boëne, B. 1
Böller, Florian 170
border regions 24
Borzillo, Laurent 8, 60, 66, 67, 69, 72n6, 72n9, 213
Boulanger, Philippe 18
Bozoudis, M. 125n7
Braudel, Fernand 21
Briand-Kellogg Pact 34
Bridgman, Percy 120
Brown, G. 125n6
Brussels, Treaty of 33

216 *Index*

Bruxelles2 34
Bundeswehr Academy for Information and Communication (AKUF) 129
Burstein, P. 194

Cabanes, Bruno 52
cabinets 176
cabinet-unit of analysis 180
calculus (Octave) 124
CAMEO (Conflict and Mediation Event Observations) classification 136
cartography 16
Castex, Raoul 19
Cattaruzza, Amaël 7, 15
Center for Advanced Armament Studies 52
Center for Defence History Studies (CEHD) 51
Center for Higher Military Studies and Research 52
Center for International Development and Conflict Management (CIDCM) 129
Center for Social Studies in Defence 52
Center for Systemic Peace (CSP) 129
Centre for Command Teaching and Doctrine 48
Centre for Strategic Aerospace Studies 48
Cerovic, Masha 52
Chapel Hill Expert Survey (CHES) 82, 183
Christiansen, Flemming J. 170
CIA 27
CIDSP 63
civic engagement 194
civilian action and resistance 130
civilian policies 76
civil-military gap 189–190; military-related opinion polls 197–198; military-related public opinion surveys 195–197, 199–203; political science research 192–195; public opinion research on security 190; security and defence policy attitudes in military sociology 190–192
civil wars 109, 114, 118; after 1993 **116**
classic international wars 132
classified documents, access to 5
Clausewitz, Carl von 16, 96
codebook content 145
cohabitation 38
Cohen, Samy 9n11
cold state of aggregation 96
Cold War 43, 110, 151, 162, 172
collaboration, databases: access to sources 147; codebook content 145–147; expanding 144; facilitating traceability 145; intersubjectivity 144; workflows 144–145
colonial anthropology 17
colonialism 21
Combat Engineer Regiment 53

Commander-in-Chief of the Armed Forces 38
Common Foreign and Security Policy (CFSP) 36
Common Security and Defence Policy (CSDP) 36, 76
Comola, M. 162
Comparative Manifesto Project (CMP) 178, 183
comparative politics 78
complete observer 101
complete participant 101
concordance theory of civil-military relations 191
confidentiality 55, 83
conflict-induced internal displacement 121
constructing "conflict" using disaggregated event data 132–134
constructivist approach 70
Contamine, Philippe 51
contentious issues 130
conventional weapons 130
CoreNLP 136
Correlates of War (COW) 129, **131**, 135
cost-benefit approach (CBA) 152, 161
Coticchia, Fabrizio 170
Countries at Risk of Electoral Violence (CREW) **131**
Court of conflicts 31
Cox, Kevin 21
Criminality Awareness System 28
crises 27, 132
critical geopolitics 21
cross-country comparisons 159
cross-disciplinary approach 53
cross-fertilization of methods 210; cyber issues and military effectiveness 211–212; data and digitalization 212–213; terrorism and defence 210–211
CSP, Polity 4 **131**
Cukier, Keneth 17
cultural liberalism 170
Cyber and International Security (CYBIS) **131**
cyberattacks 24, 43, 84, 210
Cybersecurity and International Security Databases project (CyBis) 212

Dalby, Simon 21
Darwinian evolutionary biology 115
data: Big Data 7; digitalization 7, 62; macroeconomic data 157–158; microeconomic data 158–159
databases: big data and natural language processing 136; collaboration 144–147; collaborative validation workflow *146*; constructing "conflict" using disaggregated event data 132–134; in defence studies **131**, 143–147; diversity in conflict data 130, 132;

GDELT 138–140; ICEWS 136–138; lack of interoperability 135–136; limitations of Big Data and NLP 142–143; overview 129–130; Phoenix 140–142; proliferation on armed conflicts 130–132; security 147
data limitations 160
decision-making processes 85n1, 96
decolonization: in Algeria 41; wars 18, 20
defence: action 3; in French Constitution 38; function in human societies 4; international index 7; measurement of public opinion 7; organizations 101; policy 3; qualitative interviews 8; quantification 3; quantitative methods 8–9; signification 3; social characteristic 4
Defence Advanced Research Projects Agency (DARPA) 136
defence and industrial base (DIB) 152
defence and security politicians 103
defence capabilities 153
defence clause of NATO 33
Defence Committee of the German Bundestag 195
defence economics 110, 151, 152, 161, 166; alliance and burden sharing 161; data in 129; economic impacts 164–166; industry and R&D 163–164; trade 162–163
defence industrial base (DIB) 163
defence policies 82, 210
defence spending (DS) 151, 164–165, 211
defence studies 47–48; building archives 54–56; cross-disciplinary fertilization 52; defined 3, 94–95; ethnographic methods 6; fragmentation 49; insider/outsider dilemma 4–5; internal perspective 104n1; methods research 1; multi-disciplinary approach to methods 4; public laws (*see* public laws); qualitative methods 5–6, 7; quantitative methods 6, 7; research centres 48; researcher's freedom 6; social specificity 3, 5
De jure belli ac pacis (Grotius) 34
Delbrück, Hans 50
demand channel 156
Deni, J. 3
Department of Defense (DoD) 27
deployment votes *173*, 182
Deschaux-Dutard, Delphine 1, 8, 9, 60, 66, 67, 102, 210, 213
destabilization hypothesis 163
Deutsche Foschungsgemeinschaft (DFG) 82
De Vreese, C. H. 82
DGRIS 71
diaries 54
digitalization of data 7, 62
Directorate of Military Intelligence 85, 124
disagreement issues 132
disputes 132

diversity in conflict data 132
divided government 179
domestic law in defence studies 32, 37–40
Drévillon, Hervé 52
Drian, Jean-Yves le 50
DS *see* defence spending (DS)
Dunkirk, Treaty of 33
Dunlap, C. J. 27
Dunne, J. P. 156, 165
Durando, Giacomo 16, 18

Eck, K. 130
econometrics 160
Econometric Society 110
Economic and Social Research Council (ESRC) 62
economic crisis, 2008 156
economic liberalism 170
economics methods 151–154; defence economic literature 161–166; defined 151; empirical issues 157–160; theoretical models 154–157; *see also* defence economics
economic theory 164
Economists Against the Arms Race (ECAAR) 110
Economists for Peace and Security (EPS) 110
EDC Treaty 36
EDF (the GRETS) 63
e-mails 54, 213
Estaing, Giscard d'40
European Coal and Steel Community (ECSC) 36
European Defence Community (EDC) 36
European defence system 36
European Force Training Mission (EUTM) 172
Europeanization, military aspect of 72n.3
European law 33, 37
European Security and Defence Policy (ESDP) 81
European security system 33
European Union 76
European Union Battlegroups (EUG) 66
European Union Force (EUFOR) 81
European Union law and defence issues 35–37
Eurostat **131**
excel bugs 123
Excellence Research Chair 49
external laws 33, 37

facilitating traceability 145
family-cabinet cases 171, *180*
famine, conflict 109
Fauconnet, C. 163
Feaver, Peter 191
Febvre, Lucien 50
Federal Republic of Germany 98

218 *Index*

FELIN programme 26
Ferguson, N. 159
Ferlet, J.-F 124
financial institutions 110
Flint, C. 21
FLOS (Free, Libre and Open Source) software 122–123, 124
Fonck, Daan 170, 185n14
foreign and security policy postures 199–200
foreign policy analysis (FPA) 76, 170, 172, 183
formalization, degree of 96
Foucault, Michel 21
France: academic system 35; defense and war studies 48–50, 52–53; domestic law 32; legal Code on Internal Security 43; legal system 33; military history and defence studies 50–56; Pact for Higher Education funding 50; terror attacks of 2015 2, 35, 39–40
French Air Force 49
French Constitution 38; Article 16 41; Article 36 41; defence in 38–39; Fundamental Rights 42–43; responsibility of defence 39
French-German Brigade (BFA) 66
French military history commission (CFHM) 51
French Ministry of Defence (SHD) 2, 50, 53
French National Research Center (CNRS) 9n4
French Procurement Agency 49
French Revolution 31, 32
French Superior Council for Strategic Research 49
Fundamental Rights 42–43

Galbreath D. 3
Galgano, Francis A. 23, 29n3
Galser, Barney 60
game theories 111
Gardeazabal, J. 166n3
Gaulle, Charles de 38
GDELT 138–140
GDP 156
gendering 84
genocide 132
geodata 26–28
geographers 15
Geographical Pivot of History, The (Mackinder) 20
geographic methodology 2, 15–16; battlefield digitalization 26–27; critical approaches 15, 21–22; and defence studies 20–21; as discipline 16; geodata and geospatial intelligence 26–28; geopolitical methods 24–26; geopolitics 19–20; geostrategy 18–19; human geography 22–24; military geography 18; strategic geographic knowledge 16–17

Geography of the Sea (Maury) 17
Geography of War and Peace (Flint) 21
Geoint 26–28
geopolitical methods 24–26, **25**
geopolitics 19–21
Geopolitik 28
geospatial intelligence 15, 27
geostrategy 16, 18–19
German Armed Forces 100
German Marshall Fund 195
Global Conflict Risk Index (GCRI) **131**
Global Database of Events, Language, and Tone (GDELT) **131**, 138–140
globalization 170
Global Nonviolent Action Database (GNAD) **131**
global terrorism 1
Global Terrorism Database (GTD) 121, **131**
Global Terrorism Index (GTI) 121, 210
Godlewska, Anne 17
Goffman, Erving 95
government-opposition dynamics 171
grand theories 93
Greek Defence Ministry 125n7
Grenoble Alpes 212
grey materials 37
Griffith, J. 99
gross national product (GNP) 161
Grotius, Hugo 34
Group for Research and Information on Peace and Security (GRIP) **131**
growth theory 165

Hakim, C. 61
Handbook of Defense Economics (Hartley and Sandler) 166
Hartley, Keith 79, 153, 155, 163
Harvey, David 21
Haushofer, Karl 16, 19
Heaton, J. 61
Heckman model 162
Heidelberger Institut für Internationale Konfliktforschung (HIIK) 129
Herranz-Surrallés, Anna 170
heuristics 193
"High-Reliability-Organizations" 95
Historical Defence Service 53
historical defence studies, in France 47–48
Historical Service of Defence in Paris 52
Hobbes, Thomas 93
Hoeffler, Catherine 8, 76
Holeindre, Jean-Vincent 47
Hollande, François 39, 40
Holsti, Karl 72n9
hot state of aggregation 96
Howorth, Jolyon 81
Human Development Index (HDI) 135

human geography 19, 22–24
Huntington, Samuel 190, 191
Hussein, Saddam 102
Hyman, Herbert 61
hyper-personalization of war 27
hypothetical-deductive method 109, 111–117; deductive reasoning 111; definition of assumptions 111; falsifiability and statistical modelling 113–117; predictions and falsifiability 111–113

IBC 134
ICEWS 136–138
iconographic documents 54
ideational factors 80
IMF 110
individualism 98
individual parties 178
inductive method and empirical approaches 117; case studies 117–118; comparative studies 118–119; descriptive statistics 119–120; induction 117
industrial cooperation 164
in-extremis situations 95
Information Extraction (IE) algorithm 136
ingénieurs-géographes (engineers-geographers) 17
insider/outsider dilemma 4–5
Institute for Strategic Research of the Military School in Paris (IRSEM) 2, 47, 48, 51–52, 71
institutional documents 81
institutional framework 97
insurrections 132
Integrated Conflict Early Warning System (ICEWS) 136–138, *137, 138, 139*, **142–143**
Integrated Infantryman Equipment and Communications 26
interactive data visualization (Ggobi) 124
interlocutors 69
international humanitarian law 35
International Institute for Strategic Studies (IISS) 2, 48, 157
internationalism 193
internationalization of national defence policies 79–80
international law for armed conflicts 35
International Monetary Fund (IMF) 135
International Organization for Standardization (ISO) 136
International Peace Research Institute in Oslo (PRIO) 129
International public law 35
international relations (IR) 35, 76
international security 4
International Security Assistance Force in Afghanistan (ISAF) 184n5

international Telecommunication Union (ITU) 212
interoperability: lack of 129, 135–136; of storage and analysis tools 148
interpersonal replicability 123–124
intersubjectivity 144
intertemporal replicability 123
Interuniversity Consortium for Political and Social Research (ICPSR) 129
interventions 132
I/O-model 99
Iran, elite Revolutionary Guards in 136
Iraq Body Count project 133–134, *134*
Irondelle, Bastien 81
ISAF-mission in Afghanistan 202–203
Islamic terrorism 170
isolationism 193

Janowitz, M. 102, 191
Janowitz, Morris 190
Joas, Hans 93
Johannsen, J. 162
Joint Centre for Concepts, Doctrines and Experiments 49
Judiciary Supreme Court 31

Kaarbo, Juliet 170
Kauffmann, M. 6, 8, 109, 125n2, 129, 211, 213
Keegan, John 51, 57n15
Kelsen's pure theory of law 32
KEYCRIME 28
Khanna, J. 161
Kitt, W. 94
Kitto, W. 125n6
Klein, Lawrence 124n1
Kleinfeld, R. 134
Knöbl, Wolfgang 93
Knopp, J. 125n6
Kohn, Richard 191
Kosovo 136
Kreutz, J. 132
Kuĉmáš, Kryštof 170

Lacoste, Yves 21
Lafaye, Christophe 7, 47, 57n23
La Géographie, ça sert d'abord à faire la guerre (Lacoste) 21
Lappas, I. 125n7
Lapray, Xavier 52
Lavallée, Théophile 18
Law of Nations, The (Vattel) 34
League of Nations 110
Lebensraum 20
Lefebvre, Henri 21
Leontief, Wassily 124n1
Levine, P. 162

220 Index

liberal-democratic interventionism 172
liberal-democratic politics 171
Lijphart, A. 118, 125n4
Lisbon Treaty 36, 37

Maastricht Treaty 36
machine learning (Weka) 124
Mackinder, Halford 19, 20
macroeconomic mode (Quesnay) 110
macroeconomics 151, 156–157
macro-sociological theory 93
Mahan, Alfred Thayer 19
mainstream economics 152
major wars 132
Malizard, Julien 8, 151, 156, 158, 165
managing mistrust 5
Manifesto Project 82
maps 21
marginalization 49
Marine Graduate Studies Centre 49
maritime cartography 17
market failure 154
Martel, André 51
Martinez-Zarzoso, I. 162
masculinity 98
massacre 132
mass violence 132
Maury, Matthew Fontaine 17
Mayer-Schönberger, Viktor 17
McFadden, Daniel 124n1
Mello, P. A. 170
Menon, Anand 76
Merton, Robert K. 93, 94
meta-databases 130
microeconomics 151, 154–155
micro-sociological theory concepts 93
Microsoft Excel® 123
militarism 193
militarization of cyberspace 43
Military Academy, Institute of Strategic Research 73n11
military: deployments 170, 171; effectiveness 210; geography 15, 16, 18, 22; intelligence 43; organizations 95–96, 101; secrecy 55; self-restraint 172; sociology 1, 190, 204; virtues 192
Military History Operations 55
military-related contract 103
military-related opinion polls 189–190, 195–203; motivation for 196–197; problems of 197–198; types 195–196
Ministry of Defence (MoD) 9n4, 195
missions, and units of analysis 175–176
MITRE Corporation 125n8
Mitterrand, François 38
Modigliani, Franco 124n1
monopsony 155

monothematic approach 93
Moskos, Charles 99
multilateralism 193, 198
Muscarà, Luca 16–17
Myerson, Roger 124n1

Nachtwei, Winfried 103
National Center for Scientific Research (CNRS) 85
national data 158
National Defence archives 55
National Defence Institute of Advanced Studies 49
National Geospatial Intelligence Agency 26
national Member States' defence policies 76
National Security Agency (NSA) 27
NATO 34, 36, 77, 81, 148, 158, 161, 194, 196, 199, 202, 207
Natural Language Processing (NLP) 136
natural resources, conflict 109
Naval School Research Institute 49
new wars 93
non-militarism 193

Office of the Military Government 195
Olson, M. 161
Onderco, Michal 170
OpenOffice/LibreOffice Calc 124
Open Source Intelligence (OSint) 136
open source software, at defence ministries 122, 124
operating systems 124
operational environment *24*
operationalization 109, 111, 120, 133; data storage and processing 122; interpersonal replicability 123–124; intertemporal replicability 123; open source software 122–123, 124; in security analysis 120–121; of terrorism 121–122
Operation Barkhane 40
Operation Serval 40
opportunity costs 160
optimum 152
oral testimonies, of soldiers 53
Organisation for Economic Co-operation and Development (OECD) 135
organizational communication 96
organizational embedding, of research institutions 97–98
Ostermann, Falk 8, 170
O'Tuathail, Gearoid 21
Oxford Handbook of International Security (Gheciu and Wohlforth) 1

pacifism 50
Pact for Higher Education 71
Paix et guerre entre les nations (Aron) 23

Pajon, C. 5, 6
Paris Treaty *see* EDC Treaty
ParlGov 179, 183, 185n9, 185n16
parliamentary deployment votes database (PDVD) 8, 171, 172, 178–179, 183–184
Parliamentary Participation Law 172
parliamentary systems, and collecting data 177–178
parliaments, in security and defence policy 172–173
party families per cabinet 178–181
party-family-cabinet dataset 178, 184
party-political contestation 176
party-political research agenda 171
party-votes 171, 178
peace and conflicts economics 166
Pedersen, Rasmus B. 170
Pédroncini, Guy 51
perfect competition 154
Perlo-Freeman, S. 159
Permanent Structured Cooperation (PESCO) 36–37, 44
personal e-mails 54, 213
Peters, D. 170
Peters, H. 125n8
Phoenix **140**, 140–142, *141*
Pieri, Piero 51
plenary-vote data 171
political decisions: in democracies 194; and policymaking 189
Political Geography (Ratzel) 19
political regime 130
political stability 109
politicization 170, 171
Popper, K. 112
Popperian epistemology 120
Popperian falsificationism 117
PostgreSQL 125n8
poverty, and civil war **113, 114**
power distance 98
Precobs 28
prediction of banalities 29n6
predictive policing 28
PredPol 28
primary researcher interviews 69, 73n10
private individuals 100
private law 31
private military companies 155
privatization 79, 93
process-tracing 81
procurement issue 164
professionalization: confidence 55; of defence matters 1; process 53
Professional Soldier, The (Janowitz) 191
protection of witnesses 55
public goods 155

public laws 31–32; defence law 32; defence studies in 32–44; defined 31, 43; domestic law in defence studies 32, 37–40; European Union law research 35–37; French conception of 32; international public law and 33–35; place for 32; political actuality 40–43; security 33
public opinion research on security 190
public policy 76–77, 85n1; agenda setting 77–78, 85n1; comparative politics 78; confidentiality and research 82–84; core themes 80; defence studies, contributions to 77; governs 78; implementation 78–79; internationalization of national defence policies 79–80; methodological plurality 78, 80–82; methodologies and methodological challenges 80; methods 2; national executives 79–80; power, autonomy and safety 84–85; sociological accounts of decision-making 78; specific and not so specific methodological challenges 78–85
purchasing power parity (PPP) 159

Qualidata (Qualitative Date Archival Resource Center) 62, 65
qualitative analysis: defence, interviews 8; defence studies 5–6, 7; of media coverage 82; *see also* quantitative analyses; secondary analysis of qualitative data
quantitative analyses 2, 109; comparative evolution 110; in defence and security 109–110; hypothetical-deductive method 111–117; inductive method and empirical approaches 117–120; influence on defence policies 82; methodology of statistics 110–111; operationalization of concepts for statistical analyses 120–124
quantum physics 114
Quesnay, François 110
question on constitutionality (QPC) 42

Ram, R. 156
Rathbun, B. C. 170
Rattinger, H. 204n1
Ratzel, Friedrich 19, 20
Raunio, Tapio 170
re-analysis 62
recruitment, and socialization 95
reflexivity 1, 4, 5
refugees from Syria 170
Reifler, Jason 78
relational databases (Mysql, PostgreSQL) 124
research questions, generation of 98–100
Resource Governance Index (RGI) 144
RETEX 66
Reykers, Yf 170
Ribemont, T. 85n1

Index

Richardson, L. 110, 129
Richter, Gregor 8, 93, 98, 158
risk analysis 109
Risse-Kappen, T. 194
rivalries 132
Robbins, L. 151
Roman law 31
Routledge Handbook of Research Methods in Military Studies (Soeters) 1, 9n12
R (statistical software) 122–123
Ruttan, V. W. 156

Sahel-Saharan strip 53
Saint-Cyr School Research Centre (CREC) 48
Sandler, T. 155, 161
scale of analysis, and operational environment 23
Schiff, Rebecca 191
Schmid, A. 121
Schmitt, Olivier 3, 47, 56
Schoen, Harald 82
Schumpeter, J. 156
Schwartz, M. 125n8
scientific visualization (gnuplot) 124
SCORPION program 26, 29n5
Sea Power 19, 20
secondary analysis of qualitative data 2, 8, 60–62; amplified analysis 62; anonymization of sources 68–69, 70; archiving and re-using 62–63, 70; archiving data 71; assorted analysis 62; audio recordings 71; constructivist position 72n.1; data collection and access 70; death of interviewees 64; defence studies 63–64; feedback from 67–69; French-German military cooperation 66; internal documents and grey literature 63; objective 61–62; overview 61–62; ownership of data 70; positivist position 72n.1; precautions and challenges 64–66; re-analysis 62; responsibility for data collection and access 71–72; semi-structured interviews 64, 65; social specificity of defence field 64; supplementary analysis 61; supra analysis 61; theoretical framework 68; unpublished interviews 69
secrecy-breaking 5
security 147; channel 156; and defence policy attitudes in military sociology 190–192; and defence studies 33; studies 3
Security Council 34; weaknesses 34
Seiglie, C. 125n2
semi-structured interviews 64
Sen, Amartya 124n1
Sentinelle operation, in France 4
Shaw, Martin 191
Shell, K. 194

Shils, E. 102
Singer, D. 129
Slovakia's National Council 173, 176
Small, M. 129
Small Arms Trade Transparency Barometer 130
smartphones 213
Smetana, Michal 170
Smith, R. 152, 153, 156, 165, 166n1
social bonds 18
social Darwinism 19
sociological methods 93–95; access to field 100–101; generation of research questions 98–100; institutional framework 97; military organizations 95–96; organizational embedding of research institutions 97–98; researchers, requirements for 101–102; research results 102–103
Soeters, J. L. 94, 98
Soja, Edward 21
Soldier and the State, The (Huntington) 190
Solow, Robert 124n1
Sorokin, P. 129
SOWI (Bundeswehr Institute of Social Sciences) surveys 195
spatio-temporal generalization 117
spreadsheet 124
spy drone 136
standard public policy approaches 76
state of emergency 40, 42
Steinbrecher, Markus 8, 189
Stockholm International Peace Research Institute (SIPRI) 129, 151, 159
Stouffer, Samuel A. 93
strategic autonomy 151
strategic culture 193
strategic geographic knowledge 16–17
Strava application 28
street-level bureaucrats 79
supplementary analysis 61
supply of strategic goods 110
supra analysis 61
surveys and interviewing 103
systematic empirical materials 94

technologization of defence matters 1
Tenenbaum, Elie 52
terror attacks in Paris (2015) 2, 35, 39–40, 71
terrorism 125n5, 109, 130, 210, 211
theatre of operations 23
theatre of war 23
theory of relative deprivation 94
Thomson, Catarina P. 78
Tinbergen, Jan 124n1
Tobin, James 124n1
trade data 160

Transatlantic Trends 195
transcontinental lines 29n1
transnational threats 43
transparency 160
Traversac, Anne-Sophie 7, 31
Treaty of Brussels 33
Treaty of Dunkirk 33
Treaty of Maastricht 36
Treaty of Versailles 20
trend indicator value (TIV) 158

uncertainty avoidance 98
unilateralism 193, 198
unilateral violence 132
United Nations–African Union Mission in Darfur 172
United Nations Charter 34
United Nations Interim Force in Lebanon (UNIFIL) 172
United Nations Multidimensional Integrated Stabilization Mission in Mali 172
United States Information Agency (USIA) 195
unmanned aerial vehicles (UAVs) 27/
Uppsala Conflict Data Program of Uppsala University 129

Vattel, Emer de 34
Venayre, Sylvain 52
Versailles, Treaty of 20
Vidalenc, Jean 57n16
videoconferencing 54
Viehrig, H. 194
Vietnam War 18, 21
Vignoli, Valerio 170
Vilmer, Jean-Baptiste 47, 48, 49

violence 4; against civilians 145–147
violent conflict 132
voting database 172
Vogt, Wolfgang R. 191
voting, on military missions 170–171, *177, 179, 181, 182*; agreement index 174–175; cabinets 176; drivers of deployment votes 182; individual parties 178; missions and units of analysis 175–176; parliamentary systems and collecting data 177–178; parliaments in security and defence policy 172–173; by party families per cabinet 178–181

Wagner, Wolfgang 82, 170, 184n1
war: and geodata 27; simulation 110; studies 3, 47–48; theatre of war 23; *see also* defence studies
War Powers Resolution 172
Washington Treaty of 1949 33, 34, 36
water's edge-effect 178
Weber, Claude 101
Western Union (WU) 33
White, E. 125n6
Woodward, Rachel 17, 18, 22
word processing software 54
World Bank (WB) 110, 135, *135*
World Health Organisation (WHO) 135
Wright, Q. 110, 129

Yesilyurt, F. 164
Yesilyurt, M. E. 164

Zeckhauser, R. 161
Zi, Sun 16